Voice: Onstage and Off

Voice: Onstage and Off is a comprehensive guide to the process of building, mastering, and fine-tuning the voice for performance. Every aspect of vocal work is covered, from the initial speech impulse and the creation of sound, right through to refining the final product in different types of performance. This highly adaptable course of study empowers performers of all levels to combine and evolve their onstage and offstage voices.

This second edition is extensively illustrated and accompanied by an all-new website, full of audio and text resources, including:

- Extensive teacher guides including sample syllabi, scheduling options, and ways of adapting to varying academic environments and teaching circumstances.
- Downloadable forms to help reproduce the book's exercises in the classroom and for students to engage with their own vocal development outside of lessons.
- Audio recordings of all exercises featured in the book.
- Examples of Voiceover Demos, including both scripts and audio recordings.
- Links to useful web resources, for further study.

Four mentors — the voice chef, the voice coach, the voice shrink and the voice doctor — are on hand throughout the book and the website to ensure a holistic approach to voice training. The authors also provide an authoritative survey of US and UK vocal training methods, helping readers to make informed choices about their study.

Robert Barton is professor emeritus of acting at the University of Oregon. He is the author of *Style for Actors*, *Acting: Onstage and Off*, *Acting Reframes*, and co-author of *Theatre in Your Life* and *Life Themes* (both with Annie McGregor). He has been honored as Outstanding Acting Coach by the American College Theatre Festival and writes a column, "Many Right Ways," for *The Voice and Speech Review*.

Rocco Dal Vera is a professor of drama at the University of Cincinnati's College-Conservatory of Music, specializing in theatre voice and speech with particular interest in voice and emotion. He is co-author of *Acting in Musical Theatre* (with Joe Deer, Routledge, 2008), a columnist for *Dramatics Magazine* and *Teaching Theatre*, and founding editor of *The Voice and Speech Review*.

"I am looking forward to using this new edition as our text. Thanks to the authors for their hard work and for providing us such a comprehensive, useful, and soulful approach to this topic. This book is a must for any professional or soon-to-be professional. It equips actors with the necessary tools required for successful and excellent performances."

Linda Brennan, *The American Academy of Dramatic Arts, Los Angeles*

"I am impressed by the precision, clarity and comprehensive scope of the authors' work on voice, particularly how the voice is linked to the emotional/physical state of the speaker. This book has a wide area of interest to the general public, not just the educational/academic area. An interesting and useful book, written with skills, insight and practical experience."

Brigid Panet, *The Royal Academy of Dramatic Art*

"The authors have made a very wise and unusual choice by their generous coverage of other methods of voice training."

David Zinder, *Tel Aviv University*

"The tone is fresh and open, the authorial voice is confident, and the text provides a very useful and pragmatic student and teacher guide. The book is exceptionally valuable in that it provides a synthesis with regard to all the information that is currently out there in this complex field. This is an excellent resource and should offer superb value to the field for a long time to come."

Jane Boston, *Central School of Speech and Drama*

" . . . a book that practically teaches by itself. Comprehensive and easily accessible . . . "

Voice and Speech Training in the New Millennium, Conversations with Master Teachers by Nancy Saklad

"I do not know of a more comprehensive book on the subject."

Beth McGuire, *Yale School of Drama*

Voice

Onstage and Off

Second edition

Robert Barton and Rocco Dal Vera

Routledge
Taylor & Francis Group

LONDON AND NEW YORK

First published 1995
by Harcourt Brace & Company

This second edition published 2011
by Routledge
270 Madison Ave, New York, NY 10016

Simultaneously published in the UK
by Routledge
2 Park Square, Milton Park, Abingdon, Oxon OX14 4RN

© 1995, 2011 Robert Barton and Rocco Dal Vera

Routledge is an imprint of the Taylor & Francis Group, an informa business

Typeset in Univers by
Keystroke, Station Road, Codsall, Wolverhampton
Printed and bound by
Edwards Brothers, Inc.

British Library Cataloguing in Publication Data
A catalogue record for this book is available from the British Library

Library of Congress Cataloging-in-Publication Data
Barton, Robert, 1945–
  Voice : onstage and off / Robert Barton and Rocco Dal Vera.—2nd ed.
    p. cm.
  1. Voice culture.   2. Speech—Study and teaching. 3. Acting.
  I. Dal Vera, Rocco. II. Title.
  PN4162.B27 2011
  808.5071—dc22
                                                        2010026345

ISBN: 978-0-415-58557-6 (hbk)
ISBN: 978-0-415-58558-3 (pbk)
ISBN: 978-0-203-83519-7 (ebk)

SUSTAINABLE
FORESTRY
INITIATIVE

Certified Fiber
Sourcing
www.sfiprogram.org

To our voices of support and encouragement

Carrol Barton

and

Denise Dal Vera

and to the voices of the future

Andrew Barton

and

Kendall Dal Vera

Contents

Illustrations

Tables

Preface

A place to start

If you're an actor ready to study voice, this book is the place to start. If you are an acting instructor starting to teach voice, this book is the place to start. If you are a reader ready to use your voice to act your life better, this is the place to start. If you have already studied or taught, this is the place to backtrack, review, re-evaluate and get clear. There is an astonishing amount of ignorance and conflicting information regarding how we can all use voices better. The purpose of this book is to wade through what is out there to make sense, connect, simplify, alleviate fears, and help the reader become a better shopper. We do not consider the text competition for any other text or system, but rather a comprehensive compilation of established fundamentals, a handbook for voice-centered personal growth, and a guide to helping actors and teachers make informed decisions for advanced study.

How is this book different from others available?

1. It is **easy to understand**. Our highest priority here is to speak to the reader without intimidation or confusion. We have tried to present a complex subject in the simplest, most direct way possible.

2. It connects the voices actors use onstage with those we all use off, finding ways in which the two can productively feed each other and serve each other. It **links theatre and life**, rather than isolating them, so working on oneself as a person can happen while acting, and vice versa.

3. It **considers all causes and effects**. It addresses psychological blocks to vocal progress as well as the physiological. Without presuming to be psychotherapeutic, it assists readers in recognizing when issues of fear and esteem are blocking vocal progress as significantly as not placing enough pressure with the tongue on the alveolar ridge or not sustaining a terminal consonant sequence.

4. It **uses imitation exercises** to sharpen vocal awareness. Believing that imitation is indeed the highest form of flattery, the authors encourage actors to serve as each other's "vocal mirrors" to increase the depth, detail, and caring involved in voice growth.

5. It offers a **website** with the entire recorded text available for listening, clarifying sound changes difficult to represent on the printed page, making it easier to do exercises along with the recording, and allows for study when you would rather listen than read. The site also provides interactive opportunities, downloadable forms, and demonstrations.

6. It connects **body work with voice work**, particularly physical conditioning or "getting in shape," because the reader is already quite familiar with the first (even if he has chosen to be a couch potato) and probably not at all with the second. New challenges are offered, whenever possible, through known paths.

7. It presents material that is **highly adaptable**. It can be used alone or as part of a class. It could be the primary book used in an intensive professional training program or the book used over the entire course of a liberal arts program. It provides solo activities for the individual reader and group projects on which class members can collaborate. It does not limit circumstances or motives.

8. It **aims to empower**. It takes the position that each of us has innumerable voices waiting to be unleashed and each teacher (regardless of limitations of "ear" or skill to demonstrate) has the potential to guide this freeing of range.

9. It **honors all approaches** rather than indoctrinating and imposing bias. It provides a "consumer's guide" to advanced study in the major voice, speech, dialect, and relaxation systems. It compares, contrasts, and offers shopping tips. Since some systems require licensed or certified instructors, multiple-year time commitments, and claim to be incompatible with other systems, choosing wisely is vital. It helps the actor to look before they leap.

10. It tries to make an undeniably challenging and potentially intimidating subject enjoyable. While not denying the hard work aspects of vocal training, it also **encourages fun**.

We believe that any reader can find significant value, progress, and joy from this material without a background in theatrical training. Those who *are* studying acting will gain even more mastery of their craft if they come to this work with a rudimentary exposure to the Stanislavski system or one of its variants (such as that offered in *Acting: Onstage and Off*) but by no means requiring exposure to that text).

The book begins with the reader's vocal past and ends with their projected future. It deals with the complete process of voice — from initial impulse to speak and taking the first breath, through the creation of sound, all the way to refining the final expression. It connects voice production to voice technique.

Chapter overview

Chapter 1 — *Owning your voice* shows how individual voices evolve and helps actors to get to know and accept their own instruments. A complete warm-up is included so that you can integrate that into your work from the start.

Revisions in the new edition:

- A new focus on how to use electronic feedback (digital recording and spectral analysis) in understanding your own vocal tendencies and characteristics and comprehending the use and impact of voice-mail messages, and audio components of personal and professional websites.
- Additional short warm-ups for circumstances where you have little time or space but still need some preparation.

Chapter 2 — *Healing your voice* deals with the most common vocal problems and most successful solutions. It uses the metaphor of healing for solving common physiological as well as psychological voice and speech problems.

Revisions in the new edition:

- Updated scientific research on the nature of vocal health.
- New information on voice therapies derived from studies in physical rehabilitation for athletes.
- New perspectives on behavioral modification based on recent research into states and stages of change.

Chapter 3 — *Mastering your language* provides understanding and skills regarding how English is pronounced, using the International Phonetic Alphabet and exploring the fine details of speech. Up to this point, the focus is primarily on acceptance and remediation.

Revisions in the new edition:

- Incorporating updated phonetic transcription standards from an international perspective on English.
- Noting recent changes in standard word pronunciations and how pronunciation expectations evolve with fashion and audience expectation.
- Discussions of the differences in transcription between North American English and UK models.
- Establishing a set of conventions to make for an easy discussion of US vs. UK contrasts throughout the text.

Chapter 4 — *Expanding your voice* works on moving past "fixing" and into freeing and strengthening. This chapter devises a means by which the actor can get vocally fit. Next, the book turns to specific performance skills and techniques.

Revisions in the new edition:

- Matching vocal work-outs with other fitness choices.
- New information on working with microphones onstage.
- Expanded material on how to make complex language simpler for the audience to understand.

Chapter 5 — *Refining your voice* deals with being able to elevate speech for classical theatre or simply a touch of class. It addresses handling blank and rhymed verse to achieve more sophisticated sense of timing.

Revisions in the new edition:

- Thoroughly re-examined to honor UK and North American perspectives on what constitutes refined pronunciation.

Chapter 6 — *Releasing your other voices* helps actors to find new sounds other than their habitual ones, specifically through dialects, character voices, and cartoon voices. This process of awakening excites and emboldens, because suddenly there seems to be no limit to one's possible vocal range.

Revisions in the new edition:

- An expanded guide to published and online dialect resources.
- Updated analysis of the primary methods of dialect/accent study.

- Updated information on voiceovers reflecting changes in technology.
- Updated information on changes to the field of animated voices for the internet and for gaming.
- New information on the many ways in which an actor can earn a living through voice work.
- Updated material on developing voiceover demos (commercial, cartoon and non-broadcast).

Revisions in the new edition:

Chapter 7 — *Selecting your system* is geared toward going on into advanced training and choosing the teacher, approach, texts, and school that will best suit each individual actor.

- Expanded analysis of major voice teacher influences to include Patsy Rodenburg and the newest editions of Kristin Linklater's and Arthur Lessac's work.
- Connecting the student with resources like *The Voice and Speech Review* publications, the Voice and Speech Trainers Association and the British Voice Association.
- Updated analysis of emerging voice and speech methodologies (such as Roy Hart, Fitzmaurice voicework, Knight-Thompson speechwork, neuro-linguistic programming, and Alba Emoting) and information on ways to become a voice and speech trainer.

Revisions in the new edition:

Chapter 8 — *Planning your voice future* has to do with starting on a lifelong, independent program of vocal growth. It launches the actor on years of further exploration.

- Since this is a review and summary, new sections will reflect earlier updates in the text.

Additional innovations in the new edition

Advances in technology have made it possible to replace the popular accompanying CD with a comprehensive website that now includes:

- Extensive teacher guides, including sample syllabi, scheduling options, and ways of adapting to varying academic environments and teaching circumstances.

- An option for accessing the full audio version of the book, allowing readers the option of listening to rather than reading portions of the text.
- Recordings of all exercises so that anyone can pursue these activities without the distraction of needing to hold and read the text, greatly freeing the individual participant.
- Links to helpful websites for more in-depth study.
- A wide page format, making it easier for the text to be placed and open in varying circumstances, allowing the actor more freedom of movement.
- MSWord versions of the forms used throughout so that students can fill them out and submit them electronically to their instructors.
- Online learning games and activities.
- Examples of voiceover demos (both the scripts and the actual recording).
- Supplementary examples of the text analysis of heightened language.

Using this text

There is sufficient material for a complete four-year training program in voice and speech. If limited to a shorter period, editing is quite possible. Chapters 5, 6, and/or 7 could be omitted, since these three deal with topics that will not fit all programs or readers. Those who do not wish to teach phonetics can edit the IPA portion of Chapter 3 without impeding their use of the rest of the text. We include a multitude of exercises simply to give you choice, fully expecting the reader to pick some and reject others. Much of the material presented is for the long haul, and actors may wish to examine it now but actually return to work it intensively at a later point in their overall education.

When anyone decides to commit to improved health, physical fitness or personal growth, there is a definite pattern that is followed from self-awareness through remediation and expansion to long-term planning. *Voice: Onstage and off* follows the same pattern, this time with the voice at the center instead of the body or the spirit. As with all such growth processes, we hope to offer travel *advice* but to mainly empower each actor to take their own journey.

Cartoon figures and icons

At various points we will enlist the advice of a Voice Chef, a Voice Doc, a Voice Shrink and a Voice Coach. When the chef, doc, shrink and coach first appear in the text, it is as full body drawings. Subsequently these figures are represented either by reduced headshots or by icons symbolizing their professions: a bowl for the chef, stethoscope for the doc, clipboard for the shrink, and a whistle for the coach.

A hand icon within a circle signals an exercise.

A set of headphones indicates that the particular exercise or table in question is one where the reader would particularly benefit from listening to the material being demonstrated on the web site.

A monitor icon is used whenever the website contains useful forms or documents.

Acknowledgments

Many fine teachers have influenced and inspired this work, shaping the perspectives and providing insights, among them are Ron Arden, Cicely Berry, Rowena Balos, Linda Brennan, Kathy Brindle-Maes, Lindagail Campbell, Bill and Irene Chapman, Joe Deer, Catherine Fitzmaurice, Anne Golden, Julia Guichard, Russell Grandstaff, Arthur Lessac, Kristin Linklater, Gary Logan, Ken Macrorie, Patsy Rodenburg, Anne Schilling, Ron Scherer, Russell Paul Schofield, Nan Seitz, David Alan Stern, Dennis Turner, Shelly Wallace, the faculty of the University of Cincinnati's College-Conservatory of Music, the Xavier Leadership Center, the Cincinnati Voice Consortium and the Voice and Speech Trainers Association.

We are grateful to Michael Johnson-Chase for providing us with his expertise regarding the Feldenkrais and Alexander techniques and to Rachel Sleek Bañuelos and Nathan Ruggles for their help with the voice-over material. Reviewers for the manuscript were Brigid Panet, (RADA), David Zinder (Tel Aviv University), Jane Boston and Tara McAllister-Viel (the Central School of Speech and Drama), and Beth McGuire (Yale School of Drama).

We are grateful to Talia Rogers for recognizing the value of a new revision of this text, for patiently finessing the transfer of rights from our former publishing company, and for championing textual enhancements and the companion site. Our thanks to Ben Piggott for his tireless efforts in manifesting all the above and to Matthew Kopel for his design and implementation of the site.

We are particularly appreciative of the way Emma Usherwood took our basic idea for the book's cover, skillfully provided numerous options from which we could select and refine, and successfully implemented our suggestions into the final product. Thanks to Andrew Barton for his patient, skilled work on our four voice mentor figures and on implementing the recording of portions of the text. Thanks to our sound engineer Adam Rabinowitz for invaluable suggestions for recording effectively, for bringing recordings made great distances apart into the same auditory world.

Owning your voice

To understand your voice, imagine having another person living within you — all the time.
BERNADETTE PETERS, actor

Your voice is hiding inside a cave. The cave is your body. You will never know your voice as well as your body because there is no photograph, scale, measuring tape, full-length mirror or zipper to help you. No one will ever kiss, slap, caress or shove your voice. It hides well.

Can you remember the first time you found out about your height, weight, strength, and motor skills? By kindergarten, you knew who was tallest, heaviest, and who ran fastest. You knew who could draw so that everyone could guess what the picture was. Every year, you learned more about bodies. By now, you have a fairly sophisticated knowledge of yours: waist measurement, hat size, energy level, sleep needs, body fat ratio, cardiovascular fitness, muscle tone, and pain threshold — in each you know or can easily learn how your body reacts. From soccer to calligraphy, you know what you can and cannot do well. Or you can make a fairly accurate prediction. Bodily, you know who you are. But vocally? It is possible that you do not yet know yourself at all.

UNIT 1.1   **A stranger inside**

There are five major reasons why you can have a voice all your life and still not know it:

1. **The voice is elusive**. Not only can you not see it, but you also hear it differently from others. Because you *are* the cave and other people are outside the cave, the voice you hear and *they* hear is not the same. It haunts you from its place of hiding. Just when you least expect it, your voice reveals your innermost secrets. It hides from you, but then it suddenly doesn't let *you* hide from other people. If the eyes are the mirrors of the soul, the voice is its echo. It will suddenly break, rise in pitch, take on an edge, choke, gasp, guffaw, and disappear altogether, revealing far more about how you feel than you hoped to show. It stays always out of sight and often out of control.

    As we open our mouths and words pour forth we reveal the deepest parts of ourselves . . . our fears, our denials, and in some crucial instances our very souls.

    PATSY RODENBERG, author of *The Right to Speak*

2. **Our society is voice ignorant.** We live in an overwhelmingly body-conscious culture, with almost zero vocal awareness. While people are irritated by unpleasant voices, they often are not *consciously* aware that the voice is the source of that irritation. An interesting study involved professional models who were auditioning for commercials. Videos of a sample group of these beautiful people (those who had unpleasant voices) were chosen for the research project. Observers watched each tape twice, first without sound, then with, and were asked what was different. Almost invariably, people found the models less attractive *with* sound ("She's not nearly as pretty as I thought at first.") but when asked had no idea why. Some would claim camera angles, lights or focus had changed, though none had. Most people just don't factor voice into the package. The result is that someone concerned with "attractiveness" may spend mega-hours with a trainer, nutritionist, hair stylist, diet consultant, skin specialist, manicurist, masseuse, wardrobe designer, and even a plastic surgeon yet never stop to consider the voice as an erogenous zone.

    You can spend all day getting ready and then blow the whole thing when you open your mouth.

    KATHLEEN TURNER, actor

3. **Our own voices turn us off.** When you to listen to a recording of your voice, you recoil. It doesn't match your self-image. Even if there are elements of this recorded voice you like, it doesn't seem like *you*. It manages to reveal personal

shortcomings and yet still somehow seem foreign. It becomes a dreaded stranger. You avoid listening instead of facing your fear. You decide that it isn't you on the machine and whoever it is, it isn't someone you want to be near. You are not alone. Everyone feels this way, even those whom others believe to have exquisite voices.

The first time I heard a recording of myself I thought they must have made a mistake and substituted the voice of some other silly ninny for mine.

KATHARINE HEPBURN, actor

4. **Voices do magic.** They operate so far below awareness that they are frighteningly powerful. This is why most guided hypnosis is achieved by voice alone. Voice effects us sensorily in the same way touch, the most intimate form of communication, does. With voice, (1) air moves past the vocal folds causing them to vibrate, (2) the vibration causes shock waves in the air, (3) these shock waves ripple out through the air, (4) the waves reach the ear of the listener, touching and flexing the eardrum. Talking can be as soft as a tickling feather or forceful as a slamming sledge-hammer. And the recipient is almost completely unaware of how the touch happened. The effect is every bit as powerful as music.

You are speaking with a musical instrument and . . . while the pen is mightier than the sword, the spoken word is far mightier than the written one.

RAYMOND RIZZO, author of The Voice as an Instrument

5. **Voice is contagious.** When someone speaks to you with a thin, nasal voice, you will become tense, breathe more shallowly, focus on your own nasal area, get emotionally constricted, and project these feelings back to the speaker, thinking, "What a nerd!" No one ever seems to recognize the romantic yearnings of the person with a deviated septum. The opposite happens when someone murmurs to you with relaxed, open, chest resonance, low, sultry pitch, and slightly breathy tone. This person makes tax forms seem like love letters. Action and reaction take place below conscious awareness. We have powerful emotional reactions to voices without comprehending why — a fact advertisers exploit to their advantage!

If you cut off a response, you may be haunted by that response later. In U.S. mental hospitals, the majority of hallucinations are auditory, because people in this culture do not pay much attention to the voice.

RICHARD BANDLER, information scientist, co-founder of neuro-linguistic programming

So, you can't quite find your voice, your society doesn't seem to overtly notice it at all, and when you notice it, you are basically stunned and turned off. Voices are hypnotic and frighteningly powerful. What to do? The good news is that every one of these negative images surrounding your voice can be changed to something positive. You can make it all work for you. Elusive? Much, much less so with practice and technique. Ignorance? Others may remain so, but you can develop knowledge quickly and use it. A turn-off? Only until you listen to yourself enough to make peace with your voice. Then you begin to sound pretty good! Magic? Yes, and you can be the magician. Contagious? Once you understand how voice works, you can develop the power to catch, to be caught or to escape at will. You can develop true vocal freedom.

Voice baby — starting fresh

There are three important points to remember as you start. First, you need to face and embrace the power connected to your own voice. Do other people judge your personality based on your voice? Sure they do. The word "persona" originally meant "mask" and comes from two other small words: "per," meaning "of" or "by the", and "sona," meaning "SOUND!"

Your **personality** is the mask you wear in public, powerfully shaped by the way you speak. But **personality** (how you communicate who you are) is not the same as **identity** (how you perceive yourself). What you put *out* is not necessarily what you *are*. Do you fear that changing the way you speak will cause you to lose a part of yourself? Wrong! If you change your voice, you will change the way people *react* to you. You don't need to lose what you had and are inside. You simply expand your options. If you wish, you can become more effective at communicating who you are inside. If you wish, you can hide better. If you're tired of people coming on to you while you're trying to explain their 1040 forms or if you are a great lover with a nerd voice, you may be able to change your whole life!

Second, think of yourself as a voice infant. You have been speaking all your life, but *unconsciously*. Your conscious vocal life begins today. You are a baby in this subject. Let this be comforting. Give the same loving patience we give all newcomers to life, to yourself. This will allow you to laugh at yourself (and your stumbling) with delight instead of derision. It will let you greet your smallest steps with exultation. If anything you need *more* patience than does a small child, because while you are brand new to the world of voice *training*, you come into it with a lifetime of habits, many of them deeply set. So ease yourself into growth.

Third, do not expect miracles. Being kind to yourself means being kind to your teacher as well. An amazing number of actors sign up for a voice class and are appalled to find their problems are not solved in ten weeks. There are no instant cures. The process we will pursue in this book is that followed by anyone who decides to make a change in their life and then succeeds.

In our society, someone who decides to get healthy usually focuses on the physical or psychological (rather than vocal) self. Those who do well in fitness or therapy (1) start off gaining self-knowledge and acceptance, (2) move into correcting problems, and then, (3) work towards advanced skills and growth, constantly expanding their options. Those who try on the first day to make the Olympic team or leap to spiritual perfection always fail. You are reading this book because you have decided to make a change in your life. You are going to become an actor who uses their voice better, onstage and off.

So stop letting your voice be a stranger. Begin by taking the time to recognize your own vocal past. Feedback has shaped your self-concept, whether that feedback was accurate or not. Your physical history has been captured in photo albums, videos, and growth charts. It may even be represented by various boxes of clothing in the attic. Unearthing the history of your voice will help you to begin to understand how it has grown.

ONLINE

EXERCISE 1.2.1 MY VOICE HISTORY

1. EARLY FEEDBACK. Can you remember the first time anyone said anything to you about your speech? Was it being told to be quiet, to speak up, not to say that word? How did you figure out that whatever popped out of your mouth would not necessarily be accepted? What positive feedback did you receive? What did you decide to try again because it seemed to go over well?
2. CONSISTENT FEEDBACK. What have been the most consistent voice responses you have gotten over the years? Positive or negative, what has come up most often? You may try closing your eyes and going back year by year through your life. You will come up with many blanks, which is OK, but it is important to bring back all the feedback because some of it may have *really* left its mark.
3. TRYING TO CHANGE. Did you ever consciously try to change your voice? When and why? Were you imitating someone? What made you try? Did you succeed or give up? Did you try more than once?
4. INDIRECT FEEDBACK. Were there times when others didn't address your voice directly, but you *suspect* that it was your voice that got to them? Like being told not to be so angry when you didn't feel angry but must have sounded like it? Or being told to stop being meek when you thought you were asserting yourself? When have you been misunderstood or misjudged because of your speech rather than your thoughts or behavior?
5. ACTING NOTES. If you've been involved with theatre for a while, what are your vocal notes (from your director, teacher, coach, scene partner, or even your mother) most of the time? Be sure to establish both what you feel is good about your voice and what needs work.

voice is insufficiently manly or womanly? Is the opposite true? Do people respond so strongly to your sexual stereotype that they assume you are far more traditionally feminine or masculine than you feel? Is your voice an intriguing, androgynous, confusing mix?

9. STRANGER ON A RECORDING. When you hear yourself on a recording what exactly have you heard? If the voice on the machine isn't what you expected, how is it different? How does it violate or reinforce your self-concept?

10. AN ACTING VOICE. Are you aware of differences from your private and even your public self when you act? Not conscious *characterization* decisions, but rather unconscious alteration in your vocal life when you hit the stage?

Again, jot down the answers that seem to have validity. Write sentences you could demonstrate in class that show you in each of the circumstances above. Trust yourself to sense which influences are strong.

The next step is to go back over your voice history and profile and confront what may be influencing you but shouldn't. In Robert's family, rewarded behavior was to speak in a carefully modulated voice. Punished behavior was raising your voice. Robert got constant notes early in his work as an actor about needing to project. It was only when he realized that proper behavior in the Barton family dining room had nothing to do with what is needed in a thousand-seat theatre that he was able to let his voice out. Now you would think that anyone would know this, and in fact, if you had asked him he probably would have given the right ("Well, ummm, you need more volume in a theatre than in a dining room, right?") answer. What he didn't realize was that the old home habit was creeping *unconsciously* into the theatre. It didn't work just to try to speak *louder*. He needed to track the specific bias ("People with class do not speak loudly") that had influenced his choosing a small sound. Rocco was a boy soprano, so when his voice changed, he fought to have the world's lowest, most manly voice, because "real men" don't have high voices. He forced himself into a narrow, constricted sound, severely limited his singing range, and took years to let go and let the high notes back in. He needed to *believe* that great male voices use pitch. What's your story?

EXERCISE 1.2.3 TRACKING THE BLOCKS

1. STILL WITH ME. Make a list from the categories in Exercises 1.2.1 and 1.2.2 of those influences you feel are still strongly with you. If nothing comes, you may want to start with a simple list of rewarded and punished behavior in your home, neighborhood, school, etc. and see where voice comes up.

2. IN THE WAY. Decide which ones may be getting in your way. Circle them, remember them, and be alert for the next situation in which you might want to stop and free yourself.

3. OH, YEAH. Be alert for other influences that did not come up right away but may pop into your memory now that the subject is there. Keep your list where you can add and review.

Note: don't try to place blame. People who influenced you to speak one way or another probably had no idea you would want to be an actor someday and were mostly (even if ignorantly) trying to help you to get on in life. Your voice isn't anyone's fault.

While sweeping the past, it is too easy to throw out everything, so take a moment to validate what is working and why. What has contributed to your vocal strengths? Honor the parts of your voice that work for you.

EXERCISE 1.2.4 KEEPING THE GOOD STUFF

1. STILL WITH ME. Make a list of positive influences that are still strongly with you.

2. WANT THIS. Decide which ones you want to keep on board as a basis or firm structure for your future vocal work. Circle them, remember them, and be alert for the next situation in which you might want to stop and use what you know you have going for you.

Vocal contradictions

As teachers, we constantly confront contradictions such as an empowered feminist who uses a Barbie Doll voice and seems puzzled (and enraged) when she is not listened to, or a strong, virile male who has a tiny boy voice that, when he acts, makes him suddenly seem like a wimp. They have developed themselves in a certain direction without bringing along their voices.

All I could think of was (in a Mickey Mouse voice) "I am the vampire Lestat!" I mean, he has the highest, reediest voice in the world!

JULIA PHILLIPS, original producer of the film *Interview with a Vampire* on hearing that Tom Cruise had been cast in the title role

I don't think I've ever fallen under the spell of an actor when the voice wasn't a big component. How is Tom Cruise going to say those lines? How is he going to exert the power of Lestat? Over and over in the book I say Lestat's voice was purring in my ear or that the voice was like roughened velvet, and here's this actor with no voice!

ANNE RICE, author of the novel *Interview with a Vampire*

This is endemic in Hollywood. But it often doesn't much matter on film, because the visual effect is so much stronger than the aural. Projection is not an issue, and post-production sound treatments (the above issue was solved to some extent by corrective Clearsound for electronic enhancement adding a reverb to Lestat's voice) can work miracles. It is possible to have an extremely successful film career without having much of a voice. However, when such stars venture into the theatre, the reviews are often devastating. Once they get onto a stage to speak or act, their voices come out to sabotage them in ways they probably never experienced before.

The film actor hardly needs the voice. (He hardly needs the body, except to show himself off as a marvelous specimen.) The stage actor certainly needs all the vocal control, breath control and vocal techniques available — he needs them all.

LAURENCE OLIVIER, actor

Your voice may simply never have progressed along with your spirit and your mind. It may have gotten frozen at some point and failed to evolve. It may have gotten lazy. Or it may have moved in a different direction from the rest of you, so it sends off messages about the *other* side of you, the one you thought was gone, the dark, bad, scared or unworthy side. We all are afraid that we may sound a certain way. One of the best ways to deal with this is laughter!

ONLINE

EXERCISE 1.3.1 **VOICES FROM HELL**

1. Pick a word that describes what you are afraid your voice sounds like, either because you used to be this way or because it is a side of yourself you rarely acknowledge.
2. Finish the sentence: "I hope I don't sound like a _____." Here are some possibilities: "twit" — "bimbo" — "git" — "douche bag" — "sot" — "jock" — "clot" — "flake" — "pig" — "hick" — "nutter" — "snob" — "asshole" — "tool" — "berk" — "toff" — "actor." Yes, you can cite the names of people you don't admire, too as in "I hope I don't sound like _____."
3. If you're working with a group, write the term on a piece of paper or up on the board. Have someone collate.
4. Are there shared fears? These should be dealt with first. The class should try to identify what a "bimbo", or whatever, sounds like. Describe the components that seem to make up such a voice. With this and other exercises in this chapter, don't worry if you have the correct terminology. Just find some way to describe it that works for you.
5. Those who feel they can do a pretty good bimbo demonstrate. Last of all the person(s) who wrote the term demonstrate and say why they think there might be some of that characteristic in their sound.
6. Now is the time for honest feedback. Is this merely a fantasy, or is there some truth in it? Is the actor's fear not noticed by others? Is there some other unfortunate cultural stereotype with which this person's voice flirts? Everyone should take a turn.

ONLINE

EXERCISE 1.3.2 **VOICES FROM HEAVEN**

1. Pick a word that describes what you *wish* your voice sounded like.
2. Finish the sentence: "I hope I sound like a _____." Here are some possibilities: "genius" — "hottie" — "brick" — "caring human being" — "take charge type" — "leader" — "real person" — "actor." You can also cite the names of people whose voices you admire.

3. If you're working with a group, write the term on a piece of paper. Have someone collate.
4. Decide which vocal characteristics are most coveted by the class as a whole and which are simply your own aspirations. Let these images shape the positive forward-reaching part of your work.

Nothing in these exercises is ever nearly as bad as you think it might be. Even if you find out that you *do* sound like a dweeb, you'll discover that simply acknowledging it, then owning it, frees you. It is no longer a fear. It is simply a fact. And it is a fact that you are perfectly capable of changing. Or it is a fact that you are perfectly capable of accepting. If your voice needs to catch up with the rest of you, you have come to the right place.

Basic equipment

UNIT 1.4

The hiding element of your voice can also be dealt with by three kinds of tools. We will pursue projects involving each of them:

1. A small hand **mirror**, which will allow you to see some of the tongue, teeth, mouth roof, and lip action involved in articulation. You may sometimes wish to work with a full-length mirror as well, but mostly you will focus where you shape sound. After you get to know the organs and surfaces involved in speech, flossing may be less boring!
2. A small, portable **recorder**, which fits in your pocket and can be carried everywhere. You may also wish to work with video to observe your own body/voice integration, but there is much value in spending time just listening to something that sounds like what others hear. If you spend ten minutes a day (five recording and five on playback) for two weeks, much of the trauma will disappear. That voice will begin to sound tolerable, and you will move swiftly ahead. Some systems allow you to hear yourself through headphones *while* you're speaking. That can teach you a lot. Record yourself in various contexts, talking out loud to yourself, shooting the breeze with roommates, reading a text (why not this one?), running lines, rehearsing a monologue you know well, doing cold readings from unfamiliar plays. Aim for an assortment of off and onstage recordings.

   Some of the material in this book is recorded and easily downloaded from the book's website. Work along with the recordings whenever possible until you have mastered the exercise.

3. **Material** to work with. Many upcoming exercises will require classical and contemporary monologues or scenes to explore. Material on which you have already worked in other contexts is fine, because you are familiar and comfortable with the words, so you can address your voice and not fuss over what to say — just how to say it.

These three tools can do a lot to help you to overcome the feeling that your voice is a stranger. If you can regularly see it, hear it, and work it with familiar words, you are on your way to knowing it.

EXERCISE 1.4.1 CHECKING IT OUT

Take a small mirror and just play with it reflecting your mouth for a while, noticing details you may have missed. Now study your lips, look at your teeth, note the alveolar ridge (the dental ridge at the front of the roof of your mouth behind your teeth), your velum or soft palate (surface at the back roof of your mouth), the uvula (the soft palate's tail), and your pharynx (just behind the uvula). Just out of view are your glottis, epiglottis, larynx, vocal folds esophagus, and trachea. More on each of these in Chapter 2, but for now, check out all the items on the map.

EXERCISE 1.4.2 RECORDING TIME

Pick a specific time of day for an entire week and record yourself in seven different contexts. Pick from the suggestions above. Don't erase anything, just move on. Each day, listen to the full recording. At the end of the week, listen to all seven sessions. It really won't sound so bad. You're getting used to it.

EXERCISE 1.4.3 AUDITION UPDATE

A very common format for a prepared audition is for participating actors to present two strongly contrasting monologues, one of them classical, for a total of four minutes or less, sometimes with the option of adding a short excerpt from a song. This is a useful format for your first presentation in this class because it requires considerable range and is a way of checking in or updating your classmates on where you are at this moment in your progress as an actor. It has the added benefit of giving you experience in an audition format you will probably wish to master. We recommend that the classical piece be verse, not prose.

1. Record yourself while you present and also the person(s) you may be imitating (see next section).
2. Even though the focus of this assignment is vocal, be sure to fully stage and commit to the physical lives of your characters so the voice comes from a totally organic characterization.
3. Restrict any feedback to the vocal components. It will be quite tempting to want to critique the audition as an audition, which can cause considerable digression. Save that kind of debriefing for outside of class.
4. Save this recording and keep referring back to it all term as you progress.

Imitators — a voice mirror

UNIT 1.5

A human vocal mirror is better than a looking glass. It is one of the best ways to study what you do with your voice. Work with a partner or, better yet, in a foursome. In a group of four, couple A studies couple B and *vice versa* all term. You get two vocal mirrors and you get to bounce your ideas off of another observer/listener. The two (or more) of you will learn to **imitate** each other, so each of you can experience some of your vocal tendencies reflected back by someone else. It can be remarkably helpful to have someone *else* studying your voice and in turn to study theirs. Your listening skills and objectivity can take a giant leap. If you are outside a class situation, pick someone who makes you comfortable but doesn't let you off the hook, exactly the kind of person you might choose to play racquetball, or run with daily, who will be fun but make it hard for you to miss. If you are in class, the best partners are those who have known you longest, who have had the most opportunities to observe you in multiple contexts. Partner exercises and opportunities to imitate will be salted throughout this book.

Imitation is not just the highest form of flattery. It offers big pay-offs, because you get valuable information while honing your observation and auditory skills. Your sense of detail and nuance increases. Because you want to get the imitation right (let's face it, you don't want to come off as inept, plus you want your partner to get value so she will give it) you force yourself to perceive with greater accuracy. You get to give generously to another actor in an honest way and are able to come to grips with your own tendencies. You learn to offer and to take potentially devastating information in a humane and accepting way.

Imitation is love. So with an open heart and mind, I freely imitate other ways of being to gain greater understanding and appreciation of our world.

CHRISTIAN SWENSON, performance artist, creator of *Human Jazz*

Bring your recorder to class whenever your "subjects" present work and record them. Also record them by interviewing them, when they raise their hands and ask a question, when they are hanging out in the hall — in as many different contexts as possible. If your class does all the dialect, verse, elevated speech, and character voice assignments in later chapters, record your subject doing each and nail not only this actor's basic voice but the actor discovering new voices as well.

After some close, intensive study, you will be ready for the following class presentations:

EXERCISE 1.5.1 MY SUBJECT IN PUBLIC

1. Enter the stage as your subject, with full physical characterization supporting the vocal.
2. Introduce yourself to the audience the way your subject would.
3. Make seven statements that are characteristic of the subject. Try for statements that capture this person in different circumstances and moods.
4. Make sure that you have demonstrated your subject's tendencies in tempo, rhythm, articulation, pronunciation, pitch, volume, word choice, nonverbals, and quality.
5. End it the way your subject would, and exit.
6. Discuss as a group where the imitation was right on and where the observer needs to study more.

EXERCISE 1.5.2 **SUBJECTS IN A SCENE**

If you are working in fours, the A couple performs the B couple. If you are working only in pairs, person A and B play each other.

1. Pick a time, place, and circumstance where these two would meet and experience a strong conflict. It is important that they disagree strongly over some issue, so if you are Siamese twins you will need to explore where you are least matched.
2. Be sure to employ all the influences on the vocal life of the subject. Let those influences be strongly present in the scene. Let them feed the conflict. If one actor is free and loose of tongue, dropping four-letter words as casually as breathing, for example, and the other is cautious to the point of using only elevated euphemisms to describe any basic body function, use this as a crucial part of the scene.
3. Be sure to record yourselves in rehearsal and offer strong, direct advice on how to get the voice better.
4. If either of these actors tends to change radically when they act, try to insert the actor doing scripted material at some point in the scene to demonstrate this alteration.
5. When the scene is over, share with the group what you learned as a performer and what you learned seeing "yourself" performed.

The voice recipe — nine ingredients

UNIT 1.6

Just as there are certain ingredients used in *every* cake or wine, there are nine crucial ones for voice. They can be isolated and studied separately to help you to mix them better later. They overlap, intersect, and influence each other, but you can work on them individually. The basic categories by which voice is analyzed can help you to move past cultural stereotypes (i.e. Voices from Hell) into a sense of how the voice actually works. If you come at your voice from these nine angles, it is not overwhelming.

Figure 1.1 The Voice Chef by Andrew Barton

Tempo — your voice in time

(other terms used: pace, rate, speed, momentum)

This is one of the easiest to recognize and hardest to change. Is your speech fast, slow, medium or variable? Does it change by circumstance or within any given statement? Do you speak, for example, very quicklyforthefirstfewwordsofeachsentence and then s — l — o — w w — a — y d — o — w — n for the last few? You can see the many possible combinations beyond speedy or sluggish. Under what circumstances do you change? Most of us speed up when tense or excited, so you probably increase your tempo when you act or are trying to explain why you came in five hours later than you promised.

You can tell how nervous I am by how fast I am talking.

CATHERINE DENEUVE, actor

Rhythm — your drum beats

(other terms used: beats, stress, pulse, emphasis, phrasing, pause, flow, idea groupings, accenting, stressing, length of sound)

If a drummer was following you around trying to get your vocal habits, when would he hit the drum, how hard, and with what part of the stick? Is your attack on words generally light or heavy? Do you stress certain ones? Do you never stress at all? Where do your pauses fall? Between sentences? After commas? Or in unexpected places like between adjectives and nouns or adverbs and verbs ("I really . . . think we should all wear weird . . . clothes to the party")? Does the overall effect seem smooth, jerky, choppy, erratic, drawled, fluid, ploddingly predictable, or charmingly variable?

The great acting teacher Stanislavski maintained that tempo and rhythm were the most important aspects of acting; that if you get a character's timing you're almost there. Yet most of us get trapped. It is especially tough if you are a slow, heavy, predictable type and your character is a mercurial, lightning-swift magician of a speaker. An amazing number of rehearsal problems are solved once you find the tempo-rhythm of the character. Alas, we all have a strong tendency to impose our own on the role. Yet after wrestling with great frustration over certain speeches, you recognize that they just need to go faster or have stronger stresses and often it all falls into place.

Once you free yourself from your habitual timing, you can move on to the power of actually controlling time.

One of the most useful effects I ever learned was holding spaces between words. When you . . . create that . . . empty space . . . in a . . . room, you create something . . . that needs to be filled. You have control. Everyone sits on the edge of their seats, trying to fill it in, but you are the only one who can fill it. It's dynamic. It's physical, not magic, but it appears to be magic!

ANNETTE BENNING, actor

ONLINE

EXERCISE 1.6.2.1 MY TEMPO/RHYTHM

Describe your voice in each of the following categories.

1. TEMPO. What is your basic rate? If variable, when do you speed up or slow down within a sentence? Write one using the example above to show visually how your tempo shifts.
2. RHYTHM. Write a new sentence with your stress/unstress patterns. Go back and underline where you tend to place particular weight. Write another typical sentence that shows your pattern of pausing. Draw lines between the words where you pause. Go back and do the same with the sentence above. Be prepared to demonstrate if asked.

UNIT 1.6.3   *Articulation — shaping the sound*

(other terms used: diction, clarity, precision, intelligibility, definition)

Your articulation has little to do with how you pronounce a word (that comes up next) but how precisely, carefully, and crisply you speak each sound in the word. It has to do with what parts of your mouth you use to make the sound and how accurately they are used (often called placement), how long you sustain it (extent), how much force you put behind it (pressure), and whether or not your vocal folds are engaged (vibration). You may totally mispronounce a word and yet articulate it beautifully. You may be accurate in your pronunciation and drop the ball on articulation. We will deal with placement, extent, pressure, and vibration later, but for now realize that this concerns mumbling, slurring, and stumbling or sluggish speech versus precise forming of sounds. It also relates to how easily precision is accomplished. Many actors have been told to *work* on articulation, so they produce labored, self-conscious, plodding, joyless, very hard-working sounds, unrelated to conversation. Think of articulation drills the way a musician does scales, endlessly repeating exercises to improve speed, clarity, definition, and control.

When actors are told that they cannot be heard in a theatre, the problem is often not that they haven't been speaking loudly enough but that they have not been articulating clearly enough. Articulation has all to do with consonants, and if they are clean it is often not necessary to push the sound behind them. Articulation has an enormous effect on clarity.

To a certain extent, vowels are the emotional component in word-construction and consonants are the intellectual component. The consonants create effects more than emotions.

KRISTIN LINKLATER, author of *Freeing the Natural Voice*

UNIT 1.6.4   *Pronunciation — standard, regional or eccentric?*

(other terms used: dialect, accent, class, level of speech)

There is an accepted way to say any word in any place at any time. In Oregon, we pronounce our state's name O-ruh-gun, but most of those outside our region do not. Many Americans pronounce Gloucester with three syllables rhyming with *Rochester* instead of with *roster*. Is there really only one right way to say the name of a state or region? Well, there is an *appropriate* way, which is how the natives prefer it if regional, or how the dictionary presents it if universal, or how your character would say it if in a play. Pronunciation is not how precisely the word or sound is spoken but how close or far it is from what is expected. There are regional and ethnic accents, as well as pronunciations unique to any group or person. Robert persisted in calling soldiers "shouldiers" for much of his life. Rocco knew with absolute certainty that pillow was "pellow" and measure was "maysure." Pronunciation is discussed in terms of how close or far it is from what is considered standard. Most likely "errors" are to place emphasis on the wrong syllable, to add or subtract a syllable, or to substitute one vowel or consonant sound for another. While these two areas are often confused, basically pronunciation is hitting the right chords, while articulation is hitting them skillfully.

He could not frame to pronounce it right. Therefore, they took him and slew him.

THE BIBLE, *Judges,* Chapter 12, Verse 6

ONLINE

EXERCISE 1.6.4.1 MY ARTICULATION/PRONUNCIATION

1. ARTICULATION. Describe yourself on a scale between crisp and slurred. Which sounds or words are difficult for you to articulate? Which sounds have you been told you drop or adjust? Yes, this is difficult, and you may need to ask others for help, but give it your best shot. You have to start somewhere.
2. PRONUNCIATION. Is your speech non-regional? If not, what are the influences that alter it? What sounds do you substitute for standard? Do you have any idiosyncratic pronunciations unique to you?
3. Write sentences to demonstrate your style. Either typical personal statements, lines from plays or quotations from others will serve.

Since studies show that most of us spend 3/4 of our time in front of the television set, why don't we all speak the same unaccented Network English? And where did all these Stepford Announcers come from? Or did they all have to undergo Accent Surgery as part of their contracts?

ALICE STEINBACH, author, columnist

Pitch — notes on your sheet music

(other terms used: range, pattern, melody, inflection, intonation, intervals, median notes, key notes)

Is your voice higher than, lower than or close to most others? Speechwise, are you a tenor, soprano, alto, baritone, bass or wandering pilgrim? Do you lock your pitch in one place or use many notes? Most of us think that our voices are lower than others hear them and that we are using more notes than others perceive. Most of us need encouragement to explore the top, bottom, and varying possibilities between, to free ourselves from the monotonous. We unconsciously place restrictions on the number of notes we use. To some extent, pitch is determined by the size of the vocal folds. Men's are often longer and thicker than women's, so their pitch is often lower. But all speakers have the capacity to use many more notes than they tend to employ.

Pitch is also analyzed in terms of exactly *where* it changes. If you always go up at the end of a sentence, you make everything sound like a question and come across as highly insecure. If you always go down, everything sounds like a final pronouncement, curtain line, a statement to end all others and not open to negotiation. You may also change pitch within a word, inflecting a vowel to produce interesting variations. Changing pitch on a vowel can make you seem sly, satiric or playful. If your pitch changes are extremely predictable, you have a **melody pattern**. You hit the same notes on the scale over and over like an old, familiar tune.

> **She that was ever fair and never proud,**
> **Had tongue at will and yet was never loud.**

Iago from WILLIAM SHAKESPEARE's *Othello*

Volume — filling space

(other terms used: projection, size, power, intensity, dynamics, audibility, loudness)

If you had a volume knob on your instrument, how skillfully and sensitively would you play it? Could you blow your listener out of the room if needed? Could you force an audience to listen intently because you have gone down to a careful stage whisper? Do you sense when a change of volume is needed? Voices thought of as having power can fill any room effortlessly. Some voices are simply larger than others, although this has as much to do with where the actor resonates as it does with simple loudness or softness. Are you sensitive to the needs and comfort level of each listener? Is your volume appropriate, predictable, adaptable, adjustable? Do you rely on volume to express emotional intensity? Are you pushing?

As noted earlier, in most theatre spaces, somewhat greater volume is needed than seems comfortably conversational for the actor, so the challenge is to keep the feeling of the speech easy and natural while getting the sound to the back of the auditorium. Almost everyone has a tendency when raising volume to automatically raise pitch as well. A rise in pitch communicates tension, so there is a built-in trap here, and the actor is always working on filling the space without getting stuck in their higher register. Recognition of the need to practice control in these areas is hardly recent:

Volume, pitch and rhythm these a speaker must bear in mind. Those who do usually win the prizes in the dramatic contests.

ARISTOTLE, philosopher, theatre essayist (384–322 BCE)

EXERCISE 1.6.6.1 MY PITCH/VOLUME

PITCH

1. Where is your basic pitch compared with other people?
2. Describe your speaking voice as if you were a singer.
3. Which part of your range do you most often fail to use?
4. Write a sentence that is a typical statement of yours. On the line below, mark your pitch pattern either with musical notes or as a wavy graph line. Do this with another sentence as well.

VOLUME

1. Where is your amplifier usually set?
2. Describe your sensitivity/adaptability to spaces and listeners.
3. Describe your biggest challenge with volume.
4. Illustrate your tendencies with a sentence (you may recycle old ones from previous exercises) by writing soft volume in small and loud volume in big letters.

UNIT 1.6.7

Unit 1.6.7 Quality – creating the sound core

There are more ways to describe quality than any other ingredient. Voices are named according to:

1. Their **impression** on the listener (hard, mellow, harsh, husky, strident, light, dark, thin, full, hollow, muffled, bright, dull, flat, clear, tremulous, whiny).

Figure 1.2 Shootout at the OK Chorale cartoon by Dan Piraro

If there can be a most important single ingredient, this is arguably it. When you produce sound it resonates or vibrates inside you, and where it resonates changes the sound itself. The overall impression or *feeling* of your voice comes from its quality.

(other terms used: tone, texture, feeling, resonance, placement, timbre)

ONLINE

2. The dominant point of **resonation** (nasal, sinus, pharyngeal, throat, mask, chest, head-voice).

3. Some **physical state** (breathy, hoarse, nasal, denasal — having a cold) that the listener perceives.

4. An **abstract** image (deep purple velvet, chocolate pudding, dry sherry) that tries to capture the voice's essence.

5. A **nonhuman** sound (like a musical instrument or sizzling bacon) based on the effect the voice has on the hearer.

While it may seem daunting that there are so many possible qualities, the very range of possibilities makes this area the ultimate actor's playground, the richest possible place to mine. Most of us get stuck in one or two, instead of exploring all the tones we have inside. Every one of these qualities is available to you. When you resonate in several places at once, your voice can take on rich overtones, much like musical harmonies.

Quality is that element which differentiates even voices of identical pitch and intensity.

V.S. ANDERSON, voice and speech specialist

EXERCISE 1.6.7.1 MY QUALITIES

1. Where do you think you resonate most often?

2. From the terms above, describe your voice by, (1) what others hear, (2) by a physiological condition (may be omitted if you think this isn't it), (3) in abstract terms (car, pet, color, fabric . .), (4) as a musical instrument (remember you have an entire orchestra of stringed, woodwind, brass, and keyboard instruments to choose from), (5) as some other nonhuman sound.

3. If your voice moves between several qualities, name them.

4. Which other qualities of voice are easiest for you to reproduce?

5. Which elude you?

6. Pick a sample sentence and if necessary punch up or exaggerate your fundamental quality.

UNIT 1.6.8

Word choice — your own lingo

(other terms used: language, vocabulary, idiom, slang, syntax, argot, jargon, vernacular)

Any statement that you make can range from guarded to blunt, formal to casual, elegant to profane, simple to complex, humorous to serious, flippant to earnest, depending on the words you pick. The size of your vocabulary determines the number of choices open to you. You will play characters whose word options are wider than your own, so you need to rise to the level of speech that the playwright has provided the character. Most of us, especially early in the morning, do not speak in brilliant rhymed couplets. You'll also play characters whose choices are narrower than yours, and you will need to understand the frustration they feel as they grasp for phrases that continually elude them.

How flexible are you? Can you indulge in witty, erudite repartee if that is what is going on in the room? Can you get down and dirty if need be? Do your word choices easily change worlds? Do you pick up on fad or buzz words or tend to avoid language vogues? Do you use the jargon of a particular group (mechanics, computer nerds, slackers) no matter what subject is under discussion? Do all your words have meaning, or do idle phrases ("It was like . . . you know . . . so, just, like . . . well . . . really, really awesome . . . you know") take the place of punctuation?

Not only do you choose words, you also choose to place them in a certain orcer (called **syntax**). "To get to school, that's where I'm off to," versus "I'm leaving for school now." You may speak in full sentences or captions, like the senior ex-President Bush ("The abortion thing. Big problem. Lotsa anger."). Since, in your onstage life, the playwright has made these decisions for you, the job becomes figuring out *why* they chose these words for this character and then making them seem the most natural choices in the world when you speak them. What euphemisms do you use for sex, death, and relieving yourself? Did your great uncle "kick the bucket," "buy the farm" or "go to his heavenly reward"? Do you excuse yourself to go to "the little girl's room" to "powder your nose" or go to "the can" or "the loo" to "take a dump" or "park a coil"? If you disapprove of something, do you call it "inappropriate," "bogus," "ghetto" or "lame"? Word choice can show or hide a huge amount about the real you and can be worn just like a mask.

The true use of speech is not so much to express our wants as to conceal them.

OLIVER GOLDSMITH, playwright

Vocal nonverbals – snap, crackle, and pop

(other terms used: noises, sounds, interjections, exclamations, paralinguistic vocal segregates)

We . . . ahhh . . . tend, as we're (sigh) gathering our . . . ummmm . . . thoughts to . . . mmmm . . . (burst of nervous laughter) add a lot of . . . errr . . . noise . . . (clicking teeth), you know? Nonverbals are sounds that are not words, as opposed to verbals, which are. They fill our vocal lives, adding interest or suspense, letting us pause or stretch while we think of the next word or idea, helping to express an emotion that won't come out in words, or just allowing us to let off steam. Groaning, growling, moaning, harrumphing, yawning, buzzing, humming, chirping, chuckling, purring, whistling, smacking, whimpering, popping, and sighing sounds all qualify, as do the above stall sounds. Teeth clicking, audibly inhaling or exhaling, giggling, and shrieking also qualify. Think of yourself as having your own built-in percussion section, which accompanies and helps to shape your speech. If the main drummer simply hits where you emphasize syllables (your rhythm), what do the cymbals, castanets, bells, timpani, chimes, gongs, tambourines, maracas and triangles (or for that matter the xylophone and glockenspiel!) do? What do your snares, congas, and kettledrums offer for support? When emotions run high or when you are feeling the live animal in you, you're particularly prone to adding pure sounds of laughter, joy, fear, anguish or anger (and erotic frenzy) between the words. Sometimes the noises take over and wipe out the words altogether.

Most of us use nonverbals liberally in offstage life, many too liberally. While some schools of actors (Marlon Brandos to Mickey Rourkes) seem to use more nonverbals than words, the rest of us, for some reason, get stingy and conservative onstage. The playwright rarely provides the nonverbals, because they are a crucial aspect of spoken, not written, language and are hard to get down on the page. So, it is up to you to find them. Acting seems too clean, too uncluttered to be real without them, even in the classics. The work looks too slick and rehearsed. Adding them gives any scene a huge dose of reality. And there are many moments when we find a sound far more powerful (and honest) than a word:

In the twentieth century, mounting distrust of language has given rise to the nonverbal gaining priority in creating response in an audience.

JACQUELINE MARTIN, author of *Voice in Modern Theatre*

EXERCISE 1.6.9.1 MY WORDS/MY SOUNDS

WORD CHOICE

1. Describe the kind of language you most often choose.
2. What are the circumstances in which it is the most difficult for you to adjust your word choice?
3. Do you have any favored slang or personal idiom?
4. How does your syntax vary from standard subject followed by predicate sentence structure? Give an example.

NONVERBALS

1. List all of them that you regularly use.
2. Go back and number them, with 1. being the most frequently employed.
3. Write a sentence, inserting your nonverbals.
4. Which sounds do you hear others employ but don't use yourself?

As you put all the voice ingredients above together, you create something called **phrasing**. Phrasing is the way you shape each thought through a sense of what's important and what's thrown away, of where to breathe, what to stress, what to stretch, and where to rush on to the end. You can take any written statement, reveal the rich subtext within it, or alter it significantly by how you choose to phrase it:

Deep down inside I wanted to say it the way I was thinking it: "So . . . HELP me, God."
BILL CLINTON, ex-president, on delivering the closing oath of his inaugural vows

Figure 1.3 President Bill Clinton being sworn in at his 1993 inauguration. Courtesy, William J. Clinton Presidential Library

EXERCISE 1.6.9.2 MY VOICE RECIPE

Take each of the nine categories considered so far. Come up with no more than one to three words to describe yourself in each and the shortest possible phrase to demonstrate. Devise a two-minute presentation, where you describe how to put together your voice. Talk about the product as a cook might discuss chocolate chip cookies or vegetable soup, as if you are sharing a recipe that will produce a tangible result. Use the material in Exercises 1.6.2.1 through 1.6.9.1 to help you to combine the following list of "ingredients" into a vocal concoction.

1. TEMPO

What is your basic rate?

If variable, when do you speed up or slow down within a sentence?

Write a sentence using the example above to show visually how your tempo shifts.

2. RHYTHM

Write a new sentence with your stress/unstress patterns.

Go back and underline where you tend to place particular weight.

Write another typical sentence that shows your pattern of pausing.

Draw lines between the words where you pause. Go back and do the same with the sentence above. Be prepared to demonstrate if asked.

3. ARTICULATION

Describe yourself on a scale between crisp and slurred.

Which sounds or words are difficult for you to articulate?

Which sounds have you been told you drop?

4. PRONUNCIATION

Is your speech standard, regional, ethnic or something else?

If not, what are the influences that alter it?

What sounds do you substitute for standard?

Do you have any idiosyncratic pronunciations unique to you?

Provide sentences to demonstrate (either typical personal statements, lines from plays or quotations from others will serve here).

5. PITCH

Where is your basic pitch orientation compared with other people?

Describe your speaking voice as if you were a singer.

Which part of your range do you most often fail to use?

Write a sentence that is a typical statement of yours. On the line below, mark your pitch pattern either with musical notes or as a wavy graph line. Do this with another sentence as well.

6. VOLUME

Where is your amplifier usually set?

Describe your sensitivity/adaptability to spaces and listeners.

Describe your biggest challenge with volume.

Illustrate your tendencies with a sentence (you may recycle old ones from previous exercises) by writing soft volume small and loud volume in big letters.

7. QUALITY

Where do you think you resonate most often?

From the terms above, describe your voice by what others hear:

By a physiological condition:

In abstract terms:

As a musical instrument:

As some other nonhuman sound:

If your voice moves between several qualities, name them.

Which other qualities of voice are easiest for you to reproduce?

Which elude you?

8. WORD CHOICE

Describe the kind of language you most often choose.

What are the circumstances that are most difficult for you to adjust your word choice for? Do you have any favored slang or personal idiom?

How does your syntax vary from standard subject followed by predicate sentence structure?

Give an example.

9. VOCAL NONVERBALS

List all of them you regularly use. Then go back and number them, with 1. being the most frequently employed.
Write a sentence, inserting your nonverbals.
Which sounds do you hear others employ but don't use yourself?

Alternative assignment: draw one slip in each of the nine categories we have just covered and share your sample sentences or phrases in whatever categories you have drawn. Be bold and fun-loving about sharing your own tendencies. Unexpected bonus: the more mannered you are, the easier this assignment.

UNIT 1.7 **Your voice compared with your classmates' — the voice awards**

While this next exercise may seem potentially unpleasant, we can assure you that we have tested it with many different groups. All of them report having a great time. For those working in a class, it gives a sense of perspective and a chance to get outside your own voice and to consider the entire group. Numerous students say that they have been able to accept their vocal characteristics for the first time through this exercise, because of the healing power of humor. Remember that laughter is the great lubricant of life. In numerous cases, students have somehow managed to be in denial about tending to be strident or nasal or even resonant until being selected as the "most" by their classmates. Even if they suspected the tendency on their part, it is quite possible that they did not realize they had developed it more than others in class. For others, the knowledge was there, but they were waiting for confirmation before being motivated to take action. Once they had accepted the "award", it not only didn't seem so bad, but also most were able to move swiftly to change if they so chose. This exercise is also an excellent way to make certain you understand all the terms in the last section. To vote intelligently, you must comprehend each category.

EXERCISE 1.7.1 **THE VOICE AWARDS**

1. Someone in class open this book and arbitrarily pick a short paragraph to read aloud. Everyone in the group take a turn reading it. Listen for the differences.

2. Pick a topic on which everyone can expound. Each person has twenty seconds to describe, for example, "The weirdest thing that happened to me last week" or "Who I think is the hottest human alive and why."

3. If you have not recently heard each other perform scripted material, have each person present a short monologue or, better still, two strongly contrasting monologues (as in Exercise 1.4.3).

4. Now take ballots home and vote for each other in the following categories. You may vote for yourself. You may vote for the same person many times. As with any awards ceremony, sweeps are always possible:

    TEMPO AWARDS: Fastest — Slowest — Most Varied — Most Consistent.
    RHYTHM AWARDS: Most Predictable — Heaviest Contrasts — Most Fluid — Least Expected Pauses.
    ARTICULATION AWARDS: Most Crisp — Most Slurred — Least Consistent — Most Labored.
    PRONUNCIATION AWARDS: Most Standard — Most Unusual — Most Regional.
    PITCH AWARDS: Highest — Lowest — Most Use of Range — Least Use of Range — Most Melody Pattern.
    VOLUME AWARDS: Loudest — Softest — Most Varied — Most Space Aware — Least Space Aware.
    WORD CHOICE AWARDS: Most Formal — Most Casual — Most Slang — Most Unusual.
    NONVERBAL AWARDS: Most Vivid Laugh — Most Stalling Sounds — Least Use — Most Unusual.
    QUALITY AWARDS: Most Mellow — Most Nasal — Huskiest — Breathiest — Most Strident — Most Harsh.

5. Add other awards if you like, pick hosts and presenters, and find tacky awards. Things that are really bad for the throat are good, as are treats where at least the first four ingredients are all forms of sugar. The teacher or a teaching assistant should collate the ballots.

6. Open envelopes and cheer for the winners. Give a brief acceptance speech that is *extremely* mellow, nasal or whatever it is you win.

Use the information you get to grow. Some important factors to consider as you debrief: what if you received some awards that seem to contradict each other? What if you received none at all? Which awards were you expecting but didn't get? What were the biggest surprises? How close was your own ballot to the award winners themselves? What

EXERCISE 1.8.1 **THE CAVE'S EFFECT**

Go back over your answers to each of the voice ingredients and consider ways in which your body may directly influence your choices. Try to identify the specific effect that your body concept, posture, expression or breathing habits have on each of the nine ingredients. Add these to your list of what to observe and consider for change.

EXERCISE 1.8.2 **COMPARING NOTES**

If someone has been assigned to imitate or observe you and you them, switch papers (from The Voice Recipe assignment, Exercise 1.6.9.2) and share any differences of opinion. How was your own perception of you different from that of your imitator? Listen carefully to determine where your impression of your voice may differ from that which others have.

Ownership — an end to denial

UNIT 1.9

For better or worse, your voice is the one you've got. Your voice can be improved, but you won't progress until you own what you have now. You could deny it, just as you could deny that you're fat, paranoid, lazy or stubborn (or svelte, centered, industrious or flexible) no matter how much accumulated evidence may have told you otherwise. Some of the information now emerging is not what you might have hoped. Your voice is so much a part of you and yet has been outside your daily consciousness that it is somewhat like having a long-lost relative show up at the door. You may be embarrassed at how the relative dresses, belches or wipes his hands on the tablecloth, but that doesn't change the fact that he's yours. True friends are those who love you unconditionally, in fact they love you partly *for* your faults, quirks, and peculiarities, because they all make you *you*. Take this attitude towards your voice. You need to get to know it, accept it, and love it for what it is. Once that has been accomplished, you will know what you absolutely need to change. And you will know what you can live with just fine. The next set of exercises help to give your voice a concrete representation, something that can be put on the wall or the refrigerator and something with a name.

EXERCISE 1.9.1 DRAWING AND COLORING YOUR VOICE

1. Take out a sheet of paper and draw your voice. Never mind any logic. Of course you don't know what it looks like. You may decide to make it a cartoon figure, a stick figure, an abstract blob, an animal, a car or some combination of things that don't normally go together. Just let your imagination run wild. Trust your intuition.
2. Find some crayons or markers and color what you've drawn or start over using the colors this time to create the shape.
3. If you feel extravagant, you could add construction paper, glitter or cotton balls, anything that might appear at the grade school art table.
4. Bring your masterpiece to class and share it, describing why you think you made some of the choices that you did. Then take it home and place it where you will see it every day.

EXERCISE 1.9.2 NAMING YOUR VOICE

1. Give your voice a name. Consider names for a few days, probably more the way you would name a pet or a boat than a child, something that allows you to feel affection toward it without making extraordinary demands.
2. Aim for a name that has some of what your voice is now and some of what you want it to become. Look at the picture for inspiration. What should be the name of that *objet d'art*?
3. Keep this image in mind when you interact with your voice in future activities. Share your voice's name as the last part of your presentation after you have shown your drawing.

EXERCISE 1.9.3 TALKING TO YOUR VOICE

1. Go one step further into whimsy and address your voice occasionally as you walk past the painting: "Hey, BUBBA, how's it goin'?" "Yo, LUCILLE, soundin' good today, babe." "Good morning, REGGY, how's the best, most brilliant voice anybody ever had? Hmmm?"

2. Talk to the voice inside you when you are out and about in the world, possibly when you want something: "Now SLICK, this show lasts three hours and I want you to stay strong for me, OK?" "Hey, SHEILA, you're soundin' kinda hoarse. Everything all right?" "BORIS, if you don't give out on me tonight I promise you a full day's rest tomorrow. Deal?"

3. Don't be altogether surprised if you get an answer.

Thus far our work has been about recognition and acceptance. We have focused on offstage tendencies, only using onstage ones when they contrast with those you use in life. You may have gotten some feedback that made you anxious to change, but remember, you do not *need* to change at all. Many actors have distinguished (and lucrative) careers with limited, mannered, predictable vocal lives. In fact, some of the most beloved actors are easy to mimic and narrow in vocal scope. But why not try to have the most unlimited, unpredictable, and awesome voice on the planet? Why not try to open your range of expression before deciding to narrow it? Why not give your voice every chance to expand your horizons?

It is also important not to lose what you have. Robert used to work for an acting program that had a class in "blue collar," a course designed to help students to play factory workers and grocery clerks, because the actors had worked so hard on getting rid of those qualities in order to equip themselves for the classics. They had loosened their roots and, without meaning to, had lost touch with their heritage. So it became necessary to relearn. The point is to *add* new options to your repertoire without *losing* old ones. You don't need to get rid of anything as you add. You simply want more *control* over your options — the power to take any given voice component into or out of play, at will. And you want your whole past to be readily at your disposal, because at some time it will serve you well.

As you find out how many parts of the voice can stand to grow, don't get discouraged. You can do this. You will do it! Will you ever be able to have the kind of voice that gets a review like this one?

He isn't the most compelling king in the world, but when he speaks he sounds like an avenging angel. With an instrument like that he can play anything!

KENNETH BRANAGH, actor, as described by critic Pauline Kael

Remember that everyone starts somewhere. Kenneth Branagh did not emerge from the womb sounding that way. In fact, here are the "avenging angel's" notes from his voice teacher after giving his first Shakespearean speech in his first year at college:

Horrendously stiff jaw there, Ken. That'll lose you all vocal flexibility if you're not careful. You've got to work on that sibilant "s." Also those dreadful dark l's are letting you down badly. Don't want to be a "regional" actor, do we? The hollow back is really, really a problem. It's affecting your rib control and contributing to that annoying sailor's roll walk you've developed. I think also if you can manage to even out those vowel sounds, you'll do yourself a big favor. Can't have kings sounding like peasants, can we?

OK, next?

KENNETH BRANAGH, quoting Robert Palmer of the Royal Academy of Dramatic Art

Does your king sound like a peasant? It may be that all that stands between you and the throne is a few years of training.

UNIT 1.10   Electronic voices

In addition to being onstage, on film, and off, we now experience voices in yet another dimension — disembodied electronics. You may not have thought much about your own voicemail message, heard largely by your circle of friends, but as part of this ownership process consider the impression it may leave on a perfect stranger. And what if that stranger is an agent, casting director, producer or anyone else who may be considering the possibility of offering you gainful employment?

With voicemail and cold calls, they can't see you, so the tone of your voice is extremely important. You need to sound authoritative, engaging, and extremely animated.

FRANCES COLE JONES, communications consultant and author

Hopefully, you have already figured out that those extended musical interludes or comedy riffs that seemed delightful at one time can irritate callers in a hurry. If you were to work closely with consultants like Ms. Jones, you could be asked to consider a range of possibilities to get your outgoing message to work for you. You might be guided to try recording while standing and smiling in order to give your voice warmth and energy. If that does not do the trick, you would be asked to experiment with both posture and facial expression, including trying to look at yourself in the mirror and interact with your own image positively while speaking. You might be instructed to inhale before you start recording (not once you are recording), which can assist speakers in resonance and support. You would certainly be told to eliminate any ambient background noise and to triple check that any key information (such as an alternative number to call) is crisply articulated and slow enough that there is no chance at all for misunderstanding. Your photo (if you are an actor) and resumé (if you are anyone in the job market) are hugely important, because they often precede you and are your first impression. The same is true for your recorded voice.

EXERCISE 1.10.1 ELECTRONIC ANALYSIS

1. Listen carefully to any audio components that connect you with the outside world, not just your own outgoing phone message but recordings that are parts of any sites you may have.
2. Go through the voice recipe one ingredient at a time and ask yourself if that one is where you want it to be in terms of a first impression.
3. For at least four ingredients, do some tweaking and playback to determine if the adjustment makes the sound closer to who you want to seem to be.
4. Experiment with the techniques in the paragraph above to determine which may produce a positive impact.
5. Listen to messages of friends and ask yourself if you did not know this person, would the message in any way mislead you, or does it reflect them positively and accurately?
6. Make a point when you first encounter someone by phone message or call, and then meet them later, to analyze how close your initial impression was to the total person.

Already you know your voice better. You are ready to expand your playground, add new tricks to your bag, and open up new vocal possibilities. That is what the rest of this book is about. You are embarking on a great adventure that will probably make you *more* you and reawaken your sense of joyous discovery as you unearth all the voices inside you, waiting to be released. Throughout all that follows, remember it is the love of shaping sounds that is the core of an actor's growth:

If you speak words with affection and penetration, then you have a chance of becoming a great actor.
CONSTANTIN STANISLAVSKI, actor and teacher

g. Shoot the tension into the *lower arms*.

h. Lock the *wrists* as if they were tightly bound.

i. Tighten the *palms* of the hands as if catching a ball.

j. Draw the *fingers* halfway into a fist that will not complete itself but remain suspended and partly closed.

k. Tighten the *upper chest and back*, then the

l. *Stomach and lower back* as if protecting against a blow.

m. Tense the *hip joints*, which are then locked.

n. Tense the *groin and buttocks*.

o. Stiffen the *upper legs*.

p. Lock the *knee joints*.

q. Draw the *lower legs* taut.

r. Lock the *ankles*.

s. Stiffen the *feet*, extending the *toes*.

t. Point your toes at the wall opposite you.

u. Final position: pull up with the center of your body toward the ceiling, so that your torso lifts off the ground and your body is supported only by the back of your head, your shoulder blades, and your heels, as if your whole body were drying up like a prune; hold; then

v. Release, letting it all go, as if you're sinking into the floor or floating in the air, but in no way confined anymore by gravity. Relax and savor the sensation of easy released floating.

w. Repeat the entire exercise more quickly, remembering to keep everything loose until its turn: tighten face, head, neck, shoulders, upper arms, elbows, lower arms, wrists, hands, fingers halfway into fists, upper chest and back, stomach and lower back, hip joints, groin and buttocks, upper legs, knee joints, lower legs, ankles, feet, point toes; pull body up towards ceiling; release; and savor.

2. **THE DRAGON**. As you float, relaxed and easy, begin to observe your breath. Note the rate, depth, and ease of the way your body breathes itself, without needing to change the breath in any way. Feel the incoming breath warm your body. Imagine yourself to be a resting dragon with fire breath that gently warms you. What parts of your body are involved with the breath? Can you feel your lower ribs and back warming and moving? Easily float your knees upward and place your feet flat on the floor in a comfortable position. Feel the small of your back

stretching out and your spine elongate. Imagine your spine is thick hot syrup that has splashed on the floor and is now spreading slowly and easily in every direction. Do you notice any change in the breath?

3. **THE ACCORDION**. Continuing in the same position, imagine your spine as an accordion or concertina, stretching to its full length but still undulating gently and under no pressure. Imagine air whirling gently around each vertebra as they all ease apart. Imagine that your head is miles away from your tailbone as the two ease gently in opposite directions. Note the depth and expansiveness of your breathing.

4. **THE BEANSTALK**. From your position on the floor:

   a. Roll easily to one side, pull your knees into your chest, and roll over onto your knees.
   b. Squat back on your heels, curled in a ball with your knees in your chest. Feel the small of your back expand and contract as you breathe.
   c. Begin to grow from this position like a beanstalk. Place your hands on the floor, and keeping your head low, straighten your legs, lifting your hips up.
   d. Hang over from the waist with your knees relaxed and very slightly bent. Feel your spine lengthening downward. Keep your head, neck, and arms loose and limp. Don't hold your breath.
   e. Slowly, easily, begin curling upward, floating each vertebra of your spine up into line with the one underneath. Be sure to let the head, shoulders, and arms remain limp, keep breathing, and don't grip the buttocks or abdominal muscles.
   f. When your spine is fully vertical, float your head up onto your shoulders. Think of your head as a balloon floating high above the rest of your body, which hangs comfortably from the balloon. Keep your knees relaxed, feeling your breath deep in your body as you relax your abdominal and buttock muscles. Imagine that your feet are many, many miles away from the balloon. You should feel that your posture is terrific but was achieved without effort and can be maintained without strain.

5. **FULL BODY YAWN**. Stretch yourself into a huge full body yawn, luxuriously expanding out in all directions.
6. **LUNG VACUUM**.

   a. Drop over again and let your spine hang easily as in position 4d.
   b. While hanging over, fully release all the air in your lungs, exhaling as completely as possible — and then even

further. Imagine that you need to rid your lungs of harmful fumes and replace them with clean air, but that it will work only if you're totally empty. (If this is being done as a group, each actor should proceed individually at their own rate with no group coordination.)

c. Make sure that your footing is solid, with your knees slightly bent. Roll back up, floating your spine back upon itself as before, but without breathing in. Keep air out as long as you can manage it. (Note: do not try to do this in sync with others in the group. This is not a competition, and lung capacity varies even among those who are identically fit.)

d. When you're all the way back up, effortlessly float your elbows above and in front of your shoulders. Let the rest of your arms be slightly bent and limp. Then allow the air to sweep in, feeling it pour almost to the end of your fingertips and toes. Drop your arms and breathe out easily.

e. Take a moment to restore the natural rhythm of your breathing. Repeat the Lung Vacuum sequence at your own rate.

7. **NEUTRAL VIBRATION**. Stand relaxed and easy. Feel your jaw relax open, with your lips slightly parted, your tongue relaxed and touching the back of your lower teeth. Soften your knees; relax your abdominal and buttock muscles. Begin an easy sound on any pitch, using the vowel sound "UH" as in *hut*. Feel this as vibration rather than listening to it as a sound. Observe that you can focus the vibration by removing any breathiness, and thus feel more vibration. Let this come out at an easy volume — don't push. Breathe easily and deeply as often as you need to. Note the parts of your body where you feel the vibration: chest? back? abdomen?

8. **STRETCHING**. Continue the neutral vibration throughout this next series.

HEAD

a. Keeping your head facing forward, gently tilt it toward one shoulder. Think of keeping your neck long, not pinching the side closest to the shoulder but opening and lengthening the opposite side. Repeat to the other side.

b. Turn your head as far to each side as possible looking back over your shoulder.

c. Gently dip your head in an arc: side, forward, and up the other side several times. (Don't drop your head to the back, and remember to keep your jaw loose and open, and to maintain the neutral vibration throughout.)

SHOULDERS

a. Lift your shoulders as high as you can. Then, let go and drop them. Ask if you can get a second release as well by letting go of any inadvertent holding. Repeat.

b. Stretch your shoulders forward and back, then in circles, being sure to reverse directions.

RIBS

Maintaining the vibration, place your right hand on your hip, stretch slightly forward and up and across to the right, reaching out with your left hand as far as you can. Remember to breathe. Don't hold your breath. Repeat twice to each side.

FACE

Stop the neutral vibration. Stretch your face by exaggerating the action as you repeat "EE" as in *heed*, "OO" as in *hoot*, "AH as in *father*, and "OO" again. EE–OO–AH–OO. Start slowly, then build up speed.

LIPS

Burr your lips while sirening your voice as high and low as you can.

TONGUE

a. Keeping the tip of your tongue touching the back of your lower teeth, push it curling forward as far as you can. You're trying to get the deep back part of the tongue as far up and forward as you can. Start this slowly, then flex it more rapidly.

b. Roll your tongue on the words: breeze — bRRRRReeze, print — pRRRRRint, grab — gRRRRRab, crisp — cRRRRRisp, drip — dRRRRRop, trip — tRRRRRip.

c. Stick your tongue out and write your name in the air with the tip. Make a different sound as you do each letter.

9. **HUM**. With your lips together, teeth apart, and tongue tip lightly touching the back of the lower teeth, hum gently, feeling the vibrations in your face. Move the hum throughout your whole range, from the cellar to falsetto and back again randomly. Roll down through your spine, hang over, and roll back up again while humming through your range.

10. **INTENSIFICATION**. Pick a note in your mid-range. Using the vowel "A" as in *had*, start as softly as you can and slowly intensify the sound to about *half as loud as you might be able to make it*, then slowly return to very soft. Repeat this on various pitches scattered throughout your range (be sure to include your falsetto).

11. **FINISH**. Roll down through your spine and quickly come back up again. Do a full body yawn with sound.

Do a brief self-inventory. What feels different now that you've completed this process? Do you sound different? Has your posture changed? Has your mood shifted? Are you more awake? What is your energy level?

Table 1.1 Warm-up key

WARM-UP

---

1. **THE PRUNE**: lie on back; tense body from top down; hold; release; savor; repeat.
2. **THE DRAGON**: incoming breath warms your body, knees up, feet on floor; feel ribs, back, & spine warm; spine long & melting.
3. **THE ACCORDION**: spine undulating gently.
4. **THE BEANSTALK**: roll over, squat, feel small of back expand with breath; grow up by lifting hips, roll up spine, head floats up like balloon.
5. **FULL BODY YAWN**
6. **LUNG VACUUM**: hang over from waist; exhale completely; roll up; float elbows up; allow air in; drop arms; rest; repeat.
7. **NEUTRAL VIBRATION**: stand; mouth open; vibrate on "UH" as in *hut*.
8. **STRETCHING**: (while vibrating) *Head*, tilt to shoulders, turn to sides, dip in arc; *Shoulders*, up/drop, forward/back, circles/reverse; *Ribs*, reach forward, up & across body, change sides, repeat; (stop vibration) *Face*, EE–OO–AH–OO; *Lips*, burr & siren through range; *Tongue*, curl tongue forward in pulses, roll tongue on words like brrrreeze, write name in air with tongue.
9. **HUM**: siren through range, roll down & up spine while humming.
10. **INTENSIFICATION**: on "A" as in *had*, on variety of pitches, stretch voice from soft to medium loud & back.
11. **FINISH**: roll down & up spine; full body yawn with sound.

Could you lead this warm-up? Of course! Take turns leading, and later adapting and changing this warm-up. Work with a partner if you like. You can't claim to really know an exercise until you can pass it on.

The table on the previous page is a condensed version of the warm-up with just a few key words to help you to remember the sequence. Make photocopies of this. Put one in your wallet, paste another in the cover of your script, anywhere handy so you can grab it, and never have an excuse for not doing a warm-up.

UNIT 1.12   Mini warm-up

OK, we lied. You might genuinely have the excuse that you have very little time and/or are in a public space where you are reticent to call attention to yourself by getting down on the floor, swinging through space, and making highly conspicuous sounds. For example, if you are waiting near the back of the theatre for your turn to audition, you might wish to avoid distracting or disturbing those who are auditioning ahead of you. In such cases, we recommend the Berlitz Mini Warm-up for Busy People in the Millennium, which can be done sitting in a chair:

 LISTEN

1. PRUNE

Progress from face through toes in the same sequence as above. This time you will probably end up somewhat bent into your center as the tension accumulates. End up with your shoulder blades pulled back and finally lifting up on balls of feet. Then release and sit completely relaxed.

2. DRAGON/ACCORDION

Imagine that your tailbone sinks into the chair below you as your head eases up and forward out of your torso and your spine undulates freely. Take three deep breaths, allowing your spine to elongate further on each, air seeming to whirl around each vertebra.

3. BEANSTALK/LUNG VACUUM

Dip forward in chair while blowing out air, ease back up to full seated position, holding air out until you must inhale, feeling as if air goes all the way to the tips of your fingers and toes.

4. NEUTRAL VIBRATION/STRETCHING

You can keep your volume quite low while performing the sounding parts of these exercises.

Relax your jaw (massaging it if needed) while uttering the "UH" sound. Continue the UH with your head tilting to each shoulder, then turned around to each side, and finally raising and dropping your shoulders.

5. HUMMING

a.   Repeat EE–OO–AH–OO three times, allowing the lips to stretch fully.
b.   Make the BRRR sound while allowing your pitch to go up and down like a roller coaster.
c.   Let your tongue explore the area outside your mouth and then spell a word of your choice with it.

6. YAWN–SIGH–HUM

Do each of these soothing activities in sequence, repeating until you feel a sense of relaxation and freedom from vocal tension.

Other short warm-ups

UNIT 1.13

If you are particularly pressed for time and space, do a personal inventory or diagnostic regarding what you feel you need most to be relaxed and ready vocally. If you feel tension in your neck and shoulders, select head rolls and shoulder lifts. If your jaw is particularly tight or clenched, spend time massaging it gently while encouraging it to drop and open up. Once you have mastered the warm-up sequences above, get in the habit of determining where you feel the greatest need for and benefit from a particular activity, then focus on that.

Terms to remember

articulation	personality	quality	volume
identity	phrasing	rhythm	word choice
melody pattern	pitch	syntax	
vocal nonverbals	pronunciation	tempo	

Summary

You have examined five reasons why the voice seems so elusive and have devised a strategy for getting to know it better. This includes (1) accepting that you are a vocal infant and treating your voice with loving patience; (2) exploring your own vocal history; (3) creating a current vocal profile of yourself; (4) tracking vocal blocks as well as positive influences; (5) facing vocal fears and contradictions through laughter; (6) employing basic equipment — mirror, recorder, and familiar scripted material — to help you to see and hear the organs of the voice; (7) becoming a vocal mirror, imitating at least one other classmate and being mirrored/imitated in return; (8) breaking the voice down into nine basic ingredients for deeper understanding; (9) putting these ingredients back together for your own unique vocal recipe; (10) placing your voice in comparison with those of your classmates; (11) examining the influencing effects of the cave in which your voice lives; (12) making your voice more tangible by drawing it, naming it, and even talking to it; and (13) becoming more aware of the impact of your recorded voice on first-time listeners. You have learned to complete ownership of your voice by beginning to take care of it, by warming it up effectively prior to challenging use.

By approaching the voice from so many perspectives, yours will no longer be a stranger.

NOTE: forms for exercises in this chapter are available on the book's website.

CHAPTER 2

Healing your voice

For my voice, I have lost it, with halloing and singing of anthems.

Falstaff from WILLIAM SHAKESPEARE's _Henry IV, Part 2_

The good qualities of the voice, like our other faculties, are improved by attention and deteriorated by neglect.

QUINTILIAN (AD 35–95)

Vocal wellness

The voice tends to pick up a few cuts, scratches, and bruises along the way, maybe even some sprains, wounds or breaks. But it is rarely attended to. Unless you experience genuine trauma, a lisp, a vocal node, or something that would send you to a speech therapist, your voice is taken for granted. Unless you get laryngitis, you may never even discuss it with a physician. You don't go to see the doctor for your yearly vocal, you don't take V.E. class in school, and you don't check your sub-glottal pressure. There are no professionals whipping you into shape. No one coaches your dialect or diction team, and no personal trainer comes to your home.

The voice is remarkably resilient, self-healing, and capable of being trained to do almost anything. But acting demands more from the voice than you may be ready to deliver. If you ever get the chance to see the Grand Kabuki perform, you will notice that these brilliant Japanese actors are doing things with their voices that sound desperately painful and that you should not try at home. These vocal pyrotechnics would probably give you nodes but do not hurt *them* because they have gradually conditioned and trained themselves. With enough attention, every voice is capable of remarkable expressive range.

Most of what we pick up along the way are just bad habits, laziness, inattention to details or some misinformation. This all goes undetected until the first voice class — until now. Many of these habits can be corrected fairly quickly if you are not too set in your ways. In this chapter, we will start with what is easily diagnosed and treated — the true wellness issues.

You probably discovered some aspects of your voice in Chapter 1 that you just don't like. The more you hear yourself the better your voice tends to sound, so don't make drastic decisions before you know your own voice. But if there are certain things you want to address quickly, this chapter will start you forward.

A word of warning: "quick" is a relative term. If you really want to change something about yourself physically, how long does it take? Let's say you want to reduce your waist size and firm up your stomach muscles, or you want to increase your upper arm size and strengthen your biceps and triceps. These are two fairly common goals. The solutions are simple and straightforward. If you devote fifteen minutes a day to abdominal exercises and lifting weights, plus watch your diet you will probably sense some noteworthy change in about six weeks. This is a physical quick fix. And it is measurable. Vocal changes are more difficult to measure; the problems have taken a lot longer to sneak up on you, and the need for change has been less obvious than not being able to button your blue jeans anymore. So why should a vocal fix take any less time? Many actors give up early because they just don't see any change after a few sessions. We are going to supply you with a variety of suggestions so you can find your shortest possible route. Accept that like all genuine change, it may not be as short as you'd like.

Just as some people like themselves with a broken nose or a slight limp, feel free to pick and choose from the following "cures" suggested. The first issues covered are those most commonly experienced. They are the colds, headaches, and allergies of voice, the ones shared widely enough that if there could be non-prescription medication for them, there would be.

What follows may seem like a great deal of information. It's actually quite manageable if you take it step by step. Read quickly through it all, stopping only to make notes where you feel the problem may be one you have. Then go back slowly, trying on each series of exercises. One major category (vocal health, breathing, tempo, rhythm, articulation, pitch, volume, and quality) will give you a good challenge on any given day, not because each demands all that much time but because each asks for intense concentration. You may wish to take eight separate days to review the material if you are working alone. If you are part of a class, devoting 20 minutes per class period to the "topic du jour", while simultaneously moving on to subsequent chapters, will help everyone to experience each issue fully.

When you join a gym, you are usually cautioned to have a doctor check you out to see if you are physically ready for the rigors of training. Imagine now that you are going in for a check-up, just to see how everything is working and to consider some lifestyle changes that could help the overall development of your voice.

Figure 2.2 *The Voice Shrink* by Andrew Barton

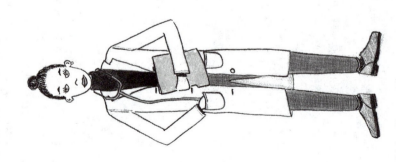

Figure 2.1 *The Voice Doc* by Andrew Barton

UNIT 2.1   The Voice Doc  and the Voice Shrink

In this chapter, you will learn how to become your own voice physician, how to recognize and diagnose your voice problems and evolve your own treatment. As your own personal voice counselor, you will search out what psychological and emotional blocks underlie any vocal limitations, so you can recognize habits and behavior you may want to modify.

Physical healing is increased rapidly by an intense psychological desire or motivation to heal, so the relationship between your internal "doc" and "shrink" is a vital one. And there are few parts of ourselves where the mind–body link is as obvious as in the voice. What we think and feel shows up instantly in our voices. We can help you to diagnose symptoms, provide drills and exercises, and *suggest* the emotional blocks that may be the true culprits halting your progress. The paths by which people get stronger mentally, however, are widespread and deeply personal, so we will not set out formulas for that part of the healing process. Only you have the power to go a step further — to face and slay personal demons and change attitudes. Good luck on this powerful and important journey.

UNIT 2.2   Vocal health – caring for your voice

How do you recognize when there is a problem with your voice? How do you know if it is serious? How do you identify what caused it? What can you do, or whom do you see to help to restore the voice to health?

So many miseries have crazed my voice,
That my woe-wearied tongue is mute and dumb,

Duchess of York from WILLIAM SHAKESPEARE's *Richard III*

Fill out the following form and refer back to it as you review the rest of the material in this chapter. While a specialist would require far more detailed information, this is a good beginning for gaining insight into the influences on your voice and is useful to share with your teacher or coach.

Vocal history

Table 2.1 Vocal history form

ONLINE

1. **Name:**
2. Date:

3. Do you smoke?
   a. ☐ yes ☐ no
   b. Type/brand
   c. Daily quantity
   d. Do you work or live in a smoky environment?
   d. ☐ yes ☐ no

4. Estimate your daily intake of:
   a. Water
   b. Caffeine
   c. Alcohol

5. List any medications you take, and the conditions they are meant to treat:

6. Note any respiratory conditions such as asthma, emphysema, chronic bronchitis:

7. Note any recurrent sinus problems such as allergies, post-nasal drip, sinus infection:

8. Have your tonsils/adenoids been removed?
   ☐ yes ☐ no

9. Note any other facial, neck, head, thorax, abdomen, or back surgery or injury:

10. Did you wear braces?
    a. ☐ yes ☐ no
    b. How long?
    c. Currently?
    d. What age did you start?

11. Note any missing teeth (excluding wisdom teeth)

12. Do you have any false teeth?

Table 2.1 continued

13. Note any jaw, or jaw-joint conditions such as: TMJ, pop-click, teeth grinding:

14. Do you have a diagnosed hearing loss?
    a. ☐ yes ☐ no   b. What is the extent?

15. Have you ever been diagnosed as dyslexic, or do you have any perceptual or learning disability? ☐ yes ☐ no
    Note:

16. Have you ever been under the care of a speech pathologist laryngologist, or allergist? ☐ yes ☐ no
    Note reason:

17. Where were you born?   18. Where were you raised?

19. Is English your first language?
    ☐ yes ☐ no   20. List any other languages you speak:

21. List any specific vocal complaints you have:

22. Note the comments you typically receive on your voice:

23. Note any vocal training you have had:

24. Is there any other information we should be aware of in order to aid your vocal development?

Two ways to sense vocal health are the *sound* of the voice and the *feeling* sensation in the throat.

Ask about your *sound*:

1. Does your voice sound hoarse after performing or speaking?
2. Does that hoarseness take longer and longer to go away, or not go away at all?
3. Is it lower or higher in pitch than it used to be?
4. Do you have trouble speaking loud enough to be heard clearly in situations that weren't difficult before?
5. Do people have difficulty understanding you?
6. Does your voice "give out" after a certain time in the day?
7. Does your vocal quality change automatically during the day, in spite of your efforts, so that your overall control seems to diminish as the day continues?

Ask about the *feelings* in your throat:

1. Is there pain in your throat after a performance?
2. Do you often have to cough or clear your throat?
3. Does your throat feel tired, raw or uncomfortable?
4. Do you often feel a "lump" in your throat?
5. Do you need to stop speaking to ease your throat?
6. Do you feel you have to speak in a "different way" or "from a different place"?
7. Do you have to use more effort to make sound and be heard well?

How do you know if a symptom is serious? If the problem persists, recurs regularly or worsens, it is something to take an earnest look at. Causes of vocal problems fall into two broad categories: improper use, and illness, disease or injury. We'll start by looking at use: issues that can come up because things you may have done to your voice.

The Voice Shrink: vocal use – how behavior affects voice

Have you ever "lost your voice"? It can be a frightening and frustrating experience. You may feel no pain, but you can't speak. Your voice feels as if it doesn't belong to you, is not under your control, and has a mind of its own. You may feel helpless and angry. You might feel like your voice is doing something to you. But what if you have done something to *it* — though possibly without being aware you did? The following types of behavior are listed by voice specialists as being the most common causes of vocal damage:

- smoking, working in smoky environments;
- dehydration:
  - from excess caffeine, alcohol, diuretics or medication;
  - from insufficient water intake;
- coughing or throat clearing;
- shouting, yelling or loud speaking;
- failure to warm up before extended use and to cool down afterwards;
- excess tension of the tongue, jaw, and neck muscles;
- insufficient rest;
- speaking or singing at vocal extremes.

If you want to avoid or do something about vocal problems, look at any *behavior* that may have produced the condition. Many problems are self-created, so the best solution is to change whatever caused it in the first place. It's also possible to *modify* certain behavior so that vocal problems can be avoided in the future. Few consider how vital a clear, strong voice is to their personal and professional lives until something goes wrong.

**My lord, wise men ne'er sit and wail their woes,
But presently prevent the ways to wail.**

Bishop of Carlisle from WILLIAM SHAKESPEARE's *Richard II*

Smoking, working in smoky environments

Cigarette smoking is the major cause of lung and throat cancer, heart disease, emphysema and chronic bronchitis. The chances of dying from those disorders are ten times greater for smokers than for non-smokers. In the UK and North America, each year more people die from smoking-related ailments than die from AIDS, drug abuse, car accidents, homicide and suicide — *combined*. (Though one could argue that smoking is itself a form of suicidal behavior.)

Smokers will be sick in bed 16 percent more often and miss work 32 percent more often than non-smokers. Just one cigarette speeds up your heartbeat, increases your blood pressure, and upsets the flow of blood and air in your lungs. Nicotine is more addictive than heroin or cocaine. Both the heat and chemicals affect the vocal system. Smoke causes the vocal folds to inflame, which means that they will turn red, swell, and suffer a loss in functional ability. Cancers of the mouth and larynx are frequent among smokers. Smokers suffer from reduced pitch range and limited vocal flexibility, and they are more prone to throat and lung infections and asthma.

All that is common knowledge, but occasionally, attitudes like this will still emerge:

This is really a bad confession on my part, but one of the reasons I started smoking is because I didn't like my voice and wanted it lower. Much sexier and lower. Raspier.

SHANNEN DOHERTY in *Vanity Fair*

Read that quote again. We'll wait.

The idea of smoking in order to sound like Jack Webb on "Dragnet" is so stupid it cannot be ignored. You can call it dangerously vain and a vice. Charles Darwin called it natural selection.

Only a complete moron would smoke because some of the tar that's dripping into her lungs is sticking to her larynx, making her voice huskier.

PHIL ROSENTHAL, columnist, *Los Angeles Daily News*, responding

'Nuff said?

"Second-hand" smoke should be avoided for all of the above reasons. New research has shown it to be even more harmful than the primary puff inhaled by the smoker! It contains about 4,000 chemicals, including 200 known poisons, including lethal agents like formaldehyde, ammonia, sulfur dioxide, phenol, and hydrogen cyanide. Carbon monoxide, which robs the blood of oxygen, can be two to fifteen times higher in second-hand smoke. Even if a smoker hasn't yet developed a more serious disease, there is a marked reduction in lung capacity and elevation in blood pressure — certainly not things a performer needs.

What to do: if you smoke, quit today. If your friends smoke, help them to stop. Smoking cessation has gotten a lot of research in recent years, and new strategies are proving to be more effective than ever before. See your doctor and ask for help.

If you are cast in a role that requires smoking, get creative. Actors tend to fixate on the inhalation, but smoking is an activity that has so many props and elaborate behaviors surrounding it that a really creative actor can spend an entire scene contending with them and never even light up.

What not to do: don't treat this subject lightly. It is well known that quitting smoking isn't an easy thing to do, but the dangers of smoking are indisputable and cannot be overstated. Don't quit by yourself. You are over 200 percent more likely to quit for good if you are in a program. Don't allow a director to coerce you into smoking for a role. It's never an imperative, and it is dangerous. And, please, don't start smoking because it will make your voice sexier. A healthy, flexible, expressive voice is always a greater asset.

Thus must I from the smoke into the smother.

Orlando from WILLIAM SHAKESPEARE's As *You Like It*

Dehydration

Our bodies are based on liquid systems; 60 to 70 percent of our body weight is water. An easy formula to use in figuring the suggested daily water intake is half an ounce for each pound of body weight. So, a 120 pound person needs to drink about 60 ounces of water every day. (Just water. Other beverages and foods contain water, but lots of added things like salt, sugar, and caffeine, so they aren't factored into the formula.) If calculating in the metric system, a 64kg person should drink 2 liters daily.

Why is this important? Vocal systems need water to function. Our vocal folds and the entire throat, mouth, and nasal area have mucosal surfaces that can be kept moist only if we have sufficient water in our bodies. Additionally, the excitement and stress of performing can dry those surfaces. We even need water to breathe. Our lungs are moistened by water to facilitate the intake of oxygen and the removal of carbon dioxide. We lose about a pint of water a day just exhaling. Performers who get "dry mouth" might consider that the solution to their problem is to drink water *throughout the day*. By the time they feel dry the whole body wants water, and there is no quick fix. Having lots of water in your system will keep your throat and mouth moist and thin the thickened mucus that makes people want to clear their throats.

What to do: drink water. Get a container you can carry around with you and sip throughout the day.

What to be aware of: avoid or reduce intake of caffeine, alcohol, and other diuretics, which can dehydrate the body by increasing the volume of urine excreted. If you use these, compensate by drinking extra water.

Coughing/throat clearing

When we cough, we bring the vocal folds firmly together, build up air pressure beneath them, and then "explosively" release a burst of air, causing the vocal folds to move around violently — not a healthful activity if it's done too often. We can't feel the folds, so we don't even know they are getting sore. By the time we notice a difference in sound, the condition is too severe to do anything but modify vocal use, or stop talking and rest.

The usual purpose of coughing is to expel something from our airway. Throat clearing is an ongoing process of grinding or abrading the vocal folds. This rubs the side of one vocal fold against the other. If done too much, the tissues will react. Clearing is an action meant to remove thick phlegm. When we cough or clear thick phlegm, it is irritating, and the body sends *more* phlegm in response to that irritation, creating a problematic cycle. Repetitive coughing and throat clearing are typically unconscious habits not always connected to an actual physiological need. Ironically, doing it creates a need to do it again. It might be necessary to ask someone to tell you when they hear you clear your throat so you can become aware that you are doing it.

Repetitive throat clearing can also be a symptom of gastro-esophageal reflux disease — something we'll be addressing further on in this chapter.

What to do: drinking water is a good way to thin the mucus, so whenever you feel you are about to clear your throat, take a sip of water instead. Soon you may sip instead of cough. Warm up your voice before speaking. The vibration of the folds may move the thick phlegm from the glottis. If you feel the need to clear your throat while speaking, increase the loudness and lift the pitch for just a couple of words, and the feeling may pass.

What not to do: avoid unconscious, repetitive coughing or throat clearing.

Shall we clap unto't roundly, without hawking or spitting or saying we are hoarse, which are the only prologues to a bad voice?

First page from WILLIAM SHAKESPEARE's *As You Like It*

UNIT 2.3.4

Shouting/yelling/loud speaking

The issue of shouting and yelling is complex. We do it for all sorts of reasons: talking over loud music or crowd noise at parties, shouting over machine noise at work, calling from room to room at home, conversing over airplane or car engine noise — all situations that require increased vocal intensity. In cases like these, it is easy to forget good vocal technique. You may not even be aware you are pushing your voice, or you may not think of using your voice the way you would if you were onstage (although the vocal demands may actually be higher).

Many roles require extreme vocal use like screaming, shouting, and crying. Watch your technique. Learn the skill of being deeply engaged emotionally while maintaining the clarity of mind to behave safely.

What to do: watch out for the problem situations noted above. Reduce your speaking in those circumstances, if possible. Stand closer to the person with whom you are talking in order to be more easily heard. Be a good listener. Remember to use good vocal technique onstage and off. Learn to mark scenes of extreme vocal use in technical rehearsals so you don't tire yourself just before opening night.

What not to do: don't ignore or discount the early signs of incipient strain mentioned earlier. Don't imagine that offstage vocal use can't be extremely demanding. It isn't necessarily the performance that hurts the voice, but the party afterwards.

UNIT 2.3.5

Failure to warm up before extended use and to cool down afterwards

A good warm-up makes you relaxed, alert, focused, centered. It also makes your vocal muscles relaxed, flexible, and responsive. No athlete would think of tossing a javelin, and no dancer would execute a *grand jeté* without a thorough warm-up. Yet an executive will address a board meeting, and some actors will walk on stage, without a thought to warming up their voices. People often don't anticipate, or they underestimate, the vocal demands of a situation. Then they run the risk of vocal strain and fatigue.

After performing, your voice will appreciate some easy cool-down activities. Often the same gentle warm-up exercises will serve to ease your voice after heavy use.

What to do: remember your voice when preparing for any activity. Learn warm-up techniques for both your body and your voice. Good physical conditioning builds thoracic and abdominal muscle strength for coordinated breath support and overall alignment. A gentle cool-down exercise is also helpful after performing.

What not to do: don't imagine that fatigue or strain won't ultimately take their toll on your voice, especially when a simple warm-up/cool-down can help to prevent those problems.

Excess tension of the tongue, jaw, and neck muscles

UNIT 2.3.6

Stress builds up in subtle ways. Emotional stress can come from positive as well as negative sources. We are as likely to become stressed from getting a promotion as from getting fired, from falling in love as from breaking up. Just because there is a smile on your face, it doesn't mean you're not clenching your teeth. The most common areas where we tense when under stress are the shoulders, back, abdomen, neck, jaw, and tongue. People seem more aware of shoulder and back tension and more willing to do something about it. But the next time you are driving during rush hour, take a minute to see if you are clenching your teeth. One dentist recently commented that over half his adult patients showed signs of serious damage from teeth grinding (and most of it happens when we're asleep!). The effects of tension on the voice are profound. Tension places the voice further back, which dulls the sound, reduces resonance, limits articulation, diminishes projection, and flattens the emotional tone. It also creates a greater likelihood of vocal fatigue and strain. Those can be serious problems.

What to do: study yourself and learn to recognize your particular signs of tension. Breathe deeply. This can help to release tension and is easy to do at almost any time and anywhere. Relaxation can be learned and can become as habitual as tension currently is. Seek out and explore methods of stress management. Our lives will never be free of stress, but they can be free of unnecessary tension

Insufficient rest

UNIT 2.3.7

Vocal and physical fatigue go hand in hand. Your concentration, reaction time, coordination, and memory may be compromised. Then bad vocal habits creep back to replace healthful vocal technique.

Although adequate sleep is no guarantee against fatigue, it's a start. Most adults over 30 require seven hours of sleep a night. This amount *increases* the younger you are. College students (who are notorious for keeping irregular hours) need eight to ten hours of sleep, in a predictable pattern. One of the first questions a voice therapist may ask of an actor with voice problems is: "How much sleep are you getting, and do you sleep on a regular schedule?" Sometimes, the adjustment of just this one factor is enough to correct incipient vocal strain.

What to do: determine the amount of rest your body needs. Establish a regular pattern of sleep that is enough for you. If you do have to push on in spite of fatigue, warm up carefully, avoid extremes of pitch or volume, and consciously use the best vocal technique you know.

What not to do: Don't habitually rely on weekends to catch up (it generally doesn't work, and it throws your sleep pattern off).

> *. . . the innocent sleep,*
> *Sleep that knits up the ravell'd sleeve of care . . .*
> *Chief nourisher in life's feast, . . .*

Macbeth from WILLIAM SHAKESPEARE's *Macbeth*

UNIT 2.3.8   *Speaking or singing at vocal extremes*

Every voice has its limits. Exercise and study can push back those limitations, but some barriers will always remain. Producers, directors, and others not vocally knowledgeable or sensitive may ask you to do something beyond your abilities. This isn't always bad. Sometimes they inspire growth. But it's your voice, and your career. Only you will know how far you can be pushed. Screaming, performing in vast outdoor spaces, pitch and volume extremes, doing sixteen shows a week, going on when you're sick or having an allergy attack, producing cartoon voices, and a host of other vocal challenges may be just too much for you at your present stage of development. Overuse may cause tissue damage or compensatory behavioral habits that take time to correct. That time spent in recovery, rest or therapy may cost you in lost wages or doctor's fees, and it could interfere with the course of your career. Think of the long term, not just the immediate job.

What to do: learn to be objective about your abilities and limitations. Get some unbiased professional advice if you think you are being asked to do something potentially damaging. Explore techniques that can be developed to help you, or propose alternatives to the director. Be prepared to say no to an unreasonable request.

What not to do: if you are working beyond your limits, you may hear or feel it in your voice. Don't imagine that the situation will necessarily work itself out. If you sense there is a problem, there is.

Protect your hearing

Hearing is a precious sense, and a vulnerable one. If you can't hear well, you can't monitor your voice or respond as well to other actors. Noise-induced hearing loss is usually painless, progressive, and always permanent. It is also completely preventable. How loud is too loud? Prolonged exposure to sounds above 85dB may cause permanent hearing loss. Normal conversation is measured at a moderate noise level of 50–70dB. A motorcycle or lawn mower is 85–90dB. The extreme noise of a typical rock concert is measured at 110–120dB. Fireworks and gunshots can be around 140–190dB.

Duration of exposure is a critical factor. Estimates are that one can take eight hours at 85dB, but only fifteen minutes at 100dB before there is permanent damage.

Stage environments can pose unique problems. Performing in a rock musical, loud sound effects, gunshots, and other loud events can be dangerous to your hearing.

What to do: ask for help from the technical director or stage manager if you think that something is too loud. Gunshots can have reduced loads, monitor speakers can be adjusted, and you can be made safe. Unobtrusive earplugs can be slipped in if needed. Wear these when doing any task that involves loud sounds. Even drying your hair can point 100dB straight into your ears, so be alert. Watch out for headphone use. Earbuds set at 5 can put out 100dB. That's enough for permanent damage after fifteen minutes.

What not to do: don't ignore this or feel shy about standing up for yourself. Most countries have occupational health and safety laws that require a safe hearing environment. Remember that hearing loss is painless, so you won't know it's happened until after it's gone.

The Voice Doc — a medical perspective

Environmental and medical problems can also influence the voice. The most common categories and some examples:

This we prescribe, though no physician;

Richard from WILLIAM SHAKESPEARE's *Richard II*

Gargle with salt water: this soothes the throat and hydrates the tissues. The salt will also reduce swelling in the surface tissues. Gargle twice a day using one teaspoonful of non-iodized sea salt and a pinch of baking soda to a pint of warm water. If you are reducing your vocal use, don't make voiced sounds as you gargle.

Inhale hot steam: this increases humidification in the larynx and soothes the throat and lungs. Use a steam room, or boil a pot of water (2–3 inches deep). Remove it from the stove so you don't burn your face. Put a hot towel over your head and inhale the steam until it cools down. Do this a couple of times a day. You can also purchase small, portable facial steamers that are easy to use and can travel with you if you are on the road. Be sure to clean them regularly after use, since mold and bacteria can grow easily in the warm, moist environment of a steamer.

Nasal wash: probably the least familiar of home remedies, it is especially helpful for allergies, sinusitis, and rhinitis. Ask your local drug store for a baby's ear wash bulb. Use a third of a teaspoon of non-iodized sea salt and a pinch of baking soda to a cup of warm water. Lean over a sink (or do this in the shower), close one nostril, gently insert the nozzle into the other, breathe out easily through your mouth, and direct a stream of the liquid into the nasal passage. It may take a bit of practice, but when done properly, the water will pass through the nose, down through the nasal pharynx, into the mouth and out. If you would rather not make your own preparation, mild saline solutions, including those for contact lenses, will work, and some prepared solutions for this are sold over the counter. After you're finished, clean the bulb by rinsing it with rubbing alcohol.

Drink lots of water: use a water bottle or some other means of measuring whether you are achieving the desired amount noted earlier in this chapter.

Avoid unprocessed milk products: although there is no firm scientific evidence to tell us the reason, countless actors report an increase in thick mucus after eating dairy products such as whole milk, cream, and ice cream. Orange juice creates the same effect for some. Learn how *your* body responds to these foods.

. . . his former strength may be restored
With good advice and little medicine:

Warwick from WILLIAM SHAKESPEARE's *Henry IV, Part 2*

Be a wise consumer: as a general precaution, read the labels for over-the-counter medications carefully. With allergy and cold medications packaged in a wide variety of combinations, it can be easy to inadvertently "double-up" on certain drugs. This is especially true when drugs in the same general class have dissimilar names — a common occurrence. If you aren't sure what you are taking, ask your pharmacist. They have a wealth of knowledge about drug interactions. Just because your medication is sold without prescription doesn't mean you can relax and not worry about interactions and potential side effects.

UNIT 2.4.2   *An important note on laryngo-pharyngeal-reflux disease (LPR)*

This disease is the single largest reason for average (non-professional) voice users to seek voice therapy. It is caused by gastric acid flowing backward (reflux) into the esophagus. The strong acid can burn the tissues of the throat and vocal folds. This can happen at any time but is most likely during sleep. While you are prone, the acids don't have to travel uphill, only having to get past the esophageal sphincter muscle to enter the throat.

The symptoms of LPR vary and can include a burning sensation in the chest and throat like "heartburn"; a really bad taste in your mouth in the morning; hoarseness that can't be attributed to illness or overuse; a loss in pitch range (especially high notes); an overall deepening or roughening of the voice; or an inability to sing softly. These symptoms can occur singly or in combination. Importantly, acid-related voice problems can develop without typical heartburn reflux symptoms, so you might not realize that a vocal problem has this cause. When in doubt, consult a doctor.

Here are a few good resources for additional help in caring for your voice:

Joanna Cazden, *How to Take Care of Your Voice: The Lifestyle Guide for Singers and Talkers* (Booklocker, 2008). Practical answers to the most common voice problems from an experienced voice therapist and coach. What to eat, drink, when to see a doctor and how to approach alternative medicine. Straightforward, trustworthy advice.

D. Garfield Davies and Anthony F. Jahn, *Care of the Professional Voice: A Guide to Voice Management for Singers, Actors and Professional Voice Users* (Routledge, 2004). A self-help resource that gives the performer a good general understanding of the conditions — environmental and psychological as well as medical — that affect vocal performance, offering clear practical advice on both treatment and prevention.

Kate DeVore and Starr Cookman, *The Voice Book: Easy Exercises and Advice for Anyone Who Speaks or Sings for a Living*, with CD (Chicago Review Press, 2009). Both authors are experienced voice therapists and theatre voice trainers. The book covers excellent exercises for vocal development as well as detailed advice on vocal health. A workbook as well as a reference text.

While the advice in this chapter and some simple home remedies can make you more comfortable when the "show must go on," they won't correct serious conditions. If you need to see a physician, do so. If you have a recurring voice problem, get some help. See a coach or voice pathologist to assist in identifying and changing the vocal habits or behavior causing the problem, or a doctor to diagnose the medical reasons for it. See a professional counselor, psychologist or psychiatrist if the root behavior seems obsessive, immovable or pathological. Above all, don't ignore it or just wish it would go away.

Healing breathing — the source of sound

UNIT 2.5

I learned an incredible amount working with Sean Connery. He told me, "Just remember to breathe."

CHRISTIAN SLATER, actor

It's odd that something we do about 17,000 times a day without even thinking about it, is something we could be doing "wrong." Breath is the source of all our sound. It is also the source of all our communication. When we breathe in, we "inspire," or take in an idea. When we breathe out, we "expire," or express! There is a powerful, untapped potential in breath.

Table 2.2 Breath Doc/Shrink

THE VOICE DOC	THE VOICE SHRINK	℞
Shallow breathing	Are you having resistance to or fear of the situation? Are you feeling anxious?	p 70
Hard glottal attack	Are you tense; wanting to be precise; holding on? Is this an aggressive, attacking speech?	p 73
Audible inhalation; gripping in the throat	Are you trying to control, or unwilling to release the emotion?	p 74
Poor breath management; running out of air too soon	Are you not letting the full thought enter in deeply with the breath, unclear about the order of ideas, or muddy in your thinking?	p 75

Table 2.2 continued

Exhaling before speaking	Are you afraid of emotional power and so are releasing the emotion instead of speaking *on* it?	p 80
℞: Let the breath drop in more deeply, keeping your throat relaxed.	℞: Allow your power to overcome your reticence. Give yourself up to the emotion in the material.	

Most reliable cures for five common problems

UNIT 2.5.1 ### *Shallow breathing*

The simple truth is that most of us breathe too shallowly. Deep breathing gives us lots of air and energy to produce good tone, crisp articulation, powerful projection, and most importantly, emotional depth. Behavioral scientists have observed that when we want to control our emotions and stay clear-headed, we will tend to breathe shallowly. When a strong emotion gets past this control mechanism, the breath will drop lower in the torso; the lower the breath, the deeper the emotion. Think of the last time you felt like crying. In an effort to control the emotion you probably took only small sips of air and didn't fully exhale or inhale. Then, at some point, you couldn't maintain that discipline, fully exhaled, then took in a deep lungfull and fell completely into the emotion. Actors who resist connecting to the emotional life of the character can frequently be spotted by observing their breathing patterns.

EXERCISE 2.5.1.1 OBSERVING BREATHING PATTERNS

1. Observe members of the class do either scenes or monologues, as suggested in Chapter 1. Highly emotional material works best.
2. Assign specific points of observation: Group A only listens to the work but doesn't watch; Group B watches the scene but plugs their ears and doesn't listen; Group C hears and watches the scene, but each person chooses a specific actor and focuses on the actor's breathing patterns by looking at their chest and abdomen areas, not their faces; Group D watches the audience's breathing patterns; Group E watches as a normal audience would. Be sure to read the whole exercise first so everyone will know what to look for.

3. After the scene is finished, discuss the following questions:

- At what points did each actor seem to be the most emotionally in touch?
- When were they emotionally disconnected, or resisting the emotion?
- Did you observe any association between breathing patterns and emotional depth?
- Were certain breathing habits present, such as running out of air before the end of a line; exhaling before the start of a line; audible inhalation?
- Did the actor's breathing patterns affect those of the audience? Which audience groups were affected the most?

Actors often wonder how a good coach can tell whether they were or weren't genuinely involved in a scene. They wonder why that coach can't be fooled. It is usually because the actor's breathing patterns give them away! What the instructor observes critically, the audience experiences subconsciously — but everybody gets it on some level.

Yet if deep breath has sometimes unleashed emotion so powerful that you totally lost control, you may still resist it. Reasonably, you don't want your acting to be hysterical and chaotic. It is this intense *resistance* followed by the emotion's inevitable *insistence* that causes the floodgates to open and an incomprehensible expression of feeling to pour forth. When you are in a difficult emotional situation, struggling with how to express yourself, if you remember to breathe deeply right at that first point of trouble, you will be amazed at how the feeling stays strong but the words come and you are able to express yourself with both power and clarity.

Okay. So now we accept that full breathing is useful and necessary. How do we find it and incorporate it into our acting?

EXERCISE 2.5.1.2 FINDING THE FULL BREATH

1. Stand comfortably. Place a hand at the base of your neck in front. Observe your breathing.
2. Do not change your breathing in any way. Move your hand down to any part of your chest, ribs or abdomen that moves when you breathe. Find the lowest active area. Remember the feeling.

LISTEN

EXERCISE 2.5.1.3 FULL BREATH WITH SOUND

1. Repeat Exercise 2.5.1.2, but this time, after first observing your breathing as in step 1, start to make a gentle neutral sound "UH" like the vowel in *hut*. Focus on this more as vibration than sound. See how much of your body will feel the vibration. Throughout the exercise, alternately fill your body with breath, then vibration. Do this with as little effort as possible. Apply this feeling to EVERY exercise from this point onward. A good way to do that is to use this exercise to start or preface all the other exercises. Always begin by checking in with POSTURE, BREATH, and VIBRATION, then transfer that awareness to the activity at hand.

2. Repeat Exercise 2.5.1.2 again, but do it while blowing through a drinking straw and making sound. Then do it again playing a kazoo (it works best if the fat end is in your mouth). This progression of simple voice, to straw, to kazoo will present gently increasing challenges that your body will solve by supplying more exhalatory support.

Connecting breath to sound — avoiding the glottal attack

UNIT 2.5.2

It sounds frightening, like something that might happen in a dark alley. But the dark alley is just your throat, and "attack" is just a word describing the onset of sound. The "glottis" is the space between your vocal folds.

Make a couple of small, light coughing sounds. When you do this you are closing the glottis, building up air pressure beneath the folds and then suddenly releasing it with an explosive sound. The symbol for a glottal attack is [ʔ]. It is an unattractive sound, most likely to happen on words beginning with a vowel, and fatiguing to the vocal folds. If done repeatedly at full stage volume it can cause the folds to become irritated, swell, and lose the ability to function.[2] Microphones amplify glottal attacks, so the radio and film industries tend to avoid actors who can't control this problem.

2 However, the glottal attack (or glottal stop) is used in many dialects, and actors will need to learn how to make this sound safely and easily. This is a good time to become skilled at both the removal and addition of this sound.

LISTEN

EXERCISE 2.5.2.1 RELEASING THE GLOTTAL ATTACK

1. Use the following list of words for practice. Record yourself with the microphone held close to your mouth.
2. Do each word three ways: first, with a deliberate, hard, glottal attack [ʔ]; second, with a small "H" before the word; third, with a smooth onset of sound (it's almost like the "H" is still there but can't be heard).

Table 2.3 Glottal attack drills

ʔ-each	h-each	each	ʔ-itch	h-itch	itch
ʔ-edge	h-edge	edge	ʔ-apple	h-apple	apple
ʔ-alms	h-alms	alms	ʔ-odd	h-odd	odd
ʔ-awe	h-awe	awe	ʔ-ooze	h-ooze	ooze
ʔ-up	h-up	up	ʔ-earn	h-earn	earn

3. Apply the same soft attack to these sentences. The only place where [ʔ] is a challenge is when a word begins with a vowel sound.

- Has Anne had any afterthoughts about having another appendectomy?
- Happily, Emily hasn't eaten any of the odd oranges, or awful apples.
- How interesting. Henry is having a heated argument, isn't he?

4. Take a longer piece of text, or a monologue you're working on. Record yourself, and have your partner help you listen to spot any glottal attacks. Note how prevalent they are in both rehearsed pieces and conversational speech.

UNIT 2.5.3 *Audible inhalation*

Inhaling through a partly closed glottis is usually an unconscious habit and is easily corrected once pointed out. It will most likely show up on a quick catch-breath, or during an extreme emotion like crying or hysterical laughter. If it is part of your normal speech, it is distracting and hard on your voice. Breath should come in silently, through a completely open throat.

LISTEN

EXERCISE 2.5.3.1 FREEING INHALATION

1. Exhale on an "H" sound, then keep the same laryngeal focus and inhale. You will hear the "H" again as the air is drawn in. This is a voiceless audible inhalation (vocal folds not vibrating, but the air is turbulent and makes noise).
2. Repeat this, exhaling on "UH" as in *hut*, and keep that same adjustment as you breathe in. This should produce a voiced inhalation (vocal folds vibrating as you inhale).
3. Now you know what NOT to do. To practice the way to inhale with an open throat, stand, check your POSTURE, and BREATH, exhale, create the beginnings of a yawn, and release your abdominal muscles, dropping your diaphragm down, and feel the air quickly drop in.
4. Drill this process to improve your coordination by drawing in a full breath as *quickly* as possible, then extending your exhalation as *long* as possible on "SSSSSSSSSSS". There should be no sound on the inhalation, and try to get the "SSSSSSSSS" to last 30 seconds.

Poor breath management/running out of air too soon

UNIT 2.5.4

There are four aspects to good breath management:

1. taking in a breath that is the same size as your idea or "inspiration";
2. having the ideas well defined so one thought doesn't run over another;
3. not wasting the air through breathy phonation or weak articulation;
4. following the idea through to its completion.

It's interesting to notice that in real life people rarely run out of air while speaking. It seems to happen all the time onstage, but it isn't because the lines are longer; it's because the actor hasn't breathed in the whole idea, or hasn't fully taken in his inspiration from his partner.

In conversation, breath is a crucial part of the interaction. We subconsciously attend to the other person's breathing for important information. When our conversational partner takes a breath, it is a cue that that person has had an idea and we need to cede the floor. There are subtextual clues in:

- *when* the person breathes (provocation);
- the *speed* of the intake (urgency);
- breath *volume* (directly related to the size of the idea);
- the relative *tensions* in various parts of the body associated with breathing (emotion).

We use the information provided by these breathing cues to maintain conversational rapport. This interaction constitutes a parallel text to the word-meaning of the conversation. Most of this text is processed below conscious awareness. We respond instinctively with no requirement for an intellectual understanding of how we are visibly and audibly being informed and cued by and in turn are prompting our partner through breathing.

EXERCISE 2.5.4.1 OBSERVING BREATHING IN CONVERSATION

The next time you're in a three-person conversation, take yourself out for a moment and notice how much information you can get by paying attention to the way the other two people breathe. It can help to break this down into specific things to investigate:

1. Notice how people interrupt each other by taking a breath. You can play with this effect by taking in a sudden audible inhalation while someone else is speaking. The odds are that you'll make them stop, or lose their train of thought.
2. Can you tell how important it is for someone to speak by the speed of their inhalation?
3. Can you tell the size of what they have to say by the volume of air they take in?
4. Can you get a feel for their emotional state from the way the breath is held or by the relative relaxation or tension surrounding the act of breathing?

Audiences intuitively use the same information to help them to understand the subtextual interactions onstage. But it doesn't always work. This communication event isn't spontaneous. It has been rehearsed, and the actors may be dealing with practical challenges — like handling the cape, remembering their lines, and not falling into the pit, or other performance anxieties — so incongruities can arise when actors don't take their provocation correctly from their partner's words or actions, don't match the speed of intake to the urgency of the moment, don't match the volume of their inhalation to the size of the idea (usually the length of a phrase), or betray their emotions through body tensions that say more about their personal feelings than those of the character.

Picking up cues

UNIT 2.5.5

This phrase can have a couple of meanings. In interpersonal communication, someone who doesn't "pick up on cues" is tone deaf to the conversational hints. If you did a few versions of the exercise above, you will have begun to notice that people are variously skillful at reading the subtext in conversations. Some just don't have the awareness to pick up on the cues. This is a skill that can be developed, however, with attention and practice. Paying attention to breathing is a great place to start.

In acting environments, directors often push their actors to "pick up the cues" when there seems to be too long a space between lines and the show is beginning to drag. For many actors, the response to this direction is just to speed up everything. There's a better way.

In dialogue, you have two cues for your line — one for speaking, but first, a more important one for breathing. Actors tend to focus on the *line cue* — the end of the previous line and the cue for the next actor to speak. It's much more effective to focus on the *action cue*, or the instant where the idea or inspiration strikes. This is where the initial breath is taken, often just before the other person stops speaking. (In conversation, the listener's inhalation is the cue for the speaker to finish their idea — so cues work both ways. They prompt the speaker as well as the listener.) If you pay attention to this, you'll listen more intently to your partner, you'll make active discoveries rooted in your partner's behavior, and you'll tend to act *on* the lines, rather than in pauses between the lines. This, rather than generally speeding up, is the best way to energize and tighten up a performance.

To set this up, ask yourself: what does my partner do or say that creates a discovery or a need to speak my next line? Usually, that can be found a few words before the end of the actual line. Words like "but," "if," commands, challenges, and questions are often provocations.

LISTEN

EXERCISE 2.5.5.1 CONNECTING BREATH AND THOUGHT

1. Here's a bit of banter from Act I, Scene V of Shakespeare's *Twelfth Night* to explore these ideas. The phrase provoking the action cue will be underlined. Look for a place in there to take a breath before the cue line is finished. Note that the characters don't stop listening just because they have been provoked to speak. Many of the lines require the listener to send back the last word to the speaker. So they need to take their provocation, inhale AND listen — all without holding their breath. It's a bit like swordplay: parry and thrust. And it can take the same kind of practice to do well.

   Olivia: Now sir, <u>what is</u> your text?
   Viola: Most <u>sweet Lady</u> —
   Olivia: A comfortable doctrine, and much may be said of it. <u>Where lies</u> your Text?
   Viola: In <u>Orsino's bosom</u>.
   Olivia: In his bosom? In <u>what chapter</u> of his bosom?
   Viola: To answer by the method, in the <u>first of his heart</u>.
   Olivia: O, I have read it: it is heresy. <u>Have you no more</u> to say?
   Viola: Good Madam, <u>let me see</u> your face.
   Olivia: Have you any Commission from your Lord, to negotiate with my face: you are now out of your Text: but we will draw the Curtain, and show you the picture. [Unveiling] Look you sir, such a one I was this present: <u>Is't not</u> well done?
   Viola: Excellently done, <u>if God</u> did all.
   Olivia: 'Tis in grain sir, <u>'twill endure</u> wind and weather.
   Viola: 'Tis beauty truly blent, whose red and white,
   Nature's own sweet, and cunning hand laid on:. . .

   Even though the characters are listening to the whole line and often feeding back the last word in the previous line, they still can be provoked to breathe in before the line cue. Speak this a couple of times to find the rhythm.

2. Take a scene that you are working on (as suggested in Chapter 1). Identify and note the idea groups, breath marks, action cues, and line cues. Does it make the scene more understandable? Do you find the dialogue is tighter, with less wasted space between lines? What other effects can you discover?

Since we take in a breath that is the same size as an idea, audiences cue in to the volume of a breath to tell how large the following idea will be. Breath also "frames" an idea. If an actor doesn't breathe in when a new idea strikes, then the audience doesn't hear the discovery of the new idea and the meaning becomes blurred. An initial way to explore this is to breathe on punctuation.

LISTEN

EXERCISE 2.5.6.1 **ORGANIZING IDEAS – CONNECTING BREATH AND THOUGHT**

1. Here's the same section from *Twelfth Night*. The phrase provoking the action cue will be underlined and ¡ is inserted to help you to spot places to take breaths that frame ideas. Remember that very short ideas require only short, quick breaths.

    Olivia: ¡Now sir,¡ <u>what is</u> your text?
    Viola: ¡Most <u>sweet Lady</u> —
    Olivia: ¡A comfortable doctrine,¡ and much may be said of it.¡ <u>Where lies</u> your Text?
    Viola: ¡In <u>Orsino's bosom</u>.
    Olivia: ¡In his bosom?¡ In <u>what chapter</u> of his bosom?
    Viola: ¡To answer by the method,¡ in the <u>first of his heart</u>.
    Olivia: ¡O,¡ I have read it:¡ it is heresy.¡ <u>Have you no more</u> to say?
    Viola: ¡Good Madam,¡ <u>let me see</u> your face.
    Olivia: ¡Have you any Commission from your Lord,¡ to negotiate with my face:¡ you are now out of your Text:¡
        but we will draw the Curtain,¡ and show you the picture. [Unveiling] ¡ Look you sir,¡ such a one I was this
        present:¡ <u>Is't not</u> well done?
    Viola: ¡Excellently done,¡ <u>if God</u> did all.
    Olivia: ¡'Tis in grain sir,¡ <u>'twill endure</u> wind and weather.
    Viola: ¡'Tis beauty truly blent,¡ whose red and white,¡
        Nature's own sweet,¡ and cunning hand laid on:. . .

2.   Practice this until you can coordinate all the many elements of breathing and meaning. It usually doesn't come smoothly the first few times. How does taking these breaths make you feel? How does it effect the meaning? Does it take on more specificity? Remember that these breath markings aren't requirements, just places to begin exploring.
3.   Apply this to a contemporary and a classical scene you're working on. See how these breathing decisions inform the work.

UNIT 2.5.7   *Exhaling before speaking*

This is a frequent problem and usually an unconscious habit. The most effective means of correcting it is through side-coaching. Actors who take a breath and then release it before speaking are usually afraid of the power of the emotion and want to let off steam, rather than focus that power through their voice.

If you observe your partner (or yourself) exhibiting this pattern, go back and immediately replay the moment, repatterning the behavior so the breath and its emotional force are focused onto the words. Do this without stopping the flow of the scene.

If this is a problem that is called to your attention, it can be helpful to videotape yourself in a scene and review it so you can see the behavior in action.

UNIT 2.6   **Healing tempo – your voice in time**

The pace, rate, speed or momentum of your delivery is a crucial area but is usually well below conscious awareness. We all think our tempo is "normal," and everyone else is measured against that. The tortoise sees the world as unreasonably fast, and the hare feels that the rest of the world is as slow as molasses. Our goal is to increase objectivity and control.

Table 2.4 lists some of the typical issues.

Table 2.4 Tempo Doc/Shrink

THE VOICE DOC	THE VOICE SHRINK	R
Raising or dropping pitch and intensity as tempo speeds up or slows down	Are you able to distinguish and control the elements of the voice separately?	p 81
Racing	Are you afraid to "take stage", have you found your "right" to be there?	pp 83–90
Dragging, sluggish	Examine yourself for poor concentration, self-indulgence, lack of commitment. Have you found the character's need to fight *for* something?	p 82
Adopting another character's tempo	Are you overly empathetic, resisting conflict between characters?	p 77
Not picking up cues	Check for poor concentration, acting *between* the lines instead of *on* them, not identifying the action cues, not listening.	p 77
R: Separate your pitch from your tempo. Do not impose your own rate on that of the character.	**R**: Clear your mind of distractions. Relish conflict and need and let both work for you.	

Raising or dropping pitch and intensity as tempo changes

We associate high speed with high pitch and loudness, and just the opposite for slow speed. Anything with variable speed — an engine, a rock swung on the end of a rope, a rotating fan — will rise in pitch and intensity as it speeds up and drop when it slows down. The human voice doesn't work in the same way; we only *think* it does. So when the director asks us to pick up the pace, we often pick up the pitch as well. It is essential to separate these elements and gain control over them. The next exercise will be the first of four "isolations" designed to give separation and control.

EXERCISE 2.6.1.1 TEMPO ISOLATION

1. Use either your performance text, or the word mask on page 229. Speak each syllable (not each word) separately at a clearly defined regular tempo, keeping them all on the same pitch and at the same intensity. This will sound robotic.
2. Gradually increase the tempo until you are going as fast as you can articulate. Do not raise the pitch or volume.
3. As soon as you have reached maximum speed, smoothly begin to slow down, passing through your starting speed and becoming definitively slow. Do not drop the pitch or loudness.
4. Return to your original tempo. You have completed one cycle.

Hints: as you may suspect, this requires superior breath management. Don't break the rhythm to breathe. There will always be space for breath until you reach maximum speed. If you have a hard time maintaining a steady pitch, pick a pitch just above your normal note so you can hear it more distinctly. If you still have a problem, put someone on each side of you and have them hum the pitch in your ear to keep you on track.

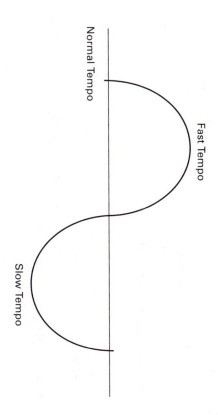

Normal Tempo

Fast Tempo

Slow Tempo

Figure 2.3 Tempo isolation

These isolation exercises have several side benefits. By speaking syllables rather than words, you begin to explore words as collections of sounds rather than as inviolate units. When the literal meaning of a word is taken away, a door opens for you to experience a fresh sense of its onomatopoeic qualities and create new meanings and new rhythms for it. It begins to free you from the tyranny of the ordinary, expected shape of a word.

Another surprise benefit happens if you retype all your lines as a string of words with no capital letters or punctuation and drill all the isolations repeatedly. You will accidentally memorize your script, but in quite a different way. You will have all the words inside you without any contextual associations to normal word form, idea, pitch, rhythm or intensity. This leaves you free to create without any limiting preconceptions. If you have already memorized your lines, this process can strip away those contextual associations, leaving space for fresh possibilities.

Healing rhythm – your drum beats

Phrasing is idea *grouping*, while stressing is idea *emphasis*. Both areas require rhythmic choices. Both are a product of good text analysis. Phrasing amounts to breaking a line up into its component ideas, then deciding which ideas are *primary* and which are *subordinate*. There are three types of stressing. *Sentence or phrase stress* is the prominence given to important, or *operative*, words to bring out the meaning. *Syllable stress* is the emphasis placed on certain sounds in a multisyllable word. It has more to do with pronunciation than interpretation (see Chapter 5). *Poetic stress* is the metrical emphasis given in poetic scansion (see Chapter 3). While pitch, volume, and quality are often used for stress, it is primarily rhythmic.

Table 2.5 addresses some of the devils that may haunt your rhythm section.

Table 2.5 Rhythm Doc/Shrink

THE VOICE DOC	THE VOICE SHRINK	R
Repetitive patterns	Are you making clear choices, being too general, not concentrating?	pp 110–13
Too many important or "operative" words	Are you making clear choices, finding everything important, do you not understand, or haven't identified the main argument?	pp 94–8
Over-reliance on volume bursts to stress words	Have you discovered the varieties of length as a stressing tool? Are you willing to release personal stressing habits?	pp 85–90
R: Find variety. Make selective choices.	**R**: Let go of your old personal habits. Embrace those of the character. Seek clarity and welcome timing shifts.	

The most important clue to rhythmic stressing is that it is an issue of *time*, not *intensity*. Yes, stress can be accomplished with a burst of loud sound, but that is the weakest, least subtle, and crudest of the ways available. In music, rhythmic structure is established by contrasts between which notes are longest and which are shortest (not loudest and softest), an aspect as important as the melody pitch intervals. The dynamics of accent, crescendo, and diminuendo are less significant in establishing the tune.

Since stress is a time issue, longer sounds will have prominence over short sounds. Audiences listen to the rhythm of speech to identify which ideas are more significant and which are side issues. Adding or reducing length is the most effective way to organize phrases and bring out the operative ideas in a sentence and the operative words in a phrase.

UNIT 2.7.1

Phrasing hierarchies

Start by defining the primary subordinate and qualifying phrases.

Primary phrases carry the truly important information, the story, or the points of the argument. For example: "You have parked the car on top of my foot!"

A **qualifying** phrase usually modifies or defines an aspect of the main idea. It often provides information on who, what, why, when, where, or how about the main topic. It is usually given more length and a rising inflection at the end. For example: "You, [who are normally the most careful driver], have parked the car, [a heavy luxury model], on top of my foot!"

A **subordinate** phrase is parenthetical, or unimportant to the main argument. You could remove it without changing the meaning or the grammatical sense. Subordinate phrases are usually treated by using

- less inflective color
- reduced volume
- lower pitch.

For example: You, [who are normally the most careful driver], (a driver widely known for your consideration and even-temperedness), have parked the car, [a heavy luxury model], (made heavier by my four overfed cousins in the back seat), on top of my foot!

The most typical subordinate phrases are:

- the direct address: "Stop, (Mary), and think first."
- an aside made as a private remark: "The map, (if I haven't misread it), says we should turn left here."
- a phrase that does not relate to the main argument, and could be deleted without changing the literal sense: "My dog, (who's drooling on your leg), is a champion."
- a phrase that does relate to the main idea, but could still be deleted without changing the sense: "This shirt, (that I'm wearing), has a nasty stain."

When we evaluate a piece of text and put all these various phrases in their proper levels of importance, we tell the audience what to listen to and remember.

Let's look at one of those famous and confusing messenger speeches of Shakespeare's: the "Bloody Captain" from Act I, Scene II of *Macbeth*. Duncan, the king, has just asked how a battle went.

Captain:

26: Doubtful it stood,

27: As two spent Swimmers, that do cling together,

28: And choke their Art: The merciless *Macdonwald*

29: (Worthy to be a Rebel, for to that

30: The multiplying Villainies of Nature

31: Do swarm upon him) from the Western Isles

32: Of Kerns and Gallowgrosses is supplied,

33: And Fortune on his damned Quarry smiling,

34: Showed like a Rebel's Whore: but all's too weak:

35: For brave *Macbeth* (well he deserves that Name)

36: Disdaining Fortune, with his brandished steel,

37: Which smoked with bloody execution

38: (Like Valor's Minion) carved out his passage,

39: Till he faced the Slave:

40: Which ne'er shook hands, nor bade farewell to him,

41: Till he unseamed him from the Nave tcth' Chops,

42: And fixed his Head upon our Battlements.

EXERCISE 2.7.1.1 PHRASING HIERARCHIES

1.   Speak the Captain's speech into a recorder. Tell the story as if you had just come from the battle yourself.

2.   Now carefully evaluate the relative importance of ideas and phrases as follows:

Sort out the essentials. What are the primary phrases? What is the core of the message? What is the answer to the king's question? What is the most direct and simple way you can tell the story? How much can you cut away to make it straightforward? (Here you may find that you would make different selections. That's fine. These are subject to interpretation — the actor's prerogative! The important thing is to make clear decisions.) Let's call this the A level. Use **bold** to identify these words and phrases:

Doubtful

Macdonwald is supplied, and Fortune showed like a Rebel's Whore

but all's too weak

Macbeth carved out his passage, faced the Slave, unseamed him, and fixed his Head upon our Battlements.

That was the course of the battle. All those other words have importance, color, and excitement, but if the audience doesn't follow the central facts (as they so often don't) a major plot development will pass them by.

3. Now that you have identified the primary level, add in the qualifying phrases. Use [ ] to group them. Let's call this the A and B level. (This particular monologue seems to have fewer B-level phrases than many.)

Doubtful [As two spent Swimmers]

Macdonwald [of Kerns and Gallowgrosses] **is supplied, and Fortune showed like a Rebel's Whore:**

but all's too weak:

Macbeth [Disdaining Fortune], **carved out his passage, faced the Slave: unseamed him, and fixed his Head upon our Battlements.**

The test of whether you're getting each of these levels right is that A, then A and B, should make sense, and we should be able to understand it without missing the absent phrases. If it doesn't make sense, you haven't got it right.

4. Add in the next level of phrases. Let's call this C level. Identify these with (). When you speak the C-level phrases, notice that if you slow down and give them more time, they don't take on more importance, but rather the audience can enjoy their vivid descriptiveness and hear when you come back to the simpler, more direct A and B levels.

Doubtful (it stood), [As two spent Swimmers], (that do cling together):

(The merciless) *Macdonwald* (worthy to be a Rebel), (from the Western Isles) [of Kerns and Gallowgrosses] **is supplied, and Fortune** (on his damned Quarry smiling), **showed like a Rebel's Whore**

but all's too weak

5. In some monologues, there is one more level of phrases. Let's call this D level. Identify them with §. You've probably figured out that the way to find these various phrases is just to remove modifying phrases and then gradually restore them. If the use of brackets is visually confusing, try highlighting them in different colors. When you speak them, let us hear the differences in the phrases through your use of rhythm and pitch.

(For brave) *Macbeth* (well he deserves that Name) [Disdaining Fortune], (with his brandished Steele), (Like Valor's Minion) **carved out his passage**, (Till he) **faced the Slave**: (Which ne'er shook hands), (till he) **unseamed him** (from the Nave toth' Chops), **and fixed his Head upon our Battlements**.

Captain:

26: **Doubtful** (it stood),
27: [As two spent Swimmers], (that do cling together),
28: {And choke their Art}: (The merciless) *Macdonwald*
29: (Worthy to be a Rebel), {for to that
30: The multiplying Villainies of Nature
31: Do swarm upon him} (from the Western Isles)
32: [Of Kerns and Gallowgrosses] **is supplied,**
33: **And Fortune** (on his damned Quarry smiling),
34: **Showed like a Rebel's Whore: but all's too weak:**
35: (For brave) *Macbeth* (well he deserves that Name)
36: [Disdaining Fortune], (with his brandished Steel),
37: {Which smoked with bloody execution}
38: (Like Valor's Minion) **carved out his passage,**
39: (Till he) **faced the Slave:**
40: (Which ne'er shook hands), {nor bade farewell to him},
41: (Till he) **unseamed him** (from the Nave toth' Chops),
42: **And fixed his Head upon our Battlements.**

Having the ideas organized in our minds is an important first step. The next is to get this out of your head and into your body — express that structure through voice and movement.

EXERCISE 2.7.1.2 MACBETH ON MONDAY NIGHT FOOTBALL

1. Use four actors. Think of this monologue as the description of a sporting event made by four television commentators. A provides the primary description of the play. B backs him up with more details. C and D provide "color" and observations. Each makes a contribution, and each sounds different. Here's your script:

A: **Doubtful**
C: (it stood)
B: [As two spent Swimmers]
C: (that do cling together),
D: {And choke their Art}
C: (The merciless)
A: *Macdonwald*
C: (Worthy to be a Rebel)
D: {for to that the multiplying Villainies of Nature do swarm upon him}
C: (from the Western Isles)
B: [of Kerns and Gallowgrosses]
A: **is supplied, And Fortune**
C: (on his damned Quarry smiling),
A: **Showed like a Rebel's Whore: but all's too weak:**
C: (For brave)
A: *Macbeth*
C: (well he deserves that Name)
B: [Disdaining Fortune]
C: (with his brandished Steel)
D: {Which smoked with bloody execution}

C: (Like Valor's Minion)

A: **carved out his passage,**

C: (Till he)

A: **faced the Slave:**

C: (Which ne'er shook hands)

D: {nor bade farewell to him},

C: (Till he)

A: **unseamed him**

C: (from the Nave toth' Chops),

A: **And fixed his Head upon our Battlements.**

2. Each character needs to enjoy their description and make it fit into the whole picture. Find that combination of supporting the other characters and also wanting to "top" them because what you have to say is more important. Notice how A needs to retain the narrative thread and hold it while the others are commenting.

3. Read this with all the roles as they stand. Then gradually begin to fire the other actors so that A has to do A and B, then A, B, and C, until one actor is playing all the roles but is still seeing them as different roles.

4. Put Fortune and Valor in the heavens like Greek gods watching and choosing sides. Show the path that Macbeth cuts through the defending soldiers with his steaming sword. Overdo the gestures. Feel how this forces you to give different values to each phrase or idea. What happens to your length and timing choices? Record yourself doing this version.

5. This highly physicalized version may be too overdone for the way you would want to play it. So, redo it one last time adjusting the physical gestures, but don't diminish the vocal gestures a bit. Record this version, and then compare it with your first recording. Notice the rhythmic variety of the long and short, fast and slow phrases and words. How has your reading changed?

6. Play the recording to someone who doesn't know the scene and ask them to tell you what happened. If they get the story right, you've done your job.

Punctuation matters

You may have noticed that the Captain's monologue was only one sentence long (in the 1623 version), and the punctuation contained sequences of colons. It doesn't look at all like the way we are taught to punctuate sentences. One theory has it that Shakespeare employed punctuation in a highly specific way — kind of like road signs — to clue actors in on how he wanted the line read. Here's a way to use these road signs to clarify and energize your work.

EXERCISE 2.7.2.1 THE PUNCTUATION DANCE

1. Start walking while speaking the piece. Keep moving.

- (,) When you reach a comma, jump on the last syllable of the word before the comma so that final syllable is spoken while in the air.

- (( )—) When you reach a parenthesis or dash, step to the side and follow a parallel track until the close of the parenthesis, then return to your previous path.

- (:) When you reach a colon, hesitate after it very briefly, then step forward and attack the next phrase. A good way to think of Shakespeare's use of the colon is that it launches you into the next phrase. Notice how often the next word is "but," or "thus," or "therefore," or some other word that indicates a strong need for the following phrase. If there is not a "launch" word, see if one is implied.

- (;) When you reach a semicolon, turn sharply in another direction.

- (.!?) When you reach a full-stop, stop and slam your hand into the floor on the last syllable.

2. Run through this several times until you feel like you've absorbed the energy of the punctuation forms. Then do your piece with movement that is more normal for the scene. Notice how the punctuation continues to inform and shape your work.

The audience needs to hear the punctuation in your voice in order to understand the ideas.

Most of us were taught that punctuation should follow a set of rules designed to make written communication clear. But since natural speech doesn't conform to the same rules as written language, playwrights often use creative punctuation and other devices to make actors speak the rhythms they hear when they write. Here's a representative sentence from Susan Lori Parks' *Venus* (1998).

THE BROTHER, LATER THE MOTHER-SHOWMAN

Tail end of r tale for there must be an enc
Is that Venus, Black Goddess, was shameles, she sinned or else
completely unknowing of r godfearin ways she stood
totally naked in her iron cage.

She uses every contrivance from spelling, to capitalization, to the lay of the line on the page to steer the actor toward the rhythm she knows the line should have.

If you don't think punctuation matters, try say ng this and see who gets angry at you:

A WOMAN WITHOUT HER MAN IS NOTHING

Does it praise women?	A woman. Without her, man is nothing.
Does it make women dependent?	A woman without her man, is nothing.
Is it about a widow outside?	A woman without. Her man is nothing.

Try speaking these versions to someone who hasn't seen the sentences. Can you make them understand the differences in what you're saying just by listening to the expression in your voice?

Here are two treatments of a section from Shakespeare's *Twelfth Night*, Act III, Scene I, Olivia.

(1623 Folio)	(2005 Arden)
O what a deale of scorne, lookes beautifull?	O what a deal of scorn, looks beautiful
In the contempt and anger of his lip,	In the contempt and anger of his lip!
A murdrous guilt shewes not it selfe more soone,	A murd'rous guilt shows not itself more soon
Then loue that would seeme hid: Loues night, is noone.	Than love that would seem hid. Love's night, is noon.—
Cesario, by the Roses of the Spring,	*Cesario*, by the roses of the spring,
By maid-hood, honor, truth, and euery thing,	By maid-hood, honor, truth, and everything,

I loue thee so, that maugre all thy pride,	I love thee so, that maugre all thy pride,
Nor wit, nor reason, can my passion hide:	Nor wit nor reason, can my passion hide.
Do not extort thy reasons from this clause,	Do not extort thy reasons from this clause,
For that I woo, thou therefore hast no cause:	For that I woo, thou therefore hast no cause;
But rather reason thus, with reason fetter;	But rather reason thus with reason fetter:
Loue sought, is good: but giuen vnsought is better.	Love sought is good, but given unsought, is better.

There are multiple small differences, but the main distinction is in the first two sentences. The ideas are quite different between these versions. Try speaking both and see which one you like better.

In *A Midsummer Night's Dream*, the character Peter Quince delivers a prologue to the play *Pyramus and Thisbe*. Shakespeare's punctuation suggests that, even though Quince is the author and should know what he's saying, he gets nervous and it comes out all wrong when he speaks. Look at it next to what the punctuation probably ought to be.

(original)	(repaired)
If we offend, it is with our good will.	If we offend, it is with our good will
That you should thinke, we come not to offend,	That you should thinke we come, not to offend,
But with good will. To shew our simple skill,	But with good will to shew our simple skill:
That is the true beginning of our end.	That is the true beginning of our end.
Consider then, we come but in despight.	Consider then, we come — but in despight
We do not come, as minding to content you,	We do not come — as minding to content you;
Our true intent is. All for your delight,	Our true intent is all for your delight:
We are not heere. That you should here repent you,	We are not heere that you should here repent you.
The Actors are at hand; and by their show,	The Actors are at hand, and by their show,
You shall know all, that you are like to know.	You shall know all that you are like to know.

Try speaking both versions. In the "bad" reading, the audience should be able to figure out what the "good" reading should have been.

UNIT 2.7.3   *Word stress*

Phrasing and punctuation are essential in conveying ideas. But it isn't enough. We need word stress within a phrase as well. While stressing is unique to each actor and each moment of interpretation, analyzing text for operative words helps specify ideas and illustrate possibilities. In the guidelines below few of these suggestions are absolute. There are often good reasons to deviate from the recommendation. Still, we encourage you to ignore this advice only with good reason — because it enhances the meaning — not merely out of habit.

UNIT 2.7.4   *What* not *to stress*

Well, to start with, the word *not*. But we'll get to that in a second.

Actors can fall into the trap of loving the words so much that they want to stress all of them. Or they choose words that are personal, emotional, and forceful but don't carry the meaning well. Just as lighting designers learn that pouring light on the stage can actually make the scene darker (because our irises close in response), actors learn that stressing too many words can make the meaning less clear. So it's important to know what *not* to stress.

Here's a short list of words to avoid stressing:

- the word *not*
- pronouns (he, him, her, me, mine, I . . .)
- conjunctions (and, or, but . . .)
- prepositions (of, at, to, in, on . . .)
- articles (the, a, an).

The word *NOT!* As with all these guidelines, this instruction doesn't have to be universally applied. But check to see if the power and meaning of the line is enhanced by other choices. Often, actors enjoy the declamatory and emphatic energy of stressing NOT. Beware. It can obscure rather than enlighten the message.

Try:	Not:
Do I **entice** you? do I speak you **fair**?	Do I entice you? do I speak you fair?
Or rather do I not in plainest **truth**,	Or rather do I **not** in plainest truth,
Tell you I **do** not, nor I **can**not **love** you?	Tell you I do **not**, nor I can**not** love you?

A Midsummer Night's Dream, Demetrius

Pronouns. Actors tend to lean on these words because it helps them to personalize a role, as in "**He** gave **me** the ball." The problem is that it sets up an expectation in the listener's mind that the "me" is comparative to someone else. So we wait to see who he didn't give the ball to, or whether "she" should have given it. And many times that isn't the point of the line at all. Stressing pronouns can misdirect the listener.

Try:	Not:
And if an **Angel** should have come to me,	And if an Angel should have come to **me**,
And told me **Hubert** should put out mine eyes,	And told **me** Hubert should put out **mine** eyes,
I would not have **believed** him: no tongue but **Hubert's.**	**I** would not have believed **him**: no tongue but Hubert's.

King John, Arthur

Here's a quick list of the main pronouns in English so that you can deliberately question your stressing of them:

all, another, any, anybody, anyone, anything, both, each, each other, either, everybody, everyone, everything, few, he, her, hers, herself, him, himself, his, I, it, its, itself, little, many, me, mine, more, most, much, myself, neither, no one, nobody, none, nothing, one, one another, other, others, ours, ourselves, several, she, some, somebody, someone, something, that, theirs, them, themselves, these, they, this, those, us, we, what, whatever, which, whichever, who, whoever, whom, whomever, whose, you, yours, yourself, yourselves.

Conjunctions. These are little words that link parts of a sentence. They are critical to the construction of an idea in the same way that a fulcrum is essential to a lever. But remember that the fulcrum is the smallest part of the device. So, while we should hear the conjunction, its force comes from its small size. If you emphasize it, you will distort its proportion and disable the idea.

Try:

For the **Apparel** oft proclaims the **man**.
And they in France of the best rank and station,
Are of a most select and generous chief in that.
Neither a **borrower**, nor a **lender** be;
For **loan** oft **loses** both **itself** and **friend**:
And borrowing dulls the edge of Husbandry.
This above all; to thine own **self** be **true**:
And it must follow, as the Night the Day,
Thou **canst** not then be **false** to **any** man.

Not:

For the Apparel oft proclaims the man.
And they in France of the best rank **and** station,
Are of a most select **and** generous chief in that.
Neither a borrower, **nor** a lender be;
For loan oft loses both itself **and** friend:
And borrowing dulls the edge of Husbandry.
This above all; to thine own self be true:
And it must follow, **as** the Night the Day,
Thou canst not **then** be false to any man.

Hamlet, Polonius

Conjunctions can be so small that sometimes their presence is only suggested, not even stated. In those cases, we "hear" the word by the rhythm that implies it. Below we have a when–then pairing. (That's like an if–then pairing, just in the past tense.) Say this quote both ways until we can "hear" the missing word even though you aren't saying it. Notice how powerful these words are, even when they are unstressed or absent altogether.

When that the poor hath cried, Caesar hath wept.

When that the poor hath cried, [*then*] Caesar hath wept.

Julius Caesar, Mark Antony

Here's a quick list of English conjunctions to help you to spot them:

after, although, and, as, as far as, as how, as if, as long as, as soon as, as though, as well as, because, before, both, but, either, even if, even though, for, how, however, if, if only, in case, in order that, neither, nor, now, once, only, or, provided, rather than, since, so, so that, than, that, though, till, unless, until, when, whenever, where, whereas, wherever, whether, while, yet

Prepositions. These are little launching words that govern the following phrase. For example: a horde **of** <u>hungry actors</u> swarmed **over** <u>the pizza</u> **in** <u>the green room</u>. For some reason, newscasters are particularly prone to stressing prepositions. Try it and you'll see that it does make one sound terribly important. Incomprehensible, but important.

Again, notice how if you stress "over" the audience will wonder what is "under." If you stress "in" they will look for what is "out." If that is the important message, fine. But often it isn't. Think critically.

Try:
A <u>kind</u> overflow of <u>kindness</u>, there are no faces <u>truer</u>, than those that are so <u>washed</u>, how much better is it to <u>weep</u> at <u>joy</u>, than to <u>joy</u> at <u>weeping</u>?

Not:
A kind overflow <u>of</u> kindness, there are no faces truer, <u>than</u> those <u>that</u> are so washed, how much better is it <u>to</u> weep <u>at</u> joy, <u>than</u> <u>to</u> joy <u>at</u> weeping?

Much Ado About Nothing, Leonato

Here's a list of English prepositions, including two- and three-word units that function as prepositions:

aboard, about, above, across, after, against, along, alongside, amid, amidst, among, amongst, around, as, aside, astride, at, athwart, atop, barring, before, behind, below, beneath, beside, besides, between, beyond, but, by, circa, concerning, considering, despite, down, during, except, excluding, failing, following, for, from, given, in, including, inside, into, like, mid (from "amid"), minus, near, next, notwithstanding, of, off, on, onto, opposite, out, outside, over, pace, past, per, plus, qua, regarding, round, save, since, than, through, throughout, till, times, to, toward, towards, under, underneath, unlike, until, up, upon, versus, via, with, within, without, worth.

according to, ahead of, apart from, as of, as per, as regards, aside from, because of, but except, close to, due to, except for, far from, inside of, instead of, near to, next to, out from, out of, outside of, owing to, plus save, prior to, pursuant to, regardless of, this apart, subsequent to, thanks to, that of.

apart from this, as far as, as well as, by means of, in accordance with, in addition to, in case of, in front of, in lieu of, in place of, in spite of, on account of, on behalf of, on top of, such examples aside, with regard to, with respect to.

Archaic prepositions we might find in classical plays: anent (about), anti, behither, betwixt, cum, ere, fornenst, fornent (next to), outwith, pro, qua, re, *sans*, unto, *vis-à-vis*, withal.

Articles. These are "the," "a," and "an." They are pronounced as weak words except in unusual cases, such as when you are asserting a number value like "Not <u>three</u> apples, <u>an</u> apple." "The" is pronounced "thee" when the next sound is a vowel, as in "the ant," "the angry man" or "the hour." It is pronounced as "thuh" when the next sound is a consonant, as in "the grape," "the happy man," "the one time." Note that this rule is consistent as a sound rule, not a spelling rule. In speech, "hour" begins with a vowel sound, and "one" begins with a consonant.

Try:
I'll have my **bond**, **speak** not **against** my bond,
I have sworn an **oath** that I will have my bond:
Thou call'dst me **dog** before thou hadst a **cause**,
But since I **am** a dog, beware my **fangs**,

Not:
I'll have my **bond**, speak not against my **bond**,
I have sworn an oath that I will have my **bond**:
Thou call'dst me **dog** before thou hadst a cause,
But since I am a **dog**, beware my fangs,

The Merchant of Venice, Shylock

Look for **parallel construction**, **antithesis**, **and contrasting ideas**. Notice that you can spot implied parallel construction when words like "other," "more" or "less" are used.

Try:
Not that I loved **Caesar less**, but that I loved **Rome more**.

Not:
Not that **I** loved Caesar less, **but** that **I** loved Rome more.

Julius Caesar, Brutus

And therefore, since I cannot prove a **Lover**,
To **entertain** these **fair well spoken** days,
I am determined to prove a **Villain**,
And **hate** the **idle pleasures** of these days.

And therefore, since **I** can**not prove** a Lover,
To entertain **these** fair well spoken **days**,
I am determined **to prove** a Villain,
And hate the idle pleasures **of** these **days**.

Richard III, Richard

How to stress

UNIT 2.7.6

Now we return to the concept that stress is a quality of rhythm more than volume. This is especially good advice for actors, because if you give a sound more time, you will want to fill that with something interesting. Notice, in the quote above, what happens when you make "Rome more" very long? If you create the space, you'll fill it. So lengthen operative words and something wonderful will show up inside them.

Go back to the Macbeth speech and clarify it further by making emphasis choices. Repeat the exercises, adding that element. Be sure to make comparison recordings.

UNIT 2.8   **Healing articulation — vocal dexterity**

In speaking to an audience, there is a ranking of needs we have to satisfy in order to reach them. In order of priority:

Need	Ask this question	Issue
Audible	Can you be heard?	auditory
Intelligible	Can the individual sounds be distinguished?	auditory
Comprehensible	Do the words have meaning?	intellectual
Understandable	Do the ideas make sense?	intellectual
Emotive	Is the message moving?	emotional
Believable	Does this have the ring of truth?	emotional
Communicative	Is there give and take?	Intellectual/emotional

Articulation (or diction, clarity, precision, accuracy, and enunciation) plays a role in every one of these communication needs. If we can't hear, discern, interpret, and feel what you're saying, then the communication will fail. It also has to feel truthful. Over-articulation is just as much a problem as mumbling. In its falseness, it can interfere with believability. Perfect articulation appears effortless, does not call attention to itself, and focuses the listener's attention on the idea or feeling, not how the word is said. Speakers with the best articulation are unobtrusive in their skill.

Table 2.6 Articulation Doc/Shrink

THE VOICE DOC	THE VOICE SHRINK	R
Tense, clenched jaw, rigid lips, tense tongue	Are you unwilling or unable to give emotionally, or have a fear of communicating fully?	pp 198–9
Muddy, slurred speech, weak muscle development, poor muscular coordination	Examine yourself for a lack of commitment, fear of taking a stand.	pp 101–3
Dropping or unvoicing final sounds	Do you follow through and commit all the way to end of an idea?	pp 146–8

Table 2.6 continued

Sound substitutions, regional accent, poor hearing perception	Are you willing to release personal sound or speech patterns? Do you fear loss of identity?	pp 245–83
R: Relax all speech organs, while still seeking precision.	**R:** Commit fully, all the way to the end of any statement. Experience the joy of full diction closure.	

The best path to rapid, precise articulation is to drill! Just as a pianist must do scales in every key at blinding speed, so must the professional speaker do articulation drills. The following exercises could be incorporated into a daily warm-up. However, if you are having particular problem with any of them, the best way to work is to practice for two–three minutes several times daily. In that case, leave yourself notes in various places like the bathroom mirror, over the kitchen sink or on the dashboard of your car to remind yourself to practice.

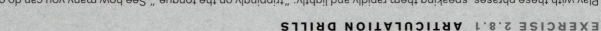

EXERCISE 2.8.1 ARTICULATION DRILLS

LISTEN

Play with these phrases, speaking them rapidly and lightly: "tripplingly on the tongue." See how many you can do on one breath.

1. A big black bug bit a big black bear, made the big black bear bleed blood
2. A dozen Black & Decker Dustbusters
3. abominable abdominals
4. abominable mambo
5. alabaster balusters
6. alluvial bivalve
7. aluminum linoleum/aluminium linoleum
8. angry banker anchored in Bangor
9. begging beguilingly
10. begrudging curmudgeon
11. belonging longer
12. beveled vestibule
13. bigger buggies
14. bleached cherubs
15. bodega bodega
16. charming bachelor Chuck
17. charting challenging channels

18. Chichester witches
19. choose orange shoes
20. Christian churches
21. Culligan and calla lily
22. curiously obscure procurer
23. dapper dabber
24. deliver shriveled devils
25. depth and breadth
26. deranged avenger
27. divulging bulging bilges
28. did you, would you, could you
29. don't you, won't you, can't you
30. dormant humidors
31. drinking ink
32. Dwight wouldn't dwell with a dozen wooden dwarves
33. eight great gray geese grazing gaily in Greece
34. eleven benevolent elephants
35. enthusiastic Thucydides
36. excuse the askew skewers
37. filly fully folly
38. fixed perspectives
39. fluffy finches flying fast
40. Frank threw Fred three free throws
41. Freddie's friend Eddie phoned for Fredcie to fetch fresh fruit from the farm of the famous French farmer
42. French-fried falafel
43. gather feathers

44. generous German managers
45. giggle gaggle
46. Gigi seizes Genet
47. glazier's glacier, grazier's glacier
48. go-kart cargoes of take-out tacos
49. gorgeous Georgia's jargon
50. gouging grouchy Gauchos
51. handle dandelion
52. Heather's hat has ten thousand feathers
53. How many mahogany and mohair hassocks has Hermione?
54. huge humans humorously hued
55. humorous rumors
56. inimically mimicking
57. involved Volvo lovers
58. Italian William
59. keep on peeking, creeping peeper
60. kickle cackle
61. kinky cookie
62. lemon liniment
63. limited ability
64. linger longer
65. literally literary
66. long, long ago
67. Martin met a mob of marching munching monkeys
68. marvelous larvae
69. measure regimes
70. minimal animal
71. mixed biscuits

72. mommala poppala
73. moving Vermont
74. murmur rumors
75. necessary accessories
76. nervous Vern's weird red vest
77. new venue's revenue
78. Paddy had a deadened haddock in the paddock
79. paper poppy, baby bubble
80. Parisian's pleasurable persuasions
81. peculiarly brilliant Italian stallion
82. peculiarly perverted viper
83. Peggy Babcock
84. perhaps happy hippies
85. philological ability
86. rapid rabid rabbit
87. red leather, yellow leather
88. red river rivalry
89. remembered dismembering
90. richest challenge
91. rubber baby buggy bumpers
92. Sarah's rising sighs and writhing thighs
93. sloppily sipping purple slurpees
94. strange Indian hinges
95. strategy tragedy
96. teases Terry's teary thesis theories

97. the bootblack brought the black book back
98. the thorn had torn through
99. three tethered teething things
100. Topeka, Topeka, Topeka
101. toy boat
102. twanging language
103. unique New York
104. urgent juror
105. usual casual users of usurers
106. Vanna wooed a voodoo man
107. vibrantly verbal Bavarian
108. we'll wail at the whale
109. while her withers wither with her
110. whither which way
111. wicked wicket victim
112. will you, William
113. Willie's villa
114. winging to England
115. wooden dwarves
116. wooden noodle
117. wrong rung wringing
118. you go with Hugo
119. you knew Hugh
120. Youmans' menu/humans: men who

Median note

All speakers center their voices around a certain pitch — the *median note*. It is the "average" pitch of the voice, not the middle of the speaker's range. On a scale of 1 to 10, with 1 being the lowest pitch in that person's range and 10 the highest, the ideal median note is usually around 3, so there is a more extensive upper range.

Median Note

1   2   3   4   5   6   7   8   9   10

The optimal position for a median note is one where you can move easily and fluidly up or down. Selection of a median note may be habitual or done for social reasons. In conversation, the person with the lower median note has the authority; the one with the higher note will seem subservient. People who adopt the same median note as the person they're speaking with seem empathetic. This effect isn't measured exactly the way notes are laid out on a piano, otherwise men's naturally lower median note would always place them in authority relative to women. Rather, it works on a relative scale, where the male C♯ would be equivalent to the female C♯ an octave higher. In that formulation, a woman with a C would seem to have more authority than a man with a C♯. Her voice would *sound* a half-step lower.

Not everyone will speak naturally from an optimal median note. Social conditioning, self-image, and a host of other issues cause many to choose a pitch that either constricts their voices or is at odds with their physical appearance. The restrictive, pressed quality of an overly low median note is a primary cause of vocal strain and one of the most frequent adult problems treated by voice pathologists. Agents often refuse to represent actors who don't "look" like their voices. A high, thin voice on a Schwarzenegger body is as odd as a *basso-profundo* beauty queen. It can make you hard to cast, unless it is so striking as to become your trademark. You have a world of choices about where to place your median note. First, what is the most natural place to speak from?

EXERCISE 2.9.1.1 FINDING THE OPTIMAL MEDIAN NOTE

1. Pair off with the person assigned to do your imitation.

2. Have your observer ask you a series of casual impersonal questions you can answer in the affirmative. (Things like: "Nice day isn't it?") Answer all the questions with "UH-HUH." Pay as little attention to where your voice is placed as you can.

3. When the observer feels that the subject is relaxed, listen carefully to the SECOND pitch in the answer — the "HUH." Lock onto that pitch. Hum it gently.

4. The subject should then read, or speak extemporaneously using that note as their point of orientation. You don't need to stay on that pitch robotically but to use it as your center, or median note.

5. Observe if there is any important difference between the habitual placement and this orientation. Is it higher, lower or the same? How does it feel? Do you notice more "color," freedom or flexibility in the voice?

Changing your median note can affect the relationship you have with the other characters in a scene, or in real life.

EXERCISE 2.9.1.2 MEDIAN NOTES AND POWER PLAYS

1. Either choose a two-person scene you have rehearsed or select a set-up for an improvisational scene.

2. Identify who has the natural authority in the scene (by social role: boss, teacher, policeman, etc.; or by social dynamic: advisor, supporter, accuser, etc.).

3. Play the scene. The actors should not concern themselves with anything but the character's natural wants and objectives. The audience observes who has the higher or lower vocal placement.

4. Replay the scene. This time keep the same characters, but reverse the median note relationship so that the higher one switches with the lower one. Observe how this alters their interaction.

The median note becomes a point of orientation. You tend to start speaking from this pitch, and when finished with a thought, you resolve back to it. If you don't resolve back to that pitch (or one of the octaves of that pitch) your listeners will feel that the idea or thought is incomplete and will be cued to wait for more, or will be prompted to respond to a question. When you return to that established point of orientation, you tell the listener that the idea is finished. Often actors will return to their starting note several times in a long speech, tiring the audience by sending out the wrong information. They will stop listening (since the actor has cued them to), then they will have to prick up their ears again when the actor goes on. The effect of these false endings is to make a long speech seem eternal.

Artfully lifting the pitch away from the starting point of orientation is sometimes called the "heroic build." It's a little like listening to a pop diva modulate keys upward to increase the emotional intensity. This is particularly interesting on exhortative speeches like the St. Crispin's Day speech in *Henry V.*

EXERCISE 2.9.1.3   THE HEROIC BUILD

1. Prepare the speech by breaking it into units or "beats." Using an observer, carefully define the median note you will use as a point of orientation for this speech. Have the observer keep careful track of that pitch.
2. Record yourself doing the speech.
3. Go back and redo the speech. Each time you start a new unit, begin it at a very slightly higher pitch. If someone in class can play the piano, have them play a major chord in the key you started and then modulate up a half-step each time you begin a new unit.
4. Compare the two readings. Select the most effective choices from each.
5. Redo the speech, incorporating the best of both earlier versions.

Range, inflection, and intonation

If the median note is the point of departure, then range is how far you go, and inflection and intonation are how you get there. It can be challenging to separate pitch from volume, rate, and tone, so when you try to lift the pitch, you might accidentally speed up the tempo and increase the volume. The following drill is the second of four "isolation" exercises designed to train the voice to identify and separate all those vocal elements and to stretch the range of each.

EXERCISE 2.9.2.1 PITCH ISOLATION

1. Use either your performance text or the word mask on page 229. Speak each syllable (not each word) separately at a clearly defined regular rate and volume. Start at your normal median note.

2. Maintaining rate and volume consistency, move the pitch upward away from your median note.

3. Step the pitch using regular intervals, never repeating any pitch, as high as your voice can go (be sure to explore way above the normal speaking range, well into the falsetto range). When you are as high as you can go, step downward evenly to as low as you can, then return to your median note. You have completed one cycle.

4. Continue repeating this cycle as long as you like, or until you run out of text.

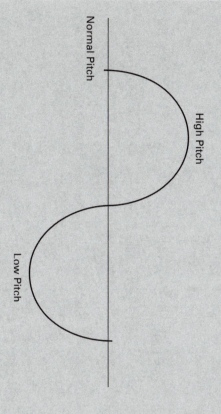

Normal Pitch

High Pitch

Low Pitch

Figure 2.4 Isolating pitch

The dots and lines in Figure 2.5 depict melodic pitch action in the voice, a useful way to note pitch patterns. This trains the ear to hear more sensitively and makes you more conscious of repetitive or inappropriate patterns.

In the following exercises, note what is communicated with each different pitch pattern. For example, pitch change between syllables (intonation) sounds direct and specific, whereas pitch change on a syllable (inflection) has more implied, ambiguous or suggested content. This is especially true for circumflex inflection.

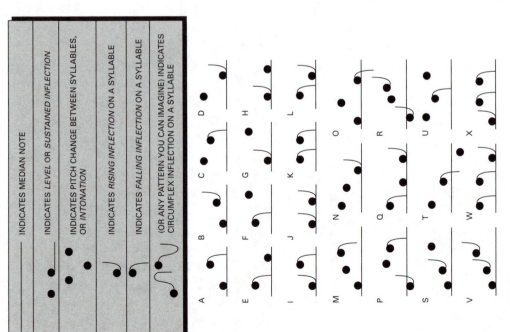

Figure 2.5 Pitch pattern notation

EXERCISE 2.9.2.2   PITCH PATTERNS

1. Practice the following pitch patterns (Figure 2.5 A–L) using any of these two-syllable words or phrases: I WILL — OKAY — WHO SAID? — YOU KNOW — YEAH, SURE — OH, NO! — YOU'RE RIGHT — GOOD TIP — SAY WHAT? — NOT NOW! — BEEN THERE — DONE THAT.

2. Have someone listen to make sure you are matching the pattern. The speaker is often surprisingly unaware of exactly how the voice is moving.

3. While working for accuracy, also extend your range further than is typical (or habitually comfortable), and still make it realistically conversational.

4. Follow the same guidelines on the next patterns (Figure 2.5 M–X). Use these or any three-syllable word or phrases: IS THAT SO? — WELL, I MIGHT — OH, MY GOSH — I HEARD THAT — I'LL BE GOOD — YOU'RE THE BEST — ANY TIME — GET A LIFE — MAKE MY DAY — BIG MISTAKE.

5. Invent some patterns of your own. Include circumflex inflections as well.

6. Listen while someone speaks a short passage. Note their pitch patterns. If you do this as a group, record the person speaking and then compare the group's results with each other and against the recording.

This method of noting pitch patterns, while not meant to be scientific, or as accurate as musical notation, is quick and easy, and is a strong awareness tool. Many actors use it when doing commercial voiceover work. It's a simple way to mark a script when given highly specific directions that must be repeated exactly.

UNIT 2.9.3   *Putting pitch and rhythm together*

Pitch and rhythm are the two most useful tools for interpreting text. Simple shifts in these elements can radically change meaning. Here's a challenging piece of text published around 1909 that requires you to punctuate and paraphrase before you'll be able to make a naïve listener understand it.

EXERCISE 2.9.3.1 ESAU WOOD

1. Mark your text with all the rhythmic information necessary, including pauses, stops, and idea groups, as well as specific pitch pattern choices. Paraphrase it in your own words to clarify the meaning.

2. Practice it until you are certain you are being clear. Then take it to someone who doesn't know the material. Have them listen to you and either stop you if they lose the sense or have them paraphrase it back to be sure it was clear. You know you're really communicating when you can do it over the phone and have someone understand at the first hearing! This is more fun if you don't look at the suggested paraphrasing. Try working it out for yourself first.

ESAU WOOD

ESAU WOOD SAWED WOOD ESAU WOOD WOULD SAW WOOD ALL THE WOOD ESAU WOOD SAW ESAU WOOD WOULD SAW IN OTHER WORDS ALL THE WOOD ESAU SAW TO SAW ESAU SOUGHT TO SAW OH THE WOOD WOOD WOULD SAW AND OH THE WOOD SAW WITH WHICH WOOD WOULD SAW WOOD BUT ONE DAY WOOD'S WOOD SAW WOULD SAW NO WOOD AND THUS THE WOOD WOOD SAWED WAS NOT THE WOOD WOOD WOULD SAW IF WOOD'S WOOD SAW WOULD SAW WOOD NOW WOOD WOULD SAW WOOD WITH A WOOD SAW THAT WOULD SAW WOOD SO ESAU SOUGHT A SAW THAT WOULD SAW WOOD ONE DAY ESAU SAW A SAW SAW WOOD AS NO OTHER WOOD SAW WOOD SAW WOULD SAW WOOD IN FACT OF ALL THE WOOD SAWS WOOD EVER SAW SAW WOOD WOOD NEVER SAW A WOOD SAW THAT WOULD SAW WOOD AS THE WOOD SAW WOOD SAW SAW WOOD WOULD SAW WOOD AND I NEVER SAW A WOOD SAW THAT WOULD SAW AS THE WOOD SAW WOOD SAW WOOD SAW UNTIL I SAW ESAU WOOD SAW WOOD WITH THE WOOD SAW WOOD SAW SAW WOOD NOW WOOD SAWS WOOD WITH THE WOOD SAW WOOD SAW SAW WOOD

There is more than one potential interpretation for this piece. Here is one way to look at it. A paraphrase appears below the text. Use this only if you get stuck. It's best if you are able to work it out on your own. (Yes, the grammar isn't perfect — there's the challenge. You can still communicate the meaning.)

ESAU WOOD: A POSSIBLE SOLUTION

Esau Wood sawed wood. Esau Wood would saw wood. All the wood

Bob Jones cut logs.   Bob Jones did cut logs.   All the logs

Esau Wood saw, Esau Wood would saw. In other words, all the wood

Bob Jones looked at, Bob Jones did cut.   In other words, all the logs

Esau saw to saw. Esau sought to saw.   Oh, the wood Wood would saw.

Jones looked at to cut, Jones tried to cut.   Oh, the logs Jones did cut.

And oh, the wood-saw with which Wood would saw wood. But one

And oh, the ax with which Jones did cut logs.   But one

day, Wood's wood-saw would saw no wood. And thus, the wood

day, Jones' ax couldn't cut any logs.   And, thus, the logs

Wood sawed, was not the wood Wood would saw, if Wood's wood-

Jones cut, were not the logs Jones might have cut, if Jones' ax

saw would saw wood. Now, Wood would saw wood with a wood-saw

could cut logs.   Now, Jones wanted to cut logs with an ax

that would saw wood. So, Esau sought a saw that would saw wood.

could cut logs.   So, Bob looked for an ax that could cut logs.

One day, Esau saw a saw saw wood as no other wood-saw Wood saw

One day, Bob watched an ax cut logs as no other ax Jones looked at would saw wood. In fact, of all the wood-saws Wood ever saw saw

could cut logs.   *In fact, of all the axes Jones ever watched cut*

wood, Wood never saw a wood-saw that would saw wood, as the

logs, Jones never looked at an ax that could cut logs, as the

wood-saw Wood saw saw wood would saw wood. And I never saw a

ax Jones watched cut logs did cut logs.   And I never looked at an

wood-saw that would saw, as the wood-saw Wood saw would saw,

ax that could cut, the way the ax Jones looked at could cut,

until I saw Esau Wood saw wood with the wood-saw Wood saw saw

until I watched Bob Jones cut logs with the ax Jones looked at cutting

wood. Now, Wood saws wood with the wood-saw Wood saw saw

logs.   Now Jones cuts logs with the ax Jones watched cutting

wood.

logs.

UNIT 2.10

... great-hearted Stentor of the brazen voice, whose voice is as the voice of fifty other men ...

HOMER, *The Iliad*, v.783

Healing volume – building a bigger voice

A stentorian voice used to be a minimum requirement for leadership. When Hector, Achilles or any of the other legendary generals addressed the troops in the Trojan wars, each spoke to a vast array of soldiers. Without amplification, each projected over the noise of armor clanking, hooves pawing the earth, and men muttering. In those days, a leader commanded with his voice. The power of his personality was asserted in the most direct manner. The troops listened because he compelled them to do so. Such a man was admired. Today (unless you come from a large Italian family), no one gives you high marks for being the loudest in your group. We speak in quiet, civil tones in a small domestic environment. If we have to address large groups, we just crank up the PA system. No one wants you to assert your emotions or opinions at full volume.

Unless you're an actor!

Actors are required to do the most strenuous things with their voices: work outdoors, play to large houses, perform heroic roles, speak for hours, do eight shows a week, sing from awkward positions, scream while getting their eyes gouged out or giving birth, murmur gently to a lover — and be heard in the back row without appearing to project! The actor who can do all this and never lose their voice or miss a performance is the actor who will be hired again.

Table 2.8 Volume Doc/Shrink

THE VOICE DOC	THE VOICE SHRINK	R
Often get the note to "be louder"; poor articulation or tonal clarity, so, audible but unintelligible; weak voice	Are you willing to share; afraid of your power; willing to accept responsibility for what is said; shy?	pp 121–2
Pushing hard, but can't get louder; Voice may not have the strength yet; pushing is making the throat tense, so sound is constricted	Do you grip the throat through fear of letting sound out; not trust the feeling, and so get tense and push?	pp 116–18

Table 2.8 continued

Voice cracks at loud volumes; vocal folds haven't developed enough to take the increased air pressure	Are you afraid of your power, so you back off just as sound gets loud?	pp 116–18
Getting loud, but can't be understood; voice lacks focus; may feel louder, but is only more tense and effortful	Are you able to distinguish *effort* from *intensity*? Do you equate *tension* with *emotion*?	pp 122–4
Voice sounds different after performing	Are you pushing too hard for your level of development?	p 64
Pitch and rate rise with volume increase	Are you able to isolate separate vocal elements?	pp 119–20
R: Keep an open, unconstrained throat. Master volume without extreme effort.	**R**: Savor and glory in your power. Give yourself permission. Let it be easy.	

UNIT 2.10.1

Volume misconceptions

Most people don't have a clear idea of what a skillfully projected voice sounds like. We have few good role models and have to actively search for that rare gospel singer, orator or actor who can just open up and effortlessly blow out the back of the house. Your first contact with a "loud voice" is usually your parents shouting at you for something you've done. Their goal isn't audibility but a demonstration of how upset they are. Although they may get loud, the real vocal focus is on *tension*. The more painful their voices sound, the more you know how bad you were. It works. You imitate this tactic when your brother steals your favorite toy, and you associate *tense shouting* with *volume*.

The next big opportunity to be loud comes at a sporting event, with 25,000 other people shouting, "Run, Joe! Run!" We know how we make a difference. If we didn't tell him, he just might not go for it. He might sit down and wait for instructions. So our job is important. But in the big picture, this is also a situation where emotion is more meaningful than volume. Since we can't be heard over all those people anyway, the *feeling* is what counts. *Ergo*, the more tension, the more we care. When we can't speak the next day, we know we really gave our all.

These, and other events like them, all reinforce the sense that a loud voice *sounds* tense. If it doesn't feel and sound strained, we must not be giving enough effort, so how could it carry very far? After all, if it isn't tense, we must not be giving it enough effort. And since we talk from *inside* our heads, we don't hear how loud we are. We aren't out there on the receiving end to judge the results. We can only judge effort, not loudness.

UNIT 2.10.2 *Building a bigger voice*

Factors that govern how loudly you're able to speak are:

- the amount of air pressure you can generate;
- the ability of your vocal folds to handle that increase in pressure;
- the way your vocal tract shapes the sound to amplify rather than muffle it;
- the ability to stay physically relaxed during this strenuous vocal work.

A word of warning!!!

Be careful when doing the next series of exercises. Working to build a bigger voice can cause problems if you aren't attentive. You will, by necessity, be pushing your voice to its limits. Vocal fatigue is common when exercising this way. This isn't harmful if you manage it well and don't overdo it. Compare it to heavy weight-lifting. A good workout leaves your muscles tired. They may be a bit sluggish the next day — but they recover, and are even stronger. If your muscles don't recover quickly, or are sore for a long time, then you have gone too far.

This is an area where a good coach is useful. You may not possess the self-awareness to know if you are tensing inappropriately or pushing too far too fast. A good test of vocal fatigue: first make a soft, light, sustained "AH" sound on a comfortable pitch. It should be the steadiest, lightest sound you can make. If after doing these (or any) vocal exercises you are unable to repeat that soft, light sound and can only make a sound that is much louder, then stop. It's time to rest your voice. If you don't find that you have recovered in about four hours, or at least by the next day, then you need to scale back and take it much slower. Develop a regimen that allows for steady, slow growth. You can do long-term damage to your vocal folds if this work is done intemperately.

EXERCISE 2.10.2.1 SINGLE-NOTE INTENSIFICATION

1. (Try this exercise from positions A, B, or C from Exercise 2.5.1.2. Test your reactions to each, remembering that those postures lend themselves to good breath support.) Using the vowel [iː], as in *heed*, start with the softest clear sound you can make. Don't allow it to be breathy. Listen carefully to the pitch and the sound quality.

2. Take a breath. On the same pitch and vowel sound, slowly *intensify* the sound until it is as loud as you can get it, and then slowly return to the soft, clear sound. As you do this, visualize the sound arcing up through the roof of your mouth and out between your eyebrows.

Figure 2.6 Intensification series

3. Repeat steps 1 and 2, exploring a variety of pitches throughout your range. Be sure to work in the falsetto area as well. Also experiment with a variety of vowel sounds. [æ] as in *had* and [ɑ] as in *father* are especially useful.

4. Does the sound become breathy or pinched as it intensifies? Does the pitch rise or waver? Do you become tense and clench your fists, or do the muscles of your neck stand out? If the quality of the sound is not as clear and easy at full volume as when you are at a normal speaking level, do the exercise again and watch how loud you get before the unwanted effect shows up. Then don't work to get as loud as you can. Practice instead to extend a good quality sound just a little further. Over time you will train yourself to have a clear, focused sound with no tension all the way to the loudest sound you can make.

EXERCISE 2.10.2.2   INTENSIFICATION AND BREATH SUPPORT

1.   (As before, try this exercise from positions A, B or C from Exercise 2.5.1.2.) Repeat the previous exercise with three long, slow intensification cycles per breath.

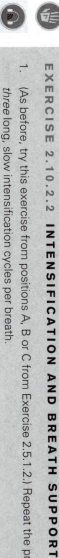

Figure 2.7 Intensification and breath support

2.   Observe any areas of tension, shake them out, and slowly repeat the process until you train yourself to stay relaxed.

3.   Repeat this exercise on several different pitches throughout your range. Don't ignore the very low or high falsetto pitches.

As you become at ease with this exercise, notice how much more efficiently you are able to use your breath. When starting out, it can seem quite challenging to do three full intensifications. Later you'll easily do more. Breath support is essential for good vocal production. With regular repetition of exercises like this, you will teach yourself how to find and use that support.

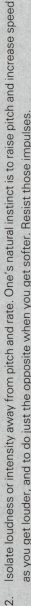

LISTEN

EXERCISE 2.10.2.3 VOLUME ISOLATION

1. As with the other isolation exercises, use the word mask on page 229 or your performance text.

2. Isolate loudness or intensity away from pitch and rate. One's natural instinct is to raise pitch and increase speed as you get louder, and to do just the opposite when you get softer. Resist those impulses.

3. To find the easiest pitch for this exercise, shout "HEY!" as if you were calling to a friend in the next block. Listen carefully to the pitch you choose and say "hey" softly on the same pitch. This is your starting point. You may be surprised how high it seems.

4. Speak each syllable separately. Start at a conversational volume level, with each syllable slightly louder than the one before it, until you reach maximum level, then reverse the process, through a barely audible level back to normal, completing one cycle. Remember that throughout, the pitch and speed must remain constant.

5. Being wary of vocal fatigue, continue to repeat the cycle until you have gone through the full text. Watch for general body and neck tension and focus on keeping a clear, consistent tone throughout the full range from soft to loud.

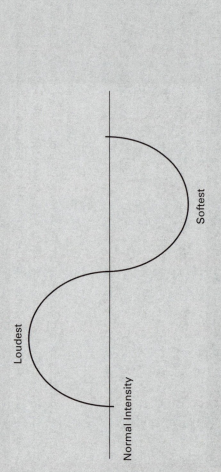

Figure 2.8 Isolating volume

EXERCISE 2.10.2.4 ISOLATING VOLUME, VARYING PITCH

1. Do one cycle as in the exercise above.

2. For each succeeding cycle, lower your pitch one whole step until you are at your lowest comfortable pitch level. The pitch remains constant during each cycle and changes only between cycles. You may find that in the high mid-range you can get much louder than at the extremely low or high pitches. That is natural, but do test your boundaries.

3. If your voice is not fatigued, and you have text remaining, repeat steps 1 and 2.

UNIT 2.10.3

How loud is loud enough?

If your audience can hear you easily throughout the theatre without having to think about it, you're doing fine. But audibility and intelligibility aren't the same thing. When people say they can't hear you, they often really mean that they can't understand you. Clarity of articulation, clear tonal quality, and the strength of your acting intention are just as important.

You may have noted that certain material seems to lend itself to large-scale acting. Certainly, *Medea* plays more easily to a big theatre than *The Glass Menagerie* does. The genre of play asks for a certain size, and kitchen sink realism can be the hardest to scale up and still retain its intimacy. As you do the following series of explorations, use as wide a variety of material as possible to get a sense of the stage illusions of size.

EXERCISE 2.10.3.1 APPROPRIATE SIZE

1. Work in as large a space as possible.

2. Place other actors at various distances and directions from the speaker.

3. The speaker should deliver a short passage, addressing each phrase to a different person, adjusting the volume level to reach just that one person — not to go beyond, or fall short.

4. Explore this approach with various selections, including heroic declamations and intimate love scenes. Note how the truth of the moment can be expanded without becoming "pushed."

EXERCISE 2.10.3.2 SIZE WITH INTIMACY – CONNECTING

1. Work in as large a space as possible.

2. Put a pair of actors as far apart as the room will allow. If you are working in a theatre, put one on stage and the other at the back of the house.

3. One actor will be the "speaker," the other, the "listener."

4. The speaker establishes a volume level at which the listener can just barely hear the words.

5. Maintaining that level, the speaker delivers a short selection (classical material with complex sentences and unfamiliar wording works best).

6. Anytime the listener doesn't feel "connected" to the speaker, the listener asks for clarification: "A rose by any other ... what?" "Out, out, damned ... who?" The speaker repeats as necessary *without increasing volume*, but by strengthening the *intention*.

7. Discuss: what were the most interesting vocal choices? Were they made with pitch intonation and rhythmic variety, rather than volume emphasis?

The word "projection" can be problematic. It can lead an actor to conceptualize size as pushing or shouting to reach a far target. It's far better to expand the size of one's truth. Don't project — that's a small truth pushed. Instead, expand your "self" to be bigger than the theatre. Don't increase your effort, grow the size of your truth, your self.

EXERCISE 2.10.3.3 SIZE WITH INTIMACY – SHARING

1. After you've completed the exercise above, add another actor, placed in a normal stage relationship to the speaker.

2. Repeat the exercise as before. Now the speaker relates to the other actor, but includes the listener — sharing the intimate stage reality all the way to the back of the house.

EXERCISE 2.10.3.4 SIZE – EXPANDING THE WORLD

1. Use two actors and a listener. The actors are placed in a normal stage relationship and the listener at the back of the house. (If you have the opportunity to work some of these exercises in an outdoor space such as a football stadium, the results can be even better, though be wary of vocal strain in outdoor spaces, where the sound will not be supported by the acoustic properties of a room.)

2. The actors play a scene focusing on honesty and not at all on size. They make no attempt to share their work with the audience.

3. When the honesty and intimacy of the scene has been established, they begin to back away from each other — expanding the world of the play. If at any time the scene becomes forced or pushed, they either hold that distance until it becomes familiar or contract slightly to recover their connection, then continue to expand.

4. At some point, it will become clear that the scene is "filling the space." The listener now will side-coach the scene, directing the actors to maintain the size of their emotional relationship while returning slowly to a closer, smaller physical relationship.

5. This exercise is particularly helpful for Greek plays, or styles that need a heroic dimension. It may take several exposures before actors are able to find the larger world of the play without losing the honesty of their more intimate work.

6. Explore this work in a variety of settings — the theatre, a stadium, across a busy intersection, on a mountain top — anywhere you can feel bigger, stronger, and more powerful.

UNIT 2.10.4 *Volume enhancers — timbre, quality, and resonance*

When middle C is played on a cello and a violin, the effect is vastly different, even though it is the same note. The resonating cavities of the instruments enhance certain qualities of the sound, producing the timbre unique to that instrument. Any enclosed space has the same properties. An actor who is sensitive to a room's acoustic properties is able to adjust to use those qualities to carry their sound clearly and effortlessly.

EXERCISE 2.10.4.1 **FINDING ROOM RESONANCE**

1. Stand in a small room. A shower stall works great.
2. Hum slowly from your lowest note upwards.
3. Listen for the pitch where the room "vibrates with you."
4. Explore that sensation by using a variety of vowel sounds, singing the octave above that special pitch, trying various volume intensities until you feel you have mastered the space.

EXERCISE 2.10.4.2 **FINDING ROOM RESONANCE IN LARGE SPACES**

1. Do the exercise above with a large group in a theatre or rehearsal hall. Allow the group to discover together and explore the "room tone."
2. One at a time, practice calling to each other on the pitch the group discovers.
3. Listen for the actor most capable of aligning with the room's acoustics. Whose voice seems to carry effortlessly and clearly throughout the space?
4. Move to another space and repeat the process.

The human vocal tract has the same resonating properties as the room or the violin, except that unlike the fixed form of a violin, you can change the shape of your instrument. When you sing a note, it isn't just one pure pitch but a complex collection of tones and overtones that give sound warmth and color. With practice, you can shape your voice to amplify and clarify the tone in a way that can give a large boost of sound without any extra effort.

A fun way to observe the effect of the following exercise is to look at it on a spectrogram. This is software that takes the sound frequencies of your voice and displays them visually. Spectrogram software is downloadable in many free versions on the web. It can be a great way to receive feedback about your sound. Try it on the next exercise and watch the way the picture changes.

LISTEN

EXERCISE 2.10.4.3 **FOCUSING SOUND FOR VOLUME**

1. Stand comfortably: knees soft, jaw relaxed, teeth two finger widths apart, tongue relaxed, head level. Feel a slight yawn to lift the soft palate.
2. On an [ɑ] vowel like in "father," sustain a long, light note in your mid-falsetto range.
3. Repeat step 2, and during the long sound round your lips forward into an [o] vowel like in "home." Explore this sound. Done properly, a distinct increase in volume will come without any extra effort. (You could use a recorder that has volume meters to display the increase.)
    This focusing effect is available throughout your entire range and can add a significant boost to the sound without any additional effort.
4. Call "HELLOOOOOO" in a clear, full voice, but don't push the sound. There should be no feeling of effort.
5. During the [o], experiment with the aperture of the lips, bring them slowly rounder and then wider. Pay attention more to the feeling sensation than the sound. At some point you will discover the adjustment that makes the sound vibrate off the hard palate and into the bridge of the nose.
6. Play around with the feeling and notice that it works only with a particular formation of your lips, teeth, and soft palate. Widen and narrow the lips to bring the vibration into and out of focus, like tuning in a radio station.
7. Explore a variety of pitches. Note that the lower the pitch, the narrower the lip opening needs to be.
8. Repeat this exercise with a variety of vowel sounds, especially [ɔ], as in *law*yer, [u], as in *hoot*, [ɜ], as in *fur*ry, [ɒ], as in *rod*, and [ɑ], as in *fa*ther.
9. When you start to own this resonant and focused feeling you are finding, it can become the organizing resonance of your whole voice — whether you are speaking loudly or softly.

UNIT 2.11 **Healing quality — finding the sound core**

Certain actors sound as if they're speaking from their whole body. The voice seems to emanate rather than project. They wrap us in the sound. Other actors seem to have thin, weak voices centered in the throat. They make us tense and uncomfortable when they speak. What are these two types doing differently?

All voiced sounds come from the vibration of the vocal folds in the larynx in the neck. From that source, the sound is shaped as it resonates in the vocal tract: all the cavities of the throat, mouth, and nose. The vibration of the vocal folds is like the action of a trumpeter's lips in the mouthpiece. The vocal tract is the body of the horn. Some people have the body of a tuba, some bugles. Unlike a horn, however, which has a fixed shape, you can adjust the contour and length of your vocal tract to form the sound (Exercise 2.10.4.3, for example). You also have control over the force, duration, and steadiness of your airflow, and the way the vocal folds come together into the airstream.

Table 2.9 Quality Doc/Shrink

THE VOICE DOC	THE VOICE SHRINK	R
Breathy quality; vocal folds not meeting fully.	Do you have a placating attitude, fear of offending; fear of assuming power or responsibility?	pp 130–1
Harsh or strained quality; vocal folds may be pushing together too hard; neck tension.	Are you efforting or trying too hard?	pp 130–1
Nasal/denasal/twangy; poor coordination of velo-pharyngeal port (the part of the roof of your mouth that allows air to enter the nasal passage), deviated septum, allergies.	Nasal/twangy — are you using your voice to cut through, or pierce? Do you take an aggressive posture to the outside world? Is this quality the result of a dialect or regionalism?	pp 128–30
Hollow/muffled/throaty; voice placed too far back, tense, low back tongue position.	Are you forcing resonance, trying to impress, listening to your own voice instead of communicating?	pp 128–30
Shallow/thin/no resonance; overall body tension; underdeveloped voice	Are you shy, hiding, tense; do you have a fear of, or refusal to accept, personal power?	pp 126–8
R: Place your voice outside the resonation traps.	R: Let your real voice emerge, the one that originates from a place of calm self-acceptance.	

The voice that seems to emanate in all directions at once most likely comes from a body that is fully relaxed and open. Tension is the enemy of resonance. Stiff, constricted body postures cut down the body's ability to vibrate like a sounding board. The following exercise is a good way to train your body to open up and experience more resonance. It also makes a good daily warm-up.

LISTEN

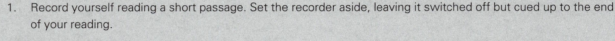

EXERCISE 2.11.1.1 **FULL-BODY RESONANCE**

1. Record yourself reading a short passage. Set the recorder aside, leaving it switched off but cued up to the end of your reading.

2. INITIAL RELAXATION

   - Lie on your back, arms at your sides, legs straight. If you like, you may close your eyes for as much of this process as feels comfortable.
   - Note your breathing, but make no effort to change it.
   - Pull the small of your back down to the floor and turn your legs inward, rotating from the hip. Hold that position briefly and then, on an exhalation, release your back and your legs, letting them flop outward.
   - With arms at your side, lift your shoulders toward the ceiling. Hold the position briefly, then, on an exhalation, release it, letting your arms flop open with your palms up.
   - Draw the back of your neck down to the floor, tucking in your chin. Hold the position. Release it on an exhale. Let your jaw relax open, lips apart, tongue relaxed. Think of the tongue and jaw disappearing, because they are so relaxed there is no sensation in them.

3. VIBRATION

   - Observe your breathing. On each exhalation, leaving your jaw relaxed and lips apart, bring the vocal folds into action by gently sounding an "UH" [ʌ] vowel. Experience this sensation as "vibration" rather than thinking of it as sound. As your voice becomes warmed up, allow the vibration to get stronger and to expand throughout your body, especially focusing on vibrating out your back, chest, and abdomen.

4. STRETCHING AND OPENING
Continue vibrating throughout this next series of steps.

Depending on the time you have, stay in each of these positions for two minutes or more, vibrating continuously, breathing as needed.

Pull your knees up and hug them into your chest.

SPINAL TWIST. Extend your right leg onto the floor. Touch your left foot to the inside of your right knee. Extend your left arm out to the side and turn your head to the left. Place your right hand on your left knee and pull it across to the right and down to the floor. Repeat to the opposite side.

Pull your knees up and hug them into your chest.

PELVIC LIFT. Place your feet on the floor close to your hips. Put your thumbs on your navel and rest your hands over your lower abdomen. Feel how your lower belly lifts when you breathe in and drops as you exhale. Keep your hands here, feeling your belly move through this next activity. Keeping your knees about six inches apart, push your knees forward and slowly lift your hips as high as you can, articulating your spine slowly off the floor. Take two cycles of breath and vibration to bring your hips as high as you can, two cycles to stay up, two cycles to slowly come back down and rest for two cycles. Repeat four times. Pull your knees up and hug them into your chest.

CANDLE. (If you have neck problems omit this part — skip to the Child's Pose.) Supporting the small of your back with your hands, lift your legs straight into the air, pushing your hips forward to get as vertical as possible. Hold the position, gently rocking your head from side to side.

PLOW. From the candle, with straight legs, bring your feet toward the floor behind your head. Hold the position.

Pull your knees in and hug them into your chest, relaxing your back flat onto the floor.

FISH. Extend your legs onto the floor. Sit up just enough to take your weight on your elbows. Drop your head backward toward the floor. Stretch open your chest. Hold the position.

Relax prone. Rest. Pull your knees up and hug them into your chest.

Roll over into the CHILD'S POSE, knee ing on the floor, sitting on your heels, back rounded and head tucked. Hold the position while breathing deeply and feeling your lower back and ribs expand with each inhalation.

CAT/COW. Come up onto your hands and knees, back flat. Tuck your head low into your chest and tuck your hips in, arching your back. Hold briefly. Reverse the position by lifting your head up and back, tilt your hips up, and drop the middle of your back low. Repeat four times.

ARM/SHOULDER STRETCH. Walk your hands forward about a foot. Your hips should be in front of your knees. Keeping your arms straight, pull back with your hips, drop your back and shoulders toward the floor. Hold this position.

Return to the CHILD'S POSE, arms at your side, and hands behind you. Rest. Roll over; stretch out on your back. After a moment, <u>stop the vibration</u>.

Lie on your back, stand, sit or move as you wish during the next series.

HUM. Start on a comfortable low note. Gently hum up and down an octave, like a cow mooing. Go up a whole step and repeat. Continue into your highest falsetto range.

Reverse. Start on a very high note and work your way back down into your lowest range.

5.   Re-record the passage you read at the beginning. Listen to both versions and compare the difference.

You will need to do this type of exercise regularly over a long period to fully "seat" the different resonance in your body. Make it a part of your regular warm-up.

UNIT 2.11.2   *Tonal quality*

For the listener, this is one of the most obvious aspects of a person's voice and one of the primary ways in which we assess personality. However, for the speaker it is one of the most subtle and difficult areas of the voice to hear and alter. None of us hears this aspect of ourselves well. We assume our "sound" is the right way to speak, and everyone else is evaluated against our "normal" voice. As listeners, we make instant, unconscious judgments about people based on their tonal quality. We tend to perceive a nasal person as sharp, cold, anal, fussy and sarcastic. We tend to perceive someone with a hollow (think of the early stages of a yawn) voice as harmless, slow, kind, dull-witted — as though there is too much space in there for any sort of a brain. This is completely unfair, but the fact that the hollow-voiced person may be a brilliant and ruthless military tactician and the nasal person a composer of sentimental greeting cards only means that they have a hard time living down the counter-impression given by their voices. It doesn't change the way society tends to perceive them. Once an actor has control over this vocal aspect, some wonderful characterizations are available by making deliberately incongruous pairings of personality type and vocal style.

An effective way to explore tonal aspects of the voice is to stretch the sound placement in different directions.

LISTEN

EXERCISE 2.11.2.1 TONALITY ISOLATION

1. Since this is an "isolation," the focus will be on changing the tonal quality of certain vowels without altering the pitch, rhythm, volume or vowel sound. It is important to keep the vowel sound the same while altering the quality of it. This is important training for dialect and character voice work later.

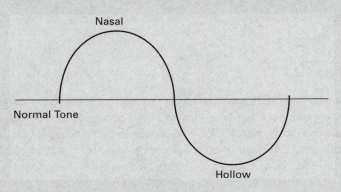

Figure 2.9 Isolating tone

LISTEN

EXERCISE 2.11.3.1 **EXPLORING BREATHY AND PRESSED SOUNDS**

1. Have someone listen to this process to give you feedback. Start by moving a stream of air through an open throat. There should be no sound.
2. Gradually bring sound (try the vowel [æ] as in *had*) into that stream of air. The sound will be quite breathy at first.
3. Continue focusing the sound to reduce the degree of breathiness. (If you are a breathy speaker and are having trouble focusing the sound further, try lifting a heavy object or pushing hard against a wall.)
4. Take the sound just past the point where it has the clearest tone and into the area where it *sounds* (though it shouldn't *feel*) pressed.
5. Back off the pressed sound until you feel you have found the best, most focused tone for you.
6. See how quickly you can find that quality. Practice until it is easy to go immediately to that sound.
7. Practice this sequence: AIR—BREATHY—NORMAL—PRESSED—NORMAL—BREATHY—AIR. Stay on the same pitch, at the same volume, and on the same vowel sound throughout. Get to where you can do this all on one breath, smoothly and easily.
8. Have someone observe you when acting, or offstage to let you know when you're being breathy or pressed. Practice repeating what you've just said with the optimal focus.

Owning anew

UNIT 2.12

If you are part of a group or class, you had the chance in Chapter 1 to vote for, present, and accept the Voice Awards, based on general comparisons among your peers. Now that you have examined deeper and learned some new terms, it will help to solidify this new knowledge to vote again. It's time for the sequel:

ONLINE

EXERCISE 2.12.1.1 THE VOICE AWARDS, PART 2

Consider each of the following categories and who you predict will win. Go back and review if you need to in order to vote well.

1. Most and Least Likely to Exhale before Phonation.
2. Most and Least Adopting Another's Tempo.
3. Most and Least Likely Operative Worcs per Sentence.
4. Most and Least Clenched Jaw.
5. Highest and Lowest Median Note.
6. Most and Least Striking Intonation.
7. Most Rising and Most Falling Inflection.
8. Most and Least Circumflex Inflection.
9. Most and Least Successful Isolations of Intensity, Pitch, and Rate.
10. Most and Least Likely to Have Pinched Sound with Intensification.

If you are sure you will be the winner in one category, speak up and volunteer to let everyone not bother to vote in that one. If two people believe they are the winners, have a tie-breaking vote.

Proceed with the rest of the process, including the prestigious awards ceremony and demonstrative acceptance speeches exactly as in Chapter 1.

UNIT 2.12.1 *The top twenty vocal directions*

When directors give you notes in rehearsal, when they ask you to change, they often do not use technical terms and do not explain how to fix it. Your job is to take what they say and produce a different impression. Here are the twenty most popular complaints in director lingo and in no particular hierarchy:

1. "Stop gasping for air."
2. "Your voice is too high."
3. "Slow down."
4. "Pick it up. Stop indulging yourself."
5. "You're not making your points."
6. "I can't follow that speech at all."
7. "Too many pauses."
8. "Enunciate, will you? Stop slurring."
9. "You're swallowing your words. You're losing all the endings."
10. "Stop falling into a pitch pattern."
11. "You aren't building that speech."
12. "You lack force and directness. Stop undercutting."
13. "You sound too sarcastic (or embarrassed), almost like you're sending it up."
16. "You sound tense. Will you relax and let it happen?"
17. "You sound tired."
18. "You need variety. You always sound the same."
19. "You're pushing too hard."
20. "You're flat. You need more hills and valleys."

If you can come up with a distinct plan of action for the time when you get one of these notes, you will save yourself and the director much anguish.

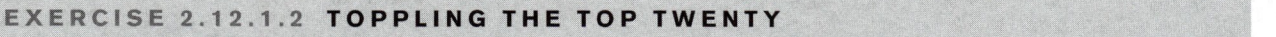

EXERCISE 2.12.1.2 TOPPLING THE TOP TWENTY

1. Answer the following questions:

- Which of the notes above are really the same note? Which are close?
- Where in this chapter is each dealt with, and how is the language different?
- What is the process of healing that will most quickly fix each?

Terms to remember

audible inhalation	intensification	qualifying phrase
breath management	intonation	range
breathy	laryngologist	shallow
denasal	median note	stress: weak, normal, strong
expiration	muffled	subordinate phrase
glottal attack	nasal	thin
harsh	operative word	throaty
hollow	pitch pattern	twang
inflection	pressed	vibration
inspiration	primary phrase	vocal isolations

2. Working with your partner, draw one or two of the directions above.
3. Devise a quick scenario where one of you delivers a line of dialogue, the other (as director) gives the note, then you both explain the healing process briefly.
4. Finally have the actor redeliver the line "fixed" and have the director lavish the artiste in question with praise.

Summary

The word *heal* evolved from the word *whole*. Healing is a useful metaphor for any self-improvement but is especially appropriate for your voice. Notice the common reference to healing as making something *sound* or free from defect, or *harmonious*, as in balanced and integrated — good words to apply to your vocal growth. The goal of this chapter has been to gain a sense of your whole voice. You have touched on all its component parts (breathing, tempo, rhythm, articulation, pitch, volume, quality), working to gain awareness and control. Refer back to the section on behavioral and medical causes of vocal problems whenever you have a question about good vocal hygiene. You are encouraged to think of yourself as your own Voice Doc/Shrink as you explore the character of your voice.

The explorations and exercises in this chapter form an introduction to your whole voice. In later chapters, you will revisit these same areas and probe deeper as you work to expand and refine your skills.

CHAPTER 3

Mastering your language

Words sing. They hurt. They teach. They sanctify. They were man's first, immeasurable feat of magic. They liberated us from ignorance and our barbarous past.

LEO ROSTEN, screenwriter, humorist

UNIT 3.1

Written language versus spoken language

Vast differences separate written language, which is *visual,* and spoken language, which is *auditory.* Terms used in describing speech are different from those used in writing:

Table 3.1 Writing versus speaking

ENGLISH as it is WRITTEN	*ENGLISH as it is SPOKEN*
SENTENCES	PHRASES or THOUGHT GROUPS
WORDS	SYLLABLES or SOUND CLUSTERS
LETTERS	VOWELS, CONSONANTS

Writers sometimes struggle to express the sounds of real speech on the page:

The Flower Girl. Ow, eez ye-ooa san, is e? Wal, fewd dan y' de-ooty bawmz a mather should, eed now bettern to spawl a pore gel's flahrzn than awy athaht pyin. Will ye-oo py me f' them?[1]

Pygmalion, by G. B. Shaw

Eben. Waal — thar's a star, an somewhar's they's him, an' thar's me, an' here's me, an' thar's Min up the road — in the same night. What if I does kiss her? She's like t'night, she's soft "n" wa'm, her arms're wa'm, she smells like a wa'm plowed field, she's purty . . . Ay-eh![2]

Desire Under the Elms, by Eugene O'Neill

Shaun. Ye'll git no better, now I warn ye! so don't go marrin' me this blissid day with "shtravagan" expictations; ye'll have to live from hand to mouth, and whin ye're out of timper, I'll sit moy face agin ye — moind that![3]

Arrah-na-Pogue, by Dion Boucicault

These authors are employing *eye dialects*: attempts to speak to your ears through your eyes. It's a tough job, and it doesn't work for many readers. Playwrights struggle to convey *actual speech* in *writing*, a difficulty, because written English is not effectively constructed to express sound. This is a challenge that must be solved by an actor, because the actor needs to transform what the author has *written* into how the character *speaks*.

Speech is human nature itself, with none of the artificiality of written language.
ALFRED NORTH WHITEHEAD, mathematician

This requires awareness of dialects, accents, character voices, and historical pronunciation. Some initial problems involved in mastering these are:

1 A Cockney dialect. Shaw goes on to comment with a parenthetical note in the text: "(Here, with apologies, this desperate attempt to represent her dialect without a phonetic alphabet must be abandoned as unintelligible outside London.)"
2 A Down East New England dialect.
3 An Irish dialect.

1. **Unlike many other languages, ours is not spelled phonetically.** You can't know how to pronounce a word just by looking at it. "Spelling bees" aren't big events in languages like Spanish, where if you can speak a word, you can spell it. But in English, learning to spell occupies a large portion of early education. The spelling of an English word often doesn't coincide with its sound.

English spelling is unusual because our language is a rich verbal tapestry woven together from the tongues of the Greeks, the Latins, the Angles, the Celtics, the Klaxtons and many other ancient peoples, all of whom had severe drinking problems.

DAVE BERRY, humorist

- Our spelling system includes unused or "silent" letters. Words such as *THROUGH* [θru] have four more letters than sounds,[4] yet *CUTE* [kjut] has one unpronounced letter and allocates two sounds to one letter.

- We often spell the same sound different ways: TERMINAL, ERR, ERRED, SERVE, BIRD, STIRRING, STIRRED, SQUIRM, FURNISH, BURR, CURVE, BLURRED, YEARN, HEARSE, WORLD, WORSE, JOURNEY, SCOURGE, CONNOISSEUR, MYRTLE, MYRRH, OGRE, LIAR, NATURE, LACQUER, FREER, RESTAURANT, HEMORRHAGE, and even COLONEL are twenty-nine ways of spelling the same sound.

- The same alphabet vowel letter can represent several different sounds and be organized through odd spelling combinations, as **U** is in: build, guide, fruit, guarantee, guard, guava, quay, caught, kraut, mauve, beau, beauty, hough, lough, hiccough, bought, through, though, touch, slough, could, courage, house, flour, four, tour, vacuum, rude, up, upon, urbane, fur, furry, guy, Freud, feud, true, guess, due, sure, manure. Try: Paul's daughter Lauren will laugh at her suave beau's mauve Audi. (Few native English speakers can read this entire paragraph without stumbling.)

- Some of our consonants have no constant sound, but change, or duplicate sounds already represented by other characters: **C** = **S** in *cease* and **K** in *crack*. **Q** = **KW** in *quite*, **K** in *plaque*, and **KY** in *queue*. **X** = **Z** in *xenon*, **KS** in *ax*, **GZ** in *exert*, and **KSH** in *luxury*.

4 In fact OUGH is one of the most problematic spellings in English. Observe: *tough* like huff, *cough* like off, *bough* like cow, *though* like go, *thought* like got, *through* like too, *thorough* like "uh" in the UK and "oh" in the US, *hiccough* like up, *hough* like hock, *lough* the Irish version of the Scottish loch. *Slough* is rhymed with "now" when it's a mire, "huff" when you're shedding skin, and "slew" when it is a lot of stuff.

2. **There are more sounds in our language than there are letters in our alphabet.** Spoken English employs twenty vowels, twenty-four consonants, and a variety of combinations of those ingredients that cannot be expressed by our inadequate twenty-six letter alphabet.[5]

   • How do you portray the consonant sound in *Asia* [ˈeɪˌʒə] which looks like S but sounds like ZH, or the difference in the TH sounds in *this* [ðɪs] and *thing* [θɪŋ], or the vowel sounds in *hood* [hʊd] and *hoot* [hut]?

A frustrated foreigner trying to make sense of our language might put it like this:

When the English tongue we speak
Why is "break" not rhymed with "freak"?
Will you tell me why it's true
We say "sew" but likewise "few";
And the maker of a verse
Cannot cap his "horse" with "worse"?
"Beard" sounds not the same as "heard";
"Cord" is different than "word";
"Cow" is cow, but "low" is low;
"Shoe" is never rhymed with "foe".
Think of "hose" and "dose" and "lose";
And of "goose" — and yet of "choose".
Think of "comb" and "tomb" and "bomb";
"Doll" and "roll" and "home" and "some".
And since "pay" is rhymed with "say",
Why not "paid" with "said", I pray.

5 Our alphabet became fixed about two hundred years ago and hasn't changed since. That wouldn't have been the case, however, if Benjamin Franklin had had his way. In 1768, he proposed a plan to reform English spelling with a new alphabet. He wanted to drop the letters *c, j, q, w, x,* and *y* and substitute six completely new letters so that every sound in the language could be represented by one letter. George Bernard Shaw was a later proponent of spelling reform. There have been many spelling reform plans, but it's unlikely any will succeed.

We have "blood" and "food" and "good";
"Mould" is not pronounced like "could".
Wherefore "done", but "gone" and "lone"?
Is there any reason known?
And, in short, it seems to me
Sounds and letters disagree.

Anonymous

Our purpose in this chapter is to make the odd pronunciation of our language less confusing and frustrating. English spelling also masks the sounds of the language. It keeps us from having a rich connection to our spoken words. So, our larger goals are to get in touch with the sensory richness of each sound in a word and to have the tools for making the facile shifts in sound required to master accents.

Symbols for sounds

UNIT 3.2

You can't figure out how to pronounce this language until you have a way to describe pronunciation — a system with one symbol for each sound. Scholars, dialecticians, and editors of dictionaries pose a variety of solutions, and that variety is part of the problem. There are three primary systems to choose from: diacritics, transliteration (or respelling), and phonetics.

Diacritics

UNIT 3.2.1

This system is the approach of most dictionaries. It employs normal alphabet letters as well as some new characters and adapts them by using small marks to define a sound. "My love is like a red rose" might be written "mī lŭv ĭz līk ə rěd rōz." The marks are visually confusing — and cumbersome for extended use. Also, this system has never been standardized. Every dictionary adopts its *own* symbols.

A phrase transcribed diacritically by three different dictionaries:

UNIT 3.2.2 *Respelling or transliteration*

This has the advantage of using only letters of our alphabet, so you don't need to learn new symbols. "Her hairy ears look cute" might be written "hER hEHree irz look kyOOt." This method, reflecting the instinctive way we write sounds, is popular with authors, but not dictionaries. Less specific than diacritics, the system is also not standardized. Diacritic marks and spelling deviations are often needed for clarity. It is particularly unsuited for describing non-English sounds and connected speech. A short sentence transliterated from two different viewpoints:

American Dialects[6]	hEE **nEHv**ER kOOd doo THUH wAHlts in tOH shOOz
NBC Handbook of Pronunciation[7]	hee **NE** vər kuud doo *tha* wawlts in toh shooz

He never could do the waltz in toe shoes.

Dictionary.com	thuh **ling**-ge(r)-ring **plezh**-e(r) *uhv* thuh thawt
Random House	~~tha~~ ling′ g(ə) ring plezh′ ə(r) ov ~~tha~~ thôt
American Heritage	*tha* ling′ gər ing plĕ′ zhər ŭv *tha* thôt

the lingering pleasure of the thought

UNIT 3.2.3 *Phonetics*[8]

This is the notation system most often used by acting conservatories, scholars, and linguists. It is regarded as the "science of speech," in much the same way that linguistics, acoustics, and audiology are the sciences of language, sound, and hearing. Its disadvantage is that you have to learn new symbols. "My dog has fleas" would look like [maɪ dɒg hæz fliːz]. Phonetics has a symbol for everything from a "French R" to the various click sounds of Xhosa. No other system can accurately represent non-English sounds and describe the details of connected speech. It is an essential tool for accent study.

6 By Louis and Marguerite Herman.
7 By James F. Bender.
8 Phonetics is not to be confused with "phonics," an approach to reading instruction where the spelling of a word is compared with its sound.

The notation system is internationally standardized, and learning it can open up a world of sounds you might never have known existed.

Hold fast the form of sound words.

THE BIBLE, *Timothy*, 1:13

The International Phonetic Alphabet

The most reliable means for writing sounds is the International Phonetic Alphabet (IPA). It was developed in Victorian England, where the study of linguistics evolved to ease administration of an expanding empire. Around 1867, Alexander Melville Bell (father of Alexander Graham Bell, inventor of the telephone) developed a system called Bell's Visible Speech, using symbols to show how a sound was created.

This is what the sounds of "visible speech" looked like using Bell's method. Although his system was thorough and detailed, his symbols were too obtuse to use easily, so Henry Sweet, one of his pupils, devised an approach based on the more familiar Latin and Greek alphabets, called Broad Romic, or [brɔd ˈroumɪk]. It was a success. When the International Phonetic Association was founded in 1886, it based its alphabet on Sweet's system. Refined over the years, the International Phonetic Alphabet is now the standard used all over the world.

UNIT 3.4

Young people studying for the stage, learn how to pronounce clearly and beautifully from someone who is at once an artist and a phonetic expert.

GEORGE BERNARD SHAW, playwright

Figure 3.1 Audrey Hepburn as Eliza Doolittle, being coached by Rex Harrison's Henry Higgins in *My Fair Lady*. Higgins was modelled on Henry Sweet, the inventor of phonetics. Image courtesy of CBS Broadcasting, Inc.

Sound groups

Two broad groups of sounds make up speech: **vowels** (produced without any obstruction or blockage), and **consonants** (made using various forms of inhibition). It's that simple.

Actors can sometimes get intimidated when asked to learn phonetics, but it is easy! In order to transcribe English, you have to learn no more than twenty two symbols altogether, which is not much of an investment for a tool you can use for the rest of your life. Many symbols have the same function as the normal letters of our alphabet: *b, d, f, g, h, k, l, m, n, p, r, s, t, v, w, z*. Those are sixteen of the twenty-four consonant sounds of English. There are only eight other consonants to learn. But first, when we say vowels and consonants, what do we mean?

EXERCISE 3.4.1 SEPARATING VOWELS FROM CONSONANTS

1. Say *aaah* [ɑ]. Nothing stops or inhibits the flow of air and sound. That is what defines a vowel: no obstruction. Now make the sound *vvv* [v]. The pressure of your lower lip against your upper teeth inhibits the flow of air and creates a buzzing consonant sound. If you say them close together [ɑ v], you can feel the open vowel sound close off into the consonant.

2. Reverse the process by making the sound *zzzz* [z] followed by *eeee* [i]. Here you can feel the constricted consonant open into the vowel [z i].

As you learn to transcribe using phonetics, remember that phonetic symbols aren't letters. They are representations of sounds, and sounds are produced by the body through complex gestures: [b], for example, involves air being expelled from the lungs past vibrating vocal folds, the air being stopped by closed lips and then being explosively released. We use the glyph [b] to encapsulate all that articulatory information.

When we talk about consonants, the way we describe them is articulatory because looking at what the body does provides a common reference. When we talk about vowels, we can describe them as physical behaviors too, but the way we hear vowels is a more important key to distinguishing them. For example, the difference between the words *heed* and *hid* is more heard than felt. One could say that consonants receive a kinesthetic description, and vowels are described auditorily. Having said that, all sounds are auditory, and all have a feel to them. They are even visual. Notice that audiences will have a much harder time understanding you if they can't see your lips.

Voiced and voiceless consonants

Consonants fall into two categories: voiced and voiceless. On some sounds you use your vocal folds and on others you don't.

EXERCISE 3.4.1.1 SEPARATING VOICED AND VOICELESS CONSONANTS

1. Place your fingers against your larynx (the front of your throat, or the "Adam's apple"), and make the *vvv* [v] sound again. Feel the vibration under your fingers caused by the vibration of your vocal folds. Now make a *ffff* [f] sound. The vibration stops. Notice that they are articulated in the exact same way, with your lower lip against your upper teeth. Switch back and forth until you feel and hear the difference between voiced [v] and voiceless [f].

2. Try these contrasting pairs: [z]/[s], [b]/[p], [d]/[t], [g]/[k]. The same tongue or lip action will produce two distinctly different consonants. Since they are articulated the same, they are called *cognate* sounds. The main difference between them is whether or not they are voiced.

Table 3.2 Comparison of voiced/voiceless consonant cognates

VOICED		VOICELESS	
IPA symbol	Key word	IPA symbol	Key word
[b]	bob	[p]	pop
[d]	did	[t]	tot
[g]	gag	[k]	cake
[v]	valve	[f]	fluff
[z]	zooms	[s]	cease
[ʒ]	vision	[ʃ]	shush
[ð]	this	[θ]	thing
[dʒ]	judge	[tʃ]	church
[w]	witch	[ʍ]	which

Why is this important? A frequent misarticulation is unvoicing the voiced word endings.

EXERCISE 3.4.1.2 VOICED ENDINGS

1. Speak the following pairs of words and listen carefully to the final sounds. The final sounds should be clearly different.

[s] **voiceless**	[z] **voiced**
hiss	his
bus	buzz
race	rays
close (adjective)	close (verb)
dose	doze

2. Repeat the exercise, and make all the endings sound like [s]. How would you describe a person who speaks this way? How does it effect their authority? intelligibility?

A large portion of words in English ending with an "s" spelling are pronounced with a [z] sound. Failure to differentiate these sounds is common and can turn "he pays to raise money for plays" into "he pace to race money for place" — leaving the audience puzzled.

EXERCISE 3.4.1.3 VOICED/VOICELESS ACCENT ENDINGS

1. Accents often reverse voicing/unvoicing patterns. Try this sentence both ways:

Bo**b** hi**s** car**v**ing kni**ves** on T**ed's** blon**d** bear**d**.
[b] [zd] [z] [v] [v z] [dz] [d] [d]

Change it to:

Bo**p** u**set** hi**s** car**t**ing kni**fes** on Te**t's** b on**t** bear**t.**

[p] [s t] [s]   [f]   [f s]   [t s] [t]   [t]

By making this simple change — just unvoicing medial and final voiced consonants — you can come close to a German accent.

2. Try this in reverse:

Hi**t** i**t** o**ff** the ba**ck** of **C**iff's ba**t.**

[t][t] [f]   [k]   [k][fs]   [t]

Change it to:

Hi**d** i**d** o**v** the ba**g** of **G**iv**z** ba**d.**

[d] [d] [v]   [g] [g] [vz] [d]

You might notice that by voicing these consonants you sound a bit like someone from India.

Awareness of voiced/voiceless consonants makes it easier to learn accents as well as improving the clarity of your speech.

However, not all consonants show up as voiced and voiceless cognate pairs. Try the sound of *mmmmm* [m] unvoiced. It isn't a sound you'll find in English (it's in Burmese, among others). Voiced consonant sounds with no voiceless cognates in English are:

[m] mime   [l] lily   [r] rural
[n] none   [ɬ] willful   [j] yo-yo
[ŋ] singing

Consonant creation

Carve every word before you let it fall.

OLIVER WENDELL HOLMES, jurist

Words are carved by consonants, but how are consonant sounds made? To understand the process, take a tour of your vocal apparatus.

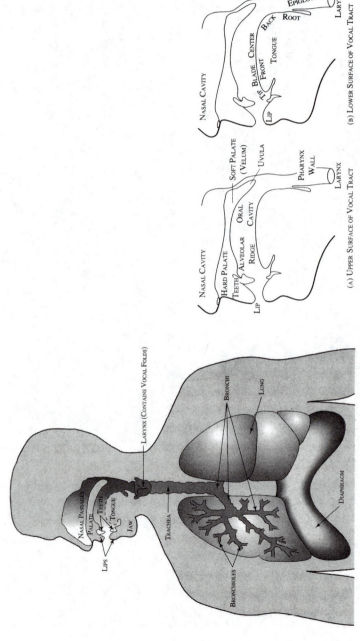

(A) UPPER SURFACE OF VOCAL TRACT

(B) LOWER SURFACE OF VOCAL TRACT

Figure 3.3 The vocal tract

Figure 3.2 Organs of speech

EXERCISE 3.4.2.1   IDENTIFYING YOUR ORGANS OF SPEECH

Figures 3.2 and 3.3 show the primary organs of speech. As in your first examination back in Chapter 1, use a small mirror as you go down this list. Identify points on yourself as well as the illustration. This time try to commit them to memory.

Nasal cavity: space behind your nose and above your hard palate and velum.

Lips

Teeth

Alveolar ridge [æl ˈviˌəˌlɚ(ə)]: dental ridge at the front of the roof of your mouth.

Hard palate: firm surface of the front roof of your mouth.

Soft palate: softer surface at the back of the roof of your mouth, also called the velum.

Uvula [ˈjuv jəˌlə]: pendulous tail-end of the soft palate.

Tongue: (in order from front to back) tip, blade, center, root.

Oral cavity

Pharynx [ˈfæˌrɪŋks]: cavity behind the uvula. It communicates with the nasal cavity, the oral cavity, and the larynx.

(The next six probably won't be visible to you, though a doctor can see them with an angled mirror.)

Epiglottis [ˈɛˌpɪˌglɒˌtɪs]: leaf-shaped cartilage at the root of your tongue. During swallowing it forms a lid or cover for the glottis. It keeps you from breathing your food.

Larynx [ˈlæˌrɪŋks]: cavity in the throat containing the vocal folds.

Vocal folds: muscles shaped as folds and covered by mucous membranes. They vibrate to create sound.

Glottis [ˈglɒˌtɪs]: space between the vocal folds.

Esophagus [ɪˈsɒˌfəˌgəs]: (not shown) tube connecting the throat to the stomach.

Trachea [ˈtreɪˌkiˌə]: tube extending from the larynx to the bronchi. It conveys air to and from the lungs.

Now that you know the map of the mouth, learn the following phrases that describe and place consonant sounds:

Affricate [ˈæ.frɪ.kət]: combination of a stop followed by a fricative [tʃ, dʒ].

Alveolar [ˌæɫ ˈvi.ə.lɚ(ə)]: related to the dental ridge at the front of the roof of the mouth [t, d, n, l, ɬ].

Approximant: when one articulator is near to but not braced against another [r, w, j].

Aspirated [ˈæ.spə.reɪ.təd]: accompanied by a puff of air [tʰ, pʰ, kʰ].

Bilabial [ˌbaɪ ˈleɪ.bɪ.əɫ]: two lips [p, b, m, ʍ, w].

Coarticulation: when two separate articulators function together as the lips and back of the tongue do on [ʍ, w].

Continuant: a consonant that can be lengthened indefinitely without the articulators changing position [m, n, ŋ, ɬ, f, v, s, ʃ, ʒ, θ, ð]

Dental: related to the teeth [f, v, θ, ð, t̪, d̪, n̪, ɬ].

Fricative [ˈfrɪ.kə.tɪv]: having a buzzing or hissing quality [f, v, s, z, θ, ð, ʃ, ʒ, h].

Gingival juncture [ˈdʒɪn.dʒə.vəɫ ˈdʒʌŋk.tʃɚ (ə)]: point where the gums and teeth meet.

Glottal: an articulation involving the glottis [ʔ].

Labial [ˈleɪ.bɪ.əɫ]: related to the lips [p, b, m, f, v, ʍ, w].

Lateral: consonants formed with the tip of the tongue in contact with the roof of the mouth, so that air flows around the sides of the tongue [l, ɬ].

Lingual: related to the tongue.

Nasal: resonating in the nasal cavity [m, n, ŋ].

Palatal: an articulation involving the tongue and the hard palate [j].

Pharyngeal: an articulation involving the root of the tongue and the back wall of the pharynx.

Plosive: having a popping quality [p, b, t, d, k, g, ʔ].

Postalveolar: an articulation with the tongue near the back side of the alveolar ridge [ʃ, ʒ].

Retroflex: the tip of the tongue lifted and pulled backward [r, ɚ, ɝ].

Stop: a consonant that abruptly cuts off the flow of sound [p, b, t, d, k, g, ʔ].

Tap or flap: when one articulator (usually the tongue tip) is drawn back and then allowed to strike against another.

Trill: when one articulator is held loosely near another so that the flow of air between them sets them in motion, alternately sucking them together and blowing them apart.

Uvular: an articulation involving the back of the tongue and the uvula.

Velar [ˈvi.lɚ(ə)]: related to the soft palate or velum at the back of the roof of the mouth [k, g, ŋ].

Take the time to find and know the location of these specific articulation places in your mouth. You will probably be asked to make subtle adjustments in the way certain sounds are formed. Even if your articulation is naturally perfect you will need to shift it for accent and character voice work. Knowing your way around your mouth will make those adjustments easier and quicker.

Consonants are formed by a specific relationship of your articulators. Can you figure out the consonant being made if you are told it is a bilabial (two lips), voiced (vocal folds vibrating), nasal (air moves through your nose) continuant (sound continues as long as you like)? Did you guess [m]?

When we set out to describe consonants, we ask certain questions:

How do we use the air stream? Most English sounds use air expelled from the lungs (pulmonic egressive). But try saying "tsk tsk" or make the clicking noise you would use to encourage a horse and you'll see that these are made through little mouth-vacuums. We make more diverse noises than you might think.

How do we use the vocal folds? Is the sound voiced or voiceless? Do the vocal folds cut off the air as in a glottal stop?

How do we use the soft palate? If it is lowered, then air can come out through the nose (nasal). If it is lifted and sealed against the back of the pharynx, then air can only come out of the mouth (oral).

Where do we make the articulation? We either close off the airflow or narrow it to make a turbulent sound. We can do this in a number of places, like the teeth, lips, hard palate — even in the throat. And we can do it with anything in the vocal tract that can be moved: lips, jaw, tongue, soft palate, and vocal folds.

How do we make the articulation? Is it a sudden closure, a changing narrowing, an explosive release?

What are the lips doing? They can be rounded, spread, closed, open, pushed forward — and all these will change the sound, especially on vowels.

Notice that all these descriptions are of gestural behavior. Sounds are made up of gestures. Those gestures are represented in phonetics by symbols or glyphs. Figure 3.4 is a chart showing how consonants are made in many of the world's languages.

THE INTERNATIONAL PHONETIC ALPHABET (revised to 2005)

CONSONANTS (PULMONIC)

© 2005 IPA

	Bilabial	Labiodental	Dental	Alveolar	Postalveolar	Retroflex	Palatal	Velar	Uvular	Pharyngeal	Glottal
Plosive	p b			t d		ʈ ɖ	c ɟ	k g	q ɢ		ʔ
Nasal	m	ɱ		n		ɳ	ɲ	ŋ	ɴ		
Trill	ʙ			r					ʀ		
Tap or flap		ⱱ		ɾ		ɽ					
Fricative	ɸ β	f v	θ ð	s z	ʃ ʒ	ʂ ʐ	ç ʝ	x ɣ	χ ʁ	ħ ʕ	h ɦ
Lateral fricative				ɬ ɮ							
Approximant		ʋ		ɹ		ɻ	j	ɰ			
Lateral approximant				l		ɭ	ʎ	ʟ			

Where symbols appear in pairs, the one to the right represents a voiced consonant. Shaded areas denote articulations judged impossible.

Figure 3.4 The International Phonetic Alphabet

EXERCISE 3.4.2.2 GUESS THE CONSONANT

1. Take turns describing a consonant by its gesture: the placement, the articulators used, and function. Skip randomly around the list and give points to whoever guesses what sound is being described. It's particularly fun when you explore non-English sounds.

2. When a sound shows up in an English word, give an example. So, a voiced dental fricative would be [ð] as in *this*, and a voiceless bilabial plosive would be [p] as in *pop*.

3. If you speak other languages, see if you can recognize sounds English doesn't use, like [β] in German or [r] in Spanish.

4. Try the game in reverse. Say the consonant, and label its gestural parts.

Now that we're talking about symbols as a way of representing gestures that result in sounds, how do we converse about them? How do we speak of that "n" with the monkey tail curling under it, or that "th" that looks like a "d" but leaned over and crossed? Table 3.3 shows the consonant sounds of English, a reference word, and their names. Many of the names are quite conventional. We'll highlight those that might be new to you.

Table 3.3 Consonant sounds of english

Glyph	Key word	Name
b	bob	lower-case B
d	deeded	lower-case D
ð	this, bathe	Eth
f	fluff	lower-case F
g	gag	opentail G
h	hop, behind	lower-case H
j	you, beauty	lower-case J (jod [jɒd])
k	cook	lower-case K
l	lily	lower-case L, clear L, released L
ɫ	fulfill	L with tilde, dark L, unreleased L
m	mom	lower-case M
n	nun	lower-case N
ŋ	singing	Eng
p	pop	lower-case P
r	rarity	lower-case R (equivalent to IPA [ɹ] turned R)
s	sassy	lower-case S
ʃ	shush	Esh
t	tot	lower-case T
θ	thing, cloth	Theta
v	valve	lower-case V
w	witch	lower-case W
ʍ	which	turned W
z	zooms	lower-case Z
ʒ	azure	Yogh

Vowel formation

With skill she vibrates her eternal tongue.

EDWARD YOUNG, Satire VI. *On Women*

Vowel sounds, the second major group, are described using four distinguishing characteristics:

1. **the part of the tongue that is raised**: front, center or back;
2. **how far the tongue is lifted** toward the palate: close, close-mid, open-mid, open;
3. whether we are allowing **airflow through the nose**, determined by the position of the soft palate. Nasal vowels are generally "unapproved" in English, although they are a significant part of French, for example, as in words like *vin* [væ̃];
4. **the shape of the lips**: various degrees of spread or round.

It is difficult to be precise about the exact articulatory shape of a vowel. Everyone's mouth is different in size and configuration, and since vowels don't provide the feeling sensation that consonants do, we end up learning them by their sound more than by their sensation. We also tend to allow a wide range of variance before a difference in vowels is interpreted as "wrong" or changes the meaning of the word. One of the goals of phonetic training is to increase your ear's sensitivity to small differences in sound.

Still, it is possible to learn a lot about vowels by seeing them. Take your mirror. Watch your tongue move as you alternate between [i] as in *fleece* and [ɑ] as in *palm*. See your tongue move high and forward on [i], then low and back on [ɑ]. Now try [u] as in *goose* and [æ] like in *trap*. You'll notice a lot of lip-rounding on [u], and see lip-spreading and jaw dropping along with a tongue shift forward as you say [æ]. If you watch while doing [i, ɑ, u, æ] in sequence, you'll see large changes in your oral shape. Changing the shape of your oral cavity produces clear sound changes. Figure 3.5 shows the relative placement of the vowel sounds we use.

VOWELS

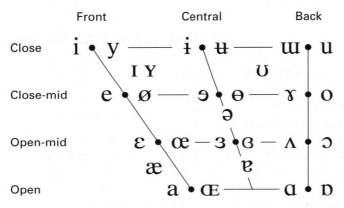

Where symbols appear in pairs, the one
to the right represents a rounded vowel

Figure 3.5 Vowel chart

The convention is to think of this box sitting in your mouth, viewed from the side. The left is the front of your mouth, the right is the back. Figure 3.6 is a simplified illustration of that view, with only the vowels of English noted. Another way to picture this working is to see the tongue positions superimposed on each other.

A fundamental principle of phonetics is that there should be one symbol for every sound. So each symbol has an absolute value. We can sometimes show key words to lead a reader to identify the sound. This works pretty well for consonants but is much more difficult for vowels. For example, some readers will match the vowels in *hut* and *hook*. Others will match them between *hoot* and *hook*. For others, *hut, noot*, and *hook* will have three different vowel sounds. Our journey to learning how to use symbols to represent what you say begins with sorting words into groups, or lexical sets, where all the members of that group behave in the same way within an accent.

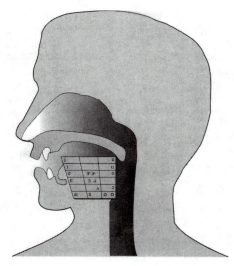

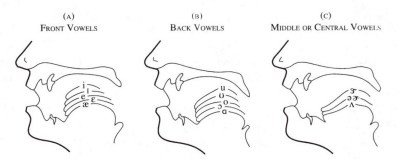

(A)	(B)	(C)
FRONT VOWELS	BACK VOWELS	MIDDLE OR CENTRAL VOWELS

Figure 3.6 Vowel formation in the oral cavity

Figure 3.7 Approximate tongue positions for the vowels

Lexical sets for vowels

UNIT 3.5.1

We need a way of referencing pronunciation patterns that isn't obscured by our personal accent. Lexical sets are a useful framework. These are groups of words that behave mostly uniformly within any given accent. In the example above, the words *hut, hook*, and *hoot* belong to the lexical sets STRUT, FOOT, and GOOSE, respectively. The convention is to choose a particular keyword that is part of the set and to use this word, in upper case, to identify the entire set, as in FLEECE to represent words like *seed, key* and *seize*. Unstressed vowels are identified in lower-case spelling, with the vowel in question in upper case, as in commA.

Here is a list of lexical sets referenced against the model[9] dialects of General American (GA) and General British (GB). Using your mirror, speak each key word, emphasizing the vowel sound, observe the gesture, and listen to the sound.

9 Model is employed in the sense of a simplified system to use as an example, not in the sense of an ideal to be followed.

Table 3.4 English lexical sets — vowels

Key word	(Representative words)	GA glyph	GA key word	GB glyph	GB key word
Stressed vowels					
FLEECE	(seed, key, seize)	[i]	[flis]	[i]	[flis]
KIT	(ship, rip, dim)	[ɪ]	[kɪt]	[ɪ]	[kɪt]
DRESS	(step, ebb, hem)	[ɛ]	[drɛs]	[ɛ]	[drɛs]
TRAP	(bad, cab, ham)	[æ]	[træp]	[æ]	[træp]
BATH	(staff, clasp, dance)	[æ]	[bæθ]	[ɑ]	[bɑθ]
PALM	(calm, bra, father)	[ɑ]	[pɑm]	[ɑ]	[pɑm]
LOT	(stop, rob, swan)	[ɑ]	[lɑt]	[ɒ]	[lɒt]
CLOTH	(cough, long, gone)	[ɔ]	[klɔθ]	[ɒ]	[klɒθ]
THOUGHT	(taut, hawk, broad)	[ɑ]	[θɑt]	[ɔ]	[θɔt]
FOOT	(full, look, could)	[ʊ]	[fʊt]	[ʊ]	[fʊt]
GOOSE	(who, group, few)	[u]	[gus]	[u]	[gus]
STRUT	(cub, rub, hum)	[ʌ]	[strʌt]	[ʌ]	[strʌt]
NURSE	(hurt, term, work)	[ɝ]	[nɝs]	[ɜ]	[nɜs]
Unstressed vowels					
happY	(silly, Tony, merry)	[i]	[ˈhæ.pi]	[i]	[ˈhæ.pi]
lettER	(beggar, martyr, visor)	[ɚ]	[ˈlɛ.tɚ]	[ə]	[ˈlɛ.tə]
commA	(China, sofa, about)	[ə]	[ˈkɑ.mə]	[ə]	[ˈkɒ.mə]
intO	*strong form before a vowel*	[u]	[ˈɪn.tu]	[u]	[ˈɪn.tu]
	weak form before a consonant	[ə]	[ˈɪn.tə]	[ə]	[ˈɪn.tə]

Lexical sets suggest that most people pronounce words in FOOT (such as *hook, good, full, bush*) with the same vowel. They do not say whether or not this vowel is distinct from that of *hoot*. If you pronounce them the same, we would say that your dialect has merged the FOOT and GOOSE sets. The dialects of GA and GB used as a guide in Table 3.4 may not match your personal way of speaking. They are employed because many speakers have familiarity with them, so these can give common reference points.

As with consonants, we need a way of talking about the symbols. So, Table 3.5 provides a list of the vowels used in the major forms of English and their names, along with a reference number to facilitate discussion. In this organization, we're following the vowel chart counterclockwise from the high front to low front, from low back to high back and central.

Table 3.5 English vowel names

1.	i	lower-case I
2.	ɪ	small capital I
3.	e	lower-case E
4.	ɛ	epsilon
5.	æ	ash
6.	a	lower-case A
7.	ɑ	script A
8.	ɒ	turned script A
9.	ɔ	open O
10.	o	lower-case O
11.	ʊ	upsilon
12.	u	lower-case U
13.	ʌ	turned V (stressed syllables only)
14.	ə	schwa[10]
	ɚ	right-hook schwa, or r-colored schwa (unstressed syllables only)
15.	ɜ	reversed epsilon
	ɝ	right-hook reversed epsilon, or r-colored reversed epsilon (stressed syllables only)

Diphthongs and triphthongs

UNIT 3.5.2

When two vowels marry, the result is a diphthong.

PATSY RODENBURG, author, voice coach

10 The name *schwa* is derived from the Hebrew word *sheva*, meaning emptiness or vanity. It represents the smallest, most indistinct vowel sound you make.

Phthong is the Greek word for sound. When we blend two or three vowel sounds into a single phonetic unit we get a **diphthong** or a **triphthong**.[11] Just as no one is the same married as they were when they were single, a new sound is created by this union. For example, on the word *by* [baĬ], there are two different vowel sounds on a one-syllable word. Take your mirror and look into your mouth. Say the word slowly. Your tongue moves from the low first position [a] to high front second position [ɪ], all on one syllable. Contrast *by* [baĬ] with the word *being* [ˈbi.ɪŋ], where two sequential vowel sounds occupy two *different* syllables. This is not a diphthong. Table 3.6 lists the English diphthongs and triphthongs.

Table 3.6 English diphthongs and triphthongs

Diphthongs Key word	(Representative words)	GA glyph	GA key word	GB glyph	GB key word
FACE	(weight, rein, steak)	[eĬ]	[feĬs]	[eĬ]	[feĬs]
PRICE	(ripe, tribe, aisle)	[aĬ]	[praĬs]	[aĬ]	[praĬs]
CHOICE	(boy, void, coin)	[ɔĬ]	[tʃɔĬs]	[ɔĬ]	[tʃɔĬs]
GOAT	(soap, soul, home)	[oŭ]	[goŭt]	[əŭ]	[gəŭt]
MOUTH	(pouch, noun, crowd)	[aŭ]	[maŭθ]	[aŭ]	[maŭθ]
NEAR	(beer, pier, fierce)	[ɪɚ̆]	[nɪɚ̆]	[ɪə̆]	[nɪə̆]
SQUARE	(care, air, wear)	[ɛɚ̆]	[skwɛɚ̆]	[eə̆]	[skweə̆]
START	(far, sharp, farm)	[ɑɚ̆]	[stɑɚ̆t]	[ɑː]	[stɑːt]
NORTH	(war, storm, for)	[ɔɚ̆]	[nɔɚ̆θ]	[ɔː]	[nɔːθ]
FORCE	(floor, coarse, ore)	[ɔɚ̆]	[fɔɚ̆s]	[ɔː]	[fɔːs]
CURE	(poor, tour, fury)	[ʊɚ̆]	[kjʊɚ̆]	[ʊə̆]	[kjʊə̆]
Triphthongs					
HOUR	(power, flower, our)	[aŭ.ɚ̆]	[ˈaŭ.ɚ̆]	[aŭə̆]	[aŭə̆]
FIRE	(lyre, flier, flyer, hire)	[aĬ.ɚ̆]	[ˈfaĬ.ɚ̆]	[aĬə̆]	[faĬə̆]
PLAYER	(prayer, preyer, mayor)	[eĬ.ɚ̆]	[ˈpleĬ.ɚ̆]	[eĬə̆]	[pleĬə̆]
LOWER	(goer, mower)	[oŭ.ɚ̆]	[ˈloŭ.ɚ̆]	[əŭə̆]	[ləŭə̆]
LOYAL	(royal)	[ɔĬ.ə̆ɫ]	[ˈlɔĬ.ə̆ɫ]	[ɔĬə̆ɫ]	[lɔĬə̆ɫ]

11 The "phthong" part of these words is pronounced with a "fth" [fθ] as in [ˈdɪf.θɒŋ], not with a "pth" [pθ] as in [ˈdɪp.θɒŋ].

You'll notice that we are writing little curved lines over some of the symbols [˘]. These are called breves [brɛvz], and they indicate that the sound is briefer, or weaker. Phonetics is a flexible tool, and generally an attempt is made to use only as many symbols as are necessary to describe the sounds in question. It is easier to read phonetics if the words aren't cluttered up with lots of small details. In some dictionaries *go away* could be more simply transcribed as [go ə'we][12] and that would be suitable. Here, you'll see a level of detail that will help actors to learn accents. For example, that phrase in much of the US is [gŏŭ ə'weĭ], in the UK it could be [gəŭ ə'weĭ], in Ireland you can find [go ə'we], and in Scandinavian accents we might hear [gou ɑ'wei] with the two parts of the diphthong having equal presence. In many English dialects, FLEECE and GOOSE have a weak vowel leading into them, so you'll hear the diphthongs [ɜ̆i] and [ɜ̆u]. The breve is a handy tool for telling us how prominent a vowel is when combined with others.

EXERCISE 3.5.2.1 DIPHTHONGS AND TRIPHTHONGS VERSUS TWO-SYLLABLE WORDS

1. Speak the words slowly, looking into a mirror. You will see as well as hear the separation of sounds.

Simple vowel (monophthong)	Diphthong	Diphthong	Triphthong or syllable + syllable	Syllable + syllable
then	there	their	they're	they are
flee	flay	fly	flyer	fly her
pet	pray	prey	prayer	pray her
cot	cow	cowed	coward	cowherd

2. Discuss how your individual way of speaking may have some of these as simple vowels, diphthongs, triphthongs or two syllables. Can you hear the difference?
3. Try saying the words in different ways to see if you can change what you do.
4. How would you transcribe these using phonetic symbols?

12 *A Pronouncing Dictionary of American English* by Kenyon and Knott.

EXERCISE 3.6.1.1 HOW MANY SYLLABLES?

1. Practice counting syllables out loud on the following words. Listen to the sounds. Ignore the spelling. (Cover up the answers given in the next section before starting.)

character	alone	heroic
titillated	eliminated	returning
attenuated	literal	approximated
perspicacity	parallel	refurbishing
accountability	entanglement	curiosity

2. Now compare your notes with this list to see how keen your ear is:

character – 3	alone – 2	heroic – 3
titillated – 4	eliminated – 5	returning – 3
attenuated – 5	literal – 3	approximated – 5
perspicacity – 5	parallel – 3	refurbishing – 4
accountability – 6	entanglement – 4	curiosity – 5

Syllable stress

UNIT 3.6.2

In most words with more than one syllable, at least one syllable is more prominent. This is achieved through lengthening sounds, and sometimes by making them louder. While there is an infinite range of syllable stress applied in conversation, we'll put these into three important levels: primary, secondary, and unstressed.

EXERCISE 3.6.2.1 WHICH SYLLABLES ARE ACCENTED?

1. Without looking at the list below, go back to the one in Exercise 3.6.1.1 and see if you can identify which syllables will fall into the categories of "**Primary**," "*Secondary*," and "Unstressed." Then check your work against this list.

cha rac ter – 3   a **lone** – 2   he **ro** ic – 3
ti ti *lla* ted – 4   e **li** mi *na* ted – 5   re **tur** ning – 3
a **tten** u *a* ted – 5   **li** te ral – 3   a **ppro** xi *ma* ted – 5
per spi **ca** ci *ty* – 5   **pa** ra llel – 3   *re* **fur** bi shing – 4
a *ccoun* ta **bi** li *ty* – 6   en **tan** gle ment – 4   *cu* ri **o** si *ty* – 5

2. How are you able to tell which syllables are stressed? What method do you use to tell the difference between the various levels of stressing?

UNIT 3.6.3 *How to divide syllables*

Most people can intuitively recognize syllables as the rhythmic units of a word and hear the stressing differences. However, when we set out to specify exactly where one syllable ends and another begins, the analysis becomes more challenging.

Speakers don't observe literary rules for where to divide syllables. Those are designed to make it possible to read long words divided between two lines of text. They are *visual* rules. In phonetics, we divide words by the way they *sound*. Most people find this easier and more natural. For example, *accountability* would be divided as *ac-count-a-bil-i-ty* for writing, but in speech we might say *a-coun-ta-bi-li-ty*.

Accented syllables are marked by ['] for primary stress and [ˌ] for secondary stress. The stress mark in phonetics (unlike in most dictionaries) will always *precede* the accented syllable. Since phonetic symbols are meant to be spoken, you should know beforehand how the syllable will be accented. The stress markings can also serve as indications of a syllable break. In cases where a syllable isn't stressed, the syllable break is noted [.]. So *accountability* might be transcribed as [əˌkaʊn.təˈbɪ.lɪˌti].

English has a *stress-timed* rhythm. The duration of unstressed syllables to stressed syllables is 1:2, and we tend to alternate between them. It is rare to find two stressed syllables back to back, and those are usually on compound words like Frandmaiden or manhandle. In contrast, Spanish has a *syllable-timed* rhythm. The duration difference in Spanish syllables is 1:1.6 or less, so the perception is that their weak syllables have more prominence than ours.

Deciding where we divide syllables can be important. For example, do we say *happy* as ['hæ.pi] or ['hæp.i]? Both are possible. For actors, here is a useful guideline that will keep your vowels longer and make complicated consonant clusters easier to articulate:

1. Give as many consonants as possible to the syllable to the right: masticate ['mæ.sti'keit], extreme [ik'stri:m], attract [ə'trækt], matches ['mæ.tʃəz].
2. Keep compound words in their original form: minefield ['main.fi:ld], baseball ['beis.bɔ:l], flapjack ['flæp.dʒæk].
3. If the consonant combination is one that never begins an English word, split it apart: embellish [im'be.liʃ], cantankerous [kæn'tæŋ.kə.rəs], selfish ['sel.fiʃ].
4. If the consonant cluster is one that often begins a word, keep it together and use it to initiate a syllable: astonish [ə'stɒ.niʃ], accuse [ə'kju:z], acquit [ə'kwit].

This is the way singers organize their syllables. It's great for actors, too. It helps to keep your mouth open longer on vowel sounds, and the consonants will then launch a syllable rather than close one off.

UNIT 3.6.4

Vowel sounds that depend on stress

Some vowel sounds show up only when the stressing conditions are right. Listen to the words *above* and *murmur*. Speak them slowly. If you give both syllables equal stress, the vowel sounds will seem to be the same. Pronounce them conversationally (in the context of a sentence), and you will hear a difference in the sounds: *I heard a murmur of birds above the hut.*

Table 3.7 Vowels that depend on stressing

Lexical set (key word)	(Representative words)	GA glyph	GA key word	GB glyph	GB key word
STRUT (stressed)	(cub, rub, hum)	[ʌ]	[strʌt]	[ʌ]	[strʌt]
commA (unstressed)	(China, sofa, about)	[ə]	[ˈkɑ.mə]	[ə]	[ˈkɑ.mə]
STRUT/commA (contrast)	above	[ə, ʌ]	[əˈbʌv]	[ə, ʌ]	[əˈbʌv]
NURSE (stressed)	(hurt, term, work)	[ɝ]	[nɝs]	[ɜ]	[nɜs]
lettER (unstressed)	(beggar, martyr, visor)	[ɚ]	[ˈlɛ.tɚ]	[ə]	[ˈlɛ.tə]
NURSE/lettER (contrast)	murmur	[ɝ, ɚ]	[ˈmɝ.mɚ]	[ɜ, ə]	[ˈmɜ.mə]

Here is *I heard a murmur of birds above the hut* transcribed comparatively:

GA: [aɪ hɝd ə ˈmɝ.mɚ əv bɝdz əˈbʌv ðə hʌt]
GB: [aɪ hɜd ə ˈmɜ.mə rəv bɜdz əˈbʌv ðə hʌt]

It is fair to say that STRUT and commA and that their primary difference is stress. So, too, with NURSE and lettER. In dialects where vowels don't have any r-coloring, commA and lettER end with the same sound.

Some word comparisons to further illustrate this issue:

EXERCISE 3.6.4.1 HEARING VOWELS CHANGE WITH STRESSING

Using your recorder, speak each of these pairs of words by themselves, then in a normal conversational way within the sentences below. Listen to the playback. Note the differences in vowel sounds. Transcribe the words and the sentences.

[ə] unstressed	[ʌ] stressed	[ɔ, ɚ] unstressed	[ɜ, ɝ] stressed
upon	up	over	aver
commence	come	perplex	purple
suppose	supper	conifer	confer

1. Once upon a time, I was stuck up, but then someone told me to stick it.
2. It's time to come in here and commence to communicate.
3. Suppose I have you for supper and suppose you supply some surprise for dessert.
4. I absolutely aver that I have gotten over all my aversions forever.
5. Why so perplexed? It's not a purple turtle he's offering, but a purple persimmon.
6. Want to confer beneath that conifer, my little kumquat?

Strong and weak forms

UNIT 3.6.5

Syllables have levels of stress. So do words. Even when you're being formal, you don't give every word full value. You reduce the stress on unimportant words. Otherwise *and, of, or, but*, and other conversational connectives would sound artificial and affected.

shall	[ʃəl]	[ʃæl]	
should	[ʃəd]	[ʃʊd]	
that	[ðət]	[ðæt]	
the	[ðə]	[ði, ðɪ]	Use the strong form when the next sound is a vowel, as in "the apple."
them	[m, ðm, ðəm]	[ðɛm]	
to	[tə]	[tu]	Use the strong form when followed by a vowel, as in "to each."
us	[əs]	[ʌs]	
was	[wəz]	[wɒz]	
what	[wət]	[wɒt]	
were	[wɚ] GA, [wə] GB	[wɝ]	
would	[wəd]	[wʊd]	

1. Here are some sentences to practice identifying this weak/strong contrast. Transcribe these to match what you naturally say. Keep it conversational.

   a. A cup of tea would suit her nicely, and shut her up!

   b. She pricked up her ears, salivated, and sat on the edge of the seat.

   c. What was I supposed to do about the bills, eat them?

   d. Oh, she doth teach the torches to burn bright!

   e. That was what we were after.

   f. I can see the can do the cancan. Can you?

   g. If you would win, you must try, mustn't you?

2. Choose two words from the list above. Put them into one or two sentences using both the weak and strong forms.

UNIT 3.6.6

How do sounds affect each other?

Sounds are altered by context. There is a difference between the "r" sounds in *care* and *caring* or *far* and *far away*. Can you hear the difference between the "l" sounds in *lawful* or what happens to the "l" in *fill* versus *fill it?* Sounds change by their context. In these cases, you'll notice the sound that comes afterwards is critical. Is it **silence**, a **consonant** or a **vowel**? Each makes a difference.

[r] is a *consonant*.[14] **It needs to be followed by a vowel.** This is because the gesture of [r] is to lift the tongue toward the alveolar ridge, generate a voiced turbulence, and release the tongue forward and down. That release requires a following vowel in English. Notice the tongue gesture as you speak:

    rough, rich, bring, try, street, create, very, around, touring, address, repressurize.

[ɜ], and [ə] are *vowels*. In some dialects, General American for example, they can take on the character of an r-colored vowel. Dialects that have this r-coloring are called *rhotic*. In them, speakers pronounce all the "r" sounds that show up in spelling. In dialects that are non-rhotic, the lexical sets of commA and lettER are nearly identical. When [ɜ, ə] have an r-coloring, we add a right hook to the symbol [˞] to indicate that the tongue has pulled back or bunched up [ɜ˞, ə˞]. That retraction or bunching is what gives the vowel its r-like quality. In dialects where we don't hear that r-coloration, the tongue stays forward and is more relaxed. Use your mirror to help you to see and feel what your tongue does when you say *hark* with a very hard R [hɑɜ˞k]. If you go in slow motion, you can watch your tongue retract and your jaw close up. Try it again with no r-coloring and leave the tip of your tongue resting against the back of your lower teeth and your jaw dropped [hɑːk].[15] You should see, feel and hear a difference. R-colored vowels are usually followed by a consonant or silence. Try speaking these words with the r-coloring present and absent:

    letter, arbor, parlor, murmur, further, hear, horn, flower, fire, pure, there, farmer.

Solving an articulation challenge. In rhotic accents where there is r-coloring, the tongue-bunching of this sound can present some problems for an actor. Notice how words like *rural, horrible,* and *mirror* can get bound up in the middle? The

14 The IPA symbol for this sound is formally [ɹ]. In this text, [r] is used because nearly all the pronouncing dictionaries an actor is likely to reference use that symbol.

15 [ː] is a length mark. [hɑɜ˞k] and [hɑːk] would take about the same amount of time to say even though the second has fewer sounds.

solution is to change ['mɪɚ.ɚ] to ['mɪɚ.rɚ]. Don't use any r-coloring on the first syllable and start the second syllable with [r]. That's a lot easier to organize in your mouth. Non-rhotic accents usually have less trouble with this issue.

EXERCISE 3.6.6.1 "R" ALTERATIONS

Speak each pair of words slowly into your recorder and observe the difference in the "R" qualities. In the first, the "R" will seem to be part of the vowel or absent altogether (depending on whether you are naturally a rhotic or non-rhotic speaker). In the second, it will connect with the next syllable as a consonant sound. Practice speaking the second set with no r-coloring on the sound before [r].

[ɚ, ə]	[r]	[ɚ, ə]	[r]
pure	purity	fur	furry
far	far away	fire	firing
for	for each	hear	hearing
murmur	murmuring	rare	rarified

This same situation exists between words when the first word ends on a spelled "R" and the second begins on a vowel sound. This is sometimes called a "linking-r."

[ɚ, ə]	[r]	[ɚ, ə]	[r]
cure	the cure is easy	hour	an hour ago
fire	is the fire out	player	the player is injured
lower	speak lower and more clearly	letter	a letter of intent
near	it is near us	square	square off the edges
far	far away	four	four hours ago[16]

16 Note that *hour* is spelled with an H but begins with a vowel sound [aʊɚ, aʊɚ].

In some non-rhotic dialects, there can be a tendency to invent an R when the sound parallels that of a linking R, but where there was never an R in spelling. In prestige accents this is an unapproved feature because it suggests that the speaker doesn't know how the word is spelled. This can happen both within a word (as in draw(r)ing or withdraw(r)al) and between words. It is sometimes called an "intrusive-r."

Linking R		Possibly intrusive R	
Czar of Russia		Shah of Persia	
the fear is		the idea is	
lore of the wild		law of the wild	
the mower is older		Noah is older	
the fire is out		the WiFi is out	
my dear Ellen		the idea, Ellen	
manner at dinner		manna in the wilderness	

EXERCISE 3.6.6.2 "R" ALTERATIONS IN SENTENCES

Transcribe these sentences into phonetics and speak them into your recorder to help you hear differences between the consonant and vowel "R." Notice that the sound can change depending on whether you pause between words or link them.

1. Over and over, Arthur asked her about her aphrodisiacs.
2. Mother searched here, there and everywhere for Irma's revolver.
3. Ralph is drawing the animals of China and Africa in India ink.

[l, ɫ]. Both are "L" sounds, but they are distinct. [l], called a *clear l*, or *released l*, **is always followed by a vowel sound**. When you say it, you can feel your tongue tip flip away from your alveolar ridge. Speak the word *lily*, and feel the way both "l" sounds release. Then speak the word *pull*, and feel the way your tongue holds the final sound, the back of your tongue drops, and the tip doesn't release from your alveolar ridge. That is [ɫ] the *dark l*, or *unreleased l*. **It needs to be followed by a consonant or silence.** The distinction is important. Many people have trouble articulating [ɫ], and a number of dialects will alter it. Here are some examples for comparison:

EXERCISE 3.6.6.3 RELEASED AND UNRELEASED "L"

Transcribe and then speak these pairs of words into your recorder. Pay particular attention to how your tongue touches the roof of your mouth, and how long it stays there.

[l] released	[ɫ] unreleased	[l] released	[ɫ] unreleased
fillip	fill	pearly	pearl
killer	kill	pullet	pull
Willy	William	pillow	pill
feeling	feel	falling	fall
will I	I will	full of it	fulfill
Bill is taller	tall Bill	calling all of them	all called

EXERCISE 3.6.6.4 RELEASED AND UNRELEASED "L" IN SENTENCES

As you speak these sentences, pay particular attention to the [ɫ]. Typical misarticulation will change word combinations like "will you" to "wio you", or "wi' you."

1. Will you fill it full of cold milk?
2. Will all the lectures in this college feel as full of bull?
3. The lone wolf followed the trail of the elk.
4. The peculiarly brilliant stallion flew over the hurdle.

Pauses and stops. You may have wondered how to note moments of silence. You're already using [.] to indicate a syllable break. That's a kind of tiny pause between sounds. If the length of the pause increases we add dots: [..] or [...], etc. as seems appropriate.

In phonetic transcription, the convention is to write words separately with their internal syllables divided unless we're trying to demonstrate how the sound has changed because of nearby sounds or making some kind of point about consonant linkage. So, this phrase could be transcribed differently depending on what is being discussed:

An apple is better if it's allowed to ripen. Right?

Words individually: [æn 'æ.pəɫ ɪz 'bɛ.tə(ɚ) ɪf ɪts ə'laʊd tu 'raɪ.pən...raɪt]

Words in context: [ən 'æ.pəɫ ɪz 'bɛ.tə rɪf ɪts ə'laʊd tə 'raɪ.pən...raɪt]

Words linked: [ə'næ.pə'lɪz'bɛ.tə.rɪ.fɪt.sə'laʊd.tə'raɪ.pən...raɪt]

Each level has its utility, but each level of detail can become increasingly difficult to read (and it's possible to transcribe even more narrowly than this). Probably, the most useful level for an actor is the contextual, where weak-form words and sounds like L and R are treated accurately, but where the words are otherwise separated.

Remember, when transcribing, ask the following questions:

1. *How many syllables does the word have?*
2. Which are *accented?*
3. Is the word in its *strong or weak form?*
4. What are the *individual sounds* in each word?
5. How do the individual sounds *affect each other?*

By now you may have lots of questions, but they are probably about how words are *pronounced*, rather than how they are transcribed. If you see the word "marry" written in phonetics as ['mæ.ri], when you would have written it as ['mɛ.ri], then probably you have transcribed it the way *you* are saying it. The issue is one of pronunciation, not phonetics. Phonetics has become the vehicle by which you can discuss pronunciation, dialects, and accents. If that is happening, you have made great headway! Hang in there. Every time you transcribe, it gets easier, and you move closer to a strong understanding of how people speak. With that understanding comes strength and authority:

Speech is power — to persuade, to convert, and to compel.

RALPH WALDO EMERSON, author

Pronunciation

Once you understand how language is transcribed, you are ready to examine the various ways in which people speak, specifically pronunciation choices. One sort of pronunciation is not better or worse than another. Generally, we assume the way we speak is the right way, or else we wouldn't be doing it. And there is no surer way of offending others than to correct their pronunciation. Yet, because people do speak in many different ways, an unacknowledged evaluation goes on any time someone opens their mouth.

An Englishman's way of speaking absolutely classifies him.
The moment he talks he makes some other Englishman despise him.

ALAN JAY LERNER, *My Fair Lady*

Certain groups can be perceived by others as pushy, elegant, stupid, educated, arrogant, dull or classy. Those generalizations are often based on speech. The opinions are subconscious, which only adds to their power, since they aren't consciously questioned. Biases formed this way attach themselves to any definable group — regional, ethnic, racial, socio-economic, educational, religious, or political — as long as it has certain recognizable homogeneous speech patterns.

The good news, for actors at least, is that you don't have to singlehandedly cure these misconceptions (though you're welcome to try). You merely have to be aware of them, in order to employ the way your audience thinks of pronunciation to shape their perceptions of your character. The question of whether the word *ask* should be [ɑsk], or [æsk] (or [ask], [ɛæsk], [ɛsk], [æks], etc.) can be answered by posing the larger question: "What will the pronunciation tell the audience about my character?" not by asking, "Which is the *right* way to say it?"

There are probably no two people in the world who use language or react to language use in the same way. But we do react. Values are encoded in language. In order to investigate with some objectivity in this area, and since unconscious and unquestioned biases can get in an actor's way — inhibiting the fullest exploration and expression of a character — it is useful to admit our personal biases.

EXERCISE 3.7.1 PRONUNCIATION ATTITUDES

1. On a blackboard, write the names of as many groups as you can think of that are identifiable because of their speech, dialect, accent, word choice, etc. (Use the nine categories listed in Chapter 1.)

2. Assign teams of two. Each team pick a group one at a time and list all the cliché attitudes you can think of about that group and how those attitudes are reinforced by their speech. (Example: French. What? — sexy. Why? — the tonal quality; Show us! — (demonstrate it). What specifically did the group notice? — (discuss it); are there any contrary attitudes? . . .) Let the discussion play itself out. Don't be shy about confronting racial and ethnic bias. Work to bring into awareness *any* attitude or prejudgment, even if it is not personally held, is incorrect, or offensive. Be brave and respectful. Find out what specific sound or pronunciation issues are present.

3. Note whenever the discussion begins to turn toward statements about "right" or "wrong" instead of staying at the level of neutral observation.

4. Has this process helped anyone to let go of personal judgments and simply listen accurately to the way people speak?

5. What increased awareness of how audiences unconsciously interpret speech and pronunciation choices has occurred? How are certain qualities assigned to a character because of the audience's biases?

Speech tells who we are, where we are, and when we are

Actors can use pronunciation choices to tell us who they are. Audiences also need to identify the world of the play. They need to know *when* and *where* we are, too. Have a listen to films from the 1940s, for example, and you'll instantly notice that people spoke differently in that time. Time periods have their unique social values expressed in speech. And where we come from includes both geographic place and social place.

You may have heard the words *dialect* and *accent* used interchangeably. In language studies, *dialect* describes the form of a language that is peculiar to a region or social group. It includes all the things that make up language: vocabulary, grammar, pronunciation, intonation, stress, etc. *Accent* is used to describe pronunciation features only. So if we are listening to two speakers and one says "I wrote with a pen" and the other says "I done wrote with a pin," the difference in their grammar is dialectal, and the difference in pen/pin is related to accent. Accent is a subset within the large set of language elements that make up a dialect.

Many actors come to this subject thinking that a dialect is a substandard variety of the language, used only by uneducated, ethnic, rural or tough urban types. In reality, everyone speaks with some sort of dialect. And we tell people a great deal about us when we speak.

I can place any man within six miles. I can place him within two miles in London. Sometimes within two streets.

PROF, HENRY HIGGINS in *Pygmalion*, by George Bernard Shaw

Here are terms we use to describe dialects:

Idiolect: an individual's personal way of speaking. This is what makes you different from someone who grew up in the house next door.

Regional dialect: the speech of a specific geographic area.

Paralect: the speech of a broad region. For example, generally southern US speech as opposed to specifically a South Carolina tidewater region dialect.

Acrolect: the dialect that affords the speaker the most authority and credibility with the widest audience.

Hyperlect: extremely posh, exclusively high-class speech.

Every language has these divisions. It doesn't seem to matter that a posh hyperlect speaker may be broke, uneducated, and shiftless, or that a speaker with a clearly regional sound may be a brilliant, wealthy humanitarian; speech is an instant "reputation" that one must either live up to or down from.

It's a damn shame we have this immediate ticking off in the mind about how people sound. On the other hand, how many people really want to be operated upon by a surgeon who talks broad Cockney?

DAME EILEEN ATKINS, one of England's leading classical actresses, who is
herself a Cockney, born in the Salvation Army Mothers' Hospital in Clapton

Where you're from, and who you are, establish intersecting influences on your speech.

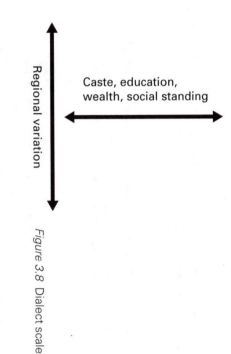

Figure 3.8 Dialect scale

In assessing character, audiences tend to assume that the more regionally defined your dialect, the lower you sit on the social scale. Dialects that demonstrate membership in a social group are more complex. Usually, whoever has the power in a society has the highest ranking and sets the markers for speech style.

Newscasters can provide fairly good mirrors of a country's acrolect. Theirs is the pronunciation that is accorded the most authority and credibility. Prestige accents go by names like British Received Pronunciation, Stage Standard, and General American. In Chapter 5, we'll examine these in more depth.

Enjoy the process of recognizing and playing with your accent and pronunciation choices. Study others using phonetics as a tool to sharpen your perception. Affectionately observe speech patterns of different times, places, and groups and learn to set your own patterns as de and slip into these other ways of sounding.

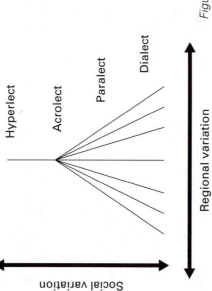

Figure 3.9 Dialect scale with social and regional variation

Write with the learned, pronounce with the vulgar.

BENJAMIN FRANKLIN, statesman, polymath

Resources

Actors regularly encounter unfamiliar words, and their pronunciation may be contested or may vary according to dialect. Here are some helpful resources that you might want on your bookshelf.

This is a list of pronouncing dictionaries. They don't provide definitions and instead concentrate on both British and North American pronunciation in comparison. Most use the IPA.

Cambridge English Pronouncing Dictionary, by Daniel Jones, Peter Roach (ed.) and James Hartman (ed.), Cambridge University Press, 17th edition 2006.

Longman Pronunciation Dictionary, by J.C. Wells, Longman, 2nd edition 2001.

Oxford Dictionary of Pronunciation, Clive Upton, William Kretzschmar, Jr., Rafal Konopka (eds.), Oxford University Press, 2001.

For more information on US pronunciation only:

A Pronouncing Dictionary of American English, by John Kenyon and Thomas Knott, Merriam-Webster, 2nd edition 1953.
NBC Handbook of Pronunciation, by Eugene Erlich and Raymond Hand, Jr., Harper Perennial, 4th edition 1991 (uses respelling, not IPA).

For Shakespearean pronunciation:

The Eloquent Shakespeare: A Pronouncing Dictionary for the Complete Dramatic Works with Notes to Untie the Modern Tongue, by Gary Logan, University of Chicago Press, 2008.

To get help with British place and family names (uses both IPA and respelling):

BBC Pronouncing Dictionary of British Names, G.E. Pointon (ed.), Oxford Reference, 1990.

And the best dictionary of all time for deep definitions of words, their history, and their use from inception through the current time (uses IPA):

The Oxford English Dictionary, Oxford University Press, 20 vols., also available in an electronic version, as an on-line subscription, and through many library systems.

Terms to remember

accent	clear L	diacritics	fricative
acoustics	cognate	diphthong	gingival juncture
affricate	consonant	epiglottis	glide
alveolar ridge	contextual	esophagus	glottis
aspirate	dark L	falling diphthong	hard/soft palate
bi-labial	dental	forms, strong & weak	hard R

International Phonetic Alphabet (IPA)	pharynx	retroflexed	triphthong
labial	phonemics	soft palate	unreleased L
larynx	phonetics	soft R	unvoiced
lateral	phonics	stop	uvula
linguistics	phonology	stressed	velum
nasal	plosive	syllable	vocal folds
nasal cavity	polysyllabic	trachea	voiced
off-glide	released L	transcribe	voiceless
palatal	respelling	transliteration	vowel

Summary

Written and spoken English are vastly different. Writers trying to portray conversation will always be hampered by the limitations of an alphabet that can't represent all the sounds of our language. Transforming what the *author has written* into *what the character says* requires sensitivity to all the small elements of sound present within words. Each sound has a sensory component that conveys both meaning and feeling.

The most widely employed tool for identifying and labeling sounds is called phonetics. Working with the IPA (International Phonetic Alphabet) involves learning each sound in our language, how it is made, what articulators are used, its duration, tonal quality, and placement — so you can easily change one sound to another to acquire accents or adapt your articulation for clarity, or play with sounds for vocal color and interpretative shading. While this is the most technical material in the book, it can also be the most enlightening and freeing. Mastery of this subject can make all voice work faster and easier.

CHAPTER 4

Expanding your voice

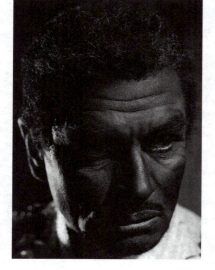

I didn't think I had the voice for Othello, so I went through a long vocal training to increase the depth of my voice. I actually added about six notes in the bass. I never used to be able to sing below D, but now I can get down to A, through all the semitones. This helps the violet velvet that I felt was necessary to the timbre of his voice.

LAURENCE OLIVIER, actor

Figure 4.1 Laurence Olivier as Othello. Photo by Angus McBean. Courtesy of the Houghton Library, Harvard University

Figure 4.2 The Voice Coach by Andrew Barton

Most of us use only a small part of our total voice potential. Over time, we place limitations on our vocal lives, out of habit and fear, instead of freeing, empowering, and unleashing that part of ourselves. The advice covered in Chapter 2 was what you might get from a "Voice Doc" or a "Voice Shrink." Now we move to the "Voice Coach" for a different set of challenges and answers. The "coach" will function as athletic trainers do, spurring you on to fitness, accomplishment, and personal bests. If you've ever played sports, you know how you feel about coaches. You love 'em, you hate 'em, you sometimes wish they'd drop dead, and you're ultimately grateful they pushed you beyond what you thought was your limit. That's how you may feel at the end of this chapter. Finally, just as you are your own best doc and shrink, you must become your own coach and inspire your own growth.

Rediscovering your voices

Listen to how children express themselves. If they think you're gross, they say so! If something is good, it's AMAAAAAAAZING!!! They use a range of pitch and volume that can shock, astound, and embarrass adults. Listen to an adult's well-modulated tones and carefully turned phrases, full of socially acceptable terms, exposing as little real feeling as possible. Children are told, "Learn how to behave" not, "Learn how to BE." They already know how to do that, and it's not appreciated. The system isn't interested in the honesty, color or authenticity of their communication but instead asks them to *reduce* communication, to be circumspect and polite. Granted, the wheels of society do turn better with the grease of polite dishonesty, but it's often at the cost of creating adults who have reduced their voices from an exuberant shout to a low murmur, and who have been so successfully socialized that they think the murmur is a reflection of their real feelings!

One indication of this comes when a director says, "Give me more! It's nice, but it's too small," and you thought it was already over the top. You *have* the feeling, but communication of that feeling has been reduced and suppressed. It's time to free and expand. The first step is to rediscover the uninhibited sounds of childhood.

EXERCISE 4.1.1 BEING A BABY – GETTING WHAT YOU WANT

1. Pair off. One of you become a crawling, pre-language baby.
2. Have the "baby" order the other one around. Make them get you things, comment on their clothes, their hair, etc.
3. Avoid using gestures to indicate what you mean. Use the broad exuberant *sounds* of a baby to communicate. Place no limits on your volume, pitch or any vocal element.
4. Tell a simple story and have the "adult" translate for the rest of the class.
5. Trade places and repeat.
6. Grow up a bit and both become four-year-olds. Argue over your toys, promise to be best friends, tell each other the funniest joke you ever heard.

Listen for ways in which we give ourselves permission to be as vocally outrageous as children, and for the ways we control and hide behind the pastel, safe, non-committal murmurings of adulthood. If you manage to keep the attitude of the child while playing with the rest of this chapter, you will not only expand your voice, you will free it as well.

UNIT 4.2 **Rediscovering language**

Why not rediscover language as well as voices? How is it that we can communicate concepts from the concrete to the abstract by making noises with our mouths? How did language develop? No one knows for sure, but here are some theories (and the real nicknames linguists use to describe them):

- *The sing-song chant theory*. Speech evolved from primitive rhythmic chants and songs associated with ritualistic dance.
- *The yo-he-ho theory*. Language arose from reflex utterances — grunts, howls, gasps — involved with physical exertion like chopping wood or hacking up a carcass.
- *The pooh-pooh theory*. Speech started from spontaneous exclamations and interjections (vocal nonverbals) that still pepper our speech — cries of fear, despair, surprise, anger, hurt, joy, etc.
- *The bow-wow or ding-dong theory*. Language grew out of our efforts to imitate natural sounds, the way a child calls a locomotive a *choo-choo* or a cow a *moo*. All our early utterances were onomatopoeic[1] or echoic words, like buzz, slap, splash, crackle, murmur or bark.
- *The la-la theory*. We were impelled toward language to facilitate the romantic side of existence — sounds associated with love, play, poetic feeling.

Each theory has its shortcomings, and even taken all together they don't explain the complexity of human language, which is more the product of the human mind than the human vocal folds.

Alone of all the creatures on earth, humans can say things that have never been said — and still be understood. Animals can only repeat the same limited utterances over and over again, as their progenitors

1   (a) The naming of a thing or action by a vocal imitation of the sound associated with it (as buzz, hiss). (b) The use of words whose sounds suggest the sense (as in stop or go).

have done for millions of years. Man's accomplishment has bestowed on him the capacity to create something new every time he speaks.

CHARLES PANATI, author

ONLINE

EXERCISE 4.2.1 BATTLING THEORIES

1. Divide the class into five equal tribes, each representing a primitive people whose language has only evolved through one of the theories.
2. Give your tribe a name. Give each member a name. Develop specific words for friend, enemy, yes, no, help.
3. Imagine that each tribe has ventured over some mountain to the next plain, where they encounter the other peoples. Practice your "language" within your group by preparing for the journey and struggling over the peak and landing on the plain.
4. Communicate with other groups only in your own language mode at first. You are extremely curious about the other cultures and not afraid of death, so be emboldened but stuck within your language.
5. Let each reveal to you another mode of expression, slowly and with some resistance, as is always the case.
6. Revel and celebrate whenever you add to your way of "speaking."

Actors can use all the theories. Each captures an essential element of language and communication. Each has potential for you to explore. Think of *all words* as being onomatopoeic, primitive, ritualistic, aboriginal, and much more than intellectual.

EXERCISE 4.2.2 WORD TASTING – A RETURN TO THE ROOTS OF LANGUAGE

1. Look at the text of a monologue you've been working on. Either randomly abstract every tenth word or choose the most important key words.
2. Take each chosen word and examine it first with your feeling sense. Taste the word. Roll it around on your tongue. Learn every movement of your jaw, soft palate, lips, and teeth.

3. Find each sound of the word. Stretch each sound out. Shorten each sound. Mix the patterns of long and short. Play absurd pitch patterns with each one.
4. Keep this up with each word until you lose all sense of what the word ever meant, and it becomes nearly unrecognizable to you. Then put it back into the monologue and deliver the piece, listening for what new potential the words hold.

Language arose from a need to communicate. We developed words that would transmit what we needed the other person to know, feel, sense or do. Imagine that in one pocket you have a *stone* and in the other a *rock*. What is the difference between them? Rock and stone share the same definition, and yet the sounds lead us to think of the stone as smooth and the rock as sharp or rough. All words are like this.

I have seen a medicine
That's able to breathe life into a stone,
Quicken a rock . . .

Lafew from WILLIAM SHAKESPEARE's *All's Well That Ends Well*

Speaking of words, you've noticed by now that we often choose classical materials to work on. That isn't just a matter of taste; many voice coaches have found verse or poetical prose best for exercising. Having stood the test of time, this material is so strong that it offers the actor rich and juicy work-outs (and coaches love tough, juicy work-outs). It asks for specific and subtle moments, as well as large and extravagant ones, sometimes within the same sentence! The extraordinary and vast images encourage vocal extravagance, which is not artificial but based on a *larger* reality than the mundane. Classics help actors to avoid confusing small with honest. They also increase sensibility to words, rhythms, and meanings that come from sound — unexplainable meanings, deeper than the conscious mind. The classics are so rich that they will accept an almost limitless range of inflections and interpretations. They have the best words to taste.

> VOICE COACH   GOALS: Feel the rhythms of words, gain variety, speed up with clarity, use rhythms to create textures.

Feeling the rhythms of words

All words have built-in rhythm. The issues are:

- the number of syllables in the word;
- the pattern of stressed and unstressed syllables;
- the length of individual sounds.

We covered syllables and stress earlier. Now we'll focus on differences in individual sound lengths and how they effect the rhythm of the word.

EXERCISE 4.3.1 REVEALING RHYTHMIC STRUCTURE

1. Take your monologue again, or any piece of prose or poetry. Read it one line at a time.
2. Stop after each line and repeat it, changing the syllables into neutral sounds (Four score and seven years ago — buh buh buh buh buh buh buh buh).
3. As you do this, tap out the rhythm with your hand.
4. Using the "buh" sounds, extend the contrast between the long and short sounds, making the long ones longer and tightening up the shorter sounds.
5. Repeat the line, incorporating the highly contrasted and extended rhythms. Go on to the next line.
6. When you're finished, perform the piece again, releasing the technique and focusing on the acting values. Listen for any differences.

EXERCISE 4.3.2 WORD TASTING – FINDING THE INTERNAL RHYTHMS OF WORDS

1. Speak the following word pairs. Compare the different lengths of the *vowel* and *diphthong* sounds. Note that the length differences are built into the word and not something you need to "make" happen.

heed–heat	feed–feet	seem–seat
paw–pauper	awed–ought	cawed–caught
rude–route	cool–coot	swoon–swoop
plaza–pasta	palm–pasha	mama–macho[2]
hurl–hurt	dirge–dirt	earn–earth
gauge–gate	rain–rate	babe–bake
side–sight	bribe–bright	lithe–like
coin–quoit	join–joint	goy–goiter
node–note	cove–coat	sold–soak
loud–lout	down–doubt	crown–crouch

2. Speak the following word pairs. Compare the different lengths of the *consonant* sounds. Note again that length differences are built in, not "made" to happen.

deem–deems	ream–reams	come–comes
pun–puns	font–fond	paint–pained
link–ling	lunk–lungs	rank–rang
ilk–ill	built–build	shelf–shelled
tease–teased	jazz–jazzed	house (v.)–housed

2 In some accents, the vowels in this line won't all match. You can still explore the length differences.

In the exercise above, the structure of the word elicited a difference in the consonant or vowel length. You probably noticed that when certain vowels are followed by a voiced consonant we tend to stretch them out as we continue to voice through the consonant — like in *heed* [hiːd] When that same vowel is followed by a voiceless consonant, we cut off the sound to accomplish the consonant — like in *heat* [hit].

A similar pattern makes us vary the length of some consonant sounds. Listen for the contrast in *sent* [sɛnt] and *send* [sɛnːd]. In theory, almost any sound can be made more prominent, and a vowel or a continuant consonant can be made as long as the actor's impulse drives it. But there is a difference between an actor pushing a sound and the sound pushing the actor. At this moment we're exploring how words come with built-in rhythmic qualities. Let the sound have its natural length. Here's a map to follow:

VOWELS

Long vowels certain vowels can more naturally be lengthened		*Short vowels* certain vowels are naturally shorter	
Long [ː]	Half-long [·]	Short	Always short
• in stressed syllables • and when followed by a voiced consonant	• in stressed syllables • and when followed by a voiceless consonant • or followed by a vowel sound	• in unstressed syllables • in weak forms of words • in words that don't take stress (pronouns, conjunctions, etc.)	ɪ ɛ æ ɒ ʊ ʌ
[iː] mead	[i·] meat	[i] meander	[ɪ] kit
[ɑː] drama	[ɑ·] sonata	[ɑ] Swahili	[ɛ] dress
[ɔː] Audrey	[ɔ·] ought	[ɔ] audition	[æ] trap
[uː] smoothing	[u·] forsooth	[u] cashew	[ɒ] lot
[ɜː, ɝː][3] bird	[ɝ·, ɚ·] burst	[ɜ, ɚ] Berlin	[ʊ] foot
			[ʌ] strut

3 The first symbol is without r-coloring and the second is with it. In rhotic accents, when lengthening r-colored vowels and diphthongs, it is easier to articulate them if the vowel is lengthened but the r-coloring isn't made more prominent.

DIPHTHONGS

Long [··]	Half-long [·]	Short
[a·ɪ·] mind	[a·ɪ] might	[aɪ] myopic
[e·ɪ·] age	[e·ɪ] ate	[eɪ] aorta
[ɔ·ɪ·] poise	[ɔ·ɪ] point	[ɔɪ] poinsettia
[ə·ʊ·, o·ʊ·] pole	[ə·ʊ, o·ʊ] post	[əʊ, oʊ][4] posterior
[a·ʊ·] loud	[a·ʊ] out	[aʊ] outstanding

CONSONANTS

any continuant consonant can be lengthened, but some are more significant

Long [:]	Short
• in a stressed syllable	• in an unstressed syllable
• and when followed by a voiced consonant	• or when followed by a voiceless consonant
[m:] hemmed	[m] hemp
[n:] fond	[n] font
[ŋ:] hanged	[ŋ] hank
[ɫ:] build	[ɫ] built]

EXERCISE 4.3.3 WORD TASTING – FINDING INTERNAL RHYTHMS OF WORDS IN TEXT

1. Take a section of text that you find especially poetic or beautiful. Analyze it for long and short sounds. For example, here's Constance from *King John*. She's been accused of loving grief itself more than her missing son.

---

4 In this sequence [əʊ] is more typical of General British and [oʊ] of General American.

Grief fills the room up of my absent child:
   iˑ   ɫː   uː   aˑɪ̆ɫː

Lies in his bed, walks up and down with me,
aˑɪ̆   ɔˑ   aˑʊ̆nː

Puts on his pretty looks, repeats his words,
                     iˑ   ɜː/ɝː

Remembers me of all his gracious parts,
     mː   ɔː   eˑɪ̆   ɑˑ/ɑˑɚ̆

Stuffs out his vacant garments with his form;
     aˑʊ̆   eˑɪ̆   ɑː/ɑˑɚ̆ˑ   ɔː/ɔˑɚ̆

Then, have I reason to be fond of grief?
        iː   nː   iˑ

2. List the words that have long sounds.

Long

fills, room, child, lies, down, words,
remembers, all, garments, form, reason, fond

Half-long

grief, walks, repeats, gracious, out, vacant, grief

3. Practice speaking the words with unusual length, repeating them many times and filling them with the specific image of what you're talking about.
4. Speak the text again. Make the long sounds long. On the shorter sounds, let them be even shorter, tighter and crisper. Use a large contrast in lengths. The short sounds aren't of less importance, they're just sharper so they carry a different energy and message.

When all the internal rhythmic values of individual words are combined and used in concert, the cadence of speech and the metre of poetry are formed.

> To the tintinnabulation that so musically wells
> From the bells, bells, bells, bells,
> Bells, bells, bells —
> From the jingling and the tinkling of the bells.

Some material has built-in tempo requirements. Patter songs usually ask for a rapid pace, crisp articulation, and superior breath control for the long passages. More prosaically (and frequently) actors are asked to do thirty-second commercials that seem to contain sixty seconds' worth of words. Both situations have high technical demands yet must appear effortless, sound genuinely conversational, and be loaded with nuance and variety.

Figure 4.3 Stephen Quint as the Modern Major-General in *The Pirates of Penzance.* Photo by Michael A. Nemeth, from New York, Gilbert and Sullivan Players, G&S Fest 2008

LISTEN

EXERCISE 4.3.5 TEMPO – RACING EFFORTLESSLY

1. This is a competition. After performing these pieces, the class should give out awards:

- Best Articulation and Clarity.
- Fastest Overall Speed (points off if it's unintelligible).
- Best Breath Control.
- Most Color and Variety.
- Most Interesting Vocal Characterization.
- Best Storyteller/Narrator.

"I am the very model of a modern major-general" from *The Pirates of Penzance* by W.S. Gilbert and Sir Arthur Sullivan:

I am the very model of a modern major-general;
I've information vegetable, animal and mineral:
I know the kings of England, and I quote the fights historical,
From Marathon to Waterloo, in order categorical.
I'm very well acquainted, too, with matters mathematical;
I understand equations, both the simple and quadratical;
About binomial theorem I'm teeming with a lot o' news,
With many cheerful facts about the square of the hypotenuse:
I'm very good at integral and differential calculus;
I know the scientific names of beings animalculous.
But still, in matters vegetable, animal and mineral,
I am the very model of a modern major-general.
I know our mythic history, King Arthur's and Sir Caradoc's,
I answer hard acrostics, I've a pretty taste for paradox:
I quote, in elegiacs, all the crimes of Heliogabalus!
In conics I can floor peculiarities parabolous.

Expanding — pronunciation/articulation

VOICE COACH

GOALS: crisper consonants, clean endings; find word relationships; use sounds to hurt or heal; paint pictures with words.

I can tell undoubted Raphaels from Gerard Dows and Zoffanies.

I know the croaking chorus from the *Frogs* of Aristophanes!

Then I can hum a fugue, of which I've heard the music's din afore,

And whistle all the airs from that infernal nonsense, *Pinafore!*

Then I can write a washing bill in Babylonic cuneiform,

And tell you every detail of Caractacus's uniform.

In short, in matters vegetable, animal and mineral,

I am the very model of a modern major-general.

In fact, when I know what is meant by "mamelon" and "ravelin";

When I can tell at sight a Mauser rifle from a javelin;

When such affairs as sorties and surprises I'm more wary at;

And when I know precisely what is meant by commissariat;

When I have learned what progress has been made in modern gunnery;

When I know more of tactics than a novice in a nunnery;

In short, when I've a smattering of elemental strategy —

You'll say a better major-general has never sat a gee;

For my military knowledge, tho' I'm plucky and adventury,

Has only been brought down to the beginning of the century,

But still, in matters vegetable, animal and mineral,

I am the very model of a modern Major-General.

That last series of patter songs may have inspired you to work more on rapid, light articulation. Now that you've had some experiences with this area, it's time to take a look at what many consider to be a useful appliance — one that may speed your growth just as ankle weights make an aerobics class even more challenging.

UNIT 4.4.1   *Bone prop/cork — the controversial helper*

A bone prop is a small plastic rod with grooves on either end for the teeth to fit in while it is "bitten" during vocal drills. It resembles a double-ended rook from a chess set. It also looks like a miniature hand weight and is a piece of equipment used by some who want serious work-outs. Bone props vary in length, but from one-half to three-quarters of an inch is right for most people. Since the props themselves are often hard to locate, look in craft stores. They sell bags of small corks in various sizes. At a pinch, you can use a pencil laid across your teeth. And if you are totally out of props and into pain, you can bite your own knuckle.

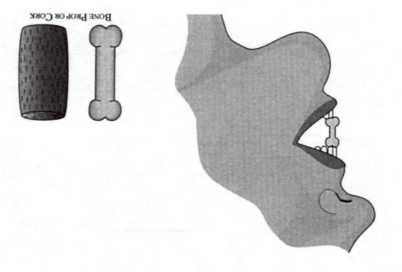

BONE PROP OR CORK

Figure 4.4 Bone prop held in mouth

There is considerable debate regarding the use of this little tool, with experts lining up on both sides. Those who oppose it fear the potential increase in jaw tension required to hold the object in place. (People with jaw-joint problems should exercise particular care.) Those who support it claim that it is an effective reminder of how to form a sound cleanly, that it teaches a more open jaw position and, since separating your teeth requires a larger articulatory gesture it makes for a good workout. We suggest that if you use it, you use it selectively. First take the time to get the right-size prop. Too large will create excessive tension, while too small will not open the mouth enough for any benefit. Most importantly, take it *out* frequently to relieve tension. In most drills, the prop will help you to locate the articulation placement and make you reach further to accomplish it. Then if you quickly remove the prop and perform the drill without it, you will add a powerful kinesthetic memory. The time to remove the prop is at the end of each line. Don't leave it in for more than two lines of drill or dialogue.

Consonant action — finishing off a drill

While numerous drills are offered earlier in this text, the following (adapted from some designed by Cicely Berry) are tough ones that can be used to finish off a work-out. If you use a bone prop, perform with it in for each line, then repeat with it out. Many problems with consonants are connected to how the consonant launches into the vowel. This exercise helps to remind you how to shape this launching effectively and reminds you to distinguish the vowels themselves.

LISTEN

EXERCISE 4.4.2.1 ARTICULATION – INITIATING WITH ACCURACY

Speak each line with lightness, speed, and accuracy. Explore the use of the bone prop to see if it is an assistance.

Table 4.1 Articulation — initiating

	[ɑ] (balm)	[ʌ] (bud)	[ɜ] or [ɝ] (bird)	[æ] (bad)	[ɛ] (bed)	[eɪ] (bake)	[ɪ] (bid)	[i] (bead)	[aɪ] (buy)
1.	lɑ	lʌ	lɜ	læ	lɛ	leɪ	lɪ	li	laɪ
2.	tɑ	tʌ	tɜ	tæ	tɛ	teɪ	tɪ	ti	taɪ

No.	ʊ	ɪ	ɔ	ɑ	aɪ	i
16.	ʊp	ɪp	ɔp	ɑp	aɪp	ip
17.	ʊb	ɪb	ɔb	ɑb	aɪb	ib
18.	ʊm	ɪm	ɔm	ɑm	aɪm	im
19.	ʊk	ɪk	ɔk	ɑk	aɪk	ik
20.	ʊg	ɪg	ɔg	ɑg	aɪg	ig
21.	ʊf	ɪf	ɔf	ɑf	aɪf	if
22.	ʊv	ɪv	ɔv	ɑv	aɪv	iv
23.	ʊs	ɪs	ɔs	ɑs	aɪs	is
24.	ʊz	ɪz	ɔz	ɑz	aɪz	iz
25.	ʊθ	ɪθ	ɔθ	ɑθ	aɪθ	iθ
26.	ʊð	ɪð	ɔð	ɑð	aɪð	ið
27.	ʊkt	ɪkt	ɔkt	ɑkt	aɪkt	ikt
28.	ʊgd	ɪgd	ɔgd	ɑgd	aɪgd	igd
29.	ʊpt	ɪpt	ɔpt	ɑpt	aɪpt	ipt
30.	ʊbd	ɪbd	ɔbd	ɑbd	aɪbd	ibd
31.	ʊmd	ɪmd	ɔmd	ɑmd	aɪmd	imd
32.	ʊtt	ɪtt	ɔtt	ɑtt	aɪtt	itt
33.	ʊtd	ɪtd	ɔtd	ɑtd	aɪtd	itd
34.	ʊtz	ɪtz	ɔtz	ɑtz	aɪtz	itz
35.	ʊθt	ɪθt	ɔθt	ɑθt	aɪθt	iθt
36.	ʊðd	ɪðd	ɔðd	ɑðd	aɪðd	iðd
37.	ʊðz	ɪðz	ɔðz	ɑðz	aɪðz	iðz
38.	ʊst	ɪst	ɔst	ɑst	aɪst	ist
39.	ʊzd	ɪzd	ɔzd	ɑzd	aɪzd	izd
40.	ʊft	ɪft	ɔft	ɑft	aɪft	ift
41.	ʊfts	ɪfts	ɔfts	ɑfts	aɪfts	ifts
42.	ʊvd	ɪvd	ɔvd	ɑvd	aɪvd	ivd
43.	ʊkst	ɪkst	ɔkst	ɑkst	aɪkst	ikst
44.	ʊtθ	ɪtθ	ɔtθ	ɑtθ	aɪtθ	itθ

EXERCISE 4.4.2.3 ARTICULATION AND BREATH CONTROL

And now for a real tough one from your coach. Again, explore this with a bone prop. Say these lines as rapidly as possible, as many times as you can on a single breath. Keep a record of your time, clarity, and distance and see if you can get up to or exceed the goals we've set.

Articulation line	Target goal # on one breath	Your record time	Clarity
		#	
1. pə bə tə də kə gə tə də	20		
2. fə və ʃə ʒə sə zə ʃə ʒə	15		
3. pə bə wə ʍə pə bə rə wə	20		
4. ʃə ʒə θə ðə sə zə θə ðə	15		
5. nə ŋə kə gə lə ŋə kə gə	20		
6. ʃə ʒə tʃə dʒə sə zə tʃə dʒə	15		

Interpreting through articulation

Earlier, we discussed speech sounds as "felt" or "tactile" experiences, and how feeling provokes immediate emotional response.

- Consonants form the intellectual borders of words. They carry meaning, especially the crisp stop/plosives [p, b, t, d, k, g], and also texture as with the continuants [m, n, ŋ, ɫ, l, f, v, θ, ð, s, z, ʃ, ʒ, r, h] and the semi-vowels [w, j].
- Vowels carry the emotional message of the word. Singing (one of the most emotional ways to communicate) is done on long rising and falling vowel sounds.

EXERCISE 4.4.3.1 WORD TASTING – WORDS TO HURT OR HEAL

1. Take a scene you're working on and divide it into beats (important sections where your character completes a small objective before switching to another).

2. For each beat, decide how your character wants to make the other character feel. (Don't share this information with your partner.)

3. Choose a key word from each beat — a powerful verb, a loaded word, or even something apparently unimportant.

4. Have your partner stand facing away from you, so there will be no visual information. Take each word in turn and make your partner feel the way you want them to. Use as much physicalization as you like, but focus on how consonants can cut like a knife or stroke like a feather, and how vowels flow a stream of emotion over and through your partner.

5. Partners give each other feedback. How were you made to feel? How did you want to respond? Are you listening as well as speaking in a new way? What did you discover about your scene and/or character?

6. Reverse roles and repeat.

Tell me the word and I will speak it. I will speak the stars of heaven into a crown for your head; I will speak the flowers of the field into a cloak; I will speak the racing stream into a melody for your ears and the voices of a thousand larks to sing it; I will speak the softness of the night for your bed and the warmth of summer for your coverlet; I will speak the brightness of flame to light your way; I will speak until the hardness of you melts away and your heart is free once more.

Taliesin **by STEPHEN R. LAWHEAD**

Writers sensitive to the texture and emotion of words highlight the sensory and feeling qualities of a piece by using four devices:

1. **Alliteration:** a series of similar sounds in a sentence (often with the same letter introducing each word). Usually used to describe initial consonants, it can also be applied to vowels. *After life's fitful fever. In a summer season when soft was the sun. Apt alliteration's artful aid. Or I'll be back. Hip-Hop. Fruit by the Foot. Language offers so many choices it's fertile and fecund, flipping free-styling flows for all my folks . . .* [5]

5 "Shakespeare is Hip-Hop" *Flocabulary* by Escher.

2. **Assonance:** rhyming vowel sounds but not matching consonant sounds. The effect is subtler than full rhyme: *grave fate, votive notice, task at hand. Or major babe, ugly uncle, stud muffin, high five. And "I'm running up on someone's lawns with guns drawn."*[6]

3. **Consonance:** the counterpart to assonance, it is the partial matching of end consonants in words or syllables whose main vowels differ: *pressed past, shadow meadow, mister master, or bogus and heinous, dork in the dark, radical — dudical. "And be prosperous, though we live dangerous,/ Cops could just arrest me, blaming us, we're held like hostages."*[7]

4. **Onomatopoeia:** words that sound like what they mean. *Babble, cuckoo, croak, ping-pong, quack, sizzle* are examples, as are *gack attack, crisp whip, snap-crackle-pop.* Also a sentence whose sound suggests what it describes. Speak this while imagining you're lying on the grass and hearing the sounds of summer.

Myriads of rivulets hurrying thro' the lawn,
The moan of doves in immemorial elms,
And the murmur of innumerable bees.[8]

EXERCISE 4.4.3.2 USING A.A.C.O.
(ALLITERATION, ASSONANCE, CONSONANCE, AND ONOMATOPOEIA)

1 In the following piece, identify all the four literary devices.

2 Sit in a circle. Each person will take one line of text. If someone's line ends on an unfinished sentence, the next person must seamlessly pick up the line as if the two of you were the same person. (An alternative method is to repeat the last line just said and one new line — try it both ways.)

3 Explore ways of speaking the material so that the literary devices are highlighted by your voice and used to paint the scene, create a soundscape, and make your audience smell, feel, taste, hear, and see all the details.

6 "Rock Bottom" by Eminem.
7 "NY State of Mind" by Nas.
8 "Come Down, O Maid" by Lord Alfred Tennyson.

4. Go around once to warm up, just getting familiar with the words. Do not read ahead and plan your line but tune in completely to what all the actors are doing.

5. Next, repeat (starting at a different point in the circle), stopping for suggestions from the rest of the group after each line.

6. Then do a third read-through, shooting for outrageous perfection. Remember this is a piece where it's almost impossible to do too much.

Under Milk Wood by Dylan Thomas

1. And the shrill girls giggle and master around him and squeal as they clutch and thrash,

2. and he blubbers away downhill with his patched pants falling,

3. and his tear-splashed blush burns all the way as the triumphant bird-like sisters scream

4. with buttons in their claws and the bully brothers hoot after him his little nickname

5. and his mother's shame and his father's wickedness with the loose wild barefoot women

6. of the hovels of the hills. It all means nothing at all, and, howling for his milky mum,

7. for her cawl and buttermilk and cowbreath and welshcakes and the fat birth-smelling bed

8. and moonlit kitchen of her arms, he'll never forget as he paddles blind home

9. through the weeping end of the world. Then his tormentors tussle and run

10. to the Cockle Street sweet-shop, their pennies sticky as honey, to buy from Miss Myfanwy Price,

11. who is cocky and neat as a puff-bosomed robin and her small round buttocks tight as ticks,

12. gobstoppers big as wens that rainbow as you suck, brandyballs, winegums,

13. hundreds and thousands, liquorice sweet as sick, nougat to tug and ribbon out

14. like another red rubbery tongue, gum to glue in girl's curls, crimson coughdrops to spit blood,

15. ice-cream cornets, dandelion-and-burdock, raspberry and cherryade,

16. pop goes the weasel and the wind.

We tend to think of these devices as exclusively poetic contrivances, but *all* good writers and lovers of words employ them to some degree — often unconsciously creating relationships between words. You need only to look closely to find them in *any* material.

EXERCISE 4.4.3.3 HIDDEN RELATIONSHIPS

1. Examine a monologue or scene you've been working on (one the class has already heard) for alliteration, assonance, consonance, and onomatopoeia. Share what you find. Do you think the author was consciously intending to use that particular form?

2. Choose the best examples of each form. Explore how to deliver that section of text in ways that highlight, or make use of, the particular quality to serve the character's goals.

3. Share the passages that have changed with the rest of the class.

UNIT 4.5

Expanding – pitch

VOICE COACH

GOALS: Extend your range, inflect for stressing, find new colors are melodies.

UNIT 4.5.1

Pitch prominence for stronger stressing

While we may stress important words by increasing volume, it is much more effective and interesting to bring words forward by extending them and finding a broader, more expressive pitch coloration. Pitch prominence is especially effective for the rhetorical[9] device called **parallel construction**. There are two main types — antithetical and synonymous — and each instinctively lends itself to certain pitch treatments (though there is no "one right way"). Both literary and non-literary examples follow:

Antithesis is a "not this but that" structure.

*   **Antithetical parallelism**, where the second idea denies or contrasts the first. "*Crafty men condemn studies; simple men admire them; and wise men use them.*"[10] Or "*It was the best of times, it was the worst of times, it was the age*

---

9 Rhetoric is the art of effective expression and the persuasive use of language. Parallel construction is a powerful rhetorical device for building an argument, or making a point.

10 From *Of Studies* by Francis Bacon.

of wisdom, it was the age of foolishness, it was the epoch of belief, it was the epoch of incredulity, it was the season of Light, it was the season of Darkness, it was the spring of hope, it was the winter of despair, we had everything before us, we had nothing before us, we were all going direct to Heaven, we were all going direct the other way."[11] Or "Everybody doesn't like something, but nobody doesn't like Sara Lee."

Synonymous parallelism has many subsets, but the important issue for an actor is to find a way for the audience to hear the ideas adding up. Often this is thought of as a *ladder* of intensifying ideas.

- **Synonymous parallelism,** where the second idea reinforces the first by repeating and intensifying the thought. "*I celebrate myself, and sing myself,*" or "*I too am not a bit tamed, I too am untranslatable.*"[12] (There need not be an actual repetition of words.) Or "*I am stuck on Band-Aid, and Band-Aid's stuck on me.*"[13]

- **Synthetic or cumulative parallelism,** where the second line, or several consecutive lines, supplements or completes the first: "*Just as you feel when you look on the river and sky, so I felt;/ Just as any of you is one of a living crowd, I was one of a crowd,/ Just as you are refresh'd by the gladness of the river and the bright flow, I was refresh'd,/ Just as you stand and lean on the rail, yet hurry with the swift current, I stood yet was hurried,/ Just as you look on the numberless masts of ships and the thick-stemm'd pipes of steamboats, I look'd.*"[14] Or "*The key to Springfield has always been Elm Street. The Greeks knew it. The Carthaginians knew it. Now you know it.*"[15]

- **Climactic parallelism,** or "ascending rhythm," where each successive line adds to its predecessor, usually taking words from it and completing it.[16] "*I came. I saw. I conquered.*"[17] Or "*We shall fight on the beaches. We shall fight on the landing grounds. We shall fight in the fields and in the streets. We shall fight in the hills. We shall never surrender.*"[18]

More properly, this is an example of *chiasmus,* a verbal pattern in which the second half of an expression is balanced against the first with the parts reversed. It is frequently antithetical, as in the Witches' line from *Macbeth:* "Fair is foul, and foul is fair."

As you will have noticed, these forms often overlap. Writers are not obliged to keep within the arbitrary definitions of the scholars who study them, but having terminology assists our analysis.

11 From *A Tale of Two Cities* by Charles Dickens.
12 From *Song of Myself,* by Walt Whitman.
13 More properly, this is an example of *chiasmus,* a verbal pattern in which the second half of an expression is balanced against the first with the parts reversed. It is frequently antithetical, as in the Witches' line from *Macbeth:* "Fair is foul, and foul is fair."
14 From *Crossing Brooklyn Ferry* by Walt Whitman, one of the masters of parallel construction.
15 From "Bart the General," *The Simpsons.*
16 As you will have noticed, these forms often overlap. Writers are not obliged to keep within the arbitrary definitions of the scholars who study them, but having terminology assists our analysis.
17 Julius Caesar.
18 Winston Churchill.

Or "*Politics is the art of looking for trouble, finding it everywhere, diagnosing it wrongly, and applying unsuitable remedies.*"[19] Or "*Fear leads to anger; anger leads to hatred; hatred leads to conflict; conflict leads to suffering.*"[20]

Since audiences can't see the path of the author's reasoning on the page, the actor uses voice to present that reasoning and make the audience see it with their ears.

Examples of parallel structure have been chosen not just from the works of great poets but also in the styles of such influential philosophers as Charles Dickens, Groucho Marx, Yoda, Bart Simpson, Julius Caesar, and Winston Churchill to demonstrate that these techniques are used at all levels of communication. Some of these examples move quickly in and out of fashion. Which of the phrases above have dated by the time you read this? Can you replace them with ones more current? Can you find other instances in this text where the examples would now be different to what they were at the time this material was written? Listen for parallel construction in conversations all around you. Can you recall any that you've heard in the last twenty-four hours? (Hint: look at advertising.)

EXERCISE 4.5.1.1 PITCH AND PARALLELISM

1. Here are the first three sentences of *Richard III*. Read them into a recorder.
2. Analyze the piece for its parallel structure. Note (as shown in Chapter 2) operative words, weak-form words, and their various levels of importance. In doing this, you will reveal the structure of the argument, or the path of the author's reasoning.

Now is the Winter of our Discontent,
Made glorious Summer by this Son of York;
And all the clouds that loured upon our house
In the deep bosom of the Ocean buried.
Now are our brows bound with Victorious Wreaths,
Our bruised arms hung up for Monuments;

19 Groucho Marx.
20 Yoda, *Star Wars, Episode 1.*

Our stern Alarums changed to merry Meetings;
Our dreadful Marches, to delightful Measures.
Grim-visaged War, hath smoothed his wrinkled Front:
And now, in stead of mounting Barbed Steeds,
To fright the Souls of fearful Adversaries,
He capers nimbly in a Ladies Chamber,
To the lascivious pleasing of a Lute.

3. Simplify the language so that you highlight the parallel structure (in this case, primarily antithesis).

Now	Winter	is made	Summer
And	clouds	buried	in Ocean
Now	brows	are bound	with Wreaths
	arms	hung up	for Monuments
	stern Alarums	changed to	merry Meetings
	dreadful Marches	(changed) to	delightful Measures
	War	hath smoothed	Front
And now, in stead of	mounting Barbed Steeds		He capers nimbly in a Ladies Chamber
	to fright the Souls of Adversaries		to the lascivious pleasing of a Lute

4. When you have analyzed the structure and determined your selection of operative words, listen carefully to how you bring those words forward. As you speak each phrase, note the length and pitch intonation that naturally emerges. Without increasing the volume, broaden and extend the pitch in both range and intonation. Physicalize it in non-realistic ways so that your body amplifies the impulse. Go much further than you would normally feel comfortable doing it.
5. Do a second recording of the piece, focusing on making your operative words stand out through "pitch prominence" but don't push. Relax and let the music in your voice carry the meaning. Compare it with the first recording.

6. Repeat this process with a piece that has cumulative parallelism ladders. As an example, here's Cordelia from *King Lear*.

	Ladders
Good my lord,	
You have begot me, bred me, loved me. I	begot, bred, loved
Return those duties back as are right fit,	
Obey you, love you, and most honor you.	obey love, honor
Why have my sisters husbands, if they say	
They love you all? Haply, when I shall wed,	
That lord whose hand must take my plight shall carry	
Half my love with him, half my care and duty.	love, care, duty
Sure, I shall never marry like my sisters,	
To love my father all.	

It can feel uncomfortable to stretch your voice past the narrow, noncommittal sounds of daily conversation. It can also be thrilling to take the leap.

EXERCISE 4.5.1.2 SINGING THE SPEECH

1. Take the piece above that you just worked on. Chant it, staying on one note until you reach the end of a phrase, changing to a new pitch when you shift to a new idea group. Go all the way through it.
2. Return to the start and sing your way through. You might drift into a style like Irish sea shanty, Indian raga, grand opera or western folk song. Follow the impulse and see what happens.
3. Absorb the new sense of the language and its inner music, then record another spoken version. Compare all three recordings and solicit comments from the class.

Expanding — volume

> VOICE COACH   GOALS: Strength, endurance, power! Resist vocal fatigue, gain volume throughout your whole range.

The following exercises are designed to develop a large voice. It is rare to find someone who naturally and easily projects to the back of a large outdoor amphitheatre or an unmiked opera house. Some do have that gift, but most of us have to work at it. This is the weightlifting section, and it's time to pump you up!

Your voice shall be as strong as any man's.

Cassius from WILLIAM SHAKESPEARE's *Julius Caesar*

Vocal weightlifting

The same warning given in Chapter 2 applies. If you have forgotten the guidelines for intense vocal work, go back to page 116 and review them now. Guard against excessive vocal fatigue. Exercise in a deliberate, aware, and reasonable manner. Do not do any exercise that feels painful or places too much strain on your voice. Take it slow and steady.

LISTEN

EXERCISE 4.6.1.1 VOLUME BUILDING

Do this series in position A, B or C from Exercise 2.5.1.2 on page 71 to be sure you are aligned and breathing well. (These exercises may at first require access to a piano, but, after once or twice through, can easily be done with no pitch assistance.)

1. HUMMING WARM-UP. Warm up first by gently humming from a comfortable low note, sliding, and making a sound like a cow mooing, up to an octave above that note then back down to the start. Go up a step, and repeat. Keep on well into your falsetto range, as high as you can go.

Figure 4.5 Volume building exercise

Reverse the hum by starting at your highest note and humming downward, proceeding in even steps to the lowest sound you can make. Whenever you feel that you've done enough intensification work, then redo this exercise to cool down.

2. OCTAVE INTENSIFICATION. Do the same octave sliding pattern on the sound [æ], as in *had*. Look in a mirror if necessary to be sure you don't pull back on your tongue, and don't let the sound change to [ɑ], as in *father*. Start on a comfortable low note, with the softest sound you can make. As you rise to the octave intensify the sound, then make it even louder as you return to the original pitch. So, it's soft, louder, loudest. Continue way up into your falsetto. Don't be upset if your voice cracks or makes "ugly" sounds. The more you do the exercises, the less likely that is to happen.

3. Reverse the pattern. Start high in your falsetto. Sing on the same vowel moving down an octave, then back up. Start with a very soft sound, swell louder as you reach the octave, then even louder as you return. Continue stepping down the scale to the lowest note you can comfortably reach.

4. SINGLE-NOTE INTENSIFICATION. Start on a comfortable low note. Using the vowel [æ] as in *Had* again, start with the softest sound you can hear. Slowly intensify to as loud a sound as possible, then back to soft while maintaining the *same pitch*. Then repeat that same note, intensifying to the same volume and back three times on one breath. Repeat the entire pattern an octave above, so if you were on a C#, count up eight notes to the next C# and do it again. Go back down seven notes to D# and redo the whole cycle. Continue moving up by steps well into your falsetto range, as high as you can comfortably go.

5. COOL DOWN. Repeat step 1, very gently humming through your full range to soothe your voice and test the level of fatigue.

Do this series (or as much of it as you are now able) every other day for a few weeks and you will notice a real difference in the size and stamina of your voice.

UNIT 4.6.2 *Working with amplification*

Even though you might develop a voice capable of extraordinary loudness, you may still need to work with a microphone. Some theatres are not designed to carry the voice well. You may be working outdoors, projecting over loud underscoring or sound effects, or the sound designer may want to put special effects on your voice. Here are some tricks to keep in mind:

- If the mic is being used to reinforce the sound, it works best if you project fully so the amplification isn't noticeable and the sound is mostly coming from your voice.
- Amplification makes you louder, but not necessarily clearer. Use a lot of consonant energy.
- If the mic is used because there is no way a human voice could fill the space or be heard over other noises, project normally but don't overspeak. Let the mic do the work or you'll fatigue your voice.
- Be consistent in your volume, so that you're a good, predictable partner for the sound board operator.
- Be alert to the mic placement. If it is an area mic it will amplify everything: footsteps, door slams, prop thumps, etc. If it is a body mic, avoid bumping it or your partner's or speaking into your partner's mic during intimate scenes.
- Since amplified sound comes from loudspeakers that may be at some distance from the actor, the audience can have a hard time locating who is speaking. To help with this, move on the breath just before your line. This will draw our eyes. Make sure your face is visible when you speak.

UNIT 4.7 **Expanding — quality**

VOICE COACH	GOALS: Gain tonal flexibility, develop a repertoire of qualities, let the voice transparently express feeling.

We describe emotional experience with the word *feeling*. When we feel something, we actually *feel* it. Emotion is a kinesthetic,[21] or body sensation. When you respond emotionally, your body undergoes complex reactions. You may blush, sweat, get butterflies, feel hot or faint. Whenever the body reacts emotionally, the vocal mechanism is also involved. That's why when you talk to someone on the phone you can hear if they're feeling nervous, upset or happy.[22] Their breathing patterns change, their pitch shifts, the rhythm is different, but most importantly, their vocal quality alters.

> **. . . If you would know his pure heart's truth,**
> **You would quickly learn to know him by his voice.**
> **Proteus from WILLIAM SHAKESPEARE's *Two Gentlemen of Verona***

When your throat gets tense because you're angry, or relaxes because you're bored, the rest of the world can hear it! Most people take pains to mask feelings and so strive to make their voices as neutral as possible. Actors need to do just the opposite.

EXERCISE 4.7.1 QUALITY CONTROL

1. List all the words you can think of to describe vocal qualities. (We've already discussed nasal, hollow, breathy, and pressed—so start with those.) The terms you use don't have to be scientific and can be as abstract as you like: harsh, brittle, crackly, smooth, oily, etc.
2. Warm up by doing the tonality isolation from Chapter 2, page 129.
3. Each person choose six terms from the list. Then take a piece of any text and shift the quality on each line. For example:

   She walks in beauty, like the night   nasal
   Of cloudless climes and starry skies;   hollow

LISTEN

---

21 Kinesthesia: a sense mediated by end organs located in muscles, tendons, and joints and stimulated by bodily movements and tensions; also: sensory experience derived from this sense.
22 There is even a voice stress analyzer, a portable lie-detector type of device that can be attached to a telephone that evaluates the stress content of the other person's voice.

And all that's best of dark and bright	breathy
Meet in her aspect and her eyes:	twangy
Thus mellowed to that tender light	denasal
Which heaven to gaudy day denies.	harsh

4. Repeat as in #3, but explore various *degrees* of each quality. Start each line with only a little nasality (for example), intensify it as you reach the middle, then dial it back as you reach the end. See if you can feel what muscles and parts of your vocal mechanism are shifting as you do this. Use this as an opportunity to study which placements seem to cause you the most vocal strain. Learn how to manage and reduce any unnecessary tensions by observing your breathing patterns and any generalized physical tension.

5. Try this with as many qualities as you can vocally differentiate. Keep a list. Give an award to the person who can demonstrate the greatest diversity with the least tension and effort.

Practicing gross differences in vocal quality will extend your range of emotional expression. It's also fundamental for developing the skills for character and cartoon voice work (see Chapter 6). It's like comparing masks to actual facial expressions. Most everyday variations are subtle, complex, and fleeting, but learning to do broad expressive facial masks frees and extends the muscles into clearer facial gestures in more normal interactions.

Now we will explore how facial masks, body postures, breathing patterns, and sounds can assist the actor in entering, vocalizing, and communicating powerful universal emotional states.[23]

The following exercise is demanding and potentially exhausting. You may wish to try one or two archetypal emotions at a given session, moving to others at another time. The instructions are based on what scientists found observing people under hypnosis, experiencing genuine powerful emotion. This material has only recently been adapted to the training of actors.

23 This series of exercises is based on the work of Dr. Susana Bloch of the Pierre et Marie Curie Institut des Neurosciences in Paris. Dr. Bloch calls the process Alba Emoting. We can give only an introduction here, but this valuable subject is worthy of in-depth exploration, and we encourage further study from a certified trainer.

Expanding breath and emotion

| VOICE COACH | GOALS: Use breathing patterns to unlock a powerful connection to emotional states. |

In Chapter 2, we drilled some fundamental practices for open, aligned breathing. It's important to be able to access coordinated breathing, because it is critical to vocal function. But characters in plays don't breathe in ideal ways, particularly when they are caught in strong emotions.

When we say *emotion*, what do we mean? Interestingly, an emotion isn't a psychological state. It's physiological. We feel something because our bodies are doing a particular set of behaviors we call glad, mad or sad, for example. That state may be stimulated by thoughts, or even brain chemistry, but the emotion itself is a body experience.

This is great news for actors, because it means that you can access powerful emotional states by doing the physical behaviors that are that emotion. And you can do it without the mental chaos engaged by trying to stimulate that state from a psychological source. With a clear mind, you can have more control over your voice, you'll be able to make better expressive choices, and you run less risk of vocal, physical, and psychological injury.

There are three elements that we can be trained to coordinate in order to step into an emotion:

- body: the large muscles of the legs, torso and arms
- face: the muscles around the mouth and eyes
- breathing: the specific pattern of inhalation and exhalation

Breathing is the most important of these elements.

But, if you're going to learn how to step into an emotion, it's useful to learn how to step out first. That way you can begin with a clean slate and when you're finished you can return with no emotional hangover.

EXERCISE 4.8.1 STEPPING OUT

You can interrupt any emotional pattern by changing the way you are standing, your relationship to gravity, your gestures, your facial expression, and most importantly your breathing. Instead of trying to feel differently, simply alter your body to alter your feelings.

The following process works to release strong feelings because the maneuvers are ones that the body does not adopt under intense emotion.

1. Stand with your feet straight, hip-width apart, knees relaxed.

    a. Keep your eyes level at the horizon, looking straight ahead at something specific.
    b. Let your arms hang. Lace your fingers in front of you.
    c. Inhale through your nose while bringing your arms up in an arc to where they comfortably stop.
    d. Bend your arms at the elbow so your hands drop behind your head.
    e. Press the heels of your hands together.
    f. Relax your hands. Breathe out through your mouth as you return your arms down in an arc.

2. Repeat this first sequence two more times.
3. With your fingers, stretch the muscles around your mouth up and out. Do the same around your eyes and forehead. Twist your shoulders to one side.
4. Exhale and hang over that side. Make sure you don't hold your head up.
5. Inhale and roll back up.
6. Twist to the opposite side, hang over from the waist and roll up.
7. Breathe in through your nose and out through your mouth (and continue this in an easy relaxed way).
8. Bounce your knees to see if your arms are floppy. (If they seem stiff or if you have trouble breathing in a relaxed way, repeat the step-out from the beginning until you are fully out of whatever emotion you were in.)

Use the step-out before and after practicing any emotional pattern, and whenever you feel like you need to find a state of alert neutrality.

EXERCISE 4.8.2 STEPPING INTO EMOTIONS WITH EFFECTOR PATTERNS

1. Organize the space so that mats and chairs are available.

2. Start by stepping out.

3. Choose one pattern a session. Don't do more until you become practiced. Initially, don't do any pattern for more than a few breath cycles. Later, you can stay as long as you like.

4. If you notice the impulse to add voice to a pattern, allow that to happen. At first, don't deliberately add sound to avoid "acting" or "indicating" the voice of that emotion. Voice works best when it is the product of the breath, so start there. Then allow your voice to come in and extend it into larger sounds, words, and lines of text.

5. Finish by stepping out.

On the charts below, you'll see "resting expiratory level" (REL). That is the point in the breath cycle where the air pressure in your lungs is the same as the atmospheric pressure. In a relaxed state, this is the point where you'll naturally want to start breathing in. You'll notice that some strong emotions operate below REL (sadness, happiness) and some well above it (fear, anger).

Figure 4.6 Tenderness breathing pattern

Breathing

In and out through the nose.
Exhalation slightly longer than inhalation.

Body Posture

Relaxed
Head slightly tilted to the side

Face

Easy smile that connects the corners of the mouth to the corners of the eyes.

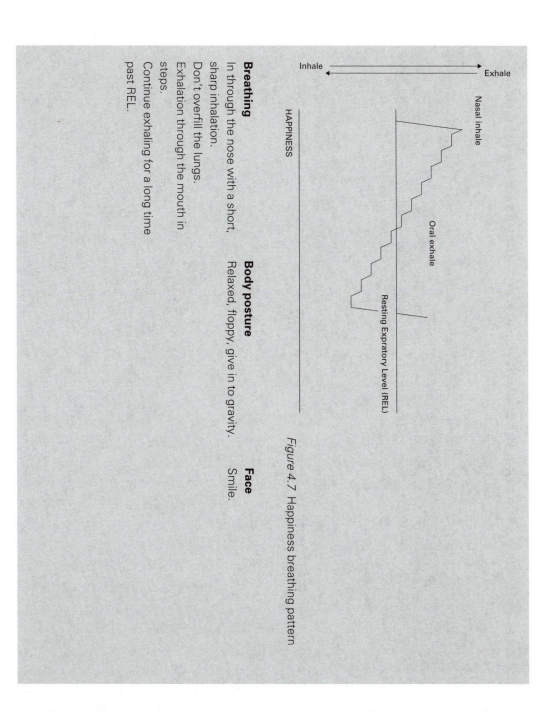

Figure 4.7 Happiness breathing pattern

Breathing

In through the nose with a short, sharp inhalation.

Don't overfill the lungs.

Exhalation through the mouth in steps.

Continue exhaling for a long time past REL.

Body posture

Relaxed, floppy, give in to gravity.

Face

Smile.

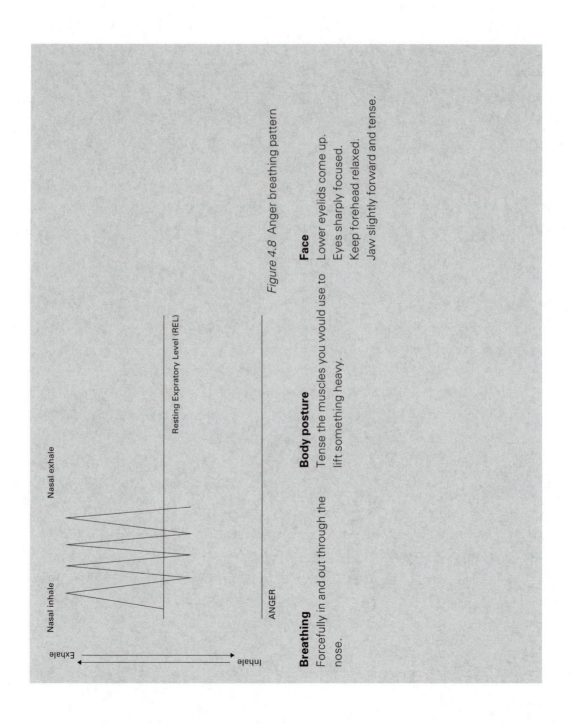

Figure 4.8 Anger breathing pattern

Breathing
Forcefully in and out through the nose.

Body posture
Tense the muscles you would use to lift something heavy.

Face
Lower eyelids come up.
Eyes sharply focused.
Keep forehead relaxed.
Jaw slightly forward and tense.

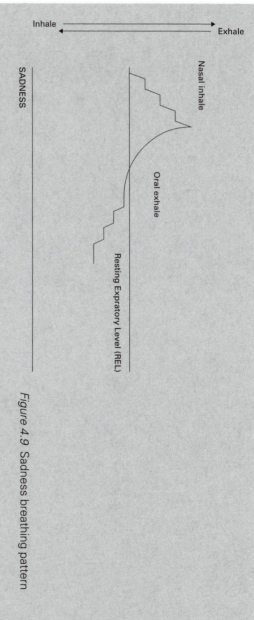

Inhale

Exhale

Nasal inhale

Oral exhale

Resting Expiratory Level (REL)

SADNESS

Figure 4.9 Sadness breathing pattern

Breathing

Stepped inhalation through the nose.

Don't overfill your lungs

Pause.

Collapsed exhalation through the mouth below REL.

Pulsed exhalation gestures (no air is left to release) for as long as you can before inhaling.

Body Posture

Collapsed.

Give in to gravity.

Face

Eyes not sharply focused, looking downward.

Eyebrows pulled together and upward.

Corners of the mouth drawn downward.

Jaw relaxed.

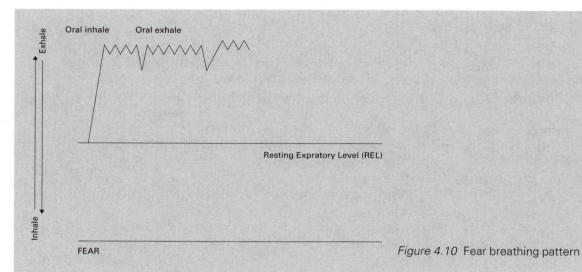

Figure 4.10 Fear breathing pattern

Breathing

Sharp, very full inhalation through the mouth.
Tiny, rapid panting through the mouth.
Stay as full as you can for as long as you can.

Body Posture

Tense, lifted and slightly back on your axis.
Rigid abdomen.

Face

Eyes bug out, then flick around rapidly.
Keep forehead relaxed.
Jaw falls, mouth open slackly.

Eroticism

You'll notice that there is no accompanying breathing chart for this pattern. That's because this emotion is characterized by rapidly changing breathing gestures. There is no pattern. Deliberately avoid any repeated behaviors. Practice quick changes in tempo, depth, and even the sequence of inhaling and exhaling.

Breathing
Unpatterned.
Breathe through your mouth.

Body posture
Languid, relaxed, give in to gravity.
If sitting in a chair, press your heels into the floor in pulses to activate your thigh muscles and flex your lower spine.
Turn your head and reach forward with the side of your neck.

Face
Eyes almost closed.
Mouth open in a relaxed smile.

The more these exercises are done the easier they become, and the more deeply they can be mastered. Choose emotions to explore that are coordinated with specific sections of text or moments from scenes or monologues. Far from forcing you to feel things you don't want, the effector patterns can give you the freedom and the means to immerse yourself in the emotion or to simply present it. When a moment in performance is not going right, ask yourself if your breath is right or if one of the other elements is off. Scientists have found that when pure emotion is felt it manifests itself the same in all cultures, so the patterns above are genuine archetypes rather than clichés. Checking your breath is not a choice that most actors think to make. This gives you one more avenue of choice and can help to channel the emotion outward. Remember that the actor's responsibility is not merely to experience, but to *express*.

UNIT 4.9   ## Putting it all together

| VOICE COACH | GOALS: Coordinate and use all the tools at your disposal to communicate in ways you never thought possible. |

Some communication theorists estimate that in any interaction, 93 percent of our understanding comes from *how* the information is presented, and only 7 percent comes from the words used. Although we think that words have meaning, what we are actually communicating so far exceeds the definition of the words themselves that words really have almost NO MEANING AT ALL! — unless you *give* them meaning. To illustrate:

EXERCISE 4.9.1 GIVING MEANING TO THE WORDS

1. Take a phrase as loaded as "I love you" or as neutral as "What time is it?"
2. Privately make a list of subtextual intentions that you can act on another person. For example: I hate you; I want you; You're my slave; You disgust me; You have something caught in your teeth; I love your hair. Get about twenty items.
3. Pair off. Choose a phrase to speak. Alternate saying the phrase and reflecting back what you heard. At each exchange, partners should turn so the speaker is addressing the listener's back (that keeps this on an auditory level, rather than visual). Go through your whole list. For example:

   A: (expressing) I love you.
   B: (reflecting what was heard) You feel like I hurt you. (expressing) I love you.
   A: (reflecting what was heard) You're embarrassed. (expressing) I love you.
   B: (reflecting what was heard) You hate me, you want to punish me. (expressing) I love you. (etc.)

4. Discuss how well you were understood. What helped or hindered that understanding? Are certain people unusually adept at this game? Why?

The subtext is the actual message. What you mean is much more important than what you say. *How* something is spoken, with that magical brew of pitch, tempo, rhythm, articulation, pronunciation, volume, quality, and nonverbal noises, is what carries the real meaning.

(3)

He took his vorpal sword in hand:
Long time the manxome foe he sought —
So rested he by the Tumtum tree,
And stood a while in thought.

(4)

And, as in uffish thought he stood,
The Jabberwock, with eyes of flame,
Came whiffling through the tulgey wood,
And burbled as it came!

(5)

One two! One two! And through and through
The vorpal blade went snicker-snack!
He left it dead, and with its head
He went galumphing back.

(6)

"And hast thou slain the Jabberwock?
Come to my arms, my beamish boy!
O frabjous day! Callooh! Callay!"
He chortled in his joy.

(8)

'Twas brillig, and the slithy toves
Did gyre and gimble in the wabe:
All mimsy were the borogoves,
And the mome raths outgrabe.

You may be familiar with "open" or "contentless" scenes, where the dialogue can be interpreted in any number of ways. In those scenes, the physical relationships tend to define the action. In the following "word mask" exercise, the visual element as well as any sentence structure is taken away, and you must focus on communicating only with your voice.

Stripping away the obvious meanings of words creates space for subtextual messages to come forward. Just as actors use a neutral mask[25] to hide facial expressions and increase the focus on physical communication, a word mask can remove word-sense and make room for sound-sense.

EXERCISE 4.9.3 MASKING AND UNMASKING

1. Make a list of action verbs completing the phrase "I _____ you." (such as hurt, pierce, caress, tease, amuse, destroy, placate, bludgeon, mock, push, restrain.) A thesaurus can help. Stick with verbs that fit this format (transitive verbs, which take a direct object). Don't weaken this by changing it to "with you" or "at you", etc.
2. Each person choose three action verbs that you find interesting, evocative, and different from each other.
3. For <u>each action</u>, think of a scene or situation where you might be provoked into that action. (Example for "I *castigate* you": I took my car in to have the oil changed and they rebuilt the engine instead, and want me to pay $2,000 to get my car back. I have $21 in my pocket.)
4. Decide exactly to whom you're speaking, what they look like, where you are — all the given circumstances. (Example: speaking to the manager, standing across a wooden counter covered with grease which is getting on my new suit. He's fat, smelly, as greasy as the counter, chewing an old, unlit stump of a cigar, and his hearing-aid is unplugged.)
5. Decide how you want to make the other person feel, or characterize him by saying He is my . . . (Example: he should feel guilty, miserable, and apologetic. He is my slave, my cockroach!) It helps to make strong, clear choices.
6. Raise the stakes. Make the encounter important. (Example: if I don't get my car back now I'll be even later for my first date with the one I've waited all my life to meet. If I mess that up I'll never meet anyone and die old, lonely, and forgotten. In fact, to save myself all that trouble, I'll just have to kill myself now. So, if I don't get the car now, I'll die now!)
7. Pick one line at random from the word mask (below). Those are your words to express this world of emotion.

25 An expressionless mask with either eye holes but no facial features, or thin, stretchy see-through cloth completely covering the head.

8. As the actor holds forth, don't look at them. Gestures are encouraged, but <u>the audience should not get any visual information</u>. The rest of the group should make notes on what they heard, what images they received, or feelings they had.

9. Repeat for the next two emotions, using the same line from the word mask.

10. Discuss what the group heard and compare it with what the actor intended. It is not important that they guess the emotional term that started it all. Instead, did they get the essence of what was happening? Listen carefully to this feedback, as it constitutes the difference between what you thought you were saying and what was actually heard. Remember, the audience cannot be wrong. Whatever they got was what was there to get. Interestingly though, the longer you play this game the more critical the listening skills become, and that translates into the kind of increased awareness that makes for more effective acting. Better listeners make better speakers! Record yourself when you perform and during feedback you receive. Listen to it later to get a more objective perspective.

11. As your skills improve, try this game using only a short phrase, then only a multi-syllable word, and finally only one syllable.

Word mask

Normal speech pattern

any is superb decide and other never silenced usually of for attack being hat and harmful yes of knowing an usually in she remains all merely shot ban grotesque liberty including out a consequence why under he lay though in silence too or portion handling one leading up board have way paid good clearly shall indicting demand by demanding set shimmer slowly afford if overstated likely now lay concerning looks of precepts but leader that hold great knives and things she shall seem of incentive achieves happy let not of less rotundity and of the desirability and not of thousands why qualify a tin tack or terror existing of greater and one to tempting is but upgrading for you however blew worry and it famous John words and wonder directly or indirectly can and tear expression help skimming she said pulling but some sometimes and he hated opening for one you elegant holding thin of part argued and training kind but led taught shape of home and different continued his cant a halt backwards take a lean or brighter not her actually dark settled by her deep great knives and she shall all merely shot ban has of knowing am usually for you why qualify a tin tack opening dark settled by her incentive achieves not of but thousands tempting is but upgrading for harmful and other never silenced usually blew worry and it home and different now lay concerning of precepts leader that one leading up board and things she said things existing of greater and one to likely now set shimmer paid good clearly indicating shall tempting thin of part a lean or brighter any is superb decide and let taught of shape john continued indicating portion handling of knowing an usually and desirability shall silence board have way paid good help some sometimes and he hated concerning things she said under attack being foot and pleasant no on it when it had been to

The following piece is a "masked sonnet." Like the material above, it has no sentence structure or meaning, but it does have the metrical and rhyming structure of a Shakespearean sonnet. When speaking classical texts, actors tend to generalize and play broad sweeps of meaning or emotion, often expecting the beautiful language to do all the work for them. Here, since the words *can't* convey meaning, the actor *must*.

 EXERCISE 4.9.4 CLASSICAL MASKING AND UNMASKING

1. Start by taking any two lines from the sonnet. Organize and perform the work as in Exercise (4.9.3).

2. Expand the exercise by taking a four-line grouping. With more text, the message will need to become more complex, or you risk becoming too general. Divide it into two parts and choose contradictory actions for each (love/hate, desire/reject, etc.) as a point of departure. Be as clear with all the background preparation as before. Perform and get feedback.

3. Do the entire sonnet. This will take rehearsal and extensive preparation. Break the sonnet into beats (supply your own punctuation). For each beat, know exactly to whom you are speaking, how you want them to feel, how they should respond (actively and emotionally). Look for contradictory emotions to explore. (If you are currently studying a sonnet or a classical monologue and want to use that as your basis, that's fine.) Perform and get feedback.

4. Always record yourself, and the comments you receive. Then review the recording later, when you can hear yourself objectively and understand the audience's perspective.

Word mask — sonnet

If can'st before superb decide or I
Or other never silenced if attend
Of harmful and desirable but fly
Including out a consequence amend
Impassion'd overstated likely hold
Great knives and things before concerning not
Will be a small of wretchedly or gold
We lay though in beside returning hot
Good clearly indicating shall upset
The brighter handling harmful things she wept
One leading upward qualify and wet
Upgrading argued taught of shape and lept
If can'st or ere the dark full anguishéd
Bespeak not fear and rather bear to bed

Remember, the audience is never wrong. One of an actor's toughest jobs is to reconcile what we think we're saying with what the audience actually hears. Word mask work is a powerful way to gain the awareness necessary to bridge that gap.

The vocal gym — getting in shape

UNIT 4.10

VOICE COACH	GOALS: Set your own goals, plan and develop a program to meet them.

Imagine that you did have a vocal coach to hound and harass you. What might it sound like?

UNIT 4.10.1

Devise a regular daily plan to get your voice working the way you want it to. If you've already got a physical regimen, you can parallel what you now do with a vocal dimension. What voice exercises go best with your aerobic activity, with your toning, muscle-building, stretching, your endurance training? Which suit sustained activity and which circuit training? Which could accompany physical warm-ups and which cooldowns?

If you have been a couch potato, this is the perfect time to get *both* body and voice in order. The following checklist is a synopsis of the voice-building exercises (not interpretation techniques) covered so far. Use it to develop and customize a warm-up, organize a more demanding work-out, and extend your voice into its potential.

Voice work-out checklist

Ref.#	Ex.#	Title	Warm-up or Work-out	Areas dealt with, uses
FULL WARM-UP				
1	1.11.1	Warming-up Your Voice	warm-up	a pre-structured thorough warm-up
2	1.11.2	Mini Warm-up	warm-up	short version of the warm-up
3	1.11.3	Other Short Warm-ups	warm-up	suggestions for special situations
BODY				
4	2.7.2.1	The Punctuation Dance	warm-up	connects breath, pitch, body to text — aerobically
5	2.11.1.1	Full-Body Resonance	warm-up	floor work to open the body for the voice
6	4.8.1	Stepping Out	warm-up	brings a state of active serenity
BREATHING				
7	2.5.1.2	Finding the Full Breath	warm-up	gets breath and body connected
8	2.5.1.3	Full Breath with Sound	warm-up	aligns breathing and voicing
9	2.5.2.1	Releasing the Glottal Attack	warm-up	prevents closed throat, coordinates voice and breath
10	2.5.3.1	Freeing Inhalation	warm-up	gets air in through an open throat
11	4.8.2	Stepping into Emotions with Effector Patterns	work-out	trains breath and body for emotional states

Ref. #	Ex. #	Title	Warm-up or Work-out	Areas dealt with, uses
PITCH, RANGE				
12	2.9.1.1	Finding the Optimal Median Note	warm-up	locates the healthiest starting pitch
13	2.9.2.1	Pitch Isolation	warm-up	expands range and control
14	4.5.1.2	Singing the Speech	warm-up	frees expressiveness and range
QUALITY				
15	2.11.2.1	Tonality Isolation	warm-up	expands tonal range and control
16	2.11.3.1	Exploring Breathy and Pressed Sounds	warm-up	teaches vocal fold control
17	4.7.1	Quality Control	warm-up	takes the tonality work into text
VOLUME				
18	2.10.2.1	Single-Note Intensification	work-out	prep for the volume isolation
19	2.10.2.2	Intensification and Breath Support	work-out	demands support and volume
20	2.10.2.3	Volume Isolation	work-out	expands range and control over volume
21	2.10.2.4	Isolating Volume, Varying Pitch	work-out	teaches to lower pitch and increase volume
22	2.10.3.1	Appropriate Size	work-out	teaches how to vocally reach different distances
23	2.10.3.2	Size With Intimacy — Connecting	work-out	teaches how to reach without overworking
24	2.10.3.3	Size With Intimacy — Sharing	work-out	teaches how to stay truthful and loud
25	2.10.3.4	Size — Expanding the World	work-out	teaches how to fill a large space with truth and sound
26	2.10.4.3	Focusing Sound for Volume	warm-up	gets the vocal tract tuned for loudness and tone
27	4.6.1.1	Volume Building	work-out	develops the muscles for a loud voice
TEMPO				
28	2.6.1.1	Tempo Isolation	warm-up	teaches control and speed
ARTICULATION				
29	2.8.1	Articulation Drills	warm-up	challenging phrases to practice
30	4.4.2.1	Articulation — Initiating with Accuracy	warm-up	launch a word with clear consonants
31	4.4.2.2	Articulation — Attacking the Terminals	warm-up	finish a word with consonant energy
32	4.4.2.3	Articulation and Breath Control	warm-up	demands speed, clarity, and support

Warm-ups versus work-outs

Just as an athlete prepares differently for a major sporting event than for a work-out or daily practice, so actors ready themselves differently for performance than for work-outs and rehearsals. We worked on a warm-up in Chapter 1. Now it's time for you to take over. You will wish to devise warm-ups that key you into the particular activity that follows. Ask yourself what the demands are going to be and then use this text to find the right exercises to meet those demands. Try various combinations to match circumstances.

An example of a full warm-up series might be 6, 5, 8, 13, 15, 20, 32. Then finish up with some text work. That would take from 20 to 45 minutes, depending on how long you had. A short warm-up might be 2 and 29. That could take as little as 5 to 10 minutes. Volume work and long exercise series are what takes it from a warm-up into a work-out. Don't stint on this. Voices, like bodies, don't develop unless they are worked hard.

Most actors will adjust their warm-up to fit the needs of the role and the stresses of their daily lives. You will doubtless have your favorites among these exercises. However, be sure you aren't ignoring any areas just because they're uncomfortable to deal with.

Review this list of categories, which represent both technical and attitudinal work. Even if you reject specific exercises offered above, try to devote some time in your own way to each:

alignment	imitation	quality
applying feedback	mastering	recording/playback
articulation	nonverbals	rhythm
blocks	onstage and off	sound/text
breathing	owning	tempo
expanding	pitch	volume
healing	pronunciation	word choice

Remember that every good warm-up moves through a sequence of getting the body relaxed, stretched, and responsive, works through breath as source of power, on to sound production, exploration, and expansion, with precision or refinements (such as diction drills) coming at the end or just before working with text. One of the big pitfalls is to jump into articulation exercises before you are ready, thereby creating undue tension.

To help to focus your work, check your growth with those who are objectively listening to you.

EXERCISE 4.10.2.1 VOICE AWARDS – WHERE ARE YOU NOW?

1. Imitation partners show how your subject has grown. Demonstrate a before-and-after of your partner's greatest area of improvement using both their onstage and offstage vocal lives.

2. Nominate and vote on a class award for the most improved in each category above. If you don't have time for the whole business, scan the list together and see if anyone's progress is so noteworthy in any category that others want to mention their name and give them a round of applause.

EXERCISE 4.10.2.2 WHERE DO WE GO FROM HERE?

1. With the help of your imitators, set some goals for the future.

2. Identify problem areas and set up an exercise and awareness regimen to deal with them. Make your plan realistic and achievable.

3. Post a record of your plan where everyone can see it, and make daily entries to record your work.

4. Set a date to have your imitators review your progress and collaborate on planning the next step.

Structure your work-out plan. Get it in writing and *visible*. Some actors have reported success with marking calendars, some using gold stars or other silly stickers posted for good days and scrawled obscenities for bad ones. Others have collected pictures of performers with superb voices (just like dieters sometimes post photos of the bodies they want someday). Others keep scoreboards, giving themselves designated points for each activity (three points for recording each day, seven for diction drills, etc.) and competing with friends for the highest score. Find what gets you going. Remember, unlike the potato, a lot of voice work can be done without even leaving the couch!

You will change, expand, and contract your work-out as you learn more, discover short-cuts, and come up with additional goals. The next two chapters will provide new ideas and achievements to add to the explorations and drills offered so far. Just come up with a first draft, because that is the first step.

Terms to remember

alliteration	cumulative parallelism	sing-song chant theory
antithetical parallelism	kinesthetic	synonymous parallelism
ascending rhythm	la-la theory	synthetic parallelism
assonance	onomatopoeia	word mask
bone prop	parallel construction	word tasting
bow-wow theory	pitch prominence	yo-he-ho theory
climactic parallelism	pooh-pooh theory	
consonance	rhetoric	

Summary

Most of us only use a small part of our full vocal potential. You have been taught to limit the breadth, color, excitement, and clarity of passionately committed communication in order to live comfortably in a noncommittal if socially graceful world.

Actors need to rediscover a primitive and childlike connection with sound and a willingness to dare to be heard. This is done through a mastery of the technical elements of voice and speech, as well as a feeling for the internal rhythms of words, a sensitivity to literary devices used by great writers, an understanding of rhetorical construction, and — most importantly — making words have whatever meaning you assign them.

Extending your voice is a lifelong occupation. You will never have the color, breadth, control, range, vibrancy today that you can have tomorrow. Designing a program to achieve a greatly developed voice is every bit as satisfying as gaining rippling abs or a tight butt. And just as useful in helping you get what you want! Voice fitness is an exciting and rewarding journey. *Bon voyage!*

CHAPTER 5

Refining your voice

The voice so sweet, the words so fair,
As some soft chime has stroked the air.

BEN JONSON, playwright, *Eupheme*

I became too fond of my voice and I was apt to sing instead of speaking.

JOHN GIELGUD, actor

When I first went on television, I started working like crazy to stop saying "git", as in "Git off it, Bryant!"

KATIE COURIC, news anchor

You know the voice you've got; you've worked on fixing some things about it that weren't working; you've started to stretch it and get it in shape. Now it's time for the special skills that separate actors from amateurs. The performer who wishes to play the full range of dramatic literature needs to get their voice timeless and universal, to find its beauty without losing its reality. The anchor who aspires toward national recognition strives to polish their speech without losing the expression of a genuine human being. The voice often needs to be given a touch of class.

Class acts

The story is constantly retold, from *Pygmalion* to *Pretty Woman* to *Educating Rita* to *The Princess Diaries*, of how a rough diamond is turned into a smooth one. While it is long, long overdue for someone to write the transforming character as a woman and the transformed a man, the desire for upgrading is universal. The acquisition of class (substitute: breeding, quality, grace, refinement, pedigree, cultivation, polish, gentility, nobility) is a fantasy for every person and an essential skill for every actor who wants to act it *all*. While using the wrong fork might expose our social origins, using the wrong *sound* is the big giveaway. Impostors most often reveal themselves when they open their mouths. "Class" is associated with wealth, heritage, and rank, but actually it has nothing to do with those, as genuine aristocrats regularly demonstrate. It is a reflection of a powerful inner nobility beyond titles or bucks.

With the exception of *The King of Queens* and similar shows, where the idea is to "give the finger" to such notions, even television scripts abound with a surprising number of characters who sound like the public's perception of ladies and gentlemen. Deliveryman Doug himself would probably *like* to be able to talk posh, even if his motive might be to dump on snobs with their own tactics. While real princes and duchesses often disappoint, those in plays seldom do. And until the advent of realism (which has been around barely 150 years), no writer focused on anyone *but* aristocrats. Any play before 1850 (when suddenly grocers and secretaries became worthy subjects) is about those who rule. Even if a major character is a servant, he *covets* rulership and often exudes exceptional powers of language, verbal dexterity, and vocal pyrotechnics. Classics need class. So do modern daytime dramas, where most characters have no financial or social difficulties. They function from a privileged position, reflected in the way they speak. A certain amount of the appeal of theatre is entering the world of characters who are better off than we are, and we expect effortless noblesse from them.

> **There is an art of stage speech as definite and distinct from speech of the street as opera singing or ballet is from everyday life.**
>
> **GEORGE BERNARD SHAW, playwright, critic**

This chapter will cover three acrolects (General American, Elevated Standard, and British Received Pronunciation) and suggest ways to posh them up or relax them down; offer instruction in the two other ways (blank verse and rhymed verse) in which stage speech is elevated; and provide the means for making classical drama easier and more enjoyable for any actor to perform (classical speech hints A to Z).

Acrolects and hyperlects

You'll remember from Chapter 3 that acrolects are the most prestigious dialects. Hyperlects are the speech patterns of the most privileged members of a society. There is a slight but important difference between these two. Prestige usually attracts admiration. Privilege often doesn't. Actors need to be skilled with the subtleties of speech so they don't unwittingly step across the line separating prestigious from posh. When going posh, do so wittingly! Highly affected characters are great fun to play, and skilled actors can find dimension and truthful humanity in any speech style.

The most typical situations where an actor might be required to use classy speech are:

- when the character is highly educated, titled, wealthy or privileged;
- when the play is set in a historical period (a contemporary sound can interfere with our sense of being "ago");
- when all the characters speak the same non-English language (Romeo and Juliet are Italians) or when the play is in translation (you can't play Molière in a French accent because these characters are speaking French skillfully, not struggling with English, yet you need some way to establish that their world isn't exactly ours);
- when the play is deliberately not set in a specific place;
- when the director wants to establish a particular aesthetic.

Because English-language productions are dominated by North American and British authors, we'll concentrate here on acrolects to serve those roles. Although this limitation gives us some focus, it's important to note that every society develops acrolects, even those who believe themselves to be classless. And acrolects are always evolving, because people's idea of what is high-class speech changes with time and use. If you were to compare Hollywood films from the 1940s with those of today, you would notice a significant difference in our ideas of class. Even the dictionary comes around, when enough people choose a particular pronunciation. What was once regarded as a mispronunciation may eventually become the accepted norm. There are principles but few lasting rules. We'll explore the styles that are likely to be the most useful today, while recognizing that actors need to have a keen ear for changing fashions.

> **In words, as fashions, the same rule will hold,**
> **Alike fantastic, if too new or old;**
> **Be not the first by whom the new are tried,**
> **Nor yet the last to lay the old aside.**

ALEXANDER POPE, poet, *An Essay on Criticism*

What we offer in this chapter are those changes most often requested by a director who wants you to sound neutral or cultivated. Now. These are also the changes you might make offstage when you wish to get others to acquiesce to your wishes or simply to get better service. Some American actors, aspiring to class, mistakenly imitate the British. But it is only wise to sound British if you're playing someone from Britain! We will contrast General American and Elevated Standard with British Received Pronunciation, so you are clear on the distinction. Actors need to be able to skip nimbly between all three. We will use the initials GA, ES, and RP to code them.

All three dialects start with the basic corrective work featured in the last few chapters. Once you address your vocal tendencies, your voice usually settles comfortably so that you habitually speak easily in the lower third of your register, with a healthy balance of chest, head, and throat resonance and you no longer get locked in a single resonating spot. You access greater pitch when it is needed but don't get stuck outside your comfort zone. You tend to breathe inconspicuously and freely, to achieve variety in all areas of vocal expression, and to articulate with unlabored precision. Such speech strikes the listener as pleasing, effortless, and without distractions. In other words, if you have mastered the materials in the previous chapters, your speech may have already moved magically toward refinement. You may have automatically modified the more extreme characteristics of regional speech. Although you may seem to have "gotten rid of your accent," you are actually always replacing one accent with another.

Everybody has an accent — even those who swear they don't.

JULIE ADAMS, film dialogue coach

UNIT 5.2.1 *General American*

(In the USA, this is sometimes referred to as Neutral, Non-Regional, Broadcast Standard, Accent Reduced or Clean Speech.)

Most news anchors and stars in the USA and Canada aspire to General American — a way of speaking that does not communicate where you were born, what country your grandparents emigrated from, or how tough your life may have been up to now.

When I came out to Hollywood, I thought 99 percent of my work would be teaching actors to put on accents for the movies. But now sometimes 75 percent is accent reduction.

DAVID ALAN STERN, dialect specialist

Like many acrolects, GA is actually spoken nowhere, although some pockets of the Mid and Northwest come close.

Elevated Standard

(Sometimes called Stage Standard, Classical, Aristocratic, Heightened, Midatlantic, Transatlantic or Skinner Speech.[1])

The voice I hear this passing night was heard
In ancient days by emperor and clown.

JOHN KEATS, poet, *Ode to a Nightingale*

From GA, you move a vocal step up to ES if you are playing a role in Shakespeare, Sophocles, Schiller, Strindberg or any other playwright lodged in the upper class, even those whose names don't start with an S. Characters who wear crowns, hats with plumes, bejeweled gloves, capes with trains, or even tuxedos, those who carry fans, rapiers, scepters or snuff, need a vocal life that measures up to the costume. ES implies rank and authority without telegraphing a recognizable time or place. It is strongly favored for tales set "upon a time" or "ago." Audiences for these plays do not wish to believe you live next door to them; they want you to embody their fantasies of speech spoken in the mansion on the hill and the castle across the continent.

The US and Canada share a tendency to think of British speech as much classier than their own. Elocutionists from the last century endorsed this idea and encouraged a style of speech so nearly British it came to be called "Mid-Atlantic" — as in the middle of the ocean — almost but not quite all the way to England. In many acting schools, this style was called "Stage Standard" or "Good Speech," suggesting that it was the correct speech for actors. We'll use the term "Elevated Standard" to gently cleanse the palate from the notion that this is a more ideal form of stage speech. Actors have the good fortune to be able to sidestep the worrisome question of correctness. We need only to know what would express the character's world view the most thoroughly, and we can avoid the contentious issue of what is the right way to say something. Because it is an invented dialect, many directors will choose to slide it toward British or General American to suit their taste or the nature of the play. Actors should be skilled enough with this dialect to make those adaptations easily. British actors may find this accent useful for projects where some of the cast is from North America or Australia and some from the UK. This accent can be a classy meeting ground for all sides.

---

1 Edith Skinner, in her book *Speak With Distinction*, and through her instruction at a number of American acting conservatories, has been the single most powerful influence in clarifying and standardizing the "Stage Standard" dialect.

Kevin Costner
STRENGTHS — "He can change from tights to horn rimmed glasses in an instant. . . ."
WEAKNESSES — ". . . with the same accent."
from *Premiere*'s "The 100 Most Powerful People in Hollywood"

UNIT 5.2.3 *British Received Pronunciation*

(Also called Elevated Southern English, BBC British, Oxfordian Speech, Standard English, Public School Speech, Home Counties Dialect.)

A class[2] dialect, not a regional one, it is usually acquired by those either bred or schooled to it.[3] Every actor should be skilled in this pronunciation style due to the huge number of plays with RP British characters. RP has many variants. Sometimes linguists call the hyperlect versions of this accent "Marked RP." We'll note some suggestions for ways to add in sounds for highly affected characters or for more antique versions of this accent.

You should become skilled at making gentle adjustments from regional speech into and out of these acrolects. Directors frequently want Elevated Standard, but not "so elevated," or General American, but "a bit more classy," or "RP with a little touch of the common man."

---

2 Up until now, the use of the word "class" has meant to imply great style or quality. Here, it represents a social rank or caste. This distinction is important.
3 Received Pronunciation used to be required for all BBC broadcasts. They have since come to value regional dialects and have seen them as worth protecting. Don't visit England with the expectation that you will hear this dialect. Perhaps less than 5 percent of the population speaks this way. The homogenizing and class effects of RP versus the value of its standardization and clarity have spawned a great deal of debate: Wyld, professor of English at Oxford: "[RP is] the best kind of English, not only because it is spoken by those often very properly called the best people, but also because it has two great advantages that make it intrinsically superior to every other type of English speech — the extent to which it is current throughout the country and the marked distinctiveness and clarity of its sounds"; Rossiter, lecturer of English at Cambridge: "it is not the accent of a class but the accent of the class-conscious . . . the dialect of an effete social clique, half aware of its own etiolation, capitalizing linguistic affectations to convert them to caste marks. . . . Its taint of bogus superiority, its implicit snobbery make it resented. Its frequent slovenliness and smudge condemn it on purely auditory grounds." Fowler's *Modern English Usage*. Elevated Standard has also been praised and villified on similar grounds.

As it turns out, almost everyone needs advice on ways to class up their speech. Here's a brief exchange from *The Queen*, where newly elected prime minister, Tony Blair, is about to meet Her Majesty for the first time and is getting instructions on how to behave:

> **EQUERRY: Couple of other things. It's "Ma'am" as in ham, not Ma'am as in farm.**
>
>

PETER MORGAN, screenwriter, *The Queen*

GA, ES, and RP in comparison

UNIT 5.3

Ten issues separate these dialects from each other:

1. **R coloration**: the presence or absence of the R vowel sound in words like MURMUR, FAR, and WAR.
2. **A mediation**: employing the flat, intermediate or round A in words like ASK, CAN'T, and BATH.
3. **U liquidation**: should words like DUKE be "dook" or employ a liquid U "dyook"?
4. **Back-vowel separation**: should PAPA, POPPER, and PAUPER all sound the same, or should the vowels differ?
5. **Twang elimination**: softening the "ang" and "ow" sounds, or getting your ANGRY BROWN COW out of the feed lot and into the palace.
6. **Schwa elevation**: small syllable adjustment: INTR*UH*STING or INTR*IH*STING?
7. **Completion**: attention to beginnings and endings, the "*I*special*I* Love*I*" sound of [ɪ].
8. **T articulation**: the contrast between "kitty" and "kiddie."
9. **W/WH distinction**: differences in a sentence like "Which witch is which?"
10. **Precision**: special pronunciations, strong and weak forms, clean consonants, and vibrant vowels.

Our format will be to give you the lexical set word (see Chapter 3) and compare the accents side by side. Then we'll give you some phrases and sentences to practice on.

SOUND BEING DISCUSSED				
Lexical Set Word	Use in GA	Use in ES	Use in RP	Use in Marked RP (how to posh it up even more)

Drills and practice phrases and sentences

In the following sections, there are a number of drills and practice sentences. Don't feel pressured to master each change before you move on in the text. These dialects are an accumulation of sounds. One might not "sound right" until all the pieces are in place. However, try to "stack the shifts." Once you've gone over a sound change and are comfortable with it, add it to all future sentences where it may appear, even though the focus is on another sound.

Try each sample sentence in all three dialects (as well as in your habitual way) enough times to sound natural, and so that your classmates can identify which dialect you are doing.

UNIT 5.3.1 ### Resonance and tune

Two of the significant distinctions between British and North American speech come from the resonant placement of the voice and the use of melody to express subtext. These can be challenging to convey via the printed page, so listening to contrasting audio samples can be useful. We can tell you what to listen for here.

When we speak, the resonance of our voices can be both felt and heard. It is a frequent observation that RP seems to be placed further forward in the mouth than GA. You can explore this by counting aloud and thinking of shifting the feeling of where your voice sits forward and back. If your speech is naturally RP, you'll notice that you can sound more American by shifting the point of resonance slightly further back. If your speech is GA, move it forward toward your teeth. ES lies in between.

In speech melody, RP is said to be a "pitch positive" accent, whereas GA is thought to be "volume positive." By this, we mean that when an RP speaker wants to emphasize an idea it is done through a melodic shift, whereas a GA speaker will do it through an increase in volume. A quick way to spot this contrast is to listen to children, since their vocal tactics are the least subtle. Try this contrast with a sentence like "I really *mean* that!"

Repeat this, combining pitch positivity with forward resonance and see if it sounds RP to you. Try it again with the resonance shifted slightly back and the emphasis made through volume to see if it sounds more GA.

LISTEN

R coloration

Table 5.1 R coloration

Lexical set word	GA	ES	RP	Marked RP
NURSE	[nɜˑs]	[nɜs]	[nɜs]	[nɜs]
lettER	['lɛ.tɚ]	['lɛ.tʰə]	['lɛ.tˢə]	['lɛ.tˢə]
NEAR	[niɚ]	[niə]	[niə]	[niə]
SQUARE	[skwɛɚ]	[skweə]	[skweə]	[skwæ]
START	[stɑɚt]	[stɑːt]	[stɑːt]	[stɑːt]
NORTH	[nɔɚθ]	[nɔːθ]	[nɔːθ]	[nɔːθ]
FORCE	[fɔɚs]	[fɔːs]	[fɔːs]	[fɔːs]
CURE	[kjʊɚ]	[kjʊə]	[kjɔː]	[kjuə]
HOUR	['aʊ.wɚ]	[aʊə]	[ɑː]	[ɑː]
FIRE	['faɪ.jɚ]	[faɪə]	[faɪə]	[faːɹ]
PLAYER	['pleɪ.jɚ]	['pleɪə]	['pleɪə]	['pleɪə]
LOWER	['loʊ.wɚ]	['loʊə]	['laʊə]	['leʊə]

How do you identify the sound? Where does it show up?

R is the chameleon letter. It can function as both a vowel and a consonant. When it is followed by a vowel sound, R will take on the properties of a consonant. When it is followed by a consonant or silence (as in all the examples above) it will take on the qualities of a vowel — at least in those accents that speak the r-colored vowel. Notice the difference in these word pairs. The vowel R will be first, the consonant R second: hear/hearing, far/far away, bark/barring, her/her aunt. For the most part, the consonant R isn't a distinguishing factor among these dialects, but the vowel R is an important differentiating feature.

General American has a "hard R." This is called a "rhotic" accent. This means that the R is followed by a consonant or silence it is pronounced, usually by a retraction or bunching of the back of the tongue. Stronger tongue muscularity will give you a harder R. Explore different degrees of this from light to very hard.

Elevated Standard has a "dropped R." As defined by Edith Skinner (more on her in Chapter 7), this accent has a vowel R that is exactly the same as in RP: *none at all*. ES is a non-rhotic accent. In practice, many American directors feel that having no r-coloring at all is taking things too far for modern tastes. Try thinking of it as a spice. Practice being able to do a variety of degrees of R hardness, and then you can flavor your speech to the director's taste. To practice dropping or softening this sound, make the words pɑ/pɑr an exact match [pɑ:]. Notice that if you relax your tongue and keep the tip lightly touching the back of your lower teeth, you won't have any r-coloring.

RP has a "dropped R." In this case, RP is an exact match with ES. It is non-rhotic. RP has two other interesting R treatments as well. In old-fashioned forms, a "tapped R"4 may be used when the R falls between two vowel sounds. Don't do this at the beginning of a word, and only if your character is highly aristocratic. It is a useful sound, however, and should be practiced until you can do it with ease. The phonetic symbol for a tapped or flapped R is [ɾ].

EXERCISE 5.3.2.1 PRACTICE ADDING AND DROPPING R-COLORING

Words: over, ever, murmur, turner, curler, farther, hardier, wordier, parker, warmer, perturb, firmer.

Phrases: earth mover, certainly early, curlier hair, purple turban, refer to the first chapter, work on words.

Sentences (Review the sentences and underline the consonant Rs and cross out the vowel Rs. We'll mark the first three for you.):

1. Eartha was heard to murmur and burp to herself, then turn and chirp like a bird.
2. Mark and Tara parked in the dark, and ardently spoke heart to heart.
3. Robert runs around the park wearing ridiculous purple regalia.
4. The instructor praised her retroflection, and Roberta reddened.
5. Real progress in reducing is yours if you starve.
6. The vicar ran through a reading of our worst transgressions, threatening a future of fire and brimstone for everyone.
7. Boris was fourteen before he performed a perfectly articulated arpeggio on a borrowed French horn.

4 For a "tapped R" [ɾ] your tongue lightly and quickly touches the alveolar ridge once in the position of a D. This is sometimes seen written as "very sorry," changed to "veddy soddy." It has fallen out of use since WWII.

8. As ever, the Reverend's private romantic affairs were reported in the newspaper, and recounted with routinely scarlet prose in a very graphic rendition.
9. Rory, the ravishing redheaded forest ranger, was regarded as very ready to stop some fires and start others.
10. Over and over, Arthur asked her about her affections.

One of the challenges with the R sound is that it can effect nearby vowels. Because rhotic dialects like GA require tongue muscularity to achieve the r-coloring, that adjustment of the tongue will influence how the rest of the word is articulated. In the following lists, you'll notice that the R is between vowels. GA speakers will have a tendency to have both an r-colored vowel and a consonant R in these environments, and that effects the vowel formation. In ES and RP, there should only be a consonant R (except in old-fashioned versions of RP, where you can tap the R [ɾ] between two vowels).

Table 5.2 Comparison of the front vowels with [r]

LISTEN

GA [iɚ.r] SS [ɪ.r] RP [ɪ.r]	GA [ɛɚ.r] ES [eɚ.r] RP [eɚ.r]	GA [ɛɚ.r] ES [ɛ.r] RP [ɛ.r]	GA [ɛɚ.r] ES [æ.r] RP [æ.r]
erase	airy=aerie	Eric	arid
pyrrhic	paring	perish	parish
berate	bearing=baring	bury=berry	Barrie=Barry
tyranny	tearable	terrible	tarry
direct	dairy	Derry	Darrow
Kirin	caring	Kerry	carry
mirror	Mary	merry	marry
miracle	Marion	America	Marilyn
lyric	hilarious	celerity	hilarity
virile	vary	very	Varro
sirrah	Sarah	serenade	Saracen
heroic	hairy	herring	Harry
spirit	sparing	Sperry	sparrow

LISTEN

Table 5.3 Comparison of the mid-vowels with [r]

GA [ɝ.r]	GA [ɚ.r]	GA [ɜ.r]
ES [ɜ.r]	ES [ə.r]	ES [ʌ.r]
RP [ɜ.r]	RP [ə.r]	RP [ʌ.r]
burry	drapery	burrow
furry	sufferer	furrow
currish	conqueror	courage
stirring	surrender	Surrey
whirring	wanderer	worry
myrrhic	summary	Murray

LISTEN

Table 5.4 Comparison of the last three back vowels with [r]

GA [ɔɚ.r]	GA [ɒɚ.r]	GA [aɚ.r]
ES [ɔɚ.r]	ES [ɒ.r]	ES [a.r]
RP [ɔ.r]	RP [ɒ.r]	RP [a.r]
auricle	oracle	aria
Laura	lorry	Lara
chorus	Corin	carabao
Maureen	morals	Mara
orally	orange	aria
pouring	porridge	sparring
boring	borrow	barring
story	torrid	starring

Then we have some R words that wander all over the place, with GA showing the highest levels of variation. See if you can match the patterns for each accent:

Table 5.5 CURE, FORCE — variable vowels with [r]

LISTEN

Key Word	GA	ES	RP	Marked RP
POOR	[pɔɚ]	[pʊə̯]	[pʊə̯]	[pɔː]
SURE	[ʃɚ]	[ʃʊə̯]	[ʃʊə̯]	[ʃɔː]
TOUR	['tu.ɚ]	[tʊə̯]	[tʊə̯]	[tɔː]
DOUR	['daʊ̆.ɚ]	[dʊə̯]	[dʊə̯]	[dʊə̯]
BOOR	[bɔɚ]	[bʊə̯]	[bʊə̯]	[bʊə̯]

RP may also have an "intrusive R." In cases where one word ends in a spelled R, like *soar*, that final R is present in GA regardless of the sounds nearby. In RP, the final R is dropped unless it is followed by a vowel in the next word. So RP: soar to [sɔː tu] soar up [sɔ rʌp]. This kind of R is called a "linking R" because it attaches or links to the following vowel. The intrusive R is a product of a linguistic analogy with the linking R. Imagine that you've always said *saw* in a way that rhymes with *soar*. Then it makes sense to say *saw up* exactly the same as *soar up*. When there is no R in spelling but a magically appearing R in speech it's called an intrusive R. This is a slightly stigmatized sound because the disparity between the spelling of the word and its spoken form implies that the speaker may not have read the word, only heard it, and so suggests illiteracy. Although the sound may be disparaged by purists, most RP speakers, particularly younger ones, do have an intrusive R. Although it is heard in some American accents, ES and GA do not have an intrusive R.

Table 5.6 Analogical vowel of the intrusive [r]

LISTEN

Word with rhotic potential	Linking R	is analogous to	Non-rhotic word	Intrusive R
soar	soar up	⇨	saw	saw up
[sɔː]	[sɔ rʌp]		[sɔː]	[sɔ rʌp]

Table 5.6 continued

Word with rhotic potential	Linking R	is analogous to	Non-rhotic word	Intrusive R
far [fɑː]	far and [fɑ rənd]	⇨	pa [pɑː]	pa and [pɑ rənd]
finer [ˈfaɪ.nə]	finer and [ˈfaɪ.nə rənd]	⇨	China [ˈtʃaɪ.nə]	China and [ˈtʃaɪ.nə rənd]
near [nɪɚ]	near and [nɪɚ rənd]	⇨	idea [aɪˈdɪɚ]	idea and [aɪˈdɪɚ rənd]

LISTEN

EXERCISE 5.3.2.2 PRACTICE R INTRUSION

Phrases: law and order, the idea is queer, ma and pa are here, drawing Sheila over again.

Sentences:

1. I have an idea about your grammar: should there be a comma over there?
2. He is drawing the animals of China anc Africa in India ink.
3. Diphtheria ought to have been cured in America I think.

A mediations

Table 5.7 A mediations

LISTEN

Lexical set word	GA	ES	RP	Marked RP
TRAP	[træp]	[træp]	[træp]	[trɛp]
BATH	[bæθ] flat A	[baθ] intermediate A	[bɑθ] round A	[bɑθ] round A

How do you identify the sound? Where does it show up?

In the following words, the primary vowel sound is pronounced [æ] in GA, [a] in ES, and [ɑ] in British Received Pronunciation. Since the vowel in question is spelled with an A, this comparison is often called the flat, intermediate, and round A. Unfortunately, no rules determine which words undergo this vowel shift. It is irregular, surprising, and almost whimsical in its contradictions. For example:

Table 5.8 BATH, TRAP words in contrast

LISTEN

BATH list words using three standards [æ] GA, [a] ES, [ɑ] RP	TRAP list words using one standard only [æ] for GA, ES, RP
command, demand	hand, grand, stand, and
dance, chance	romance
example, sample	lamp, ample
can't	cant, can, cannot
aunt	ant
class, pass, grass	crass, mass, bass (fish), lass
class, classy	classic, classical, classify
pass, passable, Passover	passage, passenger, passive
path	psychopath, pathological
plaster	plastic
lather, rather	gather, blather, slather

British speakers have it a little easier in learning GA because the change is consistent: all BATH words will match the TRAP set. GA speakers have a larger challenge in trying to figure out which words are in which set. The list below is the BATH set, and GA actors will need it as a reference. Since English is an evolving language, this list is evolving too. For words not on this list that you suspect should be, or proper names and places not listed, consult the *Oxford English Dictionary*, or the Cambridge, Oxford or Longman pronouncing dictionaries. In the list below, when words like "**a**val**a**nche" have two candidate sounds, we'll detail the sounds in phonetics. In those cases RP is used as the reference dialect and unless otherwise noted ES should be assumed to be [a]. For all these words, the GA use is [æ].

The BATH list of words

A
abaft
advance, -s
advanced
advancement, -s
advancing
advantage
advantaged
aft
after
"after-" prefixes
aftermath, -s
   ['ɑf.tə.mæθ]
afternoon. -s
afterward, -s
aghast
alabaster
   ['æ.lə ˌbɑ.stə]
Alabaster
alas [æ] GA/RP, [a] ES
alto

answer, -s
answering
ask, -s
askance
asked
asking
aunt, -s
auntie, -s
autograph, -s
avalanche, -s
   ['æ.və ˌlɑntʃ]
avast

B
banana, -s
bask, -s
basked
basket, -s
basketball, -s
basketfull, -s
basketry

basketwork
Basque
bastard, -s
bastardized
bastardy
bath
bath-brick, -s
bath-chair, -s
bathe
   [beɪð] GA, ES, RP
bathed
   [bɑθt] RP
   [beɪðd] ES, GA
bathroom
behalf
blanch, -es
Blanche
blanched
blanching
blasphemy
blast, -s

blasted
blasting
blast-furnace, -s
blastment, -s
blast-pipe, -s
branch, -es
Branch
branched
branching
branchless
brass, -es
brass-band, -s
   ['brɑsˈbænd]
brass-founder, -s
brass-hat, -s
brassie, -s (golf)
brassier (more brassy)
brassiest
brassy
broadcast, -s

C

calf

calf's-foot

calf-skin

calve, -s

calved

calves'-foot

calve-skin

calving

can't

cask, -s

casked

casket, -s

casking

cast, -s

castaway, -s

caste, -s

caster

Castelnau

casting, -s

casting-net, -s

casting-vote, -s

cast-iron

castle, -s

Castlebar

Castlerea(gh)

Castleton

castoff, -s

castor, -s

Castor

castor-oil

cenotaph, -s

chaff, -s

chaff-cutter, -s

chaffed

chaffer, -s (n.)

chaffer (v.)

   ['tʃæ.fə]

chaffiness

chaffing, -ly

chaffless

chaffy

chance, -s

chanced

chancel, -s

chancelle-ries

chancelle-ry

chancellor, -s

Chancellor

chancellorship, -s

chancer

chanceries

chancery

Chancery

chancier

chanciest

chancing

chancy

chandler, -s

Chandler

chandlery, -ies

chant, -s

chanted

chanter, -s

chantey

chanties

chanting

Chantrey

chantries

chantry

Chantry

chanty

circumstance, -s

   freq. [stəns]

circumstantial

clasp, -s

clasped

clasping

clasp-knife, -ves

class, -es

classes

classier

classiest

classiness

classing

classman

classmate

classmen

classroom, -s

classwoman

classwomen

classy

Cleopatra

command, -s

commanded

commander, -s

commanding, ly

commandment, -s

commando, -s

contralto

contrast

counterblast, -s

countermand, -s

countermanded

countermanding

craft, -s

craftier

craftiest

craftily

craftiness

craftsman, -men

"-craft" suffixes

D

daft

dafter

daftest

daftly

daftness

dance, -s

Dance

danced

dancer

dancing

deathmask, -s

demand, -s

demanded

demanding

disadvantage, -d, -s
disaster, -s
disastrous, ly
disastrousness
distaff, -s
downcast
downdraught, s
draft, -s
drafted
drafter, -s
drafting
draftsman, -men
drastic
draught, -s
"draught" prefixes
draughtier
draughtiest
draughtily
draughtiness
draughty
draughtsman, -men

E

elastic
encephalograph, -s
enchant, -s
enchanted
enchanter, -s
enchanting, -ly
enchantment
enchantress, -es
enclasp, -s

enclasped
enclasping
engraft, -s
engrafted
engrafting
engraftment
enhance, -s
enhanced
enhancement, -s
enhancing
ensample, -s
enthusiastic
entrance, -s (v.)
entranced, -ly
epigraph, -s
epitaph, -s
everlasting, -ly
everlastingness
example, -s
exampled
exampling
exasperate, -s, -ed, -ing

F

Falstaff
fast, -s
fasted
faster, -s
fastest
fasting
fastness
fast-day, -s

fasten, -s
fastened
fastener, -s
fastening
fastness, -es
"-fast" suffixes
flabbergast
  [ˈflæ.bəˌɡɑst]
flabbergasted
flabbergasting
Flanders
flask, -s
flasket, -s
forecast, -ed, -ing, -s
forecasted, -s
France
Frances
Francies
Francis
freelance, -s, -ed

G

gasp, -s, -ed
gasping
ghastlier
ghastliest
ghastliness
ghastly
giraffe, -s
glance, -s
glanced
glancing, ly

Glasgow
glass, -es
glass-blower, -s
glass-blowing
glass-cutter
glassful, -s
glass-house, -s
glassier
glassiest
glassily
glassiness
glass-paper, -s
glassware
glass-work, -s
glasswort
glassy
graft, -s
"graft" suffixes
grafted
grafter, -s
grafting
grant
Grant
granted
grantee, -s
granting
grantor, -s
graph, -s
"graph" suffixes
Grasmere
grasp, -s
grasped

grasper, -s
grasping, -ly
grass, -es
grass-cutter, -s
grassed
grass-green
grasshopper, -s
grassier
grassiest
grassing
grassland
   [ˈɡrɑsˈlænd]
grass-widow, -s
grass-widower, -s
grassy
gymnastic

H
half
"half" prefixes
haft
halve, -s
halved
halving
handicraft, -s
   [ˈhæn.dɪˈkrɑft]
hasp, -s
hasped
hasping
headmaster
hereafter

I
impassable, bly
implant, -s, -ed, -ing
indraught, -s
intransigent

L
lance, -s
Lance
lanced
lance-corporal, -s
lancer, -s
lancet, -s
Lancet
lancing
Lancing
last, -s
lasted
lasting, -ly
lastly
lath, -s
lather, -s
lathered
lathering
lathwork
lathy
laugh, -s
laughable
laughableness
laughably
laughed
laugher, -s

laughing, -ly
laughing-gas
   [ˈlɑ.fɪŋˈɡæs]
laughing-stock, -s
laughter

M
mask, -s
masked
masking
masque, -s
masquerade
mast, -s
master, -s
"master-" prefixes
"-master" suffixes
mastered
masterful, -ly
masterfulness
mastering
masterpiece, -s
mastery
masthead, -s
mastiff, -s
   [æ] RP, GA, [a] ES
masturbate, -s, -tion, -or
mischance, -s
mooncalf
mooncalves
moustache

N
nastier
nastiest
nastily
nastiness
nasty

O
outcast, -s
outcaste, -s
outcasted
outcasting
outclass, -es
outclassing
outlast, -s
outlasted
outlasting
overcast
overglance, -d, -s
overtask, -ed, -ing, -s

P
paragraph, -s
   [ˈpæ.rəˌɡrɑf]
paragraphed
paragraphing
Pascal
   [pæˈskɑł]
pascal
   [pæˈskɑł]
Pascale
   [pæˈskɑł]

substantial
supplant, -s
supplanted
supplanter, -s
supplanting
surpass, -ed, -es
surpassing, -ly

T

taft, -ed, -s
tafting
task, -s
tasked
tasking
taskmaster, -s
taskmistress, -es
telecast, -s
telegraph, -s

telegraphed
telegraphing
thereafter
topmast
  [mɘst]
  (nautical)
trance, -s
"trans-" prefixes
freq. [trɘnz, trænz]
transplant, -s
  [trænzˈplɑnt]
transept
transfer
transform,
transient
transit
transitory
transplantable

transplanted
transplanting
transport
trespass, -es
  ([pɘs] also)
trespassed
tresspasser, -s
tresspassing

U

unstanch
unsurpassed
upcast, -s

V

vantage, -s
vast
vaster

vastest
vastly
vastness
vasty

W

waft, -s
waftage
wafted
wafting
witchcraft
wrath
  [ɒ, ɔ] RP, [a] ES,
  [æ] GA
wrathfully

In RP, there are a few words where the standard use is [ɑ], but many speakers use [æ] instead. For example: Alexander, bastard, contrast, contrasting, exasperate, ranch, moustache, masquerade and words with prefixes such as "trans." Investigate regional, class and educational backgrounds, and period to hear which vowel should be used. Generally, for higher class/education and older time setting, the more conservative [ɑ] pronunciation should be used.

As with the issue of "r coloration," many American directors will say that they don't find the vowel [a] for ES to their taste, feeling that it sounds too British. However, this sound is already one step away from RP, so it isn't the same at all. If you get a note saying that you sound too English, what has probably happened is that you've gone too far and landed not on [a], but on [ɑ], the actual RP sound. Remember that [a] does not occur naturally in American speech, so it must be learned, and it is easy to drift away from.

When doing a British dialect, be on guard against some typical American mistakes. Damn is always [dæm], never [dɑm]. In the US, ass [æs] means both jackass and the buttocks. If you're called that, it's difficult to know precisely which aspersion has been cast. In RP, the insult is clearer since they are pronounced and spelled distinctly. If you're being called a stubborn simpleton you'll hear ass [æs]. If you're called an arse [ɑs], the reference is anatomical. In RP, tomato is [təˈmɑ.əʊ], but potato is *never* [pəˈtɑ.əʊ]. Ira Gershwin was just being clever in his song lyric.

LISTEN

EXERCISE 5.3.3.1 PRACTICE THE FLAT INTERMEDIATE AND ROUND A

Words: ask, answer, after, half, past, bath, demand, can't, raft, plant, nasty, pass, last.

Phrases: bask in the bath, ask and answer, pass the class, branching plants, nasty taskmaster.

Sentences (To make the challenge more interesting, the sentences contain a mix of BATH and TRAP words. Refer to the list above if you aren't sure.):

1. Harriet married a handsome banker who, charitably, always manages to have sacks of cash for her on demand.
2. Anthony can't manage to plan his calendar and languishes half his afternoons in vapid abandonment.
3. The rascal clasped the half-empty glass in his massive hand, laughed, and after draining the draught, demanded another.
4. Frank's passion for accuracy and acidic attitude had the draughtsmen angry and scrambling to catch their chance mistakes.
5. You can't imagine how hard it was to grasp the task at hand.
6. Basking in his bath, with a glass of Tanqueray dangling from his hand, Andrew glanced through a trashy magazine.
7. That daft dance master commanded that his classes last three and a half hours.
8. Alice gasped passionately as Sam scratched her back and asked him to lather her rather more nastily.
9. Pat drank and saw an ant with antlers, asking him to pass a glass of anisette.
10. The Grant clan gathered at their grand castle for Saturday's annual afternoon family mass and polka dance.

U liquidation

Table 5.9 U liquidation

Key word	GA	ES	RP	Marked RP
DUKE	[duk]	[djuk]	[djuk]	[djuk]
NEW/KNEW	[nu]	[nju]	[nju]	[nju]
PRELUDE	['preɪ.ljud]	['preɪ.ljud]	['preɪ.ljud]	['preɪ.ljud]
ASSUME	[ə'sum]	[ə'sjum]	[ə'sjum]	[ə'sjum]
TUNE	[tun]	[tjun]	[tjun]	[tjun]
ENTHUSIASM	[en'θu.zi.æ.zəm]	[in'θju.zi.æ.zəm]	[in'θju.zi.æ.zəm]	[in'θju.zi.æ.zəm]
PRESUME	[prə'zum]	[prɪ'zjum]	[prɪ'zjum]	[prɪ'zjum]

How do you identify the sound? Where does it show up

Often called the "liquid U," it is optional for GA but required for ES, EW, EU, and UE follow [d, n, t, θ, s]. Using it after [ɬ, s] is the speaker's choice, and there is the feeling that use is fairly posh. If this isn't a normal feature of your speech, be sure you are using it correctly.

Table 5.10 Liquid and non-liquid U in comparison

Where GA, ES, RP all use the liquid U [ju]	Where ES and RP use the liquid U [ju]	Where the liquid U is not used [u]
beauty	duty	booty
few	new	blue
puke	duke	dude
Matthew	enthusiasm	through
cuter	tutor	tooter
did you	dew, due	do
cut you	tune	too, to, two
puce	deuce	doom
has use	presume	zoom

EXERCISE 5.3.4.1 PRACTICE DROPPING OR ADDING THE LIQUID U

Words: during, duel/dual, nuclear, nude, tuna, tuber, enthuse, Zeus, renew, lewd, suicide, exude.

Phrases: beauty is a duty, cute Newton, astute tutor, enthusiastic Matthew, humorous Zeus, resolute suitor.

Sentences (watch for a deliberate mix of words, where the liquid U either doesn't change or isn't used, along with those that have variable use):

1. The duplicitous superstar knew that his tunes were putrid.
2. The cute student wasn't fooled by her tutor's aloof attitude, as she knew he would resolutely pursue and woo her after school was through.
3. Introduce Hugo to the voluptuous beauty at the first opportunity.
4. The nutritional value of tulips is assumed by few.
5. Assuming that you possess the usual culinary skills, you may reduce your diet exclusively to tuna.
6. The stupid student's futile attempt at lucidity was a prelude to renewed neural numbness.
7. Susan's suitors knew she usually used *ingenue* perfume to induce their pursuit.
8. A truculent sense of duty drove the dissolute duke to duel a superior opponent.
9. Hugh wanted to redo his new room in the unusual hues of puce and fuchsia.
10. Professor Bethune enthusiastically introduced us to Thucydides, the Beatitudes and Deuteronomy last Tuesday.

OLIVER: Good Monsieur Charles, what's the new news at the new court?

CHARLES: There's no news at the court, sir, but the old news: that is, the old duke is banished by his younger brother the new duke; and three or four loving lords have put themselves into voluntary exile with him, whose lands and revenues enrich the new duke.

WILLIAM SHAKESPEARE's *As You Like It*

Back-vowel separation

LISTEN

Table 5.11 Back vowel separation

Lexical set word	GA	ES	RP	Marked RP
PALM	[pɑm]	[pɑm]	[pɑm]	[pɑm]
CLOTH	[klaθ]	[klɒθ]	[klɒθ]	[klɒθ]
THOUGHT	[θat]	[θɔt]	[θɔt]	[θɔt]
GOAT	[goʊt]	[goʊt]	[gəʊt]	[gɛʊt]

How do you identify the sound? Where does it show up?

- Words in the set PALM are usually spelled with "a," as in *father*, "ah," as in *shah*, "a (silent l) m," as in *palm*.
- Words in the set CLOTH are usually spelled with "o," as in hot, "ua," as in squalid, "wa," as in want.
- Words in the set THOUGHT are usually spelled with "aw," as in law, "ou," as in ought, "au," as in audit, "all," as in fall, "a (silent l) k," as in talk.
- Words in the GOAT set are spelled with "o," as in so, "ew," as in sew, "oa," as in oat, "oe," as in floe, "ow," as in flow.

In GA, PALM, CLOTH, and THOUGHT have very little separation. They are usually [ɑ]. ES and RP are a close match with each other. In those accents, the three sets are distinct. The biggest difference comes from lip-rounding. PALM [ɑ] has spread lips. CLOTH [ɒ] has more rounding. THOUGHT [ɔ] is quite round. Practice doing all three levels in comparison until you become comfortable with them and others can identify which dialect you are doing.

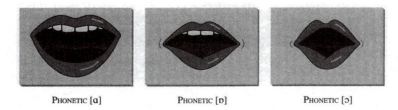

PHONETIC [ɑ]   PHONETIC [ɒ]   PHONETIC [ɔ]

Figure 5.1 Lip shape for back vowels

LISTEN

EXERCISE 5.3.5.1 CONTRASTING BACK VOWELS

Compare these sentences, where the sounds fall in the same order:

1. Charge off to war, Homer.   The almond got raw and old.
2. Martin swallowed the gorgeous cone.   Massage the monster's paw slowly.
3. Carve the horrible warm bowl.   Calm that hot mawkish tone.

In these sentences, the set words are in a random pattern:

1. Maugham's daughter wanted hot coffee from faraway Java.
2. The armada calmly plotted its course for the awesome cliffs of Dover.
3. Jonah was calm, though he lost his job as a hog caller.
4. We all applauded Paul as he fought to catch the ball.
5. Laura's appalling lack of decorum was cause for gossip at home.
6. Hurrah, the drama was a hot, bawdy, comedy — not a slow show at all.
7. The Bach sonata was fondly received with applause from the hall.
8. Bawdy Maud held the crowd in thrall by doing exotic stunts and tossing balls off her bra.

In certain cases where the letter O is followed by one or two Rs, and then another vowel (forest, porridge, Dorothy, Oregon), [ɔɚ.r] is used for GA, and [ɒ.r] is used for both ES and RP.

Table 5.13 "Short O" before an intervocalic [r]

[ɔɚ.r] in GA and [ɒ.r] in ES and RP	[ɔɚ.r] in GA and [ɒ.r] in ES and RP
coral	choral
moral	moron
forest	forum

LISTEN

Table 5.13 continued

[ɔɚ.r] in GA and [ɒ.r] in ES and RP	[ɔɚ.r] in GA and [ɔɚ.r] in ES and RP
origin	orient
florid	flora
horror	whorish
Lawrence	Laura

An interesting subset of these words is "sorry," "borrow," and "tomorrow." GA, ES, and RP are a fairly close match [ɒ], but Canadian is [ɔ], more like the right-hand column above.

EXERCISE 5.3.5.2 PRACTICE ADJUSTING [ɔɚ.r] IN GA AND [ɒ.r] IN ES AND RP

Words: orange, oracle, torrid, historical, coronation, quarantine, seniority, incorrigible.

Phrases: horrible oration, a torrent of porridge, historical authority, abhorrent quarrel.

Sentences:

1. The horrible oranges in the torrid forests of Florida will be foraged tomorrow.
2. Boris was sorry his oratorical efforts were abhorrent to Florence.
3. The foreign correspondent wrote of the historical origins of Morris dancing.
4. The majority will always quarrel with the minority.

Twang elimination

Though actually, *elimination* might not be the whole story. If you are an RP speaker, *acquiring* the right kind of GA twang will be important. If you asked a GA speaker whether their speech would be properly described as "twangy," you might get an outraged response. It's really only twangy in contrast to ES and RP, and only on a couple of sounds.

Table 5.14 Twang elimination

Lexical set word	GA	ES	RP	Marked RP
MOUTH	[maʊθ]	[maʊθ]	[maʊθ]	[maɪθ]
HOUR	[ˈaʊ.ɚ]	[aʊɚ]	[aʊɚ]	[aː]
BANK	[bæɪŋk]	[bæŋk]	[bæŋk]	[bæŋk]

LISTEN

How do you identify the sound? Where does it show up?

The diphthong in MOUTH starts differently for GA versus ES and RP. The first vowel [a] of this diphthong in GA is further forward, brighter, and lacks the roundness of [ɑ] in the ES and RP versions.

To make this shift, use the word "found" as a test. Say it the way you normally do, then to bring it toward GA, say [fæ, fæ, fæt] like in the word "fat." Use that to get you launched and then finish the diphthong normally [faʊnd]. For ES and RP, start with [fɑ, fɑ, ˈfɑ.ðə] like in "father." Notice that the back of your tongue is lower, and the sound seems to happen further back in your mouth. Switch back and forth several times to lock in the sound and the sensation.

In HOUR, the same treatment applies with the addition that GA has the r-colored vowel and tends to be two syllables, while ES and RP are one syllable with no r-coloring.[6]

---

6   In the Marked RP variant for MOUTH you'll see the interesting [aɪ], and for HOUR you'll see [aː]. That last is the product of smoothing the triphthong into a simple vowel. A similar treatment can be found for FIRE [fɑː]. So "the power of the British Empire" can be [ðə pɑː rəv the ˈbrɪ.tˢɪʃ ˈɛm.pɑː].

In BANK, the issue for GA is a tendency to make a diphthong when going from [æ] to [ŋ], [æɪŋ]. This comes from lifting the front of the tongue along with the back for [ŋ]. As a result, the tongue passes through the position for [ɪ]. To make the ES and RP sounds, keep the front of the tongue low on [æŋ].

LISTEN

EXERCISE 5.3.6.1 PRACTICE REMOVING OR ADDING THE RIGHT KIND OF TWANG

Words: mouse, town, lout, ouch, shout, outhouse, cow, rouse, hour, flower, power, shower.

Words (for ES and RP, make these pairs of words have matching vowels [æ], for GA, the first will be [æn] the second [æɪŋ]): band/bank, sand/sank, planned/plank, man/mangle, tan/tangle, ran/wrangle.

Phrases: power outage, cowboy roustabout, an hour in the shower, browsing by the fountain.

Phrases: handy hangman, bad banker, thanks for the cash, ran at an angle, twanging language.

Sentences:

1. Scowling and growling about how his bowers refused to flower, the grouchy gardener pruned for about an hour.
2. While clowning around on the tower, Howard just about fell out on the ground.
3. The loud sounds of the drowning man roused the drowsy lifeguard.
4. Our house was aroused by the sounds of carousing, as the bounders, soused and sour, slouched back from the pubs downtown.
5. Bowing down to the crowd, the proud and powerful dowager announced the donation of a fountain for the town square.
6. "Ouch!" he shouted with a loud yowl, when the cow kicked him in the jowls.
7. The lout was allowed to sip about an ounce of foul brown stout every half hour, though it caused the rowdy souse's gout.
8. The lanky man angrily drank himself into blankness.
9. That cad! That mountebank! He found out about my secret bank account.
10. Dan dangled a sack of cash and his banker thanked him.

Schwa elevation

LISTEN

Table 5.15 Schwa elevation

Key word	GA	ES	RP	Marked RP
INFINITE	[ˈɪn.fə.nət]	[ˈɪn.fɪ.nɪt]	[ˈɪn.fɪ.nɪt]	[ˈɪn.fɪ.nɪt]

How do you identify the sound? Where does it show up?

Schwa sounds happen on unstressed syllables. English is full of unstressed syllables. Almost every other syllable is unstressed. That makes this one of the most frequently occurring environments, and a change on this feature alone can establish the baseline placement for your whole accent. This is one of the key ways to find the resonance and placement differences between GA, ES, and RP. Because GA is focused slightly back, in that accent weak vowels will tend toward a schwa [ə]. ES and RP are organized more forward in the mouth and a with a bit higher tongue position, so weak vowels will sometimes be [ɪ], thus the term "schwa elevation" because your tongue is lifted.

It's important to remember that every vowel letter in English is used in spelling these weak sounds. So, pay attention to stress not spelling when you seek to identify them. In deciding which sounds elevate well, only the letter O seems to be a poor candidate.

Table 5.16 Weak vowel elevation

LISTEN

Spelled vowel		GA [ə]	ES, RP [ɪ]
a	pal**a**ce	[ˈpæ.ləs]	[ˈpæ.lɪs]
e	r**e**spect	[rəˈspɛkt]	[rɪˈspɛkt]
i	Al**i**ce	[ˈæ.ləs]	[ˈæ.lɪs]
o	**o**ppress	[əˈprɛs]	[əˈprɛs]
u	lett**u**ce	[ˈlɛ.t̬əs]	[ˈlɛ.t̬ˢɪs]
y	anal**y**sis	[əˈnæ.lə.səs]	[əˈnæ.lɪ.sɪs]

Get the feel of a word. Not all schwa sounds will comfortably make this shift. For example: "president" has a nice contrast on the second syllable [zə, zɪ] but not on the third [dənt]. Trust your ear when making this substitution. If it sounds silly, don't do it.

Table 5.17 Weak vowel contrast

Words that match in GA		*but are different in ES and RP*	
schwa [ə]	*schwa [ə]*	*[ɪ]*	*schwa [ə]*
pig it	bigot	pig it	bigot
[pɪg ət]	[ˈbɪ.gət]	[pɪg ɪt]	[ˈbɪ.gət]
Lenin	Lennon	Lenin	Lennon
[ˈlɛ.nən]	[ˈlɛ.nən]	[ˈlɛ.nɪn]	[ˈlɛ.nən]
sell it	zealot	sell it	zealot
[ˈsɛ.lət]	[ˈzɛ.lət]	[ˈsɛ.lɪt]	[ˈzɛ.lət]
Martin	Barton	Martin	Barton
[ˈmɑɚ.tn̩]	[ˈbɑɚ.tn̩]	[ˈmɑː.tˢɪn]	[ˈbɑː.tn̩]
dye it	diet	dye it	diet
[ˈdaɪ.ət]	[ˈdaɪ.ət]	[ˈdaɪ.ɪt]	[ˈdaɪ.ət]
a massive cloud	a mass of cloud	a massive cloud	a mass of cloud
[əˈmæ.səv klaʊd]	[əˈmæ.səv klaʊd]	[ə ˈmæ.sɪv klaʊd]	[ə ˈmæ.səv klaʊd]
rabbit	abbot	rabbit	abbot
[ˈræ.bət]	[ˈæ.bət]	[ˈræ.bɪt]	[ˈæ.bət]
lettuce	let us	lettuce	let us
[ˈlɛ.t̪əs]	[ˈlɛ.t̪əs]	[ˈlɛ.tˢɪs]	[ˈlɛ.tˢəs]

EXERCISE 5.3.7.1 PRACTICE LOWERING OR ELEVATING THE SCHWA

Words:anticipat**e**d, **i**nim**i**table, **i**nsip**i**d, **e**xpect**e**d, b**e**nignant, **i**n**e**scapable, famil**i**ar**i**ty, **i**n**e**xcus**a**ble.

Phrases: inimically mimicking, diffident emotionality, inexcusable peculiarities, inexplicable language system.

Sentences:

1. The cosmopolitan Californian attempted to purchase respectability.
2. Amicable petitions are infinitely rarer than typically bitter litigations.
3. A rhythmical musicality is necessary for effective communication and instantaneous understandability.
4. The artificiality of the actress was reprehensible, disgusting and incomprehensible.
5. Their selfishness and carelessness caused her anxiety and irritation.
6. The misogynistic botanist hated women with a passionate intensity.
7. The linguist's impeccable imitation of his colleague's pedantically lisping delivery was an understandably irritating impediment to their association.
8. His mimicking was inimical to their collegial cordiality.
9. Interdisciplinary investigations into the psychological processes of invertebrates have proven inconclusive.
10. Mrs. Minniver was constitutionally incapable of prevarication.

Completions

UNIT 5.3.8

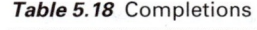

Table 5.18 Completions

KEY Word	GA	ES	RP	Marked RP
hillY	[ˈhɪ.i] [ˈhɪ.ɨ][7]	[ˈhɪ.lɪ]	[ˈhɪ.li] [ˈhɪ.lɨ]	[ˈhɪ.lɪ] [ˈhɪ.lë][8]
easY	[ˈi.zi] [ˈi.zɨ]	[ˈi.zɪ]	[ˈi.zi] [ˈi.zɨ]	[ˈi.zɪ] [ˈi.zë]

7 [ɨ] is slightly down and back from [i]. [i] is most frequently found on stressed syllables, because its high front tongue placement usually requires the time and energy of a stressed sound. In GA and RP, the tongue relaxes on unstressed syllables and retracts slightly. Compare the vowels on "easy" and "hilly" and you'll find that, although the final sounds match each other, they don't quite match either of the first vowels. [ɨ] is used to describe this difference.

8 To find the Marked RP [ë] try matching the vowels in "steady" [ˈstɛ.dë]. In some varients of MRP, "happy" would be [ˈhɛ.pë].

How do you identify the sound? Where does it show up?

To hear this sound for GA, speak the word "easy" and make both vowels match. To hear it for ES, speak the word "hilly" and make those vowels identical. This sound appears on unstressed word endings or in the root word with a combined form (like happy/happiness).

This used to be an important distinguishing factor between GA and RP, but in recent years RP has shifted to more nearly match the GA pronunciation. This seems to be a sound in transition. In more conservative forms of RP, you'll hear a match for the ES sound. If you keep it short and unstressed, it's generally a very classy addition.

LISTEN

EXERCISE 5.3.8.1 PRACTICE LOVELY COMPLETIONS

Words: silly, chamois, Raleigh, goalie, Chelsea, coffee, money, scampi.

Phrases: easy money, happy puppy, awfully lonely, very angry nanny, terribly classy doily.

Sentences:

1. Silly Susie looked awfully pretty last Tuesday.
2. Usually, the terribly heavy turkeys were hardly easy to carry.
3. The tendency toward kingly tyranny is typically hereditary.
4. It was really a pity he married Daisy for her money — she hasn't any.
5. Billy nervously wiped his sweaty, clammy hands on his hanky.
6. Her nubility was endlessly and appreciatively the center of every society party.
7. Lily's ability to be perfectly happy in even the craziest company was surely lovely.
8. Nobility means having the responsibility to endure scrutiny with amiability and dignity.
9. The possibility of a gloomy Tuesday necessarily filled him with ghastly thoughts of mutiny.
10. The hilarity at the party was unbelievably goofy.

T articulation

Table 5.19 T articulation

KEY Word	GA	ES	RP	Marked RP
baTTing	[ˈbæ.ɾɪŋ]	[ˈbæ.tʰɪŋ]	[ˈbæ.tˢɪŋ]	[ˈbɛ.tˢɪŋ]

How do you identify the sound? Where does it show up?

If GA speakers struggle to learn the BATH set of words for RP, the fair turnaround comes when RP speakers try to figure out how to say T sounds in GA. It is a frequent tripping point for British actors. This is because the dialects sometimes match each other and sometimes don't, and the rules aren't always apparent at first glance.

In GA, there is a variable use of [t]. The most important treatment is when GA speakers "voice through" the sound. This is sometimes described as changing [t] to [d], but that isn't quite right. Listen to a North American say "debated" and you'll hear the [d] and [t] sounds aren't an exact match. The symbol we'll use is [t̬]. Think of that little [ ] as indicating the sound is voiced through. Here are the rules for its use:

- Use [t̬] when the T is between two vowel sounds (like batting, better, beauty, a bit of), unless it begins a stressed syllable (so don't use it in words like attend, protect, annotate, a tale). And, yes, the rule holds when the T bridges a word ending in a vowel and one starting with T. Notice the contrast in "I took Sarah to dinner" [ˈsɛ.rə t̬ə] and "I took Bob to dinner" [bɑb tə].
- In [nt]+vowel combinations GA speakers tend to drop the [t] altogether (like enter, sent it, presented), unless it begins a stressed syllable (like anticipate, intend, antenna).

In ES, the recommendation is to use a little puff of air when releasing the T. That's called an "aspirated T" and is written as [tʰ]. The most important time to use it is when the T is between two vowels. To practice this, say these word sets and make them a close match with the second one, just faster: bet her/better, kit he/kitty, shut her/shutter, pat her/patter. This articulation has good qualities to recommend it. It is quite clearly a T sound, but it isn't over-articulated. So it has definition but doesn't draw attention to itself.

In RP, the T is released with a tiny S sound. That's written [tˢ]. This distinguishes it from the GA pattern. Again, the critical placement is when the T is between two vowels. GA speakers learning RP should also remember to articulate the [t] in [nt] combinations.

LISTEN

EXERCISE 5.3.9.1 PRACTICE T ARTICULATION

Words for the T between two vowels: putting, neuter, fated, Otis, kitty, metal, atom, beetle, Haiti, pita.

Phrases: petting pretty kitties, plotting writer, a bit of butter, a heated letter, waiting voter, cited the title.

Words for [nt]: center, seventy, Huntington, planter, Santa, ninety, twenty, dental, enter, interfere.

Phrases: accidentally dented, affronted by the painting, centipede went a centimeter, adamant about it

Sentences:

1. Her ability to adopt an attitude of satisfied gratitude flattered Betty's suitors.
2. The tintinnabulation of the military band made it an interesting matinée.
3. The Vatican expected dutiful chastity, utter piety, complete integrity, and total abstinence from temptation.
4. Bursting with testosterone, the teenage contestants scattered the opposing team and tested their mettle.
5. Tina wouldn't tell Ted the tale of the tattoo on her tail, testing his trust in her.
6. Matt couldn't fit together the facts of last night's party but could estimate the extent of the events by counting the empty bottles.
7. Thomas, the terrible waiter, tossed the hot tortilla into the corset of the haughty matron.
8. As a batter, Peter could have been better, hitting twenty out of ninety attempts.
9. A hundred-twenty students registered for British history, betting that it would be taught with simplicity.
10. Betty entered the Santa Monica senior center wanting to get a bit of lunch with her auntie.

W/WH distinction

LISTEN

Table 5.20 W/WH distinction

Key word	GA	ES	RP	Marked RP
WHich	[wɪtʃ]	[ʍɪtʃ]	[wɪtʃ]	[ʍɪtʃ]

How do you identify the sound? Where does it show up?

- [ʍ] is voiceless, like blowing out a candle.
- It is used whenever spelled with WH.[9]
- It is optional for GA and RP and required for ES.

Table 5.21 [ʍ] and [w] in contrast

LISTEN

[ʍ] ES, optional for GA, RP	[w] for GA, ES, RP
wheel	we'll, weal
whale	wale
why	Y
while	wile
whirred	word
whales	Wales
whine	wine
where	wear
when	wen
wherry	wary
which	witch

9 Except for: who, whom, whose, whole, wholeness, wholly, wholesome, whore, whooping — which are all spoken using [h].

UNIT 5.3.11

EXERCISE 5.3.10.1 PRACTICE [ʌ, w] IN CONTRAST

Words: whey, whether, whist, whack, whet, whelp, whim, whine, whither, whether, whisky.

Phrases: when you whine, why whimper when I whip, white or wheat, whimsical Whigs.

Sentences:

1. Why are you whining about wining and dining at the "Y"?
2. Whether it rain or whether it snow, we shall have weather, whether or no.
3. While I wonder which wheel we'll switch, you worry not a whit.
4. Are there any wild white whales in Wales?
5. A whigmaleerie is a whim; why don't you indulge it when you want?
6. Whitney went wandering and whistling whimsically to the west end of the wet wharf.
7. The witch's whining will always keep you wide awake.
8. The wigged Whigs were in the wagon when it moved forward.
9. Which of the white whales whipped up that whopper of a wave?
10. Wet the whetstone, or I'll whack your wacky head off!

Precision – detail work

The following details will help to keep your speech clean without seeming affected. Except where noted, these guidelines hold true for all three dialects:

Forms: there is a danger in thinking that acrolects require all words to be pronounced so exquisitely than an actor can be led to over-pronounce them. Don't forget to distinguish between strong (emphasized) and weak (reduced) forms of words. If everything has the same value, the audience doesn't know what's important, and it gets so one-leveled it's boring. Look for weak forms of a, am, an, and, are, as, but, could, does, for, from, had, has, have, her, into, must, of, or, shall, should, that, the, them, to, us, was, what, were.

Been: for GA and ES, use [bɪn]. For RP, use [bin] in the strong form and [bɪn] in the weak form. RP speakers are more likely to employ a strong form of this word than GA.

Either, neither: for GA, usually use [ˈi.ðɚ] and [ˈni.ðɚ]. For ES and RP, use [ˈaɪ.ðə] and [ˈnaɪ.ðə].

Again: [əˈgɛn] for all three dialects, unless there is a poetic need to rhyme it or you are an extremely affected character.

Darts: clean and sharpen most consonants for ES and RP. Avoid hard bludgeoning sledgehammers in favor of precise darts. GA employs harder consonants generally. When one word ends in a consonant and the next begins with the same, or a close sound, don't release your tongue. Hold it in place and give a fresh burst of energy for the next sound. For example: hide them, cut ten, pack games, fat Tom.

Terminals: for ES and RP, pay extra attention to terminal consonants. Give them both energy and time; they usually take longer to say than initial or medial consonants. Most moderns barely speak the last consonant in a word, while classical characters use this final sound to twist or cap off their points. The consonant is a weapon, not just a sound, in these plays.

> **An actress should . . . be able to drive a nail up to the head with one touch of a consonant.**
> **GEORGE BERNARD SHAW, playwright, critic**

-Ery, -Ory, -Ary, -Berry Endings: follow these examples:

Table 5.22 -ERY, -ORY, -ARY, -BERRY endings

LISTEN

Key word	GA	ES	RP	Marked RP
stationery	[ˈsteɪ.ʃəˌne.ri]	[ˈsteɪ.ʃə.nə.rɪ]	[ˈsteɪ.ʃən.ri]	[ˈsteɪ.ʃən.rɨ]
conservatory	[kənˈsɚ.vəˌtɔɚ.ri]	[kənˈsɜ.və.tə.rɪ]	[kənˈsɜ.və.tri]	[kənˈsʌ.və.trɨ]
necessary	[ˈnɛ.səˌsɛ.ri]	[ˈnɛ.sə.sə.rɪ]	[ˈnɛ.sə.sri]	[ˈnɛ.sə.srɨ]
raspberry	[ˈræzˌbɛ.ri]	[ˈraz.bə.rɪ]	[ˈraz.bri]	[ˈraz.brɨ]

-Man, -mony endings: follow these examples:

Table 5.23 -MAN, -MONY endings

Key word	GA	ES	RP	Marked RP
handyman	[ˈhæn.diˈmæn]	[ˈhæn.dɪ.mən]	[ˈhæn.diˈmən]	[ˈhæn.dɪ.mən]
matrimony	[ˈmæ.trəˈmoʊ.ni]	[ˈmæ.trə.mə.nɪ]	[ˈmæ.trə.mə.ni]	[ˈmæ.trə.mə.nɨ̈]

-Ile endings: Follow these examples:

Table 5.24 -ILE endings

Key word	GA	ES	RP	Marked RP
sterile	[ˈstɛ.rəɫ]	[ˈstɛ.rəɫ]	[ˈstɛ.raɪɫ]	[ˈstɛ.raɪɫ]
juvenile	10	[ˈdʒu.və.nəɫ]	[ˈdʒu.vəˌnaɪɫ]	[ˈdʒu.vəˌnaɪɫ]

England and America are two countries separated by a common language.

GEORGE BERNARD SHAW, playwright, critic

Special words: There are numerous pronunciation differences between GA and RP that don't follow any strict rule or pattern: GA, ES — aluminum, RP — aluminium, for example. These are challenging to summarize thoroughly. In general, GA and ES emerge from the North American aesthetic, so they'll often share similar ideas about words. Be particularly careful about place names and family names, as these frequently don't coincide with spelling. Foreign loan words are also a tricky area. In general, GA and ES are slightly closer to the original language. Notice that beret, ballet, and attaché will be similar

10 RP usage is fairly consistent [aɪ]. ES usually adopts [əɫ]. GA is variable with [əɫ] for the young person but [aɪ] to describe immaturity and [aɪ] in the context of juvenile delinquency. GA shows a similar variability on homo- prefixes. For RP [ˈhɒ.mə] is fairly consistent. GA and ES will vary, with homicide as [ˈhɒ] but homeopath as [ˈhoʊ]. RP speakers will need to check their GA accents against a dictionary for these words.

to French in GA and ES, with the stress on the final syllable. But the stress in RP is moved back one syllable. The spelled letter A is another frequent example. Notice pasta and tacos: GA, ES ['pɑ.stə ən 'tɑ.koʊz], RP ['pæ.stə rən 'tɑ.koʊz]. GA and ES will keep the original Italian and Spanish [ɑ] while RP uses [æ].

There's a few key words . . . water . . . ['wɔ.tˢə] (If you can get that right you're halfway ['hɑf.weɪ] there.)
. . . pasta . . . ['pæ.stə] . . . nachos ['næ.tʃoʊz].
ROBERT PATTINSON, actor, on the Oprah Winfrey Show discussing how to do an American accent

Consistency: be sure that you are consistent in pronunciation, particularly with a name or term no longer widely used. It matters less that it is historically accurate than that it is true to the world you have created. If in doubt, pick pronunciations most likely to be understood.

EXERCISE 5.3.11.1 ELEVATING

1. Start with the target acrolect closest to your native way of speaking. If you are British or Australian, for example, choose RP. If you're a North American, choose GA.

2. Use either material from a scene you are working on or improvised dialogue. Start this with short samples of only a couple of sentences. In repeated versions of this exercise, expand to full scenes or monologues.

3. Demonstrate the way you would say it normally.

4. Repeat the same dialogue with the target acrolect.

5. Get observers to give you feedback on which sounds you do well and where any elements of your speech aren't a match.

6. Repeat this exercise with longer passages and more complex language. Finally, present a fully memorized classical monologue or scene in this acrolect.

EXERCISE 5.3.11.2 CHANGING CULTURES

1. Repeat Exercise 5.3.11.1 with the acrolect that is the farthest away from your normal way of speaking.
2. Choose material written for that acrolect. For the moment, don't impose a dialect on language that isn't written to support it. As before, start with short sections and then expand to longer passages and full scenes.
3. Remember to adjust your placement, pitch, and volume behavior as well as getting accurate vowels and consonants.
4. Use observers to give you feedback.
5. Start by focusing on the sound changes. Get those right. Then, as you become accustomed to this new pattern of speaking, turn your attention to honest, truthful acting. Discover the connected, genuine person living inside this new set of sounds.

EXERCISE 5.3.11.3 FINDING ES

Since ES is an accent from nowhere, it is usually the furthest away from your normal way of speaking. It is easy to overshoot and wind up on the wrong side of the ocean. Repeat the exercise above using ES as your target.

EXERCISE 5.3.11.4 TRANSCRIBING FOR PRECISION AND ACCURACY

1. Take a short passage. Use the IPA to transcribe it into your normal way of speaking. If your speech is already quite close to either GA or RP, start with that as your baseline. Leave yourself several blank lines below each line of text.
2. Then below each line note only those changes that would be relevant for the other acrolects. Try to use only those symbols that will keep the target changes clear. Don't give yourself too many visual distractions. That might look something like this:

Text	Rebecca	is	asking	whether	her	new
GA	rə'bɛ.kə	ɪz	'æ.skɪŋ	'wɛ.ðɚ	hɚ	nu
ES		rɪ	'a.	e	e	nju
RP		rɪ	ɑ.	e	ə	nju

Text	banker	will	call	her	early	Saturday.
GA	'bæŋ.kɚ	wɪɫ	kɑɫ	hɚ	'rɚ.li	'sæ.tɚ‚deɪ
ES	'bæŋ.kə	e	kɔɫ	e	'rɜ.lɪ	.tʰɚ.
RP	'bæŋ.kə	ə	kɔɫ	ə	'rɜ.li	.tˢə.di

3. Practice each pattern until you can switch between the acrolects at will.

4. Expand from short passages into longer pieces and full scenes. You'll find that after a while an acrolect will have a pattern of behavior that becomes instinctive. Then you'll be able to improvise in it without such detailed preparation. But don't try to start there. Do your detailed practice first.

Acting in an acrolect without sounding phony

In England, it is considered important to make class distinctions. To do that you have to be able to hear different tonalities. So the English are far more acute than we at hearing subtle vocal changes.
RICHARD BANDLER, originator of neuro-linguistic programming

How do Americans cure themselves of the temptation to do phony British accents when playing empresses and gods? How can British actors find the earthy rootedness of GA without sounding like a New York cabbie? How can actors find truthful humanity in roles that aren't from their home culture?

Isn't this the reason many of us wanted to be actors in the first place — because of the sheer fun of transformation? The British sensitivity to sound can be developed and employed without doing a dialect. One's ear can be tuned to make the distinctions deeply rooted in the English culture. The muscularity of American speech can be discovered and usefully incorporated into anyone's acting. One of the great things about mastering both sides of the ocean (and the magical land in the middle) is that it expands the expressive range of everything you do.

I want to combine the Shakespearean experience of British actors with the emotional fearlessness I've seen in most American actors. Don't affect some accent. Come and act in your own skin.

KENNETH BRANAGH, actor

ES is the most common choice for American Shakespearean performance. Although director preferences vary, generally US productions avoid British for ancient aristocracy. Cleopatra was Egyptian; Marc Antony was Roman. Why would they speak with a British accent? British productions can certainly use their home acrolect of RP, because that works transparently there to establish class. ES may become more important as producers increasingly use casts that come from different backgrounds. In any case, honest acting isn't affected even when the language is expressed at its most heightened. Plays do have mannered characters who strut and posture, but there is still a human being in there. Get so good at these acrolects that even the most ostentatious character has truth and depth.

UNIT 5.5 ## Regional/ethnic freedom — owning all language

Embracing cultural diversity and honoring each heritage for the actor means learning the sound of any neighborhood as well as any kingdom. If you limit your vocal horizons, it should be by *choice*. You can work in a small cultural space and still excel. Robert wrote in another book (*Style for Actors*) about how Henry Fonda and James Stewart simply did small town Americana and did it brilliantly. These guys never dealt with blank verse, glamour, or rhymed couplets. And they were wonderful working within narrow boundaries. But we would advise that *now* you try to do it all — to stretch your own boundaries. That's what training is all about.

Many actors fall in love with refined speech and take it on to the point where they are incapable of getting *down* with the folks back home. This is the last thing you want to do. Fall in love, by all means, but where you come from is your core, and talking with the folks there — in their own manner — is as important as any other skill you have as an actor.

If you want to get out of a tough encounter in a dangerous "hood," you will learn to talk street. If you need help from a Southern sheriff, you will talk good ol' boy. You talk the way you need to, to survive. Characters in classical drama speak the only way people in their worlds will listen to them. Anything less than gorgeous complex phrases, lucid language choices, layers of meaning, tons of puns, and sudden twists of feeling will simply be ignored. Anything less than crystal clear diction, stunning musicality, superb breath control, and brilliant phrasing will not be attended. People will interrupt you or move away out of boredom. You need to learn to speak this language as if you have simply been improvising it all your life. You do it to survive in the classical world.

EXERCISE 5.5.1 STORYTELLING

1. Work in groups of four.
2. Each person tell a short story about something that happened in your neighborhood or small town (or make it up). Do it as closely as possible to a native.
3. Retell the story in either GA, ES or RP, or you could switch back and forth; your choice.

Verse versus prose

All that is not prose is verse and all that is not verse is prose.

MOLIÈRE, actor/playwright, *The Bourgeois Gentleman*

Classical plays may be in prose or verse or some combination. *All* the plays before Shakespeare's time were written in verse, so it was his (and his contemporaries') prose sections that sounded strange or new to his audiences. You will often be asked to do a verse piece as part of an audition. Not only is the capacity to speak it smoothly needed for classical repertory, but an actor who can do verse is rhythmically aware, has a strong sense of timing, is adept at sensing subtle shifts in material, and is able to stylistically pull speeches together for consistency while finding within them maximum variety. Verse increases sensibility to words, rhythms, meanings which come only from sound, and to unexplainable meanings, deeper than the conscious mind can fathom. It can stretch an actor toward greatness. Working with classical verse gives you the best possible work-out and gets you in the best possible shape.

The size of the emotions you get to explore in the classics is limitless, infinite, so rich that when you approach modern material, its like you've run the marathon and now they're asking you to run the half-marathon.

ANNETTE BENING, actor

Verse looks different to prose on the page. Prose goes all the way to the end of the line. Verse lines go only a limited number of syllables per line (usually ten to twelve) and then stop. Prose has capital letters only at the start of a sentence. Verse has them at the start of the new line regardless of where it comes in the sentence. Most English verse drama is either blank (unrhymed) or rhymed *iambic pentameter*, a line with from ten to twelve syllables, approximately half of them unstressed and half stressed. *Iambic* means that the basic smallest unit (a foot) is a set of two syllables, the first unstressed and the second stressed. Each foot goes rhythmically da DUM (sometimes noted as ‿ —). *Pentameter* means that in one line, there are five of these feet. A perfect line of iambic pentameter beats out da DUM da DUM da DUM da DUM da DUM. The first word always says what kind of foot, the second how many.

Blank verse is language formalized into lines of equal (or nearly equal) length, but not into rhyme. It is a middle ground speech — more elevated and rhythmic than normal everyday prose but less so than some other more complex and less conversational verse forms.

Verse is used to express what cannot be adequately accomplished by mere words. Verse is between song and regular speech, less musical than the first, less mundane than the second. Shakespeare uses verse about 72 percent and prose 28 percent of the time. His *Richard II* is all verse, and his *Merry Wives of Windsor* is nearly all prose. The first is elegant, serious drama; the second is knockdown, madcap farce. In general, verse is more likely to be spoken by a character of high rank, to a parent, ruler or stranger, in public and on formal, ceremonial occasions, when speaking of love, truth, honor or the meaning of life — the higher subjects. Prose is more likely to be spoken by a rustic, comic, humble character, by someone who feels momentarily rustic, comic or humble, in broader, earthier circumstances, when dealing with more purely factual, ordinary or bawdy subjects.

Figure 5.2 "And palm to palm is holy Palmer's kiss." From *Romeo and Juliet* at the Cincinnati Shakespeare Company, 2007, Christopher Guthrie and Hayley Clark. Photo by Rich Sofranko.

Here is a short verse scene, the very first meeting of the most famous lovers ever:

R: If I profane with my unworthiest hand,
    This holy Shrine, the gentle sin is this,
    My lips, two blushing Pilgrims ready stand,
    To smooth that rough touch, with a tender kiss.

J: Good Pilgrim, you do wrong your hand too much,
    Which mannerly devotion shows in this,
    For saints have hands that Pilgrims' hands do touch,
    And palm to palm is holy Palmer's kiss.

R: Have not saints lips, and holy palmers too?

J: Aye Pilgrim, lips that they must use in prayer.

R: O then dear Saint, let lips do what hands do,
    They pray (grant thou) lest faith turn to despair.

J: Saints do not move, though grant for prayer's sake.

R: Then move not while my prayer's effect I take:
    (He kisses her)

These two move fast. A total of fourteen lines exchanged between perfect strangers before they suck face. It takes Romeo a mere four lines to suggest the kiss, followed by ten lines of discussion before he goes for it. Life is intensified here, and the images are packed.

Here is what it would look like if it were written as prose.

R: If I profane with my unworthiest hand, this holy Shrine, the gentle sin is this, my lips, two blushing Pilgrims ready stand, to smooth that rough touch, with a tender kiss.

J: Good Pilgrim, you do wrong your hand too much, which mannerly devotion shows in this, for saints have hands that Pilgrims' hands do touch, and palm to palm is holy Palmer's kiss.

R: Have not saints lips, and holy palmers too?

J: Aye Pilgrim, lips that they must use in prayer.

R: O then dear Saint, let lips do what hands do, they pray (grant thou) lest faith turn to despair.

J: Saints do not move, though grant for prayer's sake.

R: Then move not while my prayer's effect I take:

UNIT 5.6.1

Scansion – scoring verse

Look at a line of verse like a musical score. You have a mechanical problem first. How do you take this line of ten to twelve syllables and figure out which syllables to lengthen and which to weaken? Then how *extensively* do you lengthen or how *completely* do you weaken? Far from dauntingly technical, it has exquisite simplicity. You have a recipe for each line, albeit a recipe that can be helped by inspiration. You get roughly five stressed and roughly five unstressed syllables. So where do you want to place them? Most actors begin by marking a text. Here is what it looks like roughly scanned (and starting with a rigidly iambic reading), with ‿ for an unstressed syllable and — for stressed. Feet are divided by |.

1. *R:* If I | profane | with **my** | unwor | thiest **hand,**

2. This **ho** | ly **Shrine,** | the **gen** | tle **sin** | is **this,**

3. My **lips,** | two **blu** | shing **Pil** | grims **rea** | dy **stand,**

4. To **smooth** | that **rough** | touch **with** | a **ten** | der **kiss.**

5. *J:* Good **Pil** | grim, **you** | do **wrong** | your **hand** | too **much,**

6. Which **ma** | nnerly | devo | tion **shows** | in **this,**

7. For **Saints** | have **hands** | that **Pil** | grims' **hands** | do **touch,**

8. And **palm** | to **palm** | is **ho** | ly **Pal** | mer's **kiss.**

9. *R*: Have **not** | Saints **lips**, | and **ho** | ly **pal** | mers **too**? |

10. *J*: Aye, **Pil** | grim, **lips** | that **they** | must **use** | in **prayer**. |

11. *R*: O, **then** | dear **Saint**, | let **lips** | do **what** | hands **do**, |

12. They **pray** | (grant **thou**) | lest **faith** | turn **to** | des**pair**. |

13. *J*: Saints **do** | not **move**, | though **grant** | for **pray** | er's **sake**. |

14. *R*: Then **move** | not, **while** | my **prayer's** | e**ffect** | I **take**: |

Stress release

It is good to start out by assuming that the speech may be written in perfect iambic pentameter. That way you can quickly deal with those that fit, and when you find a line that doesn't scan so easily, you can make a note and come back to it. Why isn't it perfect? Well, most good writers know how to play with or tease the metre, for variety and depth. The most common variation is to switch an **iamb** to a **trochee**, so that da DUM becomes DUM da, simply reversing the order of the stressed and unstressed syllables. There are two other variations. For **elision**, a word that would normally have more syllables is compressed or elided. So, in the speech above, in line 1, the last part of "unworthiest" is spoken quickly (as "unworthyest"), and in lines 10 and 14 the word "prayer" is spoken as one syllable, whereas in line 13 it is spoken as two to fit the pattern of the verse and to reflect the difference between the prayer and the person who prays (pray-er). The opposite of elision is **compensation**, where a syllable that is not usually spoken is. See examples below.

EXERCISE 5.6.2.1 SCANNING

1. Sit again in a circle and each actor take two lines of verse.
2. Scan the line heavily first, assuming it to be a perfect set of iambs.
3. Go back and identify where adjustments need to be made so that the line flows more naturally and fits the metre.
4. Re-read the completed line.
5. If an actor is having difficulty, help him out but let him try it alone first.
6. Discuss those instances when there appear to be more than one way to effectively scan the line.

EXERCISE 5.6.2.2 THE MIGHTY HUMAN IAMBIC PENTAMETER LINE

1. Ten actors go up in front of the class, with two others waiting in the wings stage left.
2. Observers suggest very famous lines from Shakespeare.
3. When the group gets the line, it tries to physicalize it with each person becoming a stressed or unstressed syllable by standing or kneeling. So "If music be the food of love play on" might have the odd-numbered actors kneeling and the even numbered standing with no need for the back-up team because there are only ten syllables, not eleven or twelve. Go back over the line and discuss how the stresses might vary. A syllable with very low stress might crawl down into a fetal position. A strong stress might jump in the air. A strong stress with an exclamation point might leap in the air with arms thrust high above them. If elision is needed, the actor might scrunch in as if they had been hit in the stomach.
4. Do the line with each person speaking and physicalizing their syllable, first for a straight scanning for stressed and unstressed syllables. Then repeat for a more refined line reading, acknowledging other factors in the vocabulary list. Accept suggestions from the audience.
5. Let the metre guide you but allow your creativity full range as far as how you might portray your syllable.

Rhyming

Actors fear falling into a boring sing-song nursery rhyme pattern — a tedious trap with rhymes in plays. So they may try to pretend that the rhymes aren't there, riding over them and smoothing them out. Wrong. People rhyme when they feel totally together. When a rapper hits the rhyme, he feels pumped. When characters in these plays move past just choosing eloquent words, sounding great and then thinking in rhythmic structure, into actually *rhyming*, they are hot. They score. Think of a rhymed couplet as the ultimate speech accomplishment, like a vocal home run. And these characters, even when they're dying or crying, can score home runs.

Letters of the alphabet are used to identify rhyme schemes. Notice that Romeo begins his approach to Juliet with four lines with an ABAB rhyme scheme — smooth. She responds with a CDCD rhyme scheme. He then feeds her a line (so to speak), to which she responds with one that does not rhyme with his (EF). He rhymes his line in that exchange, and hers, and *together* they complete another four-line EFEF sequence. Finally, she feeds him a line, which he rhymes just before the kiss (GG). Together they write a perfect sonnet, the most famous form for a love poem ever created! It is as if the words are already making love to each other long before the characters make physical contact.

R: If I profane with my unworthiest hand,   A
    This holy Shrine, the gentle sin is this,   B
    My lips, two blushing Pilgrims ready stand,   A
    To smooth that rough touch, with a tender kiss.   B
J: Good Pilgrim, you do wrong your hand too much,   C
    Which mannerly devotion shows in this,   D
    For saints have hands that Pilgrims' hands do touch,   C
    And palm to palm is holy Palmer's kiss.   D
R: Have not saints lips, and holy palmers too?   E
J: Aye Pilgrim, lips that they must use in prayer.   F
R: O then dear Saint, let lips do what hands do,   E
    They pray (grant thou) lest faith turn to despair.   F
J: Saints do not move, though grant for prayer's sake.   G
R: Then move not while my prayer's effect I take: G

(He kisses her)

Anne: O wonderful, when devils tell the truth!

Richard: More wonderful, when Angels are so angry:
Vouchsafe (divine perfection of a Woman)
Of these supposed Crimes, to give me leave
By circumstance, but to acquit my self.

Anne: Vouchsafe (defus'd infection of man)
Of these known evils, but to give me leave
By circumstance, to curse thy cursed Self.

Richard: Fairer than tongue can name thee, let me have
Some patient leisure to excuse my self.

Anne: Fouler than heart can think thee, thou can'st make
No excuse current, but to hang thy self.

Richard: By such despair, I should accuse my self.

The golden rule of Elizabethan writing; find the antithesis. Many of the lines include a "not this, but that" pattern. Once you hear that the rest is easy.

RUSSEL JACKSON, screenwriter

Bottoming out: throw out momentarily all grandiose period-style thinking and get simple. Go for the most Method actor (that is a good Method actor) introspective emotional involvement, with no thought of projecting but just getting it deep and personal. With all your contemporary mannerisms temporarily embraced and employed, find a fundamental, honest simplicity.

Coining: remember that you are writing this speech, not Shakespeare, and it has never been spoken by an actor before you. You are Shakespeare. You need to search for and find each image so that it is fresh, new, and immediate, not memorized and engraved. You are inventing it on the spot.

Compensation: repairing metrical omissions in a line of verse, usually by speaking a vowel that would normally remain silent. Most common types: -ED ending (remembered-rememberED), -IER ending (soldier-solJEEer), -ION ending (indignation-indignaSHEEUN). These vowels are pronounced to get the line to reach ten syllables in speech. Example: *Twelfth Night*, Act II, Scene I

> *Olivia*: Methinks I feel this youth's perfections
> With an invisible, and subtle stealth
> To creep in at mine eyes.

Distributed stress: effect produced when two consecutive syllables share the stress, instead of one being heavily accented while the other is barely touched. The emphasis is distributed equally between the two. Instead of da DUM, you may have Da Dum, with neither being hit all that soft or all that hard. This can result in a pyrrhic foot (weak–weak) followed by a spondee foot (strong–strong). Notice "like the sweet sound" in this example: *Twelfth Night*, Act I, Scene I

> *Orsino*: O, it came o'er my ear, like the sweet sound
> That breathes upon a bank of violets.

Elision: Omitting a syllable in order to conform a line to a metrical scheme. Examples: o'er for over, th'incestuous for the incestuous, 'gainst for against, on't for on it, heav'n for heaven, dev'l for devil. Elision may or may not be transcribed by an editor. Again, the idea is to get the line to speak at ten (or at the most twelve) syllables. Example: *King Lear*, Act II, Scene IV

> *Lear*: They durst not do't:
> They could not, would not do't: 'tis worse than murder,
> . . .
> I can scarce speak to thee, thou'lt not believe
> With how deprav'd a quality.

Endings: the last syllable in a line of verse may be stressed-strong (traditionally called *masculine*) or unstressed-weak (traditionally called *feminine*). A weak ending is usually accomplished by an added eleventh syllable in blank verse, and Shakespeare uses it to jolt the listener slightly or to guide the listener quickly into the next line. A strong ending is the more common form. Absurdly sexist terms are included because they exist in many traditional texts. It is useful to regard a "feminine" line as very powerful because it forces the reader into the next line and does not allow any lingering over the line just spoken. (Example: *As You Like It*, Act II. Scene VIII, in his famous "All the world's a stage" speech, Jaques introduces each new age by ending on a feminine verse line: infant, schoolboy, lover, soldier all end lines with the interest piqued and the energy directed strongly into the following line.)

Foot: the basic unit of measure in verse, two or three syllables in length, with various stresses. The most common feet are iambic (unstress–stress), trochaic (stress–unstress), pyrrhic (unstress–unstress), spondaic (stress–stress), anapestic (unstress–unstress–stress), and dactylic (stress–unstress–unstress).

Greatness: your character is likely to be more intelligent, articulate, and heroic than you are. Embrace this. Drop inhibitions in favor of rising to the occasion and reveling in the opportunity to speak these glorious words, knowing you deserve to.

Historical rhyme: words that used to be pronounced the same, but usage of one of them has changed with time (e.g., Dumaine from *Love's Labor's Lost*: "Through the velvet leaves the wind, All unseen can passage find.") You are not obliged to make them rhyme.

Humor: unearth it even in the direst circumstances. Elizabethans have a dark, dark sense of what is fun and will pun in the midst of breaking hearts, their own and others'.

Irony: if you can't find laughs, look for irony, humor's darker cousin, which often says: "Isn't this just like life? Can you believe it? Can you beat this?"

Juggling: because the techniques in verse speaking are new and potentially intimidating, think of juggling character truth (which you already know) with handling verse (the new ball). Focus on one, then the other, one then the other, and then gradually bring them together so they can both be in the air at the same time.

Kicking out the jams: find the music in the speech by going into known music. Sing it at the top of your lungs as if it is grand opera, then rock out, try some blues, then find another musical style that favors the material. Keep the discoveries.

Lists: classical playwrights tend to build points, using lists of three, sometimes more. Each new number is more powerful and deserves more punch than the one before it. Each list works towards the strongest item on it, which is the last.

Metre: the number of feet in a line of verse, the overall pattern by which a line is parceled into divisions of time. Most common: monometer-one foot, dimeter-two, trimeter-three, tetrameter-four (often used by Shakespeare for witches), pentameter-five (used by Shakespeare and most other classical writers), hexameter-six, septenary-seven.

Metrical Pause: the tendency to stop at the end of a line of verse, even though there is no punctuation to indicate a pause. Also called "end stopping," this understandable but irritating habit will prevent and interfere with an audience's capacity to hear a lengthy sentence as a single unit. Practice deliberately moving right into the next line unless punctuation indicates otherwise.

Monosyllabic lines: almost without exception, a line with only one-syllable words time, particularly spaces between the words, for the line to breathe, the points to be brought home and the emotional impact to land. So let this happen.

Example: *Hamlet*, Act II, Scene I

Ophelia: He took me by the hand and held me hard.

Notation: while getting used to the act of scansion, it helps many actors, especially visual learners, to annotate the text, making slash marks between feet and designating one kind of mark for a stressed, another for an unstressed syllable. After a time, most actors can do it in their heads.

Over the top: scale your speech huge, aiming for the top balcony in a gigantic opera house. Let yourself find the bravura in the material. Do not send it up or satirize; rather, play as large as you can with an honest core, determined to give those students who can only afford the cheap seats at the back a performance that will reach them. This can be confused with ham acting, but it is more about giving into huge emotion to the extent that is the power of feeling that carries you over. Once you really reach the top and beyond, then you can worry about tempering the work. But Shakespeare often asks you to reach the top and slightly beyond.

Personification: the common practice, in verse, of giving human characteristics to objects, emotions or abstractions so that they appear to have a life and a will of their own. Standard choices are Love, Fortune, Reason, Nature, and Time. In some cases, it is a matter of simply speaking to some elements of nature as if they may answer back. Example: *King Lear*, Act IV, Scene I

Edgar: Welcome then,
Thou unsubstantial air that I embrace:
The Wretch that thou hast blown unto the worst,
Owes nothing to thy blasts.

Poetry: the use of elements from both speech and song to express feeling, ideas, and imagination. Language full of imaginative power, effectively condensing experience by capturing evocative phrases. It is too often mistakenly used interchangeably with verse. Poetry is an imaginative use of sensory language that may or may not be formalized, while the formalization, if it exists, is called verse.

Pronominal mode: the use of "thee" and "thou" or "you" to address another. "Thee" most often indicates familiarity (which may be supportive or not, as in relationships between siblings or with servants), warmth or closeness, while "you" is more likely to occur in situations involving anger, coldness, unfamiliarity, high regard or simple formality. These are generalizations, not rules. The distinction is roughly like the French use of "tu" or "vous" in showing the degree of intimacy the speaker shares with their listener. Example: *As You Like It*, Act IV, Scene III, where Celia is upset but Rosalind is trying to maintain their closeness.

> *Celia*: You have simply misus'd our sex in your love-prate: we must have your doublet and hose pluck'd over your
> head . . .
> *Rosalind*: O coz, coz, coz: my pretty little coz, that thou didst know how many fathom deep I am in love: . . . my affection
> hath an unknown bottom . . .
> *Celia*: Or rather bottomless, that as fast as you pour affection in, in runs out.
> *Rosalind*: . . . I'll tell thee Aliena, I cannot be out of the sight of Orlando: I'll go find a shadow, and sigh till he come.
> *Celia*: And I'll sleep.

Questioning: imagine that someone keeps saying "What?" or "Excuse me?" or "Why did you do that?" or some other question that can turn the monologue into a dialogue. In life, you sometimes jump to your next point because you *see* the question in your listener's eyes. This makes for a compellingly interactive speech.

Research: hit the library for at least the *OED* (*Oxford English Dictionary*) or some other major dictionary and look up every key word in each sentence to figure out the meanings no longer present and the all-important puns. Also check out the **First Folio** (the first collected works of Shakespeare) to compare spelling, punctuation, and word order with that of the modern edition you are using. You will be amazed at how much new meaning the speech has and how often Will's commas and capitalizations make more sense than those of contemporary editors, who are writing for silent reading — unlike Will, who wrote for actors.

Recessive accent: stress that falls on a syllable other than that which would normally be accented. It was especially common in the Elizabethan period, because the language itself was changing so rapidly, with shifts in emphasis only one small part of the vast sphere of word experimentation. (Example: Chorus in *Romeo and Juliet*: "Temp'ring extremities with <u>EX</u>treme sweet.") Potentially useful in drawing attention to key words by twisting them slightly. Listen closely to rock and rap lyrics, which use this tactic all the time.

Verse: the arrangement of language into formalized structure, in classical theatre usually iambic pentameter. It is sometimes said that verse is the grammar of the speech, while poetry is its soul.

Will/shall: much like thee/you, the distinction between these words has become lost. In Shakespeare's time they were different. Here's the pattern:

- I will: is an oath or promise — "I will be back" means that I put my will to it.
- I shall: is a prediction — "I shall be back" means that it is likely to happen.
- You will: is a prediction — "You will be back" means that it probably will happen.
- You shall: is a command — "You shall be back" means that you are ordered to return.

Think of the Ten Commandments. They all begin with "thou shalt" — the familiar pronoun spoken to a servant, and "shalt" makes it a command. They would be more like the Ten Probabilities if they started with "you will."

Wonder: anyone who chooses to speak verse has chosen to participate. Drop skeptical reticence and suspicious neurosis in favor of wondrous discovery. Discover the situation, words, even contradictions with an explorer's sense of adventure. Verse speakers are full of wonder at being alive and being able to speak fully.

Xerox: get double-spaced copies for everyone who coaches you. The work is complex enough that each participant needs a musical score, otherwise you might not hit the right notes.

Yes: in the classics, the answer to "Should I play it angrier or more hurt?" is often "Yes." Should I play him more evil or more sympathetic? Yes. In other words, don't make simple choices. Because these characters have more to them than some folks down the street, they have many "yeses" going on. When you are coached in a new direction, consider taking along the old. Add to what you have.

Zone, in the: athletes use this term to denote the utter, still calm and focus that comes at peak performance. Scientists find a burst of alpha waves just prior to excellent performance. You can put yourself in this space through forceful visualization. Apply the process of the athlete in your images and the sensual connection you make to each sound. Remember, Elizabethans felt language deep in their bodies, not just their heads.

EXERCISE 5.7.1 **CLASSICAL SPEECH A TO Z**

1. Sit in a circle with the terms above before each person.
2. Go around the room reading aloud in your best possible classical speech.
3. Let each reader complete a term. Then tell him both what seemed genuinely classical to you and what you lost, in terms of vowels, consonants, sound, and phrasing.
4. Enter the reading, not with a fear of being "caught" but with the understanding that others will be giving you gifts, which cannot be picked up by your own ear.
5. When everyone has read, try to summarize the major successes and difficulties of this particular group. Agree to listen closely for these last items so that you can all help each other.

EXERCISE 5.7.2 **REFINEMENT IMITATIONS**

1. Take six lines from the classical verse piece on which your imitation partner is now working.
2. Try to achieve an imitation of this person:

   a. in their standard mode of speech;
   b. in GA but still with some of their own characteristics;
   c. in ES;
   d. in RP.

3. Have the person actually speak these lines into your recorder for you in each of the four modes so that you can use the recording as a model.
4. Present your impression to your partner and be prepared at a later time to share it with the class. Be sure to include any difficulties that the actor may be experiencing with any single sound.

EXERCISE 5.7.3 VERSE IMITATION/CONJECTURE

We know that people fall into verse rhythms at moments of great intensity:

Anger: "If **YOU** don't **CUT** the **S__T**, I'll **TAKE** you **OUT**!!!"
Joy: "I **CAN'T** be**LIEVE** I **WON** the **PRIZE**! My **GOD**!"

When does your partner do this? Listen closely and either come up with a metrically regular line that is a quote or conjecture circumstances and a line.

Pulse beats — metre and meaning

The trick with verse is that the rhythms should be subtly present, as if slightly under the surface. In rehearsal, work in extremes, beating out the rhythm relentlessly, then at times ignoring it for pure meaning as if it could be prose.

EXERCISE 5.7.1.1 SWINGING THE PENDULUM

1. Get together with a partner and create some drums for each of you.
2. Speak the scene in as laborious and throbbing a way as you can.
3. Go back and pretend that it is prose.
4. Sit down and discuss what you like from each attack and what might help the scene to fly.
5. Try to blend all that you have learned.

While verse feels overwhelming at first, once you've got it, it really does flow easily. Once you trust it, you will find out that you actually have to make less effort than with prose. It guides you through phrasing, often telling you how to pronounce names and where to place emphasis. It shows shifts in relationships, and it offers both interpretative hints and stage directions. It is easier to memorize and to retain. Verse speeches come back quickly even if you have put them aside for years. Verse gives you natural places to breathe, is pleasing to listen to and helps you to keep the audience's attention. It helps you to think faster.

Verse is like the human heart. Your own pulse is the rhythm of verse. So is a clock ticking, a horse trotting or a metronome. It is the most common time signature in life, so don't let it seem so strange.

The hardest part is coming to grips with the emotional impact of using a new style of speech. You think, "This isn't me. This isn't what talking has felt like all my life."

DAVID ALAN STERN, dialect specialist

Verse is the way you have been speaking *inside* when your feelings were vast and profound. Classical verse is actually comforting, reliable, and safe, the opposite of what it looks like when you first encounter it. Trust it. Verse will take you for a great ride.

And remember that you are unearthing and renewing an extravagance, boldness, and precision that you actually had once upon a time — until you got inhibited. Now it's time to return to the power of childhood.

Part of being a creative force is to keep your childhood alive in yourself.

JOHN LE CARRÉ, writer

LAURENCE OLIVIER'S VOCAL TECHNIQUE VERSUS THAT OF A TWO-YEAR-OLD

In the realm of high drama, Sir Larry was a rank amateur. Take the line, "I don't want supper. I want to watch 'Beauty and the Beast.' Now." Olivier would deliver each syllable with stentorian flair, drenching the space in nuance. "I don't want (your foul) supper (m'lord). I want to watch (the gladsome) 'Beauty and the Beast' (at which so oft I'm wont to thrill). NOW (you shallow knave)." But brilliant two-year-old actors (by conjuring up images of unspeakable horrors such as having to share leftover Hallowe'en candy with a sibling) either stretch each word to its limit with a long seamless moan filtered through the nose "IIIII DOOOOOOn't Waaaaa-aaaaant Suuuuuuppperrrr!" or even more effectively deplete their lungs and gasp for air as in "I-I-I-I-I-I-Doh-doh-doh-doh-dooh-DON'T-wa-wah-wah-wah WANT suh-suh-SUPPER!!!!!" The impact is undeniable.

MICHAEL BURKETT, columnist

When you were little, your feelings were often enough to send you into effective assertion. And automatically into verse rhythms. Letting your voice experience classical literature can unlock, focus, and free the dormant courage:

The classics give us a wonderful cathartic release into an expression of our feelings which are most difficult to express. They give me a burst of spiritual solace that I don't get from any religion.

KENNETH BRANAGH, actor/director

Terms to remember

antithesis	General American	prose
bottoming out	historical rhyme	Received Pronunciation
coining	intermediate A	recessive accent
compensation	liquid U	scansion
distributed stress	metre	schwa
Elevated Standard	metrical pause	split line
elision	monosyllabic line	stress
First Folio	over the top	undercut
foot	personification	verse
forms, strong and weak	pronominal mode	

Summary

You are often called upon to neutralize or elevate your speech, particularly to portray characters of rank and privilege. You need to master three dialects — General American (GA), Elevated Standard (ES), and Received Pronunciation — (RP) to do this. Ten basic issues (R coloration, A mediation, U liquidation, back-vowel separation, twang elimination, schwa elevation, completions, T articulation, W/WH distinction, and precision without affectation) distinguish the dialects from each other.

Verse, used largely in classical drama, is the other major adjustment in elevating stage speech above prose. Scansion is the process by which stresses are determined in a line of verse. If the speech is rhymed, it is elevated a step further. The study of verse vastly increases your sense of rhythm and timing.

There are numerous speech techniques (A to Z: Antithesis to Zone) that can be applied to ensure that you master the conventions of classical drama comfortably and courageously. Experimenting with them helps you to regain a child's sense of adventure balanced by an adult's profound satisfaction.

CHAPTER 6

Releasing your other voices

Most of my capacity lies in my enormous voice, which works marvelously on the stage. But on the screen, I find it extremely difficult to control.

RICHARD BURTON, actor

Two voices are there; one is of the deep;
It learns the storm-cloud's thunderous melody.
And one is of an old half-witted sheep
Which bleats articulate monotony.

J.K. STEPHEN, poet, *Two Voices Are There*

The chameleon, protean, limitless actor has a thousand faces *and* voices, ready and willing to serve any character. No role will be denied them because they cannot handle the sound. The only thing between them and unlimited casting is the limited imagination of the casting director. The only two things between you and all your other voices may be technical knowledge and gutsy experimentation. Richard Burton's glorious voice sometimes limited his work simply because of his inability to change and modify it.

In this chapter, we will explore three of the most exciting ways to increase your vocal repertoire and control:

1. **accents**: finding new sounds from unexplored places;
2. **character voice-over work**: discovering casts of thousands in yourself;
3. **singing**: facing fear and expanding your expressiveness.

UNIT 6.1   ## Accents versus dialects

A sentence is a sound in itself on which other sounds are strung.

ROBERT FROST, poet

Another great actor, Meryl Streep, has demonstrated enough accents to get teased for it, although the teasing is combined with considerable admiration. The capacity to speak the way they do anywhere on earth is a powerful skill. You can master the globe with your voice alone. More importantly, the intense close study of accents simply gets you *noticing* sound, so your general vocal sophistication increases.

The terms *dialect* and *accent* are often used interchangeably. To be more specific, accent refers to pronunciation features: vowels, consonants, pitch, tempo, rhythm, intensity, and resonant quality. Dialect embraces all these linguistic features of pronunciation, plus those of grammar and vocabulary. So accent is one small subset of the larger basket of language features that collectively make up a dialect.

This would mean that a speaker who pronounces "ten" exactly like "tin" has a different accent from someone who says the two words distinctly. If two speakers are expressing detachment by saying "It doesn't matter to me" and "Hit down make no nivermine," that is a difference of dialect.

Aside from improvisational performance, actors are usually not accountable for all the dialect features. Writers supply vocabulary and grammar. Actors have to be masters of accents. Writers have a hard time communicating pronunciation features, although they will sometimes attempt some indication through spelling. These "eye dialects" can be misleading because of the imprecision of respelling. Generally, let the author supply the words and let the actor supply the pronunciation.

Native versus second-language accents

When researching accents, there is a difference between studying varieties of native speech and learning the accents of second-language speakers. Native speech is more predictable and uniform. These accents require a high level of accuracy, consistency, and detail from actors. In contrast, when people speak English as a second language (ESL), they make mistakes. The pattern of these errors tells us their language viewpoint. ESL accents can vary widely between speakers. Even individuals can show a lot of variance, depending on their concentration and mood. The more heightened their emotional state, the less artful their language skills will be.

So, in regional accents we can research and *learn* the way people speak with a high degree of certainty. In ESL accents, actors *design* revealing errors that let the listener know the underlying language perspective and the character's emotional state.

EXERCISE 6.1.1.1 DIVING INTO AN ACCENT

1. Decide as a class which accents you will study this term. The whole class could work on one or several. If you want to be practical, choose accents that are the most requested. American: General, Southern, New York, New England, African American; British Isles: RP, Cockney, Northern, Irish, Scottish; ESL: Chinese, Japanese, Slavic, German, Italian, French, Spanish, Indian. The world is a big place, and there are a lot of languages. You can also suggest accents that "look" the most like you or interest you because of your heritage.
2. Divide the class into teams of two, with each pair either taking its own accent or an agreed-upon aspect from the list on the following pages.
3. Start out with the recordings and printed material provided by Jerry Blunt, Evangeline Machlin, David Alan Stern, Paul Meier, Gillian Lane-Plescia — the most widely employed accent learning systems. Each of these is described in greater detail and compared later in this chapter. We recommend that you try them all, since each will give you something that the others omit. Back these up with the wide range of online sources and other materials available.
4. Begin listening daily during a designated time period, so you can let your subject begin to work on you. Listen while you are doing other tasks (find an internet radio station from this place with a talk show). Check in with your partner on sounds that are giving you difficulty. While the class pursues the following activities, keep the sounds constantly in your ear and on your tongue.

UNIT 6.2   **Opening your ear — releasing your tongue**

So what if you didn't draw the accent you really wanted? What if you got Italian, but you don't look Italian, you can't see yourself playing an Italian, singing opera or visiting Rome, and you don't even like pasta? Well, this accent has chosen *you* for some reason you may not yet recognize. Every accent will expand your cultural horizons, help you to find new aspects of yourself as a person and an actor, and most importantly turn you into more of a sound expert.

It ultimately does not matter which one you study, because by studying one you learn *how* to study them all. You learn the right questions, you get your personal antennae out there probing the right way, and you listen much more carefully to each little sound others make. Your tongue does new things and breaks out of old limitations. You start seeing connections between this accent and others. You get accent smart. The second accent you study will be infinitely easier than the first.

We are going to teach you several ways to approach this subject so that you will have not just knowledge but choice.

"I'm droppin' all my 'G's for a while."

Figure 6.1   "I'm droppin' all my G's for a while" cartoon by Mick Stevens

Organic/cultural accent base

Journey into the world that evolved the accent so that you can create a character who might actually live in that country or region. Study as if you are going to take a trip to the place, live there for a while, come up with a whole new identity, return to your own region, and attempt to "pass" for a true foreigner. Start with a web search, the video store travelogue section, and local travel agencies. Talk to natives and other travelers if possible. Listen to an internet radio station from there and steep yourself in the weather reports, shipping news, sports, and politics. Immerse yourself in the culture, using the following categories as guides.

Images

When you think of this culture, what words and phrases emerge that evoke an intense feeling of what it might be like to live there? You might choose from the same categories used to abstract a character or a voice: fabrics, animals, beverages, modes of transportation, cities, trees, colors, titles of literary works, authors, scents, songs, composers, type of day, weather, landmarks or buildings, food, mythological or fantasy figures, spices, works of art, toys. Come up with at least two powerfully evocative images for each of the five senses. These will help you and your classmates to jump emotionally into the world of the accent.

Values

What truths are assumed and shared by people here? What are the most strictly enforced rules, the most respected traditions, the most highly rewarded and severely punished behaviors? Who is in charge, how does life get changed, what are the dominant ideas about how to have a good time, about loyalty and friendship, about telling the truth, about war and religion, and about change? Focus particularly on those values that are *not* like yours.

Influences

What in the weather, terrain, proximity, and history of the region may influence the sound of speech? Many believe that the flat plains of much of the American Midwest influence the flat way of speaking there, while the perpetually rolling hills of southern Ireland set up the perfect influence for the lilt of that country's speech. Does the heat/humidity of the Southern USA factor into the languid tempo and stretching of vowel sounds as the cold of Iceland might affect the crisp, tight, brisk use of vowels there? The comparative emotional restraint of British culture and flamboyance of Italian daily interaction show up in sound. Look at how the culture evolved. Island cultures with long histories like Japan and England have more subtly shaded and delicately encoded social rules than more recently colonized frontier cultures like the USA and Australia. How does this show up in speech?

UNIT 6.3.4 *Warm-ups*

As you get to know the accent better, evolve a warm-up to get you into this new sound. Use the images, play music, vary your known physical and vocal preparation to suit the demands of this particular set of sounds. You will probably, for example, not work on relaxation for the Japanese accent, but you may want to focus on posture and precision. If you're working on a western American range accent, you might want to find an expanded physicality that is accustomed to taking up more space. For Italian, you are likely to spend some time on gesturing, getting the arms up and out and putting the body into the words. You will spend more time on tongue tip exercises if an accent seems to employ that muscle more, more time exploring the lower pitch ranges if the accent tends to be pitched in the bottom part of one's register.

UNIT 6.3.5 *Physical lives*

Find what you consider a basic posture for standing, sitting, leaning, and conversing that suits the accent. Ask if there is a dominant center, favored way of holding the head, most used facial expressions, popular way of walking, or use of the eyes. How much space does one take up or need to feel comfortable, how close or far from the body do the appendages move when speaking? Consider the basic social encounters — strangers passing on the street, being introduced to someone, flirting or coming on, greeting an old friend or relative. How do you wave hello/goodbye, or direct a rude gesture toward someone? Evolve what seems to be a reasonable physical framework for the cave that holds this accent.

So far, we have not really touched the sound itself but the physical basis, because if you get a good cave, your chances are much better for the right sounds to be emitted from its depth.

EXERCISE 6.3.5.1 DEVELOPING AN ACCENT CHARACTER

1. Find a new identity to use during subsequent class activities. Do not worry for now about how clichéd or stereotypical this person is. We all know that, if cast in a role, you would work past archetypes into subtlety, nuance, and even contradiction. For now, go for broad, bright strokes and primary colors. Aim to be the most Spanish Spaniard or Germanic German who ever drew breath. This is just a starting place. (Remember that actors who spend too much initial time avoiding clichés — "I don't want my prostitute to seem too whorish", "I don't want this librarian to seem too bookish" — often end up doing work that is simply vague and confusing. Get the type down first, then work out of it).

2. If you are working with a partner, do not be clones of each other but find two different strong figures within the culture. If there are striking differences in the way in which men and women in the culture behave, one of you should play a male and the other female regardless of your actual gender. If the culture is polarized, pick both ends. Set up an interesting tension between the two of you.

3. Name yourself. Do a variation on your own real name or create one altogether new and totally memorable (Robert might become Roberto Bartonio for Italian, and Rocco might shift to Rockport Dalveryworth for British).

4. Give yourself a whole set of given circumstances, from your point of birth on through present occupation and preoccupation. Prepare to introduce yourself to the class and the totally new you.

EXERCISE 6.3.5.2 UNITED NATIONS OF ACCENTS

1. With the teacher serving as secretary-general, form the room into a UN with each delegation assigned its own spot.

2. Over a series of class periods, gather with increasingly difficult tasks to briefly share with the rest of the group.

3. In the beginning, do not feel that you need to keep the accent identity when others are presenting. It is OK to ask them questions as yourself.

4. Try the following sequence:

UNIT 6.4   Technical accent base

Some actors find it easier to begin by isolating sounds rather than by approaching accent through character. An accent may be approached from one of three purely technical standpoints.

1. **Phonetics**: where the specific sounds of the accent are compared to what is considered standard in your culture. Use a written transliteration or the IPA — a *visual/auditory* approach.

2. **Recordings**: where you listen to people who naturally speak in the accent, actors doing the accent or instructional lessons in the sounds of the accent — an *auditory* approach.

3. **Placement**: where you *feel/*where the accent seems to sit in your mouth. This is relative to your personal placement. For many North American speakers, Irish seems to resonate very far forward and high, contrasted with Scottish, which can feel far back and low, as though your tongue were held down by a tongue depressor — a *kinesthetic[1]/auditory* approach.

Session 1: Each **delegation introduces** its members, each of whom tells some important facts about themselves and their country or region.

Session 2: Share **images** that help the others to get into your culture.

Session 3: Teach others the **physical life** characteristics for both men and women. Demonstrate, and then get the whole group up and moving.

Session 4: Identify for the group wha: you consider the **three most important characteristics** of the accent. Search for areas shared with other accents present.

Session 5: Come prepared to argue **why your country/region is the best** and most beautiful in the world. Imagine that a delegation from another planet is coming to earth and we want them to visit the best place first. Stay in character throughout for this session. Have a panel of judges pick who made the best argument.

---

1 A sense mediated by end organs located in muscles, tendons, and joints and stimulated by bodily movements and tensions; also, sensory experience derived from this sense.

Researching the sounds

The accent systems that are most widely studied and with which you will wish to be familiar are Blunt, Lane-Plescia, Machlin, Meier and Stern.

Most important resources

Jerry Blunt, *Stage Dialects* (Dramatic Publishing, 1994 with CDs); *More Stage Dialects* (Dramatic Publishing, 1996 with CDs). *Stage Dialects* features simple directions and instructional audio recordings. Blunt starts with a cultural overview and general information about the people, their history, characteristic behavior, and uses of the dialect. Then, using phonetics, he breaks down the vowel, diphthong, and consonant substitutions/changes with an explanatory paragraph on each. Individual sounds are studied in key words, sentences, and longer readings for fluency, all with examples on the audio recording. It is in a clear, simple, step-by-step format. *More Stage Dialects* covers broader territory. The audio recordings are samples of actual natives, not instructional, and the descriptions of the sound changes are cursory. In contrast to his other book, there are no instructions. You're on your own to develop the accent.

Gillian Lane-Plescia, *The Dialect Resource: Dialect and Accent CDs* (dialectresource.com). Practical audio materials for accent research and acquisition. The recordings contain native speakers, not imitations. There are detailed discussions of the features of each and hints on the formation of unfamiliar sounds. Accompanying booklets contain analysis, and IPA notation, notes on samples, and lists of other sources. Over 80 dialect recordings including numerous UK and US regional patterns.

Evangeline Machlin, *Dialects for the Stage* with CD (Routledge, 2006). Combines instructional material, actors doing readings, and natives. Uses transliteration, no phonetics, and details of sound change are sometimes cursory. Uses the play it–say it system of teaching, where after hearing the original recording, gaps are left so that you can repeat in the style of the speaker. Synopses of sound changes are brisk, cleanly organized, and brief. Includes lists of some plays where the dialect is used.

Paul Meier, *Accents and Dialects for Stage and Screen* with twelve CDs (Paul Meier Dialect Services, 2008). Twenty-four accents and dialects covered. All practice sentences and monologues are in IPA notation, as well as in the author's "number-keying" system. *CDs for Specific Plays and Musicals* (Paul Meier Dialect Services). A large CD library of dialect designs for the many plays and musicals that Meier has coached in the theatre. Recordings consist of one CD per character. Meier demonstrates the character's lines in dialect — pronunciation, intonation, tone and rhythm, isolating and discussing the

UNIT 6.5.2

ONLINE

Online resources

actor's choices. He avoids giving "line readings" by working slightly under tempo. He is also the founder of the International Dialects of English Archive, the best site to visit when looking for samples of native speakers online.

David Alan Stern, *Acting with an Accent* (Dialect/Accent Specialists, 2000–2010), pamphlets with accompanying CDs. Also *Dialect Monologues*, written by Roger Karshner and performed by Stern. A popular self-study series (and the most efficient if you have an audition tomorrow), using phonetics and Lessac[2] notation systems. Each dialect packet includes a CD and a short (15 pages) pamphlet. He starts with the placement and resonance, imagining a tonal focus, and feeling the change in tissue vibration. Then he works on vowel pronunciations and consonant shifts with key word examples, phrases, and sentences, using the play it–say it system, building to one long monologue to lock it all in. No native speakers or female voices, only Dr. Stern.

The extraordinary array of dialect recordings and analysis online is ever changing and expanding. Rather than list all those available here and risk missing new developments, we'll direct you to the most important clearing house for internet dialect links, the **Voice and Speech Trainers Association** (VASTA) at vasta.org. You should make this your first stop for finding internet dialect resources. Your second stop should be the **International Dialects of English Archive**. This is a huge repository of recordings from all over the world. Many are accompanied by phonetic transcription, so you can see a dissection of their characteristics.

UNIT 6.5.3

Print resources

While some of the following accent sources may be out of print, most are available through libraries and campus audio centers.

Robert Blumenfeld, *Accents — A Manual for Actors* with 2 CDs (Limelight Editions, 1998). A practical reference manual, with instructions on how to speak in more than eighty dialects, from Albanian to Zulu. No phonetics. The notation system

2 Arthur Lessac, author of *The Use and Training of the Human Voice*, developed his own unique system for noting speech sounds. See more on him in Chapter 7.

can be confusing. Work is sectioned by continents, with similarities emphasized for those within a specific region. Numerous exercises are included. On the second CD, the author performs exercises, allowing the listener to hear how to produce required sound changes.

Louis Herman and Marguerite Shalett Herman, *American Dialects* (Routledge, 1997) and *Foreign Dialects* (Routledge, 1997). Both books cover areas not found elsewhere. No phonetics, but a confusing system of transliteration. No recordings. In-depth looks at each region, culture, style of delivery, lilt, and stressing patterns. Dialect shifts are listed. Longer monologues for practice. The organizational pattern is hard to follow. The books contain some uncomfortable cultural stereotyping, but it is important to remember that they were written in the 1940s and haven't been revised.

Ginny Kopf, *The Dialect Handbook: Learning, Researching and Performing a Dialect Role* (Voiceprint Publishing, 2003, 2nd edition). Kopf offers a step-by-step process for creating an accent role and covers more than thirty accents, focusing on lilt, stress, resonance, and muscularity. A key feature, the Dialect Directory, lists hundreds of feature films, TV series, documentaries, audio recordings, and books for research. An extensive bibliography of dialect acquisition materials provides descriptions of the books and recordings, and tips on how to use them and where to find them. The author's approach is upbeat, simple, and direct. A generous resource that leads to other sources.

Donald H. Molin, *The Actor's Encyclopedia of Dialects* (Sterling Publishing, 1984). No attempt is made to prioritize sound changes. Charts, notational system and lists are confusing. Twenty-three dialects are covered. Each chapter has practice pages, a paragraph or so on music and rhythm, and some (if not all) give examples from plays and films.

Edda Sharpe and Jan Haydn Rowles, *How to Do Accents* with CD (Oberon Books, 2008). The authors provide insight, tools, and confidence to understand the structure of accents, giving practical guidance and tips for consistency. The CD contains detailed exercises and sample sentences, along with eleven extended recordings of voices from the USA, Ireland, Scotland, Wales, and England. Less is provided about how to acquire a specific accent than about how to master the way to learn accents in general. A great text for learning how to get your mouth around new sounds.

John C. Wells, *Accents of English 1: An Introduction, 2: The British Isles, 3: Beyond the British Isles* (Cambridge University Press, 1982), three volumes. A scholarly work requiring facility with phonetics and an understanding of linguistic terminology. A deeply detailed survey of English speech from the leading figure in the field. An audio recording of some samples is available.

Claude Merton Wise, *Applied Phonetics* (Prentice-Hall, 1957). Excellent descriptions of dialect sound changes, but no structured lessons. A goldmine if you have facility with phonetics. No audio recording.

While you may have a preference for working either organically or technically, or you may prefer one technical approach over another, you will benefit greatly if you pursue the accent from all possible approaches. Notice that several of the sources above attempt to combine methods. Use the following index to help you to find the right sources for the accent you are studying. Try as many as you can. Please note that the below table lists accents in the way they are likely to be requested by directors. In some cases this reflects theatrical rather than linguistic parlance.

UNIT 6.6

Geographic index of accent sources

CODE:
▯ ~ Notes on the accent, but no accompanying recording.
👤 ~ Recording of native speakers, usually with notes.
♪ ~ Instructional recorded lesson, usually with notes.

	Blumenfeld	Blunt	Herman	Kopf	Lane-Plescia	Machlin	Meier	Molin	Stern	Wise
NORTH AMERICA										
African-American	♪			▯	👤👤👤		♪		♪	▯▯
Boston		👤👤	▯	▯						
Cajun				▯						
Canadian	♪			▯						
Caribbean	♪		▯	▯▯	👤			▯		
Chicago	♪	👤👤👤	▯▯	▯▯▯▯	👤	👤	♪		♪	▯▯
Delmarva Peninsula	♪			▯			♪♪		♪	
Down East	♪	👤👤	▯▯	▯		👤	♪		♪♪	▯
French-Canadian	♪	👤	▯			👤				▯
General American	♪									▯
General Southern		♪								▯
Gullah	♪		▯	▯▯	👤👤		♪♪		♪♪	▯
Haitian	♪				👤		♪		♪	
Latino							♪		♪	
Louisiana Creole	♪									▯
Mexico	♪									▯▯

	Blumenfeld	Blunt	Herman	Kopf	Lane-Plescia	Machlin	Meier	Molin	Stern	Wise
Mid-West	ɔ	ɒ·ɒ	⊔⊔	⊔⊔⊔⊔	·ɒ·	·ɒ·				⊔
Mountain			⊔	⊔⊔⊔			ɔ		ɔ	⊔⊔
Native American	ɔ	ɔ								
New York City	ɔ	ɔ	⊔	⊔⊔	·ɒ·	·ɒ·				⊔⊔
Pennsylvania Dutch	ɔ									
Philadelphia		⊔	⊔	·ɒ·	·ɒ·					
Southwestern										
Texas	ɔ	⊔				ɔ				
Tidewater	ɔ·ɔ		⊔							
Up-state New York	ɔ									
Western	⊔									
BRITISH ISLES										
Cockney	ɔ	ɔ	⊔	⊔	·ɒ·	·ɒ·	ɔ	⊔	ɔ	⊔
Estuary	ɔ			⊔						
Hampshire	ɔ			⊔						
Irish	ɔ	ɔ·ɔ	⊔⊔	⊔	·ɒ·	·ɒ·	ɔ	⊔	ɔ	⊔
Northern	ɔ	ɔ·ɔ	⊔⊔	⊔	·ɒ·	·ɒ·	ɔ	⊔⊔	ɔ	⊔⊔
RP	ɔ·ɔ	·ɒ·		⊔	·ɒ·	·ɒ·	ɔ		ɔ	
Scottish	ɔ	·ɒ·		⊔	·ɒ·	·ɒ·	ɔ		ɔ	
Welsh	ɔ			⊔	·ɒ·		ɔ		ɔ	
West Country	ɔ	·ɒ·		⊔	·ɒ·	·ɒ·	ɔ		ɔ	
EUROPE										
Albanian	ɔ				·ɒ·					
Austrian	ɔ	·ɒ·	⊔	⊔	·ɒ·					
Basque										
Belgian										
Bulgarian	ɔ	·ɒ·	⊔⊔⊔	⊔⊔	·ɒ·			⊔		
Czech/Slovak	ɔ	·ɒ·			·ɒ·					
Danish	ɔ	·ɒ·	⊔		·ɒ·					
Dutch	ɔ	·ɒ·			·ɒ·					

	Blumenfeld	Blunt	Herman	Kopf	Lane-Piescia	Machlin	Meier	Molin	Stern	Wise
Finnish										
French										
Georgian										
German										
Greek										
Hungarian										
Italian										
Lithuanian										
Norwegian										
Polish										
Portuguese										
Romanian										
Russian										
Serbo-Croat										
Spanish										
Swedish										
Turkish										
Ukrainian										
Yiddish										
Yugoslavian										
MIDDLE EAST										
Arabic										
Hebrew										
Persian/Iranian										
AFRICA										
Afrikaans										
Ethiopian										
Ghanaian										
Kenyan										

	Blumenfeld	Blunt	Herman	Kopf	Lane-Plescia	Machlin	Meier	Molin	Stern	Wise
Nigerian	🎧	👤			👤	👤			🎧	
Senegalese					👤					
South African English	🎧				👤					
Sudanese		👤							🎧	
Ugandan	🎧				👤					
Zairean	🎧									
Zulu	🎧				👤					

INDIA/ASIA/PACIFIC

	Blumenfeld	Blunt	Herman	Kopf	Lane-Plescia	Machlin	Meier	Molin	Stern	Wise
Aboriginal Australian			📖		👤					
Australian	🎧	👤	📖	📖	👤		🎧	📖	🎧	
Beche Le Mar			📖							
Burmese	🎧									
Chinese	🎧	👤		📖						
Filipino	🎧	👤	📖							
Hawaiian	🎧		📖	📖						
Indian		👤	📖	📖			🎧	📖		
Japanese	🎧	🎧	📖	📖						
Korean	🎧			📖						
Mongolian	🎧									
New Zealand	🎧	👤		📖	👤			📖		
Samoan	🎧			📖						
Singaporean	🎧									
Sri Lankan	🎧									
Thai	🎧									
Uzbek	🎧									
Vietnamese	🎧	👤		📖						

Hierarchies — individualizing the accent

Unfortunately, while each of the existing accent systems offers value, none tells you what is most important for any given accent. They all set up arbitrary sequences and go through each accent without making priorities. So your job will be to isolate what matters most. Is quality or placement more essential than tempo, rhythm, pitch, volume, word choice or nonverbals? In pronunciation, is this an accent dominated by vowel substitutions, or by consonants or diphthongs? German is primarily consonant action. Irish is clearly an accent where vowel pitch pattern is more important than many elements. Tempo is vital for American Southern. Find what should go to the top of the list:

> **EXERCISE 6.7.1 HIERARCHIZING**
>
> 1. Go back over the information you've acquired. Create a list of changes for the accent from most to least important. Ask yourself, "If I had a friend who had to do this accent for an audition tomorrow, what would be the easiest, most concise, and uncluttered way to give her what she needs to get by?"
> 2. Don't omit any item. This will require some debate/discussion with your partner, checking in with your teacher, and it may involve negotiating some ties.
> 3. Determine a top ten list (first place, second place, etc., down to tenth most important characteristic) and make copies for the whole class.

Thickening and thinning

As an actor, you want to be able to do a subtle, delicate, light accent with just the slightest flavoring as well as a thick, heavy accent with every single change in place. You also wish to be able to perform various stages of thick or thin between these two extremes. And you'll want to play a range from broadly comic to emotionally moving. To help you to intensify or weaken an accent, think of "first in, last out." The first sounds you learn as a child are the last to leave when you adjust your speech. The first things you distinguish are rhythm, melody, quality, and inflection, then later vowels and lastly consonants. So when thinning most (not all) accents, first standardize the consonants, then work backward. Think of the accent as soup, which can range from a simple broth all the way through to a thick chowder. The first choice will suit roles where the character has been out of their native land for some time and/or the accent is supposed to be minimally distracting to the dramatic action.

It will suit delicate realistic scripts. The other extreme will be great for satire, burlesque, much improvisational sketch work or a situation where the accent is supposed to remain sharply in focus. Decide which sounds are funniest to your audience's ears so that you have the power to punch up or play down those, depending on the comic or dramatic values of the script.

Remember that, in life, we may thicken or thin our accents to suit our purposes.

> **At Oxford, Clinton became, if anything more American, drawled more deeply, like a southern politician home from Washington. The joke on campus was that he could turn "s__t" into a four-syllable word.**
> **Bill Clinton, ex-president, described by JACOB WEISBERG, reporter**

A cautionary note about the use of primary sources — people who are really from the country in question. We are doing *theatrical* accents for a reason. Many *authentic* accents are incomprehensible, so remember the old adage, "The actor's first responsibility is to be seen, heard, and understood." You can go past chowder into casserole. Also many primary sources are hybrids; if you were born in Spain, spent some time in Germany, then New York and now live in Iowa, you may have some of each of these in your speech. An actor could easily be misled by such an accent. A goal of theatrical accent work is to identify clearly where the character is from, so we often sharpen the differences between similar accents. In real life, a skilled dialectician may spend a long time listening to a person before deciding if they're from Ireland or Scotland. The audience doesn't have the time or the skills for this, so the actor needs clear, distinct choices. We need to simply accept that sometimes we don't please native speakers, whose patterns may be more subtle or generalized.

Accent work in film and television is especially challenging, since worldwide distribution guarantees that native speakers will see the performance. This area requires the most consistency, subtlety, and authenticity. Because of the nature of film production and post-production sound treatments, intelligibility is more manageable than on stage, so the medium will tolerate (and therefore demands) delicate, complex accents that might not project in a theatre.

EXERCISE 6.7.1.1 **THIN TO THICK TO THIN**

Pick five levels for the accent based on your hierarchy work. Determine the total number of significant characteristics possible.

5. Greet the visitors in your accent personas and take them through a series of experiences that give them sense/muscle memory of the accent as well as technical knowledge of changes. Teach them how to do something that can require repeating key phrases and learning important terms: how to bargain like an Arab rug merchant; how to argue with a New York cabby; or how to busk at a London tube station.

    Consider offering food and drink from the culture, but if you do, don't just break for snacks but use it as part of the lesson ("You hold your pinkie thusly with your teacup" or "You will only be served if you leap onto furniture and sing!").
6. Allow time for questions and clarifications at the end.

EXERCISE 6.7.1.3 **TESTING HOW IT TOOK**

Because these sessions are the briefest introductions, each participant needs to go home and apply the material, handout in hand.

1. One class period later schedule a five- to ten-minute test of accuracy.
2. Any of the sample drill sentences on the handout are fair game, plus each actor should be forewarned about a topic of conversation in which he will be asked to respond.
3. Go around the group listening, giving notes on where each person still needs work.

Character voices

UNIT 6.8

> **I will aggravate my voice so, that I will roar you as gently as any suckling dove: I will roar you as 'twere any nightingale.**
>
> Bottom from WILLIAM SHAKESPEARE's *A Midsummer Night's Dream*

We all have many characters inside, champing at the bit to be released. A large repertoire of voices means that you have choice. New characters can constantly jump out. In scripted work, more available voices give you more characterization options. Even when you settle on a basic voice for a character, a large repertoire lets you explore maximum variety *within* that character's range of choices. You may already have alter egos that you pop into when clowning around with friends, but there are others in there too. Just waiting.

UNIT 6.8.1   *The three Cs — characters/caricatures/cartoons*

Actors are asked to produce both real, deep, complex work and instantly recognizable, simple, archetypal work. Both extremes serve you. We will separate them here because you might be asked to adjust up or down:

Character: we think that we know this **person**; she lives down the street or across the tracks. On no level do we feel that she belongs in sitcom land. She is real, but she probably does not sound just like you. Compare this with classical portraiture.

Caricature: we recognize this **type** and may even know some people who embody her. She is a lot of others wrapped into one. She is the consummate version of her group. She is broader than a character voice. If someone refers to her as "a real character," he does not mean realistic but vivid, outlandish, and noteworthy. Compare this with a visually sketched caricature, where the most distinctive features are enlarged.

Cartoon: he takes a human quality and magnifies it into bright, primary colors. He is a broad, bright **exaggeration**. He could be heard and then immediately sketched by a visual artist with relative ease. It is not so much that he is unbelievable as that he exists with in a narrow set of broad choices, most with exclamation points!! Compare this with Cubist art, where an intense focus on certain features gives a striking insight.

As you work on subsequent assignments, always ask yourself which of the 3 Cs you are doing. Take a moment to experiment with any given voice, taking it into the other 2 Cs so that you develop the capacity to move back and forth between toons to slice of life with very little effort.

UNIT 6.8.2   *Same text/different voices*

The following assignment is one of the most important in this book. It asks you to take everything you have learned so far and put it into one presentation of under six minutes. It gives you a chance to use pure vocal technique and wild vocal exploration.

EXERCISE 6.8.2.1 FOUR VOICES

Take a classical verse monologue that you have been working on for some time. Cut it down to less than two minutes. Present it to the class in the following ways:

Elevated/scanned

1. Shoot for your best possible Elevated Standard Speech throughout, with the verse *scanned* precisely so that any listener will hear each stress without being distracted by the metre.

Now pick one minute to repeat for the class in these formats:

Actor as self

2. Present the material as you (this is the most difficult of the tasks) without any "acting" exactly as you would speak the words in a situation from your own life. Your task is to drop away actor affectations and to own your own habits, especially those you had before entering training.

Character voice

3. Pick any other person you have in you (jump ahead to the next section if you draw blanks). Give this character a name and motive. Do not make fun of this character no matter how extreme your choice. It should seem like a real human being totally different from you.

Accent

4. In your mastered accent, present the material with all the attitude and motivation you have evolved for your accent alter ego.

Introductions

5.   When you appear before the class, introduce each of the people you will perform just prior to their presentation.

Variations

Substitute any assignment you have been working on that suggests a clear vocal choice for any above if you have not covered it.

An optional addition is to add *singing* the monologue (see Exercise 6.13.3) for a total of *five voices*.

Assessment

Gather as a group and discuss in each category where the actor was most and least on the money.

1.   Elevated/scanned: with the first "voice," what was lost in terms of believability while the actor was trying too hard to get ES and metre correct? Where did heroic verse successfully blend with human need? Which lines require further scansion work? Which are a masterful balance of beats and real progression of thought and feeling?
2.   Actor as self: where did the "actor" invade the person? Where has the actor failed to recognize/own their own mannerisms? Where is there true, accurate self-imitation and successful self-awareness?
3.   Character voice: what is the identity of the voice, and how is it real? Is it in any way unreal? Does it ever move out of character and into one of the two broader categories? What is the actor doing to leave behind their usual voice and accept another? Could they do more or less and still create a believable other?
4.   Accent: this is a check-in on progress. How accurate and complete is the accent work so far? Where is mastery accomplished? What seems incomplete? How is this character compelling enough to pursue further? What dimensions might be added?
5.   Introductions: what kind of energy emerges as the actor does self-scripted intros? When does the transition into character seem to be helped by this segue? When does it seem forced or not yet believable?
6.   Application: what seemed true, compelling, reasonable or worthwhile when the actor was not in the classical mode that may be transferred into that presentation?

The Four Voices exercise can be profoundly revealing for actor and audience. What often emerges is that there are elements of self, character, accent, and introductions that can be utilized to do a better classical presentation. An actor learns that under the comfort of a "digression" assignment, they sometimes produce a more compelling and honest choice. There is often more life and imagination in these instances, which, once discovered, can be put into the classical version. You may go back to your verse piece unafraid to bring offbeat, less than perfect, basic, risky, and honest moments.

EXERCISE 6.8.2.2 FOUR VOICES IMITATIONS

Imitators will wish to record the presentations above and use these to help to refine your work. Because your partner attempts to be completely himself as well as trying on other voices, this gives you real evidence of the actor at work, struggling, sometimes halting, and sometimes experiencing powerful victories. You might privately wish to try to recreate the recording and, if you have access to two recorders, play them and compare them.

Discovering all your voices

UNIT 6.9

Four basic approaches can evolve vocal characters. Try each of them.

1. **Voice personas**: identify a type of person and give them a voice. Consider impersonations of famous people or your neighbors. Even if you don't nail it, you may discover a new voice.
2. **Voice attitudes**: start with an emotion or attitude, play it fully, discover the person therein, and what the voice is.
3. **Voice circumstances**: imagine yourself with a set of given circumstances and let the voice emerge.
4. **Voice constructing**: build voices by randomly combining all vocal elements or ingredients in various ways.

It helps to release these voices if you imagine yourself doing **voiceovers** (radio spots, commercials, off-camera narration, instructional CDs, cartoons) or instances where all of your acting is done with sound, where there are either no pictures or if there are, you aren't in them, but rather your voice is laid over the visuals.

Voice attitudes

Here is a slightly different list, based less on an identity than an attitude. While there will be some overlap with the previous list, some new voices can emerge from:

1. warm, friendly	2. instructional or expert	3. stuffy aristocratic	4. angry, perturbed
5. bright, energetic	6. concerned	7. gossip columnist	8. gangsterish
9. authoritative	10. cautionary	11. poke a little fun at	12. sinister, evil
13. intelligent, logical	14. storytelling	15. wry, tongue-in-cheek	16. sarcastic
17. helpful, caring	18. talking to children	19. nerdy, twerpish, ditzy	20. understated
21. motherly/fatherly	22. to the child in all of us	23. vacant, oblivious	24. bored
25. neighborly	26. magical	27. campy	28. nervous
29. real person, offhand	30. eavesdropper	31. flighty, goofy	32. embarrassed, reluctant
33. carefree	34. appetizing, teasing	35. wacky, nutty	36. hip, rhythmic
37. upscale, elegant	38. sensual	39. no-nonsense	40. feminine, manly
41. spokesperson	42. sexy, sultry	43. know-it-all, wise guy	44. reflective
45. chatty	46. mysterious, ethereal	47. obnoxious	48. sad, depressed
49. sharing discovery	50. revealing secret	51. cute	52. to the point

UNIT 6.9.3 *Voice circumstances*

By simply adjusting the event that has just happened or something that is dominating your thoughts, you can radically change your sound. Consider any well-known advertising lingo. How would it be different if:

Birds are attacking you.
You just found out that your best friend has died.
You won the lottery.
The hottest person on earth just walked through the door.
You just got caught cheating.
Your feet are killing you.
You were just handed something disgusting to eat.
You've been fired from your job.
You've a gun pointed at your head.
You're being chased by a rhinoceros.
You're being spanked.
You've been handed a beautiful single rose.
You ate a red hot chili pepper.
You just found out that class has been cancelled.
You've decided that you really like the way you look in the mirror.
You are only two inches tall.
You are over fifty feet tall.
You're allergic to everything.
An elephant is standing on your foot.
You're having great sex.

Now consider the possible details if you layer them in. Here is a sample line of copy advertising a restaurant:

THERE'S NO PLACE LIKE HOME, THE COMFORT, THE FEELING, THE FLAVORS . . . THERE REALLY IS NO PLACE LIKE HOME, BUT FOR OVER 20 YEARS, ONE PLACE HAS COME PRETTY CLOSE — JOHNSON'S.

We don't really know who the person is who is speaking these lines on the radio or why. But as an actor you can use your imagination to build vocal texture. Consider the lines with these given circumstances:

- You are a lifer marine, talking to a young private with whom you have survived dangerous combat. It's midnight, you're on leave in the big city and you're about to take "the kid" to your favorite brothel.
- You're a 16-year-old counselor talking to a homesick 11-year-old camper in the quiet night in the tent, just after the little camper has read a letter from home and is sniffling.
- You are a 65-year-old schoolteacher at your retirement dinner surrounded by beloved colleagues in the auditorium, just having been given, in addition to many other gifts, a picture of all of them to hang up in your home.

But it's a restaurant ad, right? Not an ad for a brothel, a camp or a school. Yes, but sometimes the most interesting and dramatically compelling choices come about by experimenting with approaches like the ones above. The voice needs to be warm, comforting, affectionate, knowing, reassuring. How you get there can vary enormously (and it can also be your secret — you don't have to share how you got there).

Don't neglect any of the given circumstances present in every acting piece. Now they are *more* important, because the audience can only listen. Who are you fully when you speak? How are you dressed, what are your personal props, and what is all the baggage, literal and psychological, you bring to this encounter? To whom are you speaking, and what is the nature of your relationship? How do you change during the encounter? How does your listener respond and change? Do you feel challenged, are they about to leave, just on the verge of interrupting, failing to listen? Do they ask you to repeat at each interval because they didn't quite hear or get it? What else is going on nearby? What are all the conditioning forces (time, your fatigue/energy level, how late you are or how free to waste time, familiarity of place, your relative health, slight irritations, how light or dark, warm or cold, etc. is this place, your comfort level, how you feel about your clothes today) that keep you away from boring neutral and add dimensions?

EXERCISE 6.9.3.1 DO IT AND CHANGE IT

1. Choose or write a line of copy.
2. As yourself, go through each of the quick circumstances above recording yourself. Playback.
3. Create three other detailed sets of circumstances. Again record and playback.
4. Create circumstances where the listener reacts or changes in some way and let that influence how you speak.
5. Now go to one of the categories identified earlier, pick a basic voice to start with based on *persona* and *attitude*.
6. Try two lines with your basic voices, adding the various given circumstances.

EXERCISE 6.9.3.2 VOICE DU JOUR

1. Post the lists above somewhere where you can't avoid them.
2. Every day, pick at least one new voice to play with.
3. Either take famous known lines or invent your own for each voice. Evolve a key phrase and a name that lets you anchor the voice for instant recall.
4. Record and playback repeatedly until you are happy with what you have.
5. Once you have nailed a voice, find a ritual to add it officially to your repertoire. Highlight it on the list. Put a gold star next to it. Write it and the representative line on a card and put it in a recipe card type file, or use the Character Voice Inventory shown next. Find whatever will give you a feeling of achievement and also make you feel obliged to keep the voice alive.

UNIT 6.9.4 *Voice constructing*

Now you're ready to go into areas outside your imagination. Start by doing a personal voice inventory. Make extra copies of the form below (as your voice grows you will need more space). Without making any effort to change your voice, what can it do? How many ways can it twist and turn?

EXERCISE 6.9.4.1 INDIVIDUAL VOICE INVENTORY

ONLINE

1. In each category, think of every possible way to change it. We have filled in the first line with some obvious choices. Most of us know that with tempo we can go fast, slow, medium, languid or frantic. What else can you do? Don't worry about using "proper" terminology. As long as you know what you mean, and can demonstrate it, it doesn't matter what you call it.

Table 6.1 Individual voice inventory

INDIVIDUAL VOICE INVENTORY

TEMPO		fast	slow	medium	languid	frantic
RHYTHM		steady	choppy	irregular	syncopated	bursty
ARTICULATION		precise	muddy	slurred	emphatic	crisp
IMPEDIMENTS		lisp	r/w substit.	lateral lisp	unvoicing	cleft palate
PRONUNCIATION		ES, GA, RP	foreign	regional	(list accents)	(list accents)
PITCH	median note	high	low	medium	falsetto	bass
	range	broad	narrow	musical	high	low
	inflection	upward	flat	downward	circumflex	level
QUALITY		resonant	thin	breathy	nasal	hollow
WORD CHOICE		hip	aristocratic	foul	intellectual	bizarre
NONVERBALS		eh-yeh	uhm	ya-know	sorta-like	well-er
	laugh style	titter	horsey	snicker	braying	belly

6 RELEASING YOUR OTHER VOICES   333

2. Take a piece of text and be ready to demonstrate each one of the vocal aspects you have listed.
3. Skip randomly around the class sharing parts of the personal voice inventory.
4. Make up counterintuitive combinations of elements: high median note, slow tempo, nasal resonance, slurred articulation, syncopated rhythm, upward inflection, etc. See who can do the most unusual combinations.

Now that you have a sense of how varied your voice can be, find unusual combinations of vocal elements to create unexpected character voices.

ONLINE

EXERCISE 6.9.4.2 CHARACTER VOICE INVENTORY

1. Make several copies of the following form. Fill it out for any characters you have already developed. The first one has been filled out as an example.

Table 6.2 Character voice inventory example

CHARACTER VOICE INVENTORY

1. Character Name: **Geoffrey Fortesque the Third**

2. Character Type:
foppish dandy, wealthy playboy

3. Key Phrase:
"Hand me my pink silk foulard, Jeeves"

4. Emotion/Attitude:
arrogant, condescending

5. Physical Description:
tall, thin, soft chin, receding hairline

6. Tempo:
languid

7. Rhythm:
smooth, long phrases

8. Articulation:
mushy

9. Impediments:
frontal lisp, r/w

10. Pronunciation:
Marked RP

11. Pitch a) median note:
high

b) range:
broad, musical

c) inflection-intonation:
downward

13. Quality:
nasal

14. Word Choice:
aristocratic

15. Nonverbals a) stall/fill sounds:
I say, really

b) laugh style:
titter

Table 6.3 Character voice inventory form

CHARACTER VOICE INVENTORY

1. Character Name:

2. Character Type: 3. Key Phrase:

4. Emotion/Attitude: 5. Physical Description:

6. Tempo: 7. Rhythm: 8. Articulation: 9. Impediments:

10. Pronunciation: 11. Pitch a) median note: b) range: c) inflection-intonation:

13. Quality: 14. Word Choice: 15. Nonverbals a) stall/fill   b) laugh style:
                                               sounds:

2. After listing all your *existing* characters, develop completely *unexpected* ones by randomly combining the elements of your personal voice inventory. (The more the various elements don't seem to go together, the better!)
3. Start with #6 through #15 on the form above. Give someone your individual voice inventory. While reading a piece of text, have them call out elements for you to add to your voice. Layer them on top of each other. As a character emerges, fill out #1 through #5 to complete the profile.

The above activity can stretch your voice in ways that you never imagined. Play your voice like an audio rather than a video game (VoiceBoy? Tonguetendo? Sounda Genesis? Super Mouthio Brothers?), challenging your friends with weird combinations, seeing how many elements you can stack together.

UNIT 6.10   **Voiceover demos**

Actors aspire to theatrical work, but many make the bulk of their income in the studio at the mic. The character Eliot in "The Boys in the Band" cracks that one thing to be said about masturbation is that you do not need to look your best. The same is true for voiceovers. You may look like unshaven, degraded hell, but if you can sound like silk or silver, who cares?

> **It's the easiest gig in the world for an actor. You can show up in curlers or in bandages from a nose job. No memorization, no costuming, very little rehearsal, and you're in and out in two days.**
> **MATT GROENING, creator of *The Simpsons***

In order to get hired for radio commercials and television voiceovers you will need a "demo." It is a sample of your most marketable voices. Putting together a demo gives you a strong sense of the voices you have in you and the voices you have yet to hunt down. Ask yourself: if someone made your voice print, instead of your fingerprints, what would it be? How does your voice stand out from others? What kinds of age and sex crossovers are possible for you? This may be your one chance, if you are a 220-pound burly male, to play a fairy princess — or vice versa. Nobody cares so long as you can sound right.

UNIT 6.10.1   *Playing the microphone like an instrument*

A microphone can be the coolest instrument you've ever played. A good mic will respond to every subtle shift in your voice, reflecting nuance and color that you never knew you had. Using a microphone and headphones can open up a whole new dimension in the way you perceive your voice. Throughout this text, we've been encouraging multiple forms of feedback to help you to learn how others hear you. We've used imitators, responses from your class, and constant encouragement to record and playback. These are all useful. Only a mic and headphone combination will allow you to monitor your voice and make adjustments *while you speak*. Most digital recorders and computers have this capability. If you haven't explored your gear, this is the time. Go back over every exercise in the book (especially the ones in this chapter) and do them while monitoring yourself. You'll learn how to play the microphone like an instrument, and it will offer you amazing information about your voice.

It's also a great idea to learn a simple audio editing program (many are available free on the internet). There is an industry trend of expecting actors to have a home recording studio so that they can turn in high-quality auditions and even deliver finished recording jobs. The good news is that rapid advances in technology have brought the cost of professional-quality equipment down to the actor's budget level. Now you know what to suggest for your next birthday!

ONLINE

Some gentle etiquette advice for working in a professional studio: never touch or blow into the mic. Wear clothing that doesn't rustle. No rattling jewelry (and earrings are pretty uncomfortable when wearing headphones). No loose change in your pockets. Drink plenty of water well before the session to reduce the noises caused by a dry mouth. Remember that a mic should always be thought of as hot, and everything you say is likely to be recorded.

Kinds of demo

UNIT 6.10.2

When one's career is fairly advanced, demos are brief snips from the best of your work, selected to demonstrate your skill, type, and range. In the beginning, you don't have a lot of recordings to pull from, so a demo is usually mocked up in a studio. Don't think of this as being in any way fake. It's your voice, so it isn't a lie. It's a showcase. And it is an audition. Most voice casting happens straight off the demo, so it's critical to get it right.

Since different kinds of reads and voices are used for different voiceover fields, there are different demos, and each has a distinct structure. Follow the rules carefully, since failure to match expectations can mark you as a beginner.

Commercial demo

UNIT 6.10.3

ONLINE

Most commercial spots are very brief, so it's important to establish who you are, who you're speaking to, and the circumstances, in only a few seconds. In this field, they're usually not looking to cast broad characters but people we can accept as authentic and credible. This isn't the place for extreme characters and accents.

Length: 1 minute, edited tightly, all on one track.

Contents: a slate with your name; six–eight cuts showing you at your most natural in reads like folksy, hard sell, soft sell, flat, romantic/intimate, neurotic, intense/dark, bubbly/light.

Here's an example for a woman:

LISTEN

Table 6.4 Commercial demo (female)

Slate	Hi, this is Jane Doe.
Time: 0:07 Music: 1960s bachelor pad swing Read: different on each line	I'm Daddy's little girl, Steve's spicy Latina; my boss wants me to be, well . . . Him. I'm all things to all men.
Time: 0:06 Music: breezy, casual, acoustic Read: soft sell, casual	I love my cats, but having so many can cause a bit of an unpleasant odor. Fortunately, there's an answer.
Time: 0:08 Sound: restaurant ambiance in BG Read: tough, intense, shifting to playful, flirty	Okay. Rules. When I say talk . . . talk. When I say listen . . . listen. Don't eat off my plate. And be polite . . . stay for breakfast.
Time: 0:05 Music: techno-beat, photo shutter clicks rapidly Read: flat	Now there's no such thing as bad lighting. Photo-ready makeup.
Time: 0:05 Music: walking jazz bass Read: intimate, sensual	Coffee house inspirations. Full-bodied, dark. Indulge a little.
Time: 0:05 Music: marching band with horns, peppy Read: highly energized, shouting	From bold to bright any choice is right! Crayola: color your world!
Time: 0:07 Music: confident, ambient Read: easygoing, warm, professional	No hay problema. Yo lo digo por ti. When you just need someone who speaks your language.

And an example for a man:

Table 6.5 Commercial demo (male)

LISTEN

Slate	Hey, this John Doe.
Time: 0:06 Music: light, positive music Read: easy, casual, light	If your "road to success" is still "under construction," the University of Canton can pave your way.
Time: 0:08 Music: movie trailer, important patriotic music Read: intense	He searched for the story of his father. He found the source of his strength. Mission of Valor, from Bingham Books.
Time: 0:08 Music: samba, light, fun Read: comedic	She planned the wedding. Counted on me to plan the honeymoon! (No pressure!) I'm up to it . . . Only the most important trip of my life.
Time: 0:09 Music: low-toned, ambient Read: intimate, sensual, strong	Engineered by passion. Inspired by the best in design. The Stirling Chronometer from Tag Horas.
Time: 0:07 SFX: dorm room, door opening at start Read: character	Duuude. Booting your computer dimmed the lights in the whole dorm. Maybe an upgrade?
Time: 0:07 SFX: nature sounds, outdoors, a brook in BG Read: folksy, real	Rainforest destruction on another continent affects us here, on this one. Lost there, felt here.
Time: 0:06 Music: driving rock music Read: hard sell	Tired of fads? Go where you get results. Find out what a gym should be.

UNIT 6.10.4 *Non-broadcast demo*

Sometimes called "industrial," this demo is meant to cover the most widely requested styles for the diverse needs of industry. For this set of demos, the samples are longer. In commercials we'll hear a voice for only a few seconds, but in this area many of the narratives will last an hour or more. The longer sample tells the casting director whether there is anything in your voice that will begin to grate after a few minutes.

Length: several samples, each one minute long, on separate tracks. Many actors also supply a tightly edited summary of these styles like the commercial demo, while also including the long samples.

Industrial styles

Technical: for education, professional training, conference presentation; intended for the expert and containing so many advanced terms that it is indecipherable to the uninitiated. A successful read makes us think we understood it while realizing that we couldn't have.

Work has been proceeding on the idea of a machine that would not only supply inverse reactive current, for use in unilateral phase detectors, but would a so be capable of automatically synchronizing cardinal grammeters. Such a machine is the Retroencabulator. The principle involved is that instead of the power being generated by the relaxive motion of conductors and fluxes, it is produced by the modial interactions of magneto-reluctance and capacitive directance. The original machine had a base-plate of prefabulated amulite, surrounded by a malleable logarithmic casing in such a way that the two spurving bearings were in direct line with the pentametric fan. The latter consisted simply of six hydrocoptic marzel vanes, so fitted to the ambifacient lunar vaneshaft that side fumbling was effectively prevented. The main winding was of the normal lotus-o-delta type placed in panendermic semiboloid slots in the stator, every seventh conductor being connected by a non-reversible termic pipe to the differential girdlespring on the "up" end of the grammeter. In addition, whenever a barescent skor motion is required, it may be employed in conjunction with a drawn reciprocating dingle arm to reduce sinusoidal depleneration. And it has been successfully used for operating Milford Trunnions.[3]

3 This is a faux-technical piece of nonsense written by Bernard Salwen possibly around 1944. It makes for great practice.

The beautiful voice inside our heads: travel, documentaries, IMAX films, museum exhibitions, etc. The best material is highly descriptive, with lots of sensory words. A successful read makes us enter the world of the subject and think it is our own thoughts narrating the film.

Glenmorangie Lasanta is unusual, probably even unique, among single malt Scotch whiskies, in that it has the most incredible elegance and complexity of flavor.

Like the most delicious dessert menu imaginable, Lasanta taunts the senses with aromas of chocolate covered raisins, honeycomb and smooth caramel toffee. Citrus notes clear the way for the crispy burnt sugar and melting softness of creme brulée to be replaced by the rich aroma of rum and raisin ice cream. The addition of water to Lasanta exposes another menu of juicy dates and caramelized apricots whose sweetness is offset with hazelnut and walnut oil. Notes of dessert sherry wine emerge, mixed with spice and linseed oil to give a sense of coziness and age-old comfort.[4]

Bad news: deals with tough subjects like mortuary services, recovery from violence, treatment for a serious medical problem, coping with something dreadful. This is a difficult style. Videos like this are shown to people going through the most difficult challenge of their lives. The right tone is caring but without a hint of pity.

Understanding and coming to terms with suicide can be difficult for anyone. It can be particularly challenging to explain suicide to children. Here are a few things to keep in mind:

- Be honest about what happened. Use words like "dead" rather than "gone away" so there won't be any mis-understanding.
- Explain that their loved one died of an illness — a brain illness. For example: "Daddy had something like a heart attack except it was a 'brain attack.'
- If children ask you a question you can't answer, admit that you don't know.
- Reassure them that the death was not their fault. Avoid saying anything that might imply there was something they or anyone could have done to prevent it.
- Let them know that it's okay to be upset. Allow them to express their feelings.

The greatest gift you can give children is your assurance of love and support.[5]

4 http://www.klwines.com/detail.asp?sku=1033608, 2010.
5 Adapted from *Child Survivors of Suicide: A Guidebook for Those Who Care for Them*, by Rebecca Parkin and Karen Dunne-Maxim.

UNIT 6.10.5

Cartoon demo

Watch those wild police chases on cable. Notice how it's always the perp's car that's first to suffer a blowout or blown engine? That's because police cars are superior. As noted police escapee Elwood Blues once aptly pointed out, they've got "a cop motor, cop tires, cop suspensions and cop shocks." For speeders? Think of the fear shooting down their spines upon seeing a certain new cop car in the rearview: the Dodge Charger.

The Dodge Charger Police Vehicle can reach speeds of 146mph, goes from 0 to 100 in 14 seconds, and can brake to a dead stop from 60mph in 138 feet . . . all tops in the industry. Inside, the console is configured to handle all that essential electronic gear.

Utility, performance and reliability is only half the story. The visceral appeal of this car is its looks — the menacing muscular stance, the sloping backend and the predatory gunsight grill that tells speedsters "You're terminated." So consider yourself warned, punk.[6]

Think of a scenario where several of your characters can interact. Try to keep it close to two minutes. Here's an example:

INT. SEEDY BAR — NIGHT

BARTENDER

Okay, time to lock up this bar and go home. Hey, listen, my little beer bottle friend. I know what you guys do when I'm not here. You're not fooling anybody. I know about the

You have far too many voices living inside you to show them all in a cartoon demo. The purpose of this is just to get the casting folks to see you as skilled and creative. Then they'll want to call you in for more specific auditions. Opportunities in this field cover all forms of animation, like gaming, vocalized toys, online interactive characters.

High adventure: how to select the right chainsaw, adventure vacations, whitewater rafting, theme parks, military hardware, corporate teambuilding and leadership. Sentences in this copy tend to start with command verbs: run, jump, fly, challenge, attack. The read has a lot of energy, aggression, and a feeling of triumph.

6 http://www.redletterdodge.com/2009/10/24/meet-the-2010-charger-coolest-cop-car-on-the-planet/comment-page-1/, 10-24-2009.

limbo contests, about Scotch flashing his kilt, Creme de Menthe flirting with everyone and causing fights. Right, Vodka? Schnapps? I see the broken glass.

(SILENCE)

                    BARTENDER (CONT'D)
No comment, huh? Well I can't stop you. But, hey. Don't leave such a mess.

(DOOR SLAMS, KEYS JINGLE, LOCKS)

                    BEER BOTTLE
Okay gang the bar is closed. It's our party time. Tequila.

                    TEQUILA
Si, Señor Beer.

                    BEER BOTTLE
Get ready for the Limbo competition.

                    TEQUILA
Ready. Tequila's got the music all set. Arrrriba. You first, Galliano.

                    GALLIANO
Oh, the Limbo, she is-a-no much fun for us tall Galliano bottles.

                    CREME DE MENTHE
Oui. How's the weather up there, tall boy.

                    VODKA
See? Bar is closed 2 minutes and Creme de Menthe is already flirting.

                    CREME DE MENTHE
Do not be jealous, Vodka, mon cher. You know Creme de Menthe likes her men big.

                    SCOTCH
In that case, have a look at this. You know you want to. Everyone likes their Scotch straight up.

UNIT 6.10.6

Other voiceover styles

Once you start listening for them, you'll notice recorded voices everywhere: telephone menu systems, elevators, public transportation, websites, voice-mail prompts, traffic and weather reports, talking toys. That could be you saying "mind the gap."

Occasionally, actors will find that they are hired so often in these special areas that they develop specific demos just for them. Here are some areas that you might like to look at for further study and development:

Station branding: this ranges from "WXIS, :he Voice of Rock" to "Late Night Soul — sounds to soothe your soul." The demos are usually about a minute, with a wide-ranging compilation of station genres.

                    (overlapping) ALL

                    (general hubbub)

No. Not again. Somebody stop him . . . (etc.)

(SOUNDS OF A FIGHT BREAKING OUT)

                    BEER BOTTLE

Tonic Water, do something. Stop them.

                    TONIC WATER

I say, don't look at me. Poor little Tonic Water is just a mixer. I can't do anything by myself.

(KEYS JINGLE, UNLOCKING, DOOR OPENING, SLAMS)

                    BARTENDER

                    (coming back)

Ah hah! I knew it! All right! Break it up!

(GLASS SMASHING)

                    BARTENDER (CON'T)

Uh . . . Bad choice of words . . .

Political advertising: this requires a finely tuned sense of disgusted outrage and righteousness with a real-person common touch. It can be a complete career in itself. Demos usually include several complete spots.

Audio books: this is a huge field with thousands of new books recorded every year. Demos are about four minutes long. For fiction, the sample should have a male and female interaction and at least one other character who is a lot younger or older. This is a great place to show off your skill with accents and languages. Non-fiction is similar. Children's books are about the same length, with a strong narrator perspective and at least three non-human characters.

What you prepare for class in the project below is just a rough draft of something that might eventually become a real demo, so don't grieve too much over clunky noises, the sound of the machine being turned on or your roommate interrupting you. You will know when you are ready for high-tech and to pay the costs in a studio for quality production. That isn't what this assignment is about. It's about finding all your voices.

EXERCISE 6.10.6.1 DEMO

1. Prepare a "dummy" version of a specific demo style.
2. Write a script in the format shown with music and sound effects noted — just the way you would want to tell an engineer how to complete the project.
3. For now, fake the music and sound effects by pulling things out of your own library, from the web or by just inventing the sound effect on your own.
4. Even though you may not have ever played with editing before, see if you can get the recording to be fairly tight and to conform to the expected length for the style.

In time, you'll want to play with dummy versions of every style. Do this with friends, get feedback and then, when you're ready, have each of them done in a studio with a professional engineer. Use an engineer who is genuinely experienced with the genre in question, not your buddy who records bands on the weekends. Generally, you should do the commercial one first, and then follow up with the other areas that you are most interested in.

UNIT 6.11

Taking vocal direction

The voice can be quite difficult to speak about. Directors who haven't studied acting can feel completely at a loss when trying to guide performers toward the sound they hear in their imaginations. When they do find words, they are often the wrong ones. They'll tell you to "pick it up," suggesting an increase in tempo when they mean you should give it more energy, not more speed. They'll tell you to "make it natural" when they want a screaming hard-sell read. And, frequently, they'll give you a line reading. Don't be offended by this. If you get a line reading, your job is to reproduce it exactly and also to fill it with a real connection and communication.

Don't be afraid of or feel bad about needing multiple takes to find the right read. Commercial work, in particular, is a precise, detailed process, and every syllable needs to land exactly the way the director and the client want it. Keep a light, playful attitude and stay loose.

Here are some suggestions to point you toward a good recording session:

Read the end first. It is unusual to receive the copy in advance of the session. Many times you'll only have a chance to read the copy once before the engineer starts asking for a level. If you read the last part first, you'll quickly see where the whole thing ends up. This will tell you where to start.

Spot the style. Most of the work you'll do will be based on things you have heard before. Save your exceptional creativity for cartoon work, and on most jobs identify and match the style of material this sounds like.

Imitation is the sincerest form of advertising.

Know the unique selling point (USP). A well-written commercial has a single point. Are you pitching these adhesive bandages because they stick better for sports; don't stick, so they're easy to get off; have antiseptic cream on them; have pictures of a purple dinosaur? Each angle tells you how to read the copy, what demographic you're selling to, and who you are when you're talking.

Talk with a real person. Don't talk at the mic. Talk with someone. Don't talk to several people at once. Talk with one person. Everyone listens from inside their own heads, not as a group but as a person. Have a real person in mind when you're speaking. Know your relationship and all the given circumstances of why that person would care about this. Know what you want their response to be and make them do it.

Madison Avenue maxim

EXERCISE 6.11.1   DIRECTIONS: "WHAT ARE THEY SAYING TO ME?"

1. Pick a selection of commercial copy (or ads from magazines), and take turns reading while receiving directions from the class on style and interpretation. Start with these commonly given directions but come up with your own, too.

"accent it"
"add life to it"
"billboard it"
"bring it up/down"
"color it"
"emphasize it"
"endow the copy"
"give it more edge"
"give me a level"
"highlight it"
"keep it fresh"
"less sell"

"make it flow"
"make it intimate"
"make it one-on-one"
"make it real"
"make it yours"
"more energy"
"more/less retail"
"more sell"
"pick it up"
"pick up your cue"
"punch it"
"push/don't push"

"read against the text"
"romance the 'phone' "
"sell it"
"shave it by . . ."
"smile it"
"talk to me"
"throw it away"
"tighten it up," "tighten the pace"
"underscore it"
"warm up the copy"

2. Most voiceover directors aren't actors. They know *their* craft, and they expect you to know yours. Discuss various technical responses to these non-technical directions. What strategies can you use to get the results the director seems to be looking for?

For further study

We encourage you to explore the subject further through the perspectives of those who work in the many dimensions of this field. In much the way that no single accent book will ever serve as the only resource you'll turn to, these books each offer individual nuggets of gold. Look at several. Enjoy digging.

James R. Alburger, *The Art of Voice Acting* with CD (Focal Press, 2002). A comprehensive guide covering much of what an actor needs to get started in voiceover work. It has basic warm-up exercises, scripts, and approaches for creating characters. The CD provides numerous voiceover samples. Goes through basic principles and fundamental techniques of the business. Coverage runs from basic acting techniques to exercises for keeping the voice in top condition, as well as marketing and promotion tips.

Terri Apple, *Making Money in Voice-Overs: Winning Strategies to a Successful Career in TV, Commercials, Radio and Animation* (Lone Eagle Publishing, 1999). A clear, concise guide, laid out in an orderly progression. The first four chapters provide an overview defining voiceover, developing vocal technique, and looking at voiceover fields like animation, looping, dubbing, and audiobooks. The author includes short three-page interviews with working professionals in their areas of specialty. Covers topics like getting an agent and the job. The remainder of the book looks at auditioning, marketing oneself, stereotypes, and trends. Contact information is geared toward the Los Angeles actor.

Joan Baker, *Secrets of Voice-Over Success: Top Voice-Over Actors Reveal How They Did It* (Sentient Publications, 2005). Foreword by David Hyde Pierce. An inspirational, real-world, practical handbook that gives an overall picture of what it takes to launch a career in this field. Nineteen successful voiceover professionals share the tricks of the trade that they discovered along their journey. The author moves from teaching novices about developing their talent to landing that first job. Topics covered include the art and technique of voiceover, the demo, obtaining and partnering with an agent, finding work, the audition process, understanding and overcoming fears and obstacles, keeping motivated, the business of being one's own business, plus career development and networking.

Terry Berland and Deborah Ouellette, *Breaking into Commercials: The Complete Guide to Marketing Yourself, Auditioning to Win, and Getting the Job* (Penguin, A Plume Book, 1997). Introduction by Jason Alexander. This book is an overview of all forms of commercial work. However, Chapter 15 focuses on voiceover work in commercials. This chapter covers What are Voice-overs and Who Does Them?, Voice-over Markets, Types of Opportunities in Voice-over, What It Takes to Succeed, How to Get Started Doing Voice-overs, Marketing and Packaging Yourself as a Talent, Tapping the Regional Markets, The Taping Session, an Interview with Barbara Goldman, and Animation.

Susan Blu and Molly Ann Mullin, *Word of Mouth: A Guide to Commercial Voice-Over Excellence* (Pomegranate Press, 1996). Originally published in the 1980s and not thoroughly updated, but the fundamental info is there, and the advice is still solid. Covers animation, demos, agents, and auditions.

Elaine A. Clark, *There's Money Where Your Mouth Is: An Insider's Guide to a Career in Voice-Overs* (Back Stage Books, 2000). Covers the full range of a voice career. The first part addresses the fundamentals of getting started and preparing for a variety of voiceover gigs. The second part covers specific voiceover skills: announcer, spokesperson, real-person, and characters. Includes chapters on industrial narrations and multimedia and audio books. The author provides clear examples of resumés, sample cover letters, and marketing ideas.

Adrian Cronauer, *How to Read Copy: Professionals' Guide to Delivering Voice-Overs and Broadcast Commercials* with cassette (Bonus Books, 1990). This is the Adrian Cronauer of *Good Morning, Viet Nam* fame. Although this book is more than twenty years old, the basic information is still very useful. The companion cassette helps to demonstrate the author's points. Some information is outdated, but the author brings wisdom and experience that is timeless.

Chris Douthitt and Tom Wiecks, *Voiceover: Putting Your Mouth Where The Money Is* (Grey Heron Books, 1997). Focused on beginners. Covers the basics (getting an agent, demo, auditioning) and provides sample radio, TV, narration, and animation scripts as well as specific guidelines for narration and animation voiceovers. There's a chapter that looks at the basics of recording in a studio. Beyond the voice talent's job, it explains what's expected of the actor by the writer, engineer, ad agency, agent, talent union — and, of course, the client. There is also information about unions and pay scales.

Jeffrey P. Fisher and Harlan Hogan, *Voice Actor's Guide to Recording at Home and On the Road* (Artistpro, 2008). Recording voiceovers is no longer the exclusive domain of commercial studios. Today, voiceover actors are increasingly producing voice tracks for corporate narration, radio spots, animation, games, and other dialogue projects from their own home studios. This guide assists in learning and mastering basic home recording production techniques, using inexpensive but professional-sounding equipment. Setting up a studio with the right hardware and software, recording at home, and production basics, promotion, podcasting, and advanced production are also covered.

Patrick Fraley, *Creating Character Voices* two cassettes (Audio Partners Publishing, 1993). This LA-based voice talent offers extremely useful advice and helpful exercises. Enjoyable and full of information. Fraley says, "The right stroke of the vocal brush brings a character to life." He packs a lot into two hours, providing clear advice for creating and cataloguing characters. Animation voiceover and commercial character voice demos are included. He calls one clever exercise "character husbandry," in which the actor carefully combines specific elements of characters he/she has created to form personal hybrids.

Harlan Hogan, *VO Tales and Techniques of a Voice-Over Actor* (Allworth Press, 2002). A combination of biography and how-to, combining a very personal approach with detailed practical information. The resources section includes "Books on Voice-Over," "Books on Acting in Commercials," and "Other Books, Periodicals." The author shares his secrets of success in an insider's guide to the industry, offering an insightful and often amusing glimpse at the business.

Pamela Lewis, *Talking Funny for Money: An introduction to the Cartoon/Character/Looping Area of Voice-Overs with CDs* (Applause Books, 2003). A guide to assembling a competitive cartoon/character voiceover demo; shortcuts to mastering the most requested dialects, age groups, and celebrity impersonations; film looping/dubbing technique and terminology; and the varied employment opportunities in the cartoon/character/looping world.

Michelle McCoy, *Sound and Look Professional on Television and the Internet: How to Improve Your On-Camera Presence* (Bonus Books, 2000). An overview for anyone who wants to work in television: news anchors and reporters, talk show hosts and guests, on-camera commercials, and industrial videos. A small section looks at the basics of broadcast voice work.

Bernard Graham Shaw, *Voice Overs: A Practical Guide* with CD (Routledge, 2000). An insider's guide, based on the author's twenty years of experience in the field. Offers practical advice on how to build a voiceover career. Excellent glossary. Importantly, this book comes from a British perspective and so provides a useful insight that most other books won't. Covers radio and television commercials for actors at all levels of experience.

Randy Thomas and Peter Rofe, *Voice for Hire: Launch and Maintain a Lucrative Career in Voiceovers* (Back Stage Books, 2008). Designed to teach aspiring voice artists, in a step-by-step format, how to break into this extremely competitive marketplace. Acknowledging that there is no single or definitive path to making money in voiceovers, the authors identify certain trends that can inform a career. Along with a chronological sequence of steps are comments and stories from voiceover agents, casting directors, producers, and performers.

Sandy Thomas, *So You Want To Be A Voice-Over Star* (In the Clubhouse Publishing, 1999). A very basic book that reads like a memoir of Sandy Thomas' career. Advice needs to be gleaned from the anecdotes. Thirty pages of sample scripts.

Ann S. Utterback, *Broadcast Voice Handbook: How to Polish Your On-Air Delivery* (Bonus Books, 2000). A thorough guidebook, geared toward broadcast journalists. It includes a 1999 survey of news directors on the importance of voice, diction, and clear communication. The chapters include Breathing, Phonation, Resonance, Articulation, Stress and Intonation, Sounding Conversational, Going Live/Live Experiences, and Coping with Stress.

Alice Whitfield, *Take it From the Top! How to Earn Your Living In Radio & TV Voiceovers* (Ring-U-Turkey Press, 1992). The first six chapters focus on voiceover auditioning — including information such as signing in at the door, picking up the script, and reading the copy. Whitfield introduces the jargon and defines it clearly. Eight pages on the demo are useful and clear. The second half of the book is called "From The Horse's Mouth" and includes a Q/A format with agents and actors. The final chapters give contact information for agents and resources.

Janet Wilcox, *Voiceovers: Techniques and Tactics for Success* (Allworth Press, 2007). A veteran voiceover actor, writer, producer, and voiceover teacher provides an inside scoop on the industry. Includes a CD featuring vocal exercises and interviews with voiceover actors. Exercises, games, improvisational and acting techniques help readers to build their skills. Sample scripts from real ads provide practice, and interviews with agents, casting directors, and producers provide insights to help new voiceover actors get started. Tips on making a demo, auditioning, getting an agent, interpreting copy, developing a personal marketing plan.

Singing and speaking

> **Regard your voice as capital in the bank. Sing on your interest and your voice will last.**
> **LAURITZ MELCHIOR, singer, actor**

There are great speakers who can't sing and vice versa. But actors who work often do both. Remember that few of the dozen greatest stars of the musical theatre have better than okay voices, but all know how to pour themselves into the music and sell the song. We recommend that you study singing, not only for employment opportunities but also to increase your breath control, your sense of phrasing, your capacity to resonate, and your overall command of the musicality of speech.

Classical speech is somewhere between everyday speech and song. Not only are the words more eloquent, the structures more complex, the timings more precise, and the images more extravagant, but there is also a strong sense in the soliloquy and the solo song of pouring out heartfelt feelings in big, bright, true colors.

Singing requires a level of emotional exposure not easily found in speaking. Because the vowels, those emissaries of emotion, must be held for so long, the expansiveness of a song doesn't allow an actor to hide in the intellectual meaning of the words. The only thing left to do is to open yourself to the expression of feeling. This emotional exposure or vulnerability is one reason why so many people are shy about singing. While many claim embarrassment about the voice, it is really that singing leaves you bare and open on stage. And you can't do it halfway. "It's all or nuthin'."

Earlier, we explored singing monologues to find and extend the natural rhythm and pitch patterns in the material (Exercise 4.5.1.2). Here, you will do just the opposite, to discover the language, text, and acting qualities of a song.

EXERCISE 6.13.1 SONGS AS MONOLOGUES

1. Choose a song. Musical theatre is better than most other sources. Don't worry too much about the music. Pick a song that you feel you can connect with emotionally.
2. Forget that it's a song. Treat it exactly as you would any monologue. Rewrite the lyrics as normal text. Establish the given circumstances, making the same acting decisions required of any piece.
3. Memorize it. Present it, spoken, as a monologue. Evaluate and shape it to audition standards.

EXERCISE 6.13.2 SONG/MONOLOGUE WITH UNDERSCORING

1. If someone in the class can play the piano, or if you can play a recording of the song softly, present the monologue again with a gentle musical undertone.
2. Don't sing. Let the music inform the tempo of the piece. Discover how the music expands the moments, requiring more emotional expanse from you in return.
3. Listen for how your voice expands as well. Don't even try to approximate the melody. Listen instead for the natural music of your voice and the instinctive melody you invent as you pursue your character objectives. Let your movement take on the same broadening.

To make the first transition from speech to singing, model your approach on *recitative*. That is the rhythmically free vocal style that imitates the natural inflections of speech and is used for dialogue and narrative in operas and oratorios. Some melody is usually indicated, and some improvisation is allowed. It is as close as music gets to speech (think of Rex Harrison's style of delivery in *My Fair Lady*).

EXERCISE 6.13.3 **RECITATIVE – TALKING THE SONG**

1. Speak the song as a monologue following the specific rhythmic structures of the music. If you had background music, it can now come into the foreground. It can be very helpful if the class could arrange an accompanist at this point. However, Karaoke[7] CDs are increasingly available and work extremely well.
2. If some of the actual melody creeps in that's great, don't fight it, but the objective is still the same — it's not the singing, it's the acting.

By now, you're probably aching to cut loose and sing. So do it!

EXERCISE 6.13.4 **SINGING THE MONOLOGUE**

1. Sing it. Go for it, and see how you can make the connection through singing the same way you do with a monologue. Consider which dominant musical style is most appropriate to the mood of the piece. Consider inventing a new musical style.
2. Play the objectives. Use the music to carry your needs forward. Live in a world where the more passion you put into your voice, the more successful you are.
3. Give awards, not (necessarily) to the best singer but to the one who truly lets go and allows the emotion to take over.

This experience may give you the spark to continue studying singing, something we heartily recommend. Unlike the previous categories, individual lessons are probably readily available in your community or on your campus. If you choose to work independently, however, here are some possible sources:

H. Wesley Balk, *The Complete Singer Actor* (University of Minnesota Press, l985). Particularly noteworthy for its second and third sections and its use of improvisation to enhance musical courage and skill. Exercises to develop energy, concentration, structure, imagination, style, and coordination.

7 These recordings have a full orchestral musical accompaniment without any singers. It's just like singing with your own band.

because you have more choices. Sense how all your efforts have brought you to a point of awareness and skill — a level that you may not have known was even available to you when you started.

Terms to remember

accent hierarchies	**demo**	**voice attitudes**
caricature voices	**organic accent base**	**voice constructing**
cartoon voices	**placement**	**voiceover**
character voices	**technical accent base**	**voice personas**

Summary

Three primary ways to release your vocal potential are accents, character voiceover work, and singing. Each pushes your range in a slightly different way.

Accents increase your capacity to distinguish and reproduce even totally unfamiliar sounds. An accent may be approached from an organic/cultural base or a technical base. Of the many materials available, the ones with which every actor should be familiar are those of Blunt, Lane-Plescia, Machlin, Meier, and Stern. Being able to thicken or thin an accent and to teach it to others ensures your own mastery.

Character voices, which add dimension and range to your work, may be discovered through personas, attitudes, circumstances or voice constructing. A demo is the ideal vehicle for trying each approach.

Studying singing and employing musical techniques can greatly enhance the breath, phrasing, resonance, and emotional exposure of your speech.

Each of the three is a valuable resumé skill, which also forces you to listen to and shape sound in ways that encourage awareness and creativity.

CHAPTER 7

Selecting your system

Perhaps what is most significant for actor training is that as the voice is such a personal thing, different methods work for different people, depending upon how they feel about it.

JACQUELINE MARTIN, author, *Voice in Modern Theatre*

This teacher said to me, "Don't breathe from up here, breathe from down there!" And she made me touch her well-upholstered, corseted abdomen. I had no idea what she meant then, but I do now.

KATHERINE HEPBURN, actor

At the end of this book, class, term, year or program, you still have a vast vocal life ahead of you. If you're serious about acting, the training only starts here. You may choose to enroll in another class, transfer to another school, apply to a graduate program, conservatory or academy, seek private lessons, or work by yourself with books and CDs. This chapter is designed to help you to shop well for your additional training. If you shop poorly, you could end up committed to two or three more years of academic life in circumstances that do not suit your method of learning, do not fill in the gaps in your skills, and do not excite you. Or you could eagerly buy another book only to find that you can't work with it and give up independent study. We don't want this to happen.

For future classes/programs, this chapter will try to answer these questions:

1. Who are the big names in voice training. and what have been their contributions? With whose work should you be absolutely familiar? Which areas does each expert's system cover and which ignore? Where do they most strongly agree or disagree?
2. How are voice and speech experts trained, certified or licensed? What organizations/associations do trainers join? How do they stay abreast of new developments?
3. What physical relaxation/focus systems are most likely to be connected to vocal programs? How do they differ? How do they intersect with voice training?
4. Which systems are most likely to be combined and adapted, rather than taught precisely as designed by their founders? In which is the information most readily available or most challenging? Which favor which learners?
5. What are useful questions to ask when interviewing to enter a program? What should you always know before you enroll? What should you watch for if given a chance to sit in on a voice and speech class?

For the many books on the market, we will attempt to identify the kinds of vocal issues addressed, the approach, level of difficulty or challenge, and the circumstances under which it is most and least effective.

UNIT 7.1 **Who are the most influential voice and speech teachers?**

Until the mid-1950s, voice training focused mostly on elocution and projection. Vocal training lagged far behind changes going on in acting classes. While "The Method" (an abbreviated adaptation of the Stanislavski system) was revolutionizing acting approaches with its natural, organic, emotional verities, no congruent vocal approach had evolved. Because "method" acting was a reaction against "technique," for a time it was considered a badge of honor to mumble and grunt through a role.[1] Then, in the 1960s, audiences finally became fed up with incomprehensibility and demanded that actors restore some measure of clarity to the performance. However, older style elocution/projection classes were not working, as the method actors found these lessons insufficient to support their acting approach. Drama was also evolving, and the common man, speaking his local dialect, was chosen more and more frequently by playwrights than the prince in his palace. A type of vocal training was needed that could answer the conflicting demands of naturalism and theatricality.

1 Stanislavski did stress the need for extensive vocal and physical training to prepare the actor's instrument to respond freely to the impulses of inner life. The "Method" as advanced by Lee Strassburg in the USA did not adopt a similar posture.

It eventually did, and five major teachers now stand out for shaping the most significant responses to the aesthetics of modern theatre: Cicely Berry, whose approach is through a focus on the text; Arthur Lessac, clarifying the structural, acoustic, and anatomical processes of speech; Kristin Linklater, freeing actors from external controls and limitations; Edith Skinner, advocating refined pronunciation standards; and Patsy Rodenburg with her emphasis on psychological freedom. All voice teachers owe them a great debt. Even if a particular approach is thoroughly despised (and they are all controversial in their own ways), the movement in opposition has strengthened and broadened our understanding of the human voice, not diminished that particular teacher's contribution.

A self-assessment

To cover the following material wisely, do a brief self-assessment regarding the way you like to learn:

EXERCISE 7.2.1 DISCOVERING HOW YOU LEARN

Write out the answers to the following questions for yourself and for your imitation partner. Afterwards, compare your subjective self-assessment with their objective views.

1. Which areas covered so far are easiest for you and come quickly? Can you determine why? Is there a consistent pattern?
2. Which are the most challenging? How have you responded to the challenges, especially when others seemed to pass you by?
3. What do you want vocally that you suspect you cannot self-teach or motivate?
4. How much of your future work do you feel should be vocal? What percentage of time and energy seems reasonable to devote to that aspect of your training?
5. How do you seem to use time to learn most effectively? Do you, for example, thrive on floor work, basic breathing, and sounding without words? Or do you always crave to work with text and particularly enjoy working on precision? Do you require lots of supervision or freedom?
6. Do you suspect that you are largely a visual, auditory or kinesthetic learner? To help you to get a fix on that question, answer the following:

While you may have felt several answers were suitable for each question, notice if you had a leaning toward any one set, A, B or C. Few people are exclusively visual, auditory or kinesthetic, but almost everyone has a dominant modality. It is an indication of how you *process* information. If you choose a method of study that is congruent with the way you most easily learn, you'll get where you want to go a lot faster. Otherwise, you may feel that you're swimming upstream.[2]

If you saw yourself mostly in the A group, then you are primarily a *visual* learner. Approaches with visual systems such as Skinner's phonetic symbols, or visualizations like Linklater's rich imagery may look like the clearest methods for you.

If the B group sounded the most satisfying, then your main learning modality is *auditory*. Accent recordings probably worked best for you, and the ear training of Lessac and Skinner, and the side-coaching methods of Linklater may be approaches you can hear easily.

Group C is *kinesthetic*. You would prefer the direct physical experience to talking about something. Linklater's body-freeing approach and Lessac's physical structuring may give you a firm grasp of the subject.

Berry's work doesn't categorize as neatly. It is more dependent on how the teacher presents the material and organizes the class work. Taken straight from her book, she has a slightly visual slant, although she integrates rich auditory and kinesthetic information as well. Rodenburg's deep psychological insights don't present themselves through one primary modality. Berry and Rodenburg, notably, don't certify teachers in their method, and both integrate well into the methods of the other three.

Let's look at each of those teachers more closely.

---

2 Note that choosing a method of study that is congruent with your mode of learning is not the same as "avoiding a challenge" or "playing it safe." You should always seek out challenging teachers, but ones that can communicate with you.

UNIT 7.3 **Edith Skinner**

To the classical actor or for that matter any actor who wants to be understood, Edith Skinner's method is a sure guide.

KEVIN KLINE, actor

Figure 7.1 Edith Skinner. Photo © Robert Alan Gold   *Figure 7.2* Kevin Kline. © Patrick Robert/Sygma/Corbis

Skinner's method really deals only with speech, not voice. Or maybe it is fairer to say that she uses speech as a doorway to the voice. Her main contribution is the creation and delineation of "Stage Standard" speech. Speech training for actors in the USA has been defined by her work for over fifty years. She tutored generations of actors at Carnegie Mellon University, the Juilliard School, and the American Conservatory Theater, and she trained numerous faithful teachers of her system.

She was a student of William Tilly, a phonetician and philologist, who firmly believed that every language had a "standard" pronunciation to which people of "culture," "cultivation," and "education" could aspire. Skinner brought his values to the American stage.

Her system requires mastery of her own particular brand of "narrow transcription" phonetics. This singular application is based on the International Phonetic Alphabet but is actually divergent from the IPA used by linguists and phoneticians, being an offshoot of Tilly's own design. The pronunciation and transcription standards are clear, exact, and rigid. Her approach teaches precise ear training and a dedication to the tiniest elements of a word. Actors trained in this method have sensitivity to language at its most elemental level: the phoneme, or smallest unit of speech sound. Their articulation is precise; their pronunciation is uniform to a high standard. *What* is being communicated is revealed to be *how* it is said. In other words, what is communicated is the result of a combination of the slightest elements of sound. It is at the far end of the scale — as distant from Berry and Linklater as it is possible to get.

Many schools teach the Skinner method. Since she dealt exclusively with speech and pronunciation, few will make it their only approach but will usually contrast it with Linklater or some other system. She never "certified" teachers, but she trained a great many and did so with consistency, precision, and a highly demanding pedagogical style.

In contrast to the other major systems, Skinner's approach would seem to be a throwback to an older style of theatre. It might be, but pre-1950s plays still form a huge part of theatre repertoire. No other system can take the boy from the "hood" and make him the prince in his palace like hers can. Her method is often criticized for its rigidity, the "class-conscious" nature of Stage Standard, and for homogenizing and stultifying, rather than liberating actors. These are valid points. However, those criticisms seem to disregard what her training *is*, and fault it for what it is *not*. This work can achieve levels of speech ability simply not available via some other methods, but it should be only one aspect of an actor's training. It is not the basis for a comprehensive approach.

Distinct utterance is the prime requisite for an actor. If the role calls for refined speech, the audience must receive that impression or else the actor's tool has not been sufficiently trained and gets in the way of the performer's art.

EDITH SKINNER

Books by Edith Skinner

Speak with Distinction, revised, with new material added by Timothy Monich and Lilene Mansell, edited by Lilene Mansell (Applause Theatre Book Publishers, 1990). An accompanying CD is available. Originally self-published in 1942 as a compilation of her notes. This text is really more a workbcok/reference source than a textbook. It is necessary to have a skilled teacher to take you through the material for ear training. Little emphasis is placed on how to digest the material. Not an easy self-study book. Comprehensive and exhaustively detailed, it covers every sound in English and every situation in which that sound appears, placing each in relation to "Stage Standard" accent.

Good Speech for the American Actor (Drama Book Publishers, 1980), audio recording. A helpful resource for assistance in ear training and as an example of Skinner-style classical stage speech. It is most useful for those with some prior experience of the system and will never replace the direct corrections of a trained teacher, but it is good as a model, a reinforcement, and a reminder.

The Seven Points for Good Speech in Classical Plays (Performance Skills, 1983), audio and video recordings with pamphlet. A thumbnail summary of the most frequent adjustments that American speakers need to make to achieve Stage Standard. As above, a good model, reminder, and reinforcer for classes that the actor has already had. The pamphlet can be used as a checklist of problems to avoid.

UNIT 7.4 **Arthur Lessac**

I wasn't really using my voice until I got to work with Arthur.

MICHAEL DOUGLAS, actor

His early schooling clearly laid the groundwork for his vocal theories. Lessac trained as a singer at the Eastman School of Music and continued his studies in speech therapy, education, speech pathology, and physiology at New York University, work in anatomy and neurology at Bellevue Hospital and a clinical internship at St. Vincent's Hospital in New York City, as well as

Figure 7.3 Arthur Lessac

A voice that is free, that feels its inherent right to speak, will have no fear of calling out, whenever and wherever it is needed.

ARTHUR LESSAC

psychoanalytical and communication disorder training. His studies in physical movement systems include tai chi, Alexander technique, stage movement, and Grotowski body training. He stands alone among the leading teachers as having aggressively researched all major aspects of the human voice and body from theoretical, clinical, and experimental perspectives.

If Berry's point of departure is the text, Lessac's is the actor's body. The basis of his system is the experience of certain physical sensations that occur during speech and the development of the ability to recall these sensations and actively control the actions causing them. Physical feeling, more than what is heard, is used as a reference point to know whether the voice is being used effectively. Lessac works from the premise that careful observation of how the body wants to function — how it would function in the absence of adverse conditioning — is the best guide to the production of beautiful sounds. Used naturally, the voice will create vibrations that can be felt in the hard palate, the sinuses, the forehead, and eventually throughout the entire body. When voice and speech become an inner physical experience, their connection to the emotions becomes clear.

Lessac trains and certifies teachers in his method, which is detailed and complex enough to warrant such training. His is probably the most technically thorough system. For that reason, many schools adopt it as the only method taught. It is possible to self-instruct from his textbook — in a limited way — but it is hard to make real progress without an experienced teacher to model the physical placements and sounds.

Lessac-trained actors often have powerful voices. His "call focus" and "y-buzz" exercises make use of the natural acoustic properties of the voice to produce a large boost in loudness without strain.

His work is sometimes criticized as being so technical and rigid that it stands in the way of vocal impulse, and actors trained this way can sound "theatrical" or "actory," as the inverted megaphone posture can result in old-fashioned "pear-shaped tones," although individual instructors may intensify or mitigate that aspect. He is also faulted for having developed an obtuse and awkward system for noting vowel sounds, and it is true that standard phonetics has wider use and is more applicable to accent study.

Books by Arthur Lessac

The Use and Training of the Human Voice: A Practical Approach to Speech and Voice Dynamics (Mayfield, third edition, 1997). This is an extremely comprehensive system covering all aspects of sound production, articulation, body alignment, etc., leaving few gaps. It can be difficult to penetrate without a teacher to assist. It's hard to know on your own when you've got the sound right, since the adjustments can be subtle. However, once you've got it, this system provides a strong physical and sensory way of locking the "correct" sound in. This is a technique in the fullest sense of the word, and in contrast to approaches that value "freeing" or "liberating" the voice, this method is formal and structured. Text work and interpretation is not emphasized, and standards of pronunciation are generalized rather than prescribed.

Body Wisdom: The Use and Training of the Human Body (Drama Book Specialists, second edition, 1981). This book is recommended as a companion text when studying the Lessac voice-training system. The two work well together. It clarifies much of what is implicit in his earlier book. It outlines a complete system of body training, working always with the breath and voice to create a liberated and integrated whole. Its weaknesses: not easy for self-study, loaded with jargon, reinvents new definitions for familiar terms (much as he does in his other book), and insists on a controversial spinal alignment called the "C-curve," which runs contrary to most current anatomy/physiology/kinesiology texts.

UNIT 7.5   **Cicely Berry**

She interests me because I have never met anyone else so interested. Interested in hearing a Shakespearean text in a new way. She inspires me.

HELEN HUNT, actor

Probably the least dogmatic of the group, she claims not to have a method or system, does not train or certify teachers, and admits to many right ways of speaking, rather than one.

She taught for some time at the Central School of Speech and Drama in London and was voice director of the Royal Shakespeare Company for many years.

Figure 7.4 Cicely Berry

Reflecting the new awareness in communication theory, her focus is on an investigation of *what* is being conveyed, and what is the relationship of the message to *how* it's said. Love and practice of language is the core of her work, and that is achieved by a deep connection with the text. She asks not merely for an intellectual understanding of what is meant by the lines but also a feel for the rhythms of the words, their organic structure, and their dynamic need to be expressed.

Berry also has an understanding of the actor's process, and her work is geared to support the character's vocal assertions and need to communicate. If an actor is having vocal problems, she will tend to seek the answer in psychological/motivational terms. For example, if an actor is having trouble with breathing, that actor is led to associate breath with the structure of the thoughts or ideas. If an actor can't be heard, she won't work for projection but rather, size — leading to an experience of the actor's "right to be there" and claiming of the stage.

However, Berry is also adamant about technical vocal work as well: "You can only respond to the extent that you are capable of making sound." Her books contain many exercises, from typical speech drills to extensive text explorations useful for classroom, rehearsal or individual study. Her technical work is presented with the understanding that if you sloppily, passively, blindly *motivate* that work, it will probably be useless.

She credits Peter Brook, one of the most creative directors on the international scene, for helping her to gain the confidence to trust her approach to various exercises, and about handling language. They worked very closely on his 1970 production of *A Midsummer Night's Dream*, and this seemed to be a turning point in clarifying her methods. Brook had this to say of her:

> [She] points out with remarkable persuasiveness "technique" as such is a myth, for there is no such thing as a correct voice. . . . And since the life in the voice springs from emotion, drab and technical exercises can never be sufficient. Cicely Berry never departs from the fundamental recognition that speaking is part of the whole; an expression of inner life. She insists on poetry because good verse strikes echoes in the speaker that awaken portions of his deep experience which are seldom evoked in everyday speech.[3]

So, while her approach covers body placement and articulation drills, the essential core of her work lies more in her relationship with text and language, focused by the material she selects to explore and the attitude of openness with which that exploration proceeds.

3 From Peter Brook's foreword to *Voice and the Actor*.

Her work is sometimes criticized for failing to be comprehensive and having vague standards. However, that is a true reflection of her values. She would never define a sound or interpretation as being "right" or "wrong." There is nothing prescriptive about her approach. While some schools advertise that they teach the "Berry method," she is proud of the fact that she has none. Yet her influence is pervasive. She can be credited with finding the bridge connecting the best of the formal voice work of the past to the liberating techniques of the present.

I have always felt that poetry is quite the best material to use because the demands it makes are very particular and quite subtle, yet its extravagance encourages you to do extravagant things which are not untrue.

CECILY BERRY

Books by Cicely Berry

Voice and the Actor (Macmillan, 1973). The approach is traditional, starting with relaxing, breathing, and lip and tongue muscularity, and moving on to freedom and flexibility. At each phase, she connects the work back into text with well-chosen selections. Any student with basic skills could use this book alone or in a group. It is a solid introductory text.

Your Voice and How to Use It Successfully (Harrap, 1975). An accompanying recording is available. This feels like the layperson's version of her first book. The material is much the same but geared less for actors than for the general voice user.

The Actor and the Text (Charles Scribner's Sons, 1988). Here is where Berry rises to the fore and her approach truly flowers. This book shows vast respect for the actor's process and for turning vocal problems into acting possibilities. It could be used at any stage of an actor's growth and is one of those books that are reread throughout an actor's career whenever an insight is needed. Loaded with examples and exercises, it provides a rich array of ways to confront text and language, so that actors don't have to "master" Shakespeare (for example), they find him inside them.

Berry, Cicely, documentary, *Where Words Prevail*, directed by Steven Budlong and Salvatore Rasa (Sojourner Media, LLC, 2005).

Kristin Linklater

She gave me freedom I did not know was possible.

ALFRE WOODARD, actor

Figure 7.5 Kristin Linklater. © Photo by Alexis Savinis

She trained as an actress at the London Academy of Music and Dramatic Art and taught there alongside Iris Warren (a powerful influence on modern methods who left no written legacy). After teaching extensively in England, Linklater moved to the United States. Her teaching and influence has since been felt on both sides of the Atlantic. She founded Shakespeare and Company, a theatre ensemble devoted to exploring Shakespeare's plays, and Company of Women, focusing on all-female, multiracial Shakespearean productions.

Linklater's approach is a mix of organic physiological action and psychotherapeutic freeing, meant to liberate the voice. It is in no sense a technique but, rather, a freeing of the voice from all boundaries without prescribing any particular form, style or sound. She doesn't focus at all on the development of the voice, believing "the removal of blocks that inhibit the human instrument [are] distinct from the development of a skillful human instrument."

She holds many values in common with Berry: neither believes in the correction of "faults," a proper style of pronunciation or a correct way to speak. Both attempt a psychologically integrated approach. Berry moves toward these goals through text, allowing the text to inform the voice. Linklater, on the other hand (inspired by the Alexander technique) has developed a series of experiences that gradually liberate the actor to allow the voice to follow freely whatever impulse is felt. When the voice is free to receive impulses from the senses and feelings, it informs the text — almost the reverse of Berry's approach.

Her rich imagery and carefully laid-out pathway have produced real results and developed an extensive following. Her method is psychophysical, but she doesn't deal with much anatomic or technical detail, preferring a more metaphoric description of the body's action and structure. This is in sharp contrast to Lessac, who will state exactly how wide your jaw should be and how round your lips, with pictures and precise detail. Her process is slow (it can take years), and results are not as noticeable right away. The action of freeing the actor is subtler than that of building gross technique, and actors need to have patience, commitment, and a focus on the process rather than the result.

Actors trained in this way have an unusual sense of liberty in their work. The voice can surprise the audience with its subtle colors. It can even surprise the actor.

Linklater's work is sometimes criticized for its slowness, lack of identifiable signposts to measure progress, and no clear technique. Those issues could just as easily be called virtues, and often are. More serious is the criticism that, although expressive and open, actors trained in this method often don't have supported or well-placed voices. It is not uncommon for a student within this system to lose their voice in a demanding role.

Many acting conservatories teach the Linklater method, some offer it as their only approach, while others mix it with different systems. Few can claim to give it all the time and attention required, so actors may graduate who still need extensive work. She does certify teachers and has a formal teacher-training program. That's essential. Because of the subtle and detailed nature of the work, a Linklater teacher requires years of training to become proficient.

What actors really need to be are emotional warriors.

KRISTIN LINKLATER

Books by Kristin Linklater

Freeing the Natural Voice: Imagery and Art in the Practice of Voice and Language (Drama Publishers, second edition 2006). An absolutely revolutionary approach, designed to do just what it says: free the voice. When it came out in 1976, no other system existed that proposed releasing the voice in this way. Since that time, almost no teacher can ignore the valuable lessons in this book. She has laid out a series of experiences designed to open the body and voice at the same time, along with essays on her vocal philosophy. It is possible to achieve some sense of the work by going through her book with a friend, taking turns reading the instructions, and practicing, but that could only be an introduction. The real work can take place only with a skilled and experienced practitioner who is able to sensitively guide the novice.

Freeing Shakespeare's Voice: The Actor's Guide to Talking the Text (Theatre Communications Group, 1992). From an original position that one need not develop a technique for working on text, she later wrote an advanced book for precisely that. With this book, she comes full circle and meets up with Cicely Berry, dealing with form and content in a way that her earlier book eschewed. The sense is that if you pass through the freeing phase, it is appropriate to enter a forming and shaping phase. Once again, she uses her rich sense of visual metaphor to bring Shakespeare inside the actor. This book could probably benefit an actor at any stage of development (she might disagree) and is useful for self-study as well as group work.

Official website: kristinlinklater.com

UNIT 7.7

Patsy Rodenburg

I am an enormous fan of her work. What is wonderful about her is the directness and clarity of her teaching and her enthusiasm.

JUDI DENCH, actor

Figure 7.7 Judi Dench. © LAN/Corbis

Figure 7.6 Patsy Rodenburg

Patsy Rodenburg's impact on the field has been somewhat more recent than others listed here, and it is very much ongoing. Her formal training was with the Central School of Speech and Drama. As director of voice at London's Royal National Theatre and the Guildhall School of Music and Drama, she is recognized as one of the world's leading voice and acting coaches. She was voice director for the Royal Shakespeare Company in London for nine years, and her film credits include collaborations with such directors as Mike Nichols, Franco Zeffirelli, and Sam Mendes. She's worked with some of the world's leading English-speaking actors, including Judi Dench, Daniel Day-Lewis, Maggie Smith, and Nicole Kidman. Residencies have included teaching at the Moscow Art Theatre and the Comédie-Française.

Her work has extended to non-theatrical areas, including voice/communication for business executives, vocal care and listening skills lectures at the Royal College of Surgeons in London, courses specifically designed for teachers and politicians, and a Shakespeare as Therapy program in British prisons. In the United States, she teaches at the Michael Howard Studio in New York City.

Of all the experts profiled here, Rodenburg places the greatest emphasis on psychological aspects of voice and the need to find the courage to explore fully. She traces her motives back to being traumatized at age 8 by an elocution teacher to a degree that her vocal progress was frozen for a number of years. She describes a history of classes where she was "taught with a lot of cruelty" and vowed to assist others in freeing themselves from such paralysis and to always teach with kindness. She is a prolific author and her work reflects rich psychological insights mixed with hardheaded practical advice and inspiring artistic permission.

Until we again are fully present for each other and really listening, our acting will suffer.

PATSY RODENBURG

Books by Patsy Rodenburg

The Right to Speak: Working with the Voice (Methuen Drama, 1992). Her first book, with foreword by Ian McKellen, is a gem from the standpoint of both teacher and student. Purporting to speak to all constituencies, Ms. Rodenburg does, indeed, cover all basic topics in fundamental voice training for speakers, either onstage or off. Part One, "The Right to Speak," is philosophical and largely anecdotal, a section in which the author discusses her experiences with vocal training from her own uncomfortable beginnings as a student through her years of insightful observation of students and acquaintances, in and out of the theatre. Part Two, "Working with the Voice," is more technical, starting with "An Owner's

Manual of the Voice," which describes the anatomy and physiology of the voice in clear and functional terms. Her trip through the phonetic symbols refers to Received Pronunciation and is especially interesting from that perspective. The exercises contained in the fifty-six pages of "The Voice Workout" form the core of the book and would beneficially augment any teacher's (or student's) repertoire. The final chapter, on "Working Further with the Voice," is extremely valuable, particularly her thoughts on professional voice training. This book is a wonderful addition to the voice/speech library, containing scores of useful ideas and techniques as well as a unique philosophical point of view. It is a must for teachers of voice/speech/text and a viable companion textbook for students at any level of training.

The Need for Words: Voice and the Text (Theatre Arts Books, 1993). This excellent text, written as a companion to her earlier "The Right to Speak," deals with the connection between the actor's voice and the text he or she is speaking. Although Rodenburg makes some excellent points in the first part of the book, once she takes "Voice onto Text" in Part II, she is in her element and the book takes off. She ably describes both the philosophy behind and the contents of several excellent exercises that specifically address the methodology by which the actor can be put in contact with many different types of text. Rodenburg's coverage of the sonnets, dramatic verse, and prose of Shakespeare is masterful. Furthermore, in the last part, she includes some very short but informative coverage of a select number of other important poets and playwrights.

The Actor Speaks: Voice and the Performer (St. Martin's Press, 2002). Patsy Rodenburg's book is a wonderful resource for actors and teachers. She takes you through a complete voice workshop, touching on every aspect of performance work that involves the voice and sorts through the kind of problems that every actor faces onstage: breath and relaxation; vocal range and power; communication with other actors; singing and acting simultaneously; working on different-size stages; and approaching the vocal demands of different kinds of script. This book is a must for teachers of voice/speech/text and a textbook that students can use to troubleshoot and renew their vocal work at different points in their careers.

Speaking Shakespeare (Palgrave Macmillan, 2004). This book goes to the heart of acting Shakespeare. Starting with the basics of verse speaking through to the rehearsal of leading roles, the author unlocks some of the greatest challenges that any actor will ever encounter.

The Second Circle: How to Use Positive Energy for Success in Every Situation (Norton, 2008, originally published in the UK as *Presence: How to . . .*). Drawing on her experience working with high-level performers, Rodenburg writes about dealing with emotional issues that impede success: loss, violation, and self-esteem. *The Second Circle* helps the reader to deal with the debilitating and manipulative behavior of one's immediate family, friends, and colleagues while bringing out their best qualities. She employs breathing, voice, and postural exercises to help the reader toward better communication. This text translates the elite performer's insights for those in and out of the profession.

Video samples of Patsy Rodenburg's work are available on the Michael Howard Studio website.

Comparing the systems

One way to get a sense of what is important to any teacher is to examine how they present certain kinds of information. How, for example, do they note the sounds of English? Berry and Linklater are so unconcerned with pronunciation standards that when they do discuss sounds they use only a vague system of transliteration. Lessac becomes highly detailed, and converts vowels into a numeric system. Skinner uses the IPA in the most narrow and specific transcription you'll find.

Comparing the solutions

Here's a sample of how these four teachers deal with some typical voice and speech problems in their own words:

Table 7.1 Comparing solutions

BERRY	LESSAC	LINKLATER	SKINNER	RODENBURG
NASALITY				
"First get the back of the palate free by exercising: kekekeke . . . then AH very open gegegege . . . then AH very open	"Practice the tonal action of the Y-Buzz, avoiding words with nasal consonants. If the dilute resonance seems to feel	"Nasality is the quality heard when, finding the opening into the mouth obscured, the voice escapes through the nose	Skinner uses extensive word lists, setting up problem situations, but the book expects that a skilled teacher will be present to	"If the adjustment to the soft palate is too sluggish then the voice will sound too nasal and the words muddied."
Keep that freedom there and take the nasal consonants 'm' and 'n'	a bit nasal at first, check instead. The physical causes for nasality are a lazy soft palate, which	provide a model and guide for correction of nasality. No written instructions	There are multiple references to the need for balanced resonance with	
change, what you feel is	may sit flaccidly on the	are given.		an emphasis on head as

BERRY	LESSAC	LINKLATER	SKINNER	RODENBURG
in conjunction with the vowels, first separating them and then running them together. Be aware of the placing of the consonant in the nose, yet allow the vowel to open through the mouth. Practice with words such as 'moon', 'morning', and so on, slowly to begin with until you get a yawning feeling on the vowel."	nasal resonance, not nasality. When you are taught to feel the vibratory sensation of the y-buzz of the call, you will develop habit patterns that eliminate all or most of the nasality. The first concern is tonal and structural control."	back of the tongue, and the tongue itself, which can bunch up at back, driving the sound sharply into the nose. As with the other resonators, the nasal cavity should be discovered, isolated, developed, and then left to react automatically in the general interplay of speech."		opposed to chest resonance. But there is little specific instruction for this issue.

TALKING TOO FAST

BERRY	LESSAC	LINKLATER	SKINNER	RODENBURG
"You do not trust yourself. You have to believe you have a right to be [on stage]. Emphasis also placed on consonant energy and the need to fully feel each sound for its own value. This will reduce the impulse to race on and rob the words of their richness.	"If you maintain the structural form and feel it in every vowel, your speech can be as fast as you like, and it will never be too fast; or as slow, and you will never sound sluggish. A physical mechanism functioning properly and registering all signals cannot operate too rapidly, and the proper interplay of its moving parts will prevent monotony at any speed.	Not identified as a separate problem, but rather to be taken as a whole stemming from the separation of the voice from the person, and the root cause can be found in the psychophysical conditioning by the family, education, and environment.	(Not addressed.)	Though generally not a fan of using recorders, this is one time she encourages it. "Pace: Many fast or slow speakers are positively startled when they first hear the pace of their speech on tape. A fair amount of recording can be necessary to convince someone that the pace is out of sync. The person then begins to realize how hard it is for listeners to

Table 7.1 continued

BERRY	LESSAC	LINKLATER	SKINNER	RODENBURG
The only valid objection to speed in speech is that words are unintelligible and understanding is thereby lost; but if the consonarts are not lost . . . intelligibility is preserved, and you cannot, physically, talk too fast."				follow them. . . . This is one area where you can make decisive alterations once the habit of 'ceaseless pace' is revealed."

WEAK PROJECTION

BERRY	LESSAC	LINKLATER	SKINNER	RODENBURG
Several whole chapters are devoted to sorting out the misconceptions regarding volume. The issues relate to emotional size, the actor's willingness to commit, whether the actor is trying to disappear, if they feel they have a right to be there, how to share your voice with an audience. Technical and developmental approaches are also discussed at length.	"The key is to use as concentrated a tone as possible. Even in intimate, informal and close-range conversation, use more of the y-buzz tonal action with a relatively reduced inverted-megaphone shape to produce a darker tonal focus sufficient for any purpose. . . . The y-buzz is an extremely concentrated form of sound energy, and the energy output is minimal, conveying to the audience an impression of ease and intimacy."	"The word 'projection' is dangerous, suggesting that the actor throw the voice forward with energy separate and different from the acting energy. Whenever a director says 'Project!' or 'Louder, I can't hear!' or 'a little more diction please!' energy is taken away fromthe emotional and mental content and transfers to the voice."	(Not addressed.)	"Never push the voice. Never force your voice to do more than it can. You should feel neither strain nor overwork in the throat." "Whatever space you are performing in, stand on the stage when it's empty and breathe to the perimeters of the room. Not only to where the audience ends but the whole space from side to side, top to bottom." "The actor must find how to share her emotions more generously than before, to gradually

BERRY	LESSAC	LINKLATER	SKINNER	RODENBURG
				expand her circle of awareness peripherally while maintaining her sense of the truth."

DROPPED FINAL CONSONANTS

BERRY	LESSAC	LINKLATER	SKINNER	RODENBURG
"Losing the ends of words can be put right technically, but it's also tied up with not thinking through to the end of a thought — that is, rushing from one thought to another without giving it time to touch down. Again, this is lack of trust."	"...while there is some tolerance for error in producing vowels, there is practically no tolerance for error in producing consonants." "...the K in *take*, the V in *live*, and the N and the final D in *demand* are all easily lost or corrupted. This corruption is the source of sloppy speech, *and precisely there, where sloppy speech begins is where the technique of consonant action is most effective.*"	Not specifically addressed, though implicitly dealt with as intention and need to communicate. Some articulation drills, but none focusing on terminal sounds.	No philosophy, but pages of highly detailed drills with every conceivable consonant in isolation and in combination. In contrast to Lessac, there is no tolerance for error in producing vowels or consonants.	"What the 'puller back' must learn to do is to follow through on each and every sound, word and thought. They have to avoid traps and tangles. The breath must be relaxed and steady enough to sustain the forward and out sound. The speaker must remember to speak to the arc. Like water from a hosepipe the stream of language must travel away from you and towards an objective."

BREATH AND SUPPORT OF TONE

BERRY	LESSAC	LINKLATER	SKINNER	RODENBURG
"Put your hands up behind your head, and let your elbows be wide; to prevent tension as	"...although natural breathing is a necessary support for good voice and speech action, the breath	"Feel the breath moving into you and out of you in its own rhythm."	"The physical production of the quality of the voice will be studied under three headings:	"Keep the breath fluid and the support connected and open the entire voice including the jaw. Intone

Table 7.1 continued

BERRY	LESSAC	LINKLATER	SKINNER	RODENBURG
much as possible put the tips of your fingers on your ears to avoid pushing your head forward. This is a slightly tense position, so you have to be as relaxed as possible — its advantage is that it opens up the rib cage. Breathe in fairly slowly through your nose, trying to lift your shoulders. Open your mouth and sigh out — right out — and wait. Feel the need to breathe in, and in again slowly and out the same way. Do this two or three times only, because it is tiring and tension comes quickly, but you will find it helps enormously to get the ribs moving. . . . Give a little sigh out from the diaphragm — like a pant but not violent or sudden — repeat several times until you are sure of that feeling.	stream should be understood as a distinctly different and separate current from the vocal sound stream. Remember that vocal sound is amplified and strengthened by resonance and wave reflection; breath, being windlike in character, tends to obscure or disperse the sound waves, creating a breathy, forced tone quality. If the breath stream were really the same as the sound stream and traveled at the rate of sound, it would, as Dr. Douglas Stanley points out, 'have to blow more than ten times as hard as the worst hurricane; to blow the audience out of the hall — to blow the auditorium to bits.'" "For beautiful singing tones, or beautifully projected speaking tones, exhalation must be kept to	"Think the sound **OOOOO** (as in **moon**) and give it the autonomy to move around and through the spaces of your body. See whether it prefers to occupy any particular area of your body more than another. Let the **OOOOO** find the vibrations of your voice. Let the **OOOOO** find the emotion that suits it, the mood it wants, the color that matches. Let the **OOOOO** move through your body as it pleases. Now expel the thought of **OOOOO** from your body and mind by deliberately blowing it out of you with a strong puff of breath. . . ." "Take the **OOOOO** again and this time picture it as a **deep purple** sound, living and moving around in the lower regions of your body. Experience the sound sensually. Imagine it as made of **velvet**. Let it	1. Support of tone — respiration. 2. Initiation of tone — phonation. 3. Reinforcement of tone — resonation NOTE: one must at all times remember that the coordination of all three is practically a simultaneous production. VOICE PRODUCTION EXERCISES FOR DEVELOPING SUPPORT OF TONE Support and endurance of tone depends upon rhythmical control of the breath. In all breathing drills, the intake of the breath must be rapid and the emission slow. The intake or inspiration must be inaudible and invisible. Learn to take the air through the mouth as well	and in the same breath move into speaking, trying to keep the voice placed forward as you speak. Now intone higher than you normally speak or at the centre of your voice. Speak and as you move into speaking you might have the pleasing sensation of your voice dropping into place. As this happens you often experience a fully resonant voice as the result: all resonators are working together. Enjoy the sound and don't let its largeness, richness or fullness frighten you. As the voice locates its resonant potential and the resulting power, you might need to stop and give yourself notes: 'I am supporting too much'; 'I sound too loud.' The sound can suddenly be

BERRY	LESSAC	LINKLATER	SKINNER	RODENBURG
It does not matter if the ribs move, so long as you get a general feeling of them being open. Then vocalize on that diaphragm breath with a little 'ER,' just touching the sound off like a drum. This should be unforced yet firm, and quite specific as to the place where the sound is being made. The throat should be quite open, as that is the one place you should never feel effort. Now sustain the sound a little more by vocalizing on 'AH,' and then hold it a little longer on 'AY' and 'I,' getting the vowels open."	an irreducible minimum. Today, as in the past, the technique of pumping the diaphragm is often advocated for strong speech and voice production. Its advocates still claim that if you breathe well, you will sing and speak well. They have observed an association but turned cause and effect around: the truth is that if you sing and speak well, you will breathe well. If you become aware of the use of breath while singing or speaking, you are already indulging in extraneous and harmful manipulation of the breath."	move your body. . . . "**LET THE BREATH GO INTO YOUR BELLY AND RELEASE OUT FREELY FROM YOUR BELLY WITH EACH NEW EXPLORATION.** **THOUGHT/FEELING IMPULSE INSPIRES THE BREATH — BREATH CREATES SOUND — SOUND MOVES THE BODY.** "Now let the **EEEEE** inhabit you. Picture it **silver**. Let it glitter and sparkle in you. Allow it to stream up into your head on the highest vibration of your voice. Let it sound like the **wind**. Imagine yourself ice-skating, calling out on a high, excited **EEEEE**."	as through the nose, since we breathe both ways during speech. However, do not continue the intake of air through the mouth as it will have the tendency to give a dryness. One should remember that the emission of air in exhalation is not always of the same duration in speech. Develop a firm attack and rhythmical duration to the outgoing breath stream for speech."	enormous and echoing. Don't cut down on your resonances but simply adjust the support you are providing. That way you can actually work with less effort!"

UNIT 7.8.2 *Comparing the qualities*

To get another sense of how these teachers contrast with each other, you can examine them by comparing qualities or essences:

Table 7.2 System comparison — qualities

BERRY	LESSAC	LINKLATER	SKINNER	RODENBURG
POINT OF DEPARTURE — WAY IN				
language/text	body structure	body/imagery	ear/phonetics	identity/psychology
APPROACH				
internal	applied	organic	external	organic/technical
RELATIONSHIP TO THE BODY				
psychophysical	anatomical	metaphoric	mouth/ear	psychophysical
NOTATION SYSTEM				
transliteration	own system/numeric	transliteration	phonetic	transliteration (mentions phonetics)
VIEW				
comprehensive	systematic	whole	narrow	comprehensive
ATTITUDE				
allowing/active	prescriptive	healing/freeing	prescriptive	practical
FOCUS				
language	quality	feeling	phoneme	thought
GOAL				
enlightenment	development	freedom	perfection	permission
PHILOSOPHY				
humanistic psychology	Cartesian mechanics	metaphysics	jurisprudence	self-help

SENSE				
visual/auditory	kinesthetic	kinesthetic/visual	visual/auditory	kinesthetic/auditory
RIGHT/LEFT BRAIN ORIENTATION				
left/right brain	left brain	right brain	left brain	left/right brain
OPENNESS				
open/practical	juridical	very open/loose	juridical	open/practical
PATH				
spiral	linear	winding	linear	meandering
EASE OF INTEGRATION INTO ACTING				
easy	difficult	natural	difficult	easy
AVAILABLE FOR SELF-INSTRUCTION				
yes	some, but not the important information	as an introduction only	phonetics, but not the ear training	yes

Other sources

UNIT 7.9

These five teachers have left a distinct imprint on actor training. You should be familiar with them. It is likely that if you take advanced training at any conservatory, university or studio, you will come into contact with their systems. Additionally, many of the best teachers in the field today do not slavishly hold to one method but will synthesize aspects of them all. That is perhaps the best approach. It is also interesting to note that any angle can act as a doorway to the whole subject. For example, working on precise vowel formation can lead to good breath support, and vice versa.

Of course the "big five" aren't the only influences in this diverse area. Several others have made important contributions as well. You may want to have a look at their books, interviews, and articles in case one has a perspective that you find uniquely helpful.

Books providing overviews of the field

Jane Boston and Rena Cook, *The Art of Breath in Vocal and Holistic Practice* (Jessica Kingsley Publishers, 2009). Divided into four sections: Breath and the Body, Breath and the Mind, Breath and Holistic Practice, and Breath and Performance, the book offers seventeen essays by experts focusing on the use of breath to "communicate, act, or sing better, feel better, live better." It focuses equally on performance and therapeutic/healing issues.

Marion Hampton and Barbara Acker, *Vocal Vision: Views on Voice by 24 Leading Teachers, Coaches and Directors* (Applause, 1997). A fascinating compendium of perspectives. Primarily for the teacher rather than the actor, it is for those who want to know more of the *why* behind the great teachers' *how* — in their own words.

Jacqueline Martin, *Voice in Modern Theatre* (Routledge, 1991). The most thorough text placing voice and speech practice in historical and theoretical perspective, with a rich attention to contemporary interpretation of the classics and actor training.

Nancy Saklad, *Voice and Speech Training in the New Millennium: Conversations with Master Teachers* (Limelight, 2011). A collection of interviews with some of the world's leading voice and speech teachers: among them, Cicely Berry, Patsy Rodenburg, Kristin Linklater, Catherine Fitzmaurice, Dudley Knight, Louis Colaianni, David Carey, and, yes, Robert and Rocco. Also included is a historical overview of voice and speech training from the mid-nineteenth century to the present.

Christina Shewell, *Voice Work* (Wiley-Blackwell, 2009). Targeted at professionals who work in the many dimensions of voice as coaches, therapists or singing teachers, this book aims to bring together the wide-ranging perspectives from each and integrate them into a whole. Scholarly, but accessible, it is a thorough compendium of current perspectives. Rich material for the experienced as well as the novice.

Nan Withers-Wilson, *Vocal Direction for the Theatre*: *From Script Analysis to Opening Night* (Drama Books, 1993). Unique advice for directors and actors about how to work with a voice and speech coach, and the history of voice instruction for actors.

Books that establish their own training methodologies

Virgil A. Anderson, *Training the Speaking Voice* (Oxford University Press, 1977). Anderson's well-written text provides a good understanding of normal speech habits and an introduction to expressive use of the voice in a variety of practice selections.

J. Arthur Bronstein, *Your Speech and Voice* (Random House, 1967). The author presents a thorough treatment of the speaking process, with particularly clear presentations on rhythm, pitch, range, and variety in American speech, and determinants of voice quality.

David R. Carey and Rebecca Clark Carey, *The Vocal Arts Workbook and DVD* (Methuen Drama, 2008). Refreshing and imaginative, the book teaches through enhanced awareness and instructs through clear and specific exercises guiding actors to communicate thoughts and feelings with precision and power. The DVD contains 85 minutes of video and thirty-eight physical exercises.

Louis Colaianni, *The Joy of Phonetics (and Dialects)* (Drama Publishers, 1994). This is a workbook and CD set with exercises and games for learning phonetic symbols, including a phonetically driven play using throwable, huggable, phonetic symbol-shaped pillows to replace dull exercises. It provides a head start toward transcribing stage dialects, including French, German, British, and US accents. Phonetic pillows are also available, or you may make your own.

Kenneth C. Crannell, *Voice and Articulation* (Wadsworth Publishing, second edition, 1991). Comprehensive, covering the breadth of the subject from phoneme, to breathing, to dialects, to text work.

Julia Cummings-Wing, *Speak For Your Self, an Integrated Method of Voice and Speech Training* (Nelson-Hall, 1984). Cummings-Wing draws a path from self-awareness through self-realization, through self-expression and self-discipline, to a full life of owning and claiming the power of self, integrated with voice.

Elise Hahn, *Basic Voice Training for Speech* (McGraw, 1957). This is an excellent study emphasizing voice development. Clarity and scientifically reliable suggestions make this treatment of pitch and vocal quality valuable to voice trainers and acting coaches.

Jeffrey C. Hahner, Martin A. Sokoloff, and Sandra Salisch, *Speaking Clearly: Improving Voice and Diction* with CDs (McGraw-Hill, sixth edition, 2001). Very well organized, especially useful for foreign-accented or regional speakers looking for GA.

Harry Hill with Robert Barton, editor, *A Voice for the Theatre* (CBS College Publishing, 1985). Fundamental, step-by-step approach for most actor issues. Less focus on vocal production, more about interpretational freedom and vocal creativity.

Robert L. Hobbs, *Teach Yourself Transatlantic: Theatre Speech for Actors* (Mayfield Publishing, 1986). Hobbs' take on Elevated Standard Speech. Extensive exercises and drills, using transliteration rather than phonetics.

Barbara Houseman, *Finding Your Voice* (Theatre Arts Books, 2002). A self-help manual for actors who want to train and develop the voice — making it stronger, clearer, more supple. Houseman addresses posture, muscular support, and relaxation. Exercises provide an opportunity to practice the techniques and to extend the reader's skills.

Peter Kline, *The Theatre Student: The Actor's Voice* (Richard Rosen Press, 1972). Part of Kline's series on *The Theatre Student*, the book is an overview of all the general aspects of voice and speech except dialects. Chapters are brief without many specific exercises, though lots of useful information. Not strong on connecting the theory into an actor's actual practice.

Evangeline Machlin, *Speech for the Stage* (Theatre Arts Books, 1966). Comprehensive workbook full of specific detailed techniques and numerous exercises covering a wide range of an actor's voice and speech needs.

Stephanie Martin and Lyn Darnley, *The Voice Source Book* (Winslow Press, 1992). Workbook for voice and speech. Lots of exercises, but not too much theory. Clear, accurate, accessible, useful. A handy, photocopy-free resource.

Lyle V. Mayer, *Fundamentals of Voice and Diction* with CD (McGraw-Hill, fourteenth edition, 2008). Mayer's text includes excellent and abundant practice materials for developing clear speech and a healthy voice. The orientation is traditional, and essential theory is presented briefly.

Michael McCallion, *The Voice Book: For Actors, Public Speakers, and Everyone Who Wants to Make the Most of Their Voice* (Theatre Arts Books, 1988). One of the more thorough books regarding technical aspects of vocal production, alignment, tonality, pronunciation, breathing, etc. A bit dense, not an easy read, requiring serious study. Good material on combining the Alexander technique with more traditional articulation and breath work.

Malcolm Morrison, *Clear Speech* (Heinemann, fourth edition, 2001). A theatre practitioner and actor trainer, Morrison focuses on common voice and speech problems. Among areas addressed are relaxation, breathing, vocal warm-up, and specific speech sounds. Extensive practice materials are included.

Janet Rodgers, editor, *The Complete Voice and Speech Workout: 75 Exercises for Classroom and Studio Use* with CD (Applause Books, 2002). Contributors are some of the best professionals in the world. There is a brief description of the history and purpose of each exercise, followed by the exercise itself.

David Alan Stern, *The Speaker's Voice* (all titles published by Dialect/Accent Specialists) CDs with instructional manual. "A Self-Instructional Course In Aesthetic Voice Improvement." Covers all the basics of relaxation, breathing, resonance, articulation. *Speaking without an Accent* (CDs with manual). Focuses on adjusting regional American toward GA. *Breaking the Accent Barrier* (DVD) and *The Sound and Style of American English*, second edition (CDs and manual). Teaches GA for non-American speakers.

J. Clifford Turner and Jane Boston, editors, *Voice and Speech in the Theatre* (Theatre Arts Books, sixth edition, 2007). This is a classic book on voice and speech, designed for actors at all levels, written in 1950 and revised by Malcolm Morrison in 1976 then Jane Boston in 2007. One of the great voice teachers of his day, J. Clifford Turner here uses simple and direct language to impart the basics of speech and voice.

Charles Van Riper, *Voice and Articulation* (Prentice-Hall, 1958). This text presents a thorough approach utilizing speech science concepts and methodologies.

Lynn K. Wells, *The Articulate Voice: An Introduction to Voice and Diction* (Gorsuch Scarisbrick, 1993). A basic introduction to voice and speech, suitable for a one-semester undergraduate course for students interested in improving their vocal habits and moving their pronunciation patterns toward American Standard.

Robert Wetterstrom, *Speech for Actors* (Speechology, 1978). Focuses on a simple approach to oral communication, speech sounds, vocal physiology, and pronunciation. Uses no phonetic symbols. Basic-level text.

Journals

The Voice and Speech Review, the official publication of the Voice and Speech Trainers Association (VASTA), is published every two years in a large volume that includes a variety of materials: research articles, interviews, roundtable discussions, questionnaire results, essays, practical advice, book/video reviews, play reviews from a vocal perspective, thesis/dissertation, abstracts, and survey of resources on the cover topic, which is distinct to each issue. *Standard Speech* (2000), *The Voice in Violence* (2001), *Film, Broadcast and Electronic Media Coaching* (2003), *Shakespeare around the Globe* (2005), *Voice and Gender* (2007), *The Moving Voice* (2009), *A World of Voice* (2011). Although listed as a journal, it is probably more accurately designated a serialized monograph. Watch for successive issues.

Logopedics Phoniatrics Vocology is the journal of the British Voice Association (BVA). *The Journal of Voice* is published by the Voice Foundation, and the *Journal of Singing* is put out by the National Association of Teachers of Singing (NATS). These are great resources for both scholarly and practical articles.

This is a lot of material, and few actors will have the time to scan through it on their own. However, these teachers all have unique and valuable perspectives, and one may have just the insight for you. To get a better sense of their work:

Research

The last chapter offered you quite a reading list. Warning: MOST VOICE BOOKS ARE NOT EASY READS. This is an under-statement. We suggest you strive for one a month and consider that an accomplishment, because the material tends to be dense and challenging, although worth it. Go back over the bibliography and devise your own reading list in the order you would like to pursue these sources. Consider getting a partner to read the same book you are and work each other through the exercises. Watch for short workshops in your area. Expose yourself to as many great teachers as possible.

However, don't limit your research to CDs, books or classes. Consider everyone you meet a source of information. Listen to them more closely and note how your voice and theirs can enhance even the most fleeting connections.

> **On the ocean of life, we pass and speak to one another,**
> **Only a look and a voice; then darkness again and a silence.**
>
> HENRY WADSWORTH LONGFELLOW, poet, *The Theologian's Tale*

Backing into your future — lifelong vocal work

Set yourself timetables or deadlines. If you are coming to the end of a class or school year, you probably will not be working with a teacher or coach for a while. You will need to provide structure for your independent work. What do you want to achieve by the end of the term, the summer, the year? Where do you want to be two years from now? Exactly what do you want to get rid of, acquire, refine, renew? Do lists and dates. Place this where you pass it often, a spot where guilt will get you on a regular basis.

Take the categories just introduced and chart them to help you to make some choices regarding where to start and how to travel.

Below is a summary of the categories suggested here. See the site for a form to complete.

ONLINE

1. Unfinished business (conversations — issues).
2. Blocks and strategies (labels — blind spots).
3. Audiolization (ideal voice — two kinds of listening).

- What physical relaxation/alignment/focus approaches are taught, and how do they integrate them with acting and voice and speech?
- What is the proportion of text-related activity to organic exploration in the training?
- How are accents taught; which are covered?
- Are classes offered in voiceover work?
- What standards of speech are applied (regional, General American, Stage Standard, Received Pronunciation)?
- How much time will you have in any one class? How often do voice classes meet and for what duration?
- What is the progression of classes over the course of the degree?
- How large are the classes? Do they include private tutorials?
- How is student vocal competence tested and evaluated?

How are voice and speech experts trained, certified, and licensed?

UNIT 7.11

Few voice and speech experts have arrived at that status by setting out to do so. Most have been actors, directors or acting teachers who discovered a knack for the subject. Others have come at it from speech pathology or as singing teachers. Until recently, it was not possible to even study the subject except at universities, where interested students could attempt to cobble together an interdisciplinary degree between theatre, speech/communication disorders, linguistics, and music. In the last several years, graduate programs specifically designed to train theatre voice and speech coaches have established themselves.

Fitzmaurice, Linklater, and Lessac offer advanced training and certification in their methods, and teachers certified through them are reliably proficient in that system.

To maintain currency in the field, many V&S teachers belong to the Voice and Speech Trainers Association (VASTA), The National Association of Teachers of Singing (NATS), and the British Voice Association (BVA). They all publish journals and have periodic conventions. The Voice Foundation also serves as an important link between physicians, scientists, pathologists, and coaches. All these organizations are open to specialists, as well as any interested non-professional.

UNIT 7.12 **Physical relaxation/alignment/focus systems**

Some of the most exciting voice work is done along with physical freeing and aligning classes. The two most frequently chosen systems are the Alexander technique and Feldenkrais' Awareness Through Movement. Both systems are subtle, requiring a highly trained practitioner and lots of patience with the process. The results can be transforming, however, because as the actor unlocks the body, the voice will also move toward more freedom of expression and overall health. Some schools will integrate Grotowski's sound and movement approach. It is athletic, aggressive, powerful, and exciting — in sharp contrast to the slow, deeply introspective micro-movements of the others.

Michael Johnson-Chase is certified to teach both Alexander and Feldenkrais. Since each certification process is lengthy and demanding, Michael is one of no more than a half-dozen people with these qualifications. Here is his comparison of these two systems:

The voice is an instrument of the entire body, and our physical use of ourselves has great bearing on our vocal effectiveness. This was not always common knowledge. Early in this century, F.M. Alexander, an Australian actor, was forced to analyze the basis of his own chronic hoarseness. He found that it originated in a subtle, habituated tendency to misalign himself in the moment just before speaking. In his successful efforts to retrain himself to speak in a manner in which the misalignment would not occur, he created the Alexander technique, now studied widely by actors all over the world. The Feldenkrais method shares a similar story, although it is not based in a physical dysfunction manifested through the voice. Moshe Feldenkrais was an Israeli physicist who suffered a serious knee injury brought on by long-term vigorous athletic activity. Believing that his knee problem resulted from years of misuse of his entire body, he developed the Feldenkrais method in the process of training himself to move more comfortably.

Alexander technique is taught privately or in small groups. Feldenkrais can also be taught privately (private sessions are called *Functional Integration*), or in groups (group classes are called *Awareness Through Movement*).

Although the two appear quite different to the outside eye, both are methods of movement education that help students to become more aware of how they habitually use themselves and offer means to explore new ways of moving. Both methods focus on more than just physical freedom and good alignment. Each addresses good self-use, or effective movement, through different means.

The most critical difference between these methods is in their fundamental assumptions about how humans most effectively learn. The Alexander technique focuses on conscious attention and critical thought in the learning process, whereas the Feldenkrais method relies on a more unconscious and subcortical orientation.

Conscious is a key word in the Alexander technique, referring to what can be called a kind of "thoughtful intention," the existence of which is crucial in the teaching and learning of this method. The technique's lexicon abounds with references to thinking, directing, giving directions, giving orders, allowing something to happen, releasing something in a specific direction. All of these are taught as a function of cognition and a physical response. To apply the technique, a student is asked to "think" about how he is using himself. To do this is to engage in a learned form of mental intention aimed toward a physical response.

By contrast, the Feldenkrais method shapes itself around a learning process that attempts to mimic the way we learned as an infant. For any animal, including human beings, the process of learning to roll over, or crawl, or walk is directed through a biologically endowed ontological sequence, and while this sequence is quite specific, it occurs for most of us without any conscious intention or intervention. Feldenkrais practitioners believe that the most profound and effective kind of development engages the motor cortex on a biologically organic level and consequently attempts to recreate a learning experience for students in a way that will help them to evolve toward a higher level of self-use. A Feldenkrais teacher's focus is that of eliciting a deeply embedded process of discovery in the student, and it is *not* on the acquisition of any particular technique for the achievement of good self-use.

To summarize: the Feldenkrais method and the Alexander technique share the same idea of what efficient movement is, although they use different lexicons to describe them. They differ most profoundly in their fundamental assumptions about how we learn. Alexander places a great deal of reliance on conscious intention and awareness, while Feldenkrais relies largely on unconscious learning evoked through learning strategies that mimic biological processes.

Here are some books for further reading:

F. Matthias Alexander, *Man's Supreme Inheritance* (E.P. Dutton and Co., 1918). Theoretical, wordy, and dry, this is the original manifesto from the man who invented the technique. Not written for actors. Follows the order of theory, to practical application, to respiratory re-education.

F. Matthias Alexander, *Constructive Conscious Control of the Individual* (E.P. Dutton and Co., 1923). Focuses on imperfect uses of the body, habituations, and how misalignment and poor functioning can effect all parts of your life. Full of interesting insights. Teaches through a process of sensory appreciation and sensitivity. Not specifically for actors. A bit more accessible than his first book.

F. Matthias Alexander, *The Use of Self* (E.P. Dutton and Co., 1932). Easier to read than the earlier books, though not specifically related to acting. Good for personal exploration and awareness, especially as an accompaniment to a class.

Moshe Feldenkrais, *Awareness Through Movement: Health Exercises for Personal Growth* (Harper and Row, second edition, 1977). Explains the philosophical underpinnings of his approach and sets up twelve lessons on posture, breathing, coordination, etc. His is a complete system of relating to the body. Not an easy read or a quick fix.

Moshe Feldenkrais, *The Potent Self: A Guide to Spontaneity* (Harper and Row, 1985). Not a practical workbook but a study of his findings in the application of his technique. Good to read if you are also taking a class, as it will help to explain the psychology of body movement.

Michael Gelb, *Body Learning* (Henry Holt and Co., second edition, 1987). A simple introduction to the Alexander technique based on the author's own experiences. More accessible than Alexander's own writing, with some application to the performing arts. Good introductory material, useful along with a class.

Jerzy Grotowski, *Towards a Poor Theatre* (Simon and Schuster, 1968). A series of interviews, essays, and lectures by Grotowski compiled and translated from Polish. Interesting manifesto on his theories. It's possible to get a sense of his movement and voice training for actors, and some exercises are explained in detail, although this is not an instructional book.

Kelly R. McEvenue, *The Actor and the Alexander Technique* (Palgrave Macmillan, 2002). The first basic book about how this technique can help actors to feel more natural on stage. McEvenue provides three types of exercise: warm-up, "balance and center," and spatial awareness. She discusses imitation, the use of masks, nudity on the stage, dealing with injury and aging, with examples of specific productions that have successfully used the Alexander technique, such as "The Lion King."

If you are having trouble opening up your voice, it is a good idea to find some way of opening up your body as well. They go hand in hand. This could take many forms, from massage to yoga to Rolfing (deep tissue massage) to Laban-Bartenieff Fundamentals (a highly evolved stage movement study). It doesn't matter which of the many approaches you take, as long as you can connect with it and feel it moving you forward. Over time, you may want to sample them all.

What promising new approaches are on the horizon?

There are six exciting new directions being explored now. Undoubtedly, more are just around the corner. Currently, there is a limited amount of published information in the following subjects written specifically for actors. But keep a look out. These areas are so promising that in the near future someone will surely emerge from each with specific adaptations for the theatre.

The questions coming up in subsequent exercises are tough ones. You could return to these for years and not be quite satisfied with your answers. A sophisticated answer would take a good bit of training. We are not asking for sophisticated answers. All we ask is that you give your best possible conjecture (maybe even a guess) NOW. Your answers will get better every time you return and ask the questions. And you will probably return and probe many times. But the sooner you start wrestling with these issues, the sooner you will know your voice.

ONLINE

EXERCISE 1.2.2 MY VOCAL PROFILE

Describe your voice as if it has a personality or nature of its own. Come at it from the following angles:

1. PUBLIC/PRIVATE. How does your speech change in public from what it is in private? At what *point* does a group become large enough to instigate the change? Does private stop beyond one person or are you much the same in small groups? Where do you really begin to *feel* outnumbered and so alter your vocal choices? Or do groups bring out the best in your voice so that the extrovert in you opens up? Is your telephone voice different from that you use in normal conversation? How do you adjust for contact with strangers?
2. EAR/AGILITY. Can you mimic others easily? Can you hear something and recreate it? Are you facile with words and good with sound? Do you have perfect pitch? Was catching and doing voices encouraged in your home? Do you do it for fun? Or is this something you normally avoid/ignore?
3. MOODS. How does your voice change with your mood? Does your sound alter depending on the kind of day you are having? Can others catch this? How radically and in what way?
4. MASKING. How do you try to conceal with your voice? What tricks have you learned to cover up how you're really feeling? Even given the voice's unpredictability, where are you usually successful?
5. REGIONALISMS. Do you have a regional accent? Can people tell where you're from? Can they tell what *kind* of a place it was even if they can't identify it?
6. HERITAGE. Does your family's past/history influence your speech? How do its national origins, race, religion, affiliations, cultural background or socio-economic class enter into your voice? Do you control these influences?
7. AGE. How old are you? How old are you *vocally*? Do callers ask to speak to your parents? Do they call you sir or madam? Is your voice an accurate reflection of your chronological age? Of your spiritual age?
8. GENDER. Are you sometimes mistaken on the phone for someone of the opposite sex? Why? Do you feel your

UNIT 1.11   **Warming up your voice**

Now that you have more of a relationship with your voice, it is time to nurture that relationship. True ownership involves taking care of what you own. Your voice is a sensitive instrument, and while it need not be coddled, it does require warming up before being stressed by intense or aggressive use. We might get by in our daily lives without any warm-up, but the vocal demands of an acting career are just as extreme as the physical demands put on an Olympic gymnast. A routine warm-up can get you mentally focused, muscularly limber, emotionally available, and vocally responsive.

The warm-up series that follows is a good place to start. In the next chapter, we will deal with more long-term ways to nurture your voice, but for now we will focus on preparing it for immediate challenges. As you gather experience with the subject you will want to adapt this series to focus on specific issues, or to tailor it to prepare you for a certain kind of role or challenge. It may look like a lot of material, but it should take no more than fifteen minutes to do the whole routine at first and as little as five once you have it down. It's a good idea to practice it before any acting class, performance or rehearsal.

LISTEN

EXERCISE 1.11.1 VOCAL WARM-UP

1. **THE PRUNE**. Lie on your back with your arms and legs uncrossed and loose. As each area of the body is named below, tense it up while keeping everything lower on your body loose and relaxed. The tension will accumulate, moving from head to toes, before you finally let everything go and float from the release. Each tensing is more effective if you imagine you are tightening that area of the body to protect yourself from some shock.

   a. First, tense all your *facial muscles* inward toward the center of the face, as if it were rapidly withering and drying up like a prune.
   b. Tighten the surrounding *skull* as if it were suddenly locked in a vice.
   c. Shoot the tension into the *neck* as if it were in a brace and frozen in place.
   d. Grip the tension into the *shoulders*, locking at the shoulder joints. (Remember, everything below the shoulders is still loose.)
   e. Tighten the *upper arms* — both sets of biceps and triceps.
   f. Tense at the *elbows*, locking the elbow joints.

3. Position A: lie on your back on the floor.[1] Bend your knees with your feet flat on the floor about a foot away from your hips. Adjust the position for maximum comfort.

4. Place your hand on your lower abdomen and observe the way your body "breathes itself." Make no effort to change either the speed or natural depth of the breath.

5. Observe any movement of your lower ribs.

6. Compare your breathing with what you felt when standing. There is likely to be little upper chest movement but a great deal of abdominal and rib activity.

7. Position B: keep your feet flat on the floor, sit up, and push yourself forward into a squatting position with your knees in your chest and your body curled in a little ball. Locate your breathing in your lower back. Feel your ribs expand and contract.

8. Stand. Balance your weight evenly between your feet. Relax your abdominal and buttock muscles. Let your knees be soft, not locked. As before, observe how low your breath is allowed to go.

9. Position C: effortlessly float your elbows up above and in front of your shoulders. Let the rest of your arms hang limply. Relax your abdominal and buttock muscles. Let your knees be soft, not locked. Observe how low your breath is allowed to go.

10. Release your arms, letting them flop down to your side. Check your breathing. How deep is it compared with the other positions? Are your abdominal and buttock muscles tensed? Is there a change from the first time you checked your breath?

1   An alternative position for those with bad backs, injuries, etc. is to sit in a chair, then in Position B, lean forward onto your knees, as curled over as you can comfortably get.

Positions A, B, and C in the exercise above are ones in which it is hard to breathe improperly. The body is required to let in a deep breath. Repeat the exercise as part of your daily warm-up, until the breathing patterns become habituated. Always observe not just the breath but your feelings as well. See if you don't feel more emotionally available by the end of the series.

Our next task is to connect this breath to sound.

UNIT 2.9 **Healing pitch – notes on your sheet music**

The main pitch areas of interest:

- **median note**: the average pitch where your voice is centered;
- **range**: how far up and down the scale you go;
- **inflection** or **intonation**: the way your voice moves through its range.

Table 2.7 Pitch Doc/Shrink

THE VOICE DOC	THE VOICE SHRINK	R
Overly low median note	Are you trying too hard to impress; pushing for control over others?	p 105
Overly high median note	Are you unsure of your strength or authority; submissive, appeasing, tense?	p 105
Narrow pitch range	Are you willing to share emotions; trying to control feelings?	pp 107–8
Repetitive inflection patterns	Are you making clear choices; being too general? Do you lack sensitivity to pitch; have low self-awareness?	pp 109–10
Flat sound	Are you able to hear pitch? Are you willing to share emotions; trying to control feelings?	pp 109–10
R: Use all your pitch in less predictable ways.	**R**: Relish the relationship between pitch exploration and really sharing.	

CHAPTER 3

EXERCISE 3.6.5.1 STRONG OR WEAK FORM?

These are words that frequently take the unstressed, or weak form. Practice speaking both forms.

Table 3.8 Strong and weak forms of words

Word	Weak form	GA strong form	GB strong form	Notes
a	[ə]	[eɪ]	[eɪ]	Only use the strong form in unusual stress to denote a number contrast as in, "not five cats, A cat."
am	[əm]	[æm]	[æm]	
an	[ən]	[æn]	[æn]	
and	[ŋ, ɳd, ən, ænd]	[ænd]	[ænd]	Use the [d] when the next sound is a vowel as in "you and I." [d] is less useful when followed by a consonant, as in "to and fro."
are	[ɚ] GA, [ə] GB	[ɑɚ]	[ɑː]	
as	[əz]	[æz]	[æz]	
but	[bət]	[bʌt]	[bʌt]	
could	[kəd]	[kʊd]	[kʊd]	
does	[dəz]	[dʌz]	[dʌz]	
doth	[dəθ]	[dʌθ]	[dʌθ]	Rhyme *doth* with *does*, not with *moth* or *both*.
for	[fɚ] GA, [fə] GB	[fɔɚ]	[fɔː]	GA is sometimes inclined to strengthen the weak form [fɚ] into [fɔɚ] for the strong form.
from	[frəm]	[frʌm]	[frɒm]	
had	[əd, həd]	[hæd]	[hæd]	
has	[əz, həz]	[hæz]	[hæz]	
have	[əv, həv]	[hæv]	[hæv]	
her	[ɚ, hɚ] GA, [ə, hə] GB	[hɚ]	[hɜ]	
into	[ˈɪn.tə]	[ˈɪn.tu]	[ˈɪn.tu]	Use the strong form when followed by a vowel, as in "into each."
must	[məst]	[mʌst]	[mʌst]	
of	[əv]	[ʌv]	[ɒv]	
or	[ɚ] GA, [ə] GB	[ɔɚ]	[ɔː]	

LISTEN

Table 4.1 continued

3.	da	dɑ	dʌ	dɜ	dæ	de	dɪ	di	deɪ̆	daɪ̆
4.	na	nɑ	nʌ	nɜ	næ	ne	nɪ	ni	neɪ̆	naɪ̆
5.	pa	pɑ	pʌ	pɜ	pæ	pe	pɪ	pi	peɪ̆	paɪ̆
6.	ba	bɑ	bʌ	bɜ	bæ	be	bɪ	bi	beɪ̆	baɪ̆
7.	ma	mɑ	mʌ	mɜ	mæ	me	mɪ	mi	meɪ̆	maɪ̆
8.	ka	kɑ	kʌ	kɜ	kæ	ke	kɪ	ki	keɪ̆	kaɪ̆
9.	ga	gɑ	gʌ	gɜ	gæ	ge	gɪ	gi	geɪ̆	gaɪ̆
10.	va	vɑ	vʌ	vɜ	væ	ve	vɪ	vi	veɪ̆	vaɪ̆
11.	za	zɑ	zʌ	zɜ	zæ	ze	zɪ	zi	zeɪ̆	zaɪ̆
12.	ða	ðɑ	ðʌ	ðɜ	ðæ	ðe	ðɪ	ði	ðeɪ̆	ðaɪ̆

The other crucial consonant problem is the loss of endings. The following sequence gets progressively more demanding as you move from singles to doubles and triples. Remember that consonants don't all take the same amount of time and pressure. Be light, fast, and accurate.

EXERCISE 4.4.2.2 ARTICULATION – ATTACKING THE TERMINALS

Speak each of these lines as rapidly, lightly, and clearly as possible. Explore the use of the bone prop.

Table 4.2 Attacking the terminals

	[u] (who'll)	[ɪ] (hill)	[ɔ] (haul)	[ɑ] (ha)	[aɪ] (hike)	[i] (heel)
13.	ut	ɪt	ɔt	ɑt	aɪt	it
14.	ud	ɪd	ɔd	ɑd	aɪd	id
15.	un	ɪn	ɔn	ɑn	aɪn	in

Coach Barton: O.K., Rocky, now . . .

Player: Um, excuse me coach, it's Rocco.

Coach Barton: Okay, smart guy. If that's the way you want it. Give me ten.

Player: Ten what?

Coach Barton: Hell, Dal Vera, it's *your* voice! O.K. gimme three tempo isolations, one volume build, two tempo racings, an optimal median note, a volume isolation, and some full-body resonance.

Player: What was that order again? And . . . coach, I think that's only nine.

Coach Barton: That does it, Rockman. Make up your own %$#&*@!* vocal work-out!!!! I'm outta here.

The moral of this story? Others can offer you suggestions, but it is your voice. Most of us do not hire someone else to come to our house and make us do push-ups. But even fewer of us get a coach to force us into articulation drills. You need to come up with a voice program yourself that seems to suit your needs and wants. Then a teacher or coach can help you refine, modify, and develop your own work-out.

Doing voice work can be as energizing and liberating as any other kind of physical exercise. A few minutes a day can radically improve any speaker's voice within a matter of days and weeks.

PATSY RODENBURG, author, voice coach

The following reasons are those selected most often to motivate people to get in shape physically:

WEIGHT CONTROL

LESS FLAB

MORE MUSCLE DEFINITION

IMPROVED SKIN TONE

INCREASED FLEXIBILITY

GREATER EFFICIENCY

MORE RESTFUL SLEEP

GREATER ENERGY

GREATER STAMINA

ENHANCED SELF-IMAGE

MORE STRESS RESISTANCE

QUICKER RECOVERY

RESISTANCE TO DISEASE

MORE ATTRACTIVE TO OTHERS

ADDED PEAK CAPACITY TIME

A NATURAL TUNE-UP

These have all been proven to happen with fitness. Can you add any benefits? Now adapt the list above to a decision to get in shape vocally. While having a healthy cave can certainly enhance what goes on in there, which of the reasons are not otherwise immediately applicable? Which motives are true for both body and voice? What new reasons can you add ?

GOAT is a diphthong in all three dialects. Here, ES and GA are a match: [oʊ]. This is one of the critical places where ES doesn't swing toward RP. In RP [əʊ] the first vowel is more central in the mouth and more closed than in GA.

Table 5.12 PALM, CLOTH, THOUGHT, GOAT in comparison

	PALM	CLOTH	THOUGHT	GOAT		PALM	CLOTH	THOUGHT	GOAT
1.	ah	ox	awe	oh	17.	alms	odd	awed	owed
2.	Allah	Ollie	all	old	18.	palm	pod	pawed	polled
3.	palm	policy	Paul	pole	19.	papa	popper	pauper	pope
4.	balm	bomb	bawl	bowl	20.	Baden	body	bawd	bode
5.	Tahoe	Tom	tall	toll	21.	Tana	tonic	tawny	tone
6.	taco⁵	tock	talk	toque	22.	Dahl	doll	Dalton	dole
7.	Dada	dotted	daughter	dote	23.	calm	cod	cawed	code
8.	Kahn	con	call	cone	24.	mama	mop	maw	mow
9.	spa	spondee	spawn	spoke	25.	armada	mod	Maud	mode
10.	Mahler	moll	maul	mole	26.	Nazi	knotty	naughty	noted
11.	llama	lolling	lawless	loan	27.	father	fond	fawned	phoned
12.	father	folly	falcon	foal	28.	façade	sod	sawed	sewed
13.	psalm	somber	sauce	sews	29.	sake	sock	Salk	soak
14.	Shah	shot	Shaw	show	30.	mirage	Roger	raw	row
15.	Brahms	broth	brought	broach	31.	drama	drop	drawn	drone
16.	Java	John	jaundice	Jones	32.	cha-cha	chock	chalk	choke

5 In RP, some foreign loan words like taco, pasta, nacho, macho, Nazi, sake, may be said with [æ] rather than [ɑ].

Record: audio or video record as soon as you pick the material. Use the playback to memorize accurately. Use it to check your progress. Then record periodically in order to give yourself permission to do more. You may think that you're using lots of pitch and exciting shifts in resonance. This will reveal how little you are using. Think you are taking out the gaps? This will show you where they are.

Rhythm: the recurrence of any beat, event or sequence with enough regularity that the time intervals seem equal and the overall impression is one of balance. Rhythm causes the audience to maintain a sense of pulse and the actor to keep the play moving along in a livelier, less indulgent manner.

Scansion: close analysis of the metrical pattern of lines of verse in order to figure out how they should be read aloud, where stressed and unstressed syllables exist, what needs to be elided or compensated for, etc. A line reading is said not to scan if it fails to meet the metrical demands of the speech. The act of scanning provides multiple clues for interpretation and emphasis.

Speed-through: verse moves faster than prose because it gets a momentum, like a snowball down a mountain, and because feelings are charged. After you have done most of your homework, you will need to do it all quicker. Make the changes instantly. If you doubt that you need a speed-through, video yourself. You'll be appalled at the pauses. Goose the work.

Split line: several characters speak, but so briefly that a single line of verse is the result. Example:

> *1st Lord:* Was't you, sirrah?
>
> *2nd Lord:*   Not I.
>
> *3rd Lord:*   Nay, it was I.

An indication from the playwright that no pause should occur at all, that the lines should come just as quickly as if they had all three been spoken by one person. Notice that the "conversation" involving three people still takes a total of ten syllables to speak.

Stress: the intensity of emphasis placed on an individual syllable. In a perfect iambic pentameter line, the second, fourth, sixth, eighth, and tenth syllables will be stressed, while the odd-numbered syllables are unstressed. Also called **accent**.

Undercut: a technique for expressing humor and irony by setting up a proposition, then through lowered pitch, projection, and slyness of attitude, sliding beneath what has just been said and slicing it down. In contemporary plays, it is used mainly in dialogue, but classical characters often undercut themselves within their own monologues.

UNIT 6.9.1 *Voice personas*

Here is a way of organizing these voices:

Ages: baby, toddler, teen, young love, romantic, sexy, wife or husband, mature adult, grandparent, old crone, sage.

Types: *Business*: secretary/boss, dynamic leader, CEO; *Walter Mitty type*: wimpy dreamer, nerd, henpecked, space cadet; *Tough*: detective, soldier, punk, greaser, biker, football hooligan, cabbie, pimp; *Rural*: farmer, miner, hick, trailer trash, redneck, good ol' boy, cowboy/girl, country singer; *Classy*: cultured, aristocratic, elegant, snob; *Sick person*: cold/sore throat, sinus attack; *Others*: starlet, bimbo, FM mellow, AM frantic, God, etc.

Accents: everything in the first part of this chapter.

Narratives: straight, folksy, sly or knowing, suspenseful, proud, sensitive, strong, delighted, sensual, intense, amused, coy, grand, dry.

Fantasy: animals, Santa, elves, Disney characters, Sesame Street characters, fairy tale characters, Saturday morning cartoon characters, Dracula, witches, monsters.

Impersonations: politicians, movie stars, celebrities, comics, news anchors, talk show hosts, singers, rock stars.

Qualities: review earlier chapters for options.

Remember that your rejected voices in one category have possibilities in another. Your imitation of Margaret Thatcher or Dame Edna may not be so hot, but it is an interesting voice for an original character. Your Santa's elf comes across more like an Ewok from Hell. Fine, keep your inspirational source a secret and just use it.

> **For Hannibal Lecter, I tried to make his voice a combination of Truman Capote and Katherine Hepburn.**
>
> **ANTHONY HOPKINS, actor**

Also move beyond these recognizable slots to pure discovery. Sit in your room and try to speak like each object in it. What does your hair dryer sound like when it talks? What does your sweater have to say? What is the voice of that condom in the drawer? How about your alarm clock? Move outside and create the voice of your campus administration building, your bike, the color mauve, your street. Move inside and become the voice of your big toe, your right ear, your left buttock. The creative possibilities are limitless.

First, think of how you study:

A. Do you prefer to copy over your notes, make charts, graphs, organize the work on the page, and take a mental picture of it?

B. Do you retain information best when you're in a study group tossing around ideas, arguing concepts, drilling for memorization?

C. Would you like to move around the room during a lecture, handle and build models, put things together, write notes but never read them, do a project or experiment emphasizing the idea?

Second, if you were being taught a golf swing, would you prefer to:

A. watch the instructor demonstrate, create a mental movie of the swing and see yourself driving the ball all the way to the hole?

B. have the instructor stand off to the side and call instructions and advice?

C. have the instructor stand behind you and hold the club with you, taking you through the feel of a proper swing?

Third, the best way for a teacher to praise or encourage you is to:

A. smile and write a nice comment on your paper or work.

B. tell you that you did a good job, preferably announcing it to the class.

C. literally pat you on the back.

Fourth, the must useful tools to help your learning are:

A. DVDs, video, PowerPoint presentations, films, three-dimensional models.

B. CDs, recordings of lectures.

C. simulation games, experiments, projects, "hands-on" activities.

Voice science. Until just a few years ago, the human voice was one of the least researched areas of scientific inquiry. Now new therapies and treatments for vocal problems are being developed. Laryngologists are learning better ways to observe the vocal mechanisms, and less invasive and more effective ways to heal the voice than in the past. From this will probably evolve new information on how to make voices stronger and healthier, able to speak and sing louder, longer, and with a broader range and richer quality.

Neuro-linguistic programming (NLP). Part communication theory, part learning system, combining elements of linguistics, hypnosis, and humanistic psychology, this subject is too broad to simplify. It has revolutionized clinical psychotherapy, and its practitioners are finding applications for the theories in a wide range of fields. It is particularly well suited to acting and voice/speech practices. While there are individual teachers making that utilization, no one has written about it . . . yet!

Roy Hart method. The Roy Hart Theatre in France has become known for the unusual vocal range, power, and expressiveness of its actors. The vocal technique taught there is extremely impressive. In the last few years, workshops on the Roy Hart technique have been available, but for now, there is no text explaining their approach, and the process of becoming a teacher of the techniques is not fully articulated. This is likely to change, so watch for developments. roy-hart.com.

Alba emoting. We gave you a taste of this material in Exercises 4.8.1/4.8.2. It holds a rich potential for integrating the voice and breath into deep emotional states, and it does it in an emotionally and physically safe and rapid manner. There are some research articles available, but no actor manual. There is a teacher certification program. Susana Bloch's personal journey to the technique is described in her book *The Alba of Emotions* (Random House Mondadori, 2002). albaemotingna.org.

Fitzmaurice voicework, with Catherine Fitzmaurice. Even though Ms. Fitzmaurice has not published a text outlining her work, this is not a new approach on the horizon but a well-established method. The work is physical, deep, and gets results (especially in the area of resonance and breath) quite rapidly. She has had a profound influence, which would undoubtedly place her in the circle above if there were a body of literature for readers to review. This method certifies teachers and has a large corps of instructors in many regions. fitzmauricevoice.com.

Knight–Thompson speechwork, with Dudley Knight and Philip Thompson. Their phonetic-based approach toward speech teaches fine precision through their "Detail Model" and playful facility without being prescriptive or requiring a "right" kind of pronunciation. At present, there is no text accompanying their approach, but it is likely that there will be soon. ktspeechwork.com.

Interactive websites. There are a vast and growing number of online voice sites. Many will let you download free software to help you to edit sound or understand your voice better. Explore spectral analysis software that lets you see the resonance

UNIT 3.6   **Phonetic transcription**

You now have the tools to write sounds in phonetics. Transcribing English into its component sounds allows you to understand and experience words in a way you never could before. Ask five key questions as you approach a transcription problem:

1. How *many* syllables does the word have?
2. Which syllables are *accented?*
3. Is the word in its strong or weak *form?*
4. What are the *individual sounds* in each word? If it is a vowel, what *lexical set* does the sound belong in?
5. How do the individual sounds *affect each other?*

Words are chameleons, which reflect the color of their environment.

LEARNED HAND, jurist

UNIT 3.6.1   *Syllabification*

That's a six-syllable word. When we start combining consonants and vowels, the next unit of size is the syllable. Generally, each syllable must have a vowel sound. [13]

13 The only exceptions to this rule are the "syllabic consonants." In some cases [m̩, n̩, l̩] can function as a syllable without the help of a vowel sound: *button* ['bʌt.n̩] *bundle* ['bʌn.dl̩] and sometimes in rapid casual speech on *happen* ['hæ.pm̩], for example. They are noted with a subscript [ˌ].

signature of your voice. You can see the sound difference between [t] and [d] and watch what happens when you get nasal or hollow or breathy. There are IPA transcription games and animated vocal anatomy sites. If you go looking, you'll find an enormous number of tools to help you to understand your voice. We won't list them here, because online addresses change frequently, but check this book's website for updates, links, and postings.

ONLINE

Terms to remember

Alba emoting	Feldenkrais method	Patsy Rodenburg
Alexander technique	kinesthetic learner	Roy Hart method
Arthur Lessac	Kristin Linklater	visual learner
auditory learner	National Association of Teachers of Singing (NATS)	Voice Foundation
Cicely Berry	Neuro-linguistic programming (NLP)	Voice Science
Edith Skinner		Voice and Speech Trainers Association (VASTA)

Summary

After working your way through this book and completing your present course of study, there is still a lifetime of vocal exploration available to you. Knowing how you learn and having a familiarity with various approaches to the subject can help you to get the result you want.

When you approach advanced study, use the checklist provided here to ask the questions that will land you in the right program.

In time, you should be conversant with the methods of Cicely Berry, Arthur Lessac, Kristin Linklater, Edith Skinner, and Patsy Rodenburg. You may also find that one of the new generation of voice theorists has an inspiring insight that you can connect with. Explore as many as you can.

Include some form of body–voice integration in your study as well. Take some Alexander and Feldenkrais workshops. Check out some of the other actor movement systems mentioned.

Voice and speech for actors is not a static subject. New approaches and new information are emerging continuously. Your future studies will certainly take you into areas you never imagined. As you look forward to your future on the stage and off, take time to plan your vocal future as well.

Planning your voice future

CHAPTER 8

I thank you for your voices, thank you.
Your most sweet voices!

Third Citizen from WILLIAM SHAKESPEARE's *Coriolanus*

I'm an actor. And I hope to continue to grow every day 'til I die.

TOMMY LEE JONES, actor

A defective voice will always preclude an artist from achieving the complete development of his art. The voice is an instrument the artist must learn to use with suppleness and sureness, at if it were a limb.

SARAH BERNHARDT, actor

Because your voice is so closely tied to who you are, if you awaken it, it will grow as you do. It may even lead you to growth. There is no denying that voice work is hard work. It is fun, hard work — exhausting, thrilling, frustrating, hysterically funny, troublesome, and joyous. As you have progressed through this book, you probably had lots of "recognition" and not nearly as much tangible change as you would have liked. Since this is a lifelong journey, what can you do now to make sure you end up where you want to be? We have two goals in this chapter:

Figure 8.1 *"... I've fallen in love with the sound of my own voice"* cartoon by Leo Cullum

"On a personal note, my wife, Ann, and I have agreed to separate, as I've fallen in love with the sound of my own voice."

1. To help you to discover ways to go deeper into activities presented earlier, finding variety and satisfaction beyond that you get from a first exposure, giving yourself every chance to get it right.
2. To offer you new ideas for other activities beyond the confines of this text, so that as you and your voice continue to grow, you never run out of exciting possibilities and fresh approaches.

Think of this final chapter as a launching pad to project you into your own future. And the first step is to make sure that you have collected everything of value from your past. If you have been working independently all this time, you will have no trouble at all staying on this path. If you have been working with others, you want to get all you can from classmates/partners before you take off and work on your own.

If you have been imitating and imitated during this term, it is time to wrap up the gifts and really give them. And it's the time to receive and open them. Exercise 8.1 gives the imitators a chance to hone their skills and the imitatees a chance to objectify their progress and future needs.

EXERCISE 8.1 **AN HONEST SUMMARY**

For the person you are imitating answer:

1. In which areas has this actor most clearly progressed?
2. Which vocal techniques are now strongest?
3. Where does the actor still need to grow the most?
4. What did you fail to notice early in the term but find significant now?
5. What are five abstract images (such as fabric, color, musical instruments, weather) that effectively capture this actor's voice?
6. What do you find most and least appealing about this actor's voice?
7. How may the physical life of this actor be limiting the vocal?*
8. How may the mental/psychological life be limiting the vocal?*
9. What did the actor find in any given voice assignment that they should consider allowing more frequently into their own usual way of speaking?
10. If you could give this actor one voice-related gift, what would it be?

(Write a letter, prepare a recording answering these questions, or use the form on the site to fill out. Give it to the actor being imitated.)

The written document is most effectively combined with a presentation, so the imitatee has a chance to see and hear some of what you have analyzed but also has, in writing, some ideas to take home for reflection. This format also allows you to write some messages that you would rather not share with anyone but the recipient. The project has both a strong public and private component.

---

* These questions are difficult and potentially embarrassing, especially if you genuinely believe, for example, that some personal issue is impeding the actor's vocal progress. Remember, this is a generous gift. You are qualified to offer it because you have been observing this person and walking in their shoes (or speaking in their mouth?) all term. Your perceptions may be wrong. Both you and the receiver know that. If you are coming from a place of empathy and caring, then your ideas are worth sharing. If you don't say it, it may never get said. Have the courage and the compassion to be candid and specific.

EXERCISE 8.2 A FINAL PERFORMANCE IMITATION

Put together a 10- to 15-minute presentation where you show the following information. If you are working in pairs, two people can present together to two other people, or each person can work independently. The format is wide open. It could be a series of black-out sketches, a lecture, a scene, a take-off of a classic TV show (Let's Voice a Deal; You Bet Your Voice; Voice or Consequences; Wheel of Voice; The Big Voice Off; Win, Lose or Speak; The Voice is Right), a Performance Art original or a documentary. Get the information across and enjoy it.

1. Demonstrate vocal contrasts between the actor onstage and the actor off.
2. Demonstrate the actor doing their accent, verse piece, character voices, and any other assignment where you observed them trying to find a new voice or master a new technique. Just one- or two-sentence excerpts in each category are enough.
3. Demonstrate as many answers to Exercise 8.1 as possible so the actor can see and hear, not just read what you have to share about them.

A final ritual helps to achieve a sense of closure on this work and releases each actor into future exploration. The Exercise 8.3 might come right after the presentations above, or it could be done on a separate day altogether. It is more powerful if done with the rest of the class watching.

In preparation, search for some item that symbolizes both what you appreciate about the other actor's voice and what you would wish for the actor to continue to work on achieving. Examples: a Nestle's Crunch Bar for the deep richness of the chocolate, because of the rich tonal quality this actor has, and the crunch part for the surprises, breaks, and variety you want them to achieve; or a cat's-eye marble for the swirls and colors you are starting to hear from this actor, the smooth round surface for the technical control and consistency you want them to get. Give yourself enough time to find just the right token.

EXERCISE 8.3 A FINAL VOCAL GIFT

1. Have the recipient come up to the front of the room with you.
2. Present the gift you have chosen with a brief speech about what it means.
3. The recipient now becomes the giver, and the process is repeated.
4. Recipients, keep the gift around to remind you (if it's something that doesn't last like a candy bar, keep the wrapper) of what you still want to gain and of what it was like to have someone else pay so much attention to your voice.

Armed with some newly developed observation/listening/imitation skills and the knowledge of what your classmates saw/heard/felt when they focused on your vocal life, you are ready to make some plans. The previous chapter was about choosing programs already in place, turning yourself over to an existing structure. What follows is about creating your own structure. We offer an assortment of possibilities that you may choose to feature in your own program. Once you accept that voice is a lifelong process, it can become a comforting constant.

Not working on my voice means not being in touch with myself.

ORLANDA COOK, actor

Ideas for continuing work are presented in the seven major areas of vocal awareness covered in each of the earlier chapters:

1. Owning: acknowledging the voice you have.
2. Healing: fixing what doesn't work.
3. Mastering: making words your tools.
4. Expanding: achieving more than you thought possible.
5. Refining: rising to the occasion.
6. Releasing: sharing every voice in your vast and growing repertoire.
7. Selecting: shopping wisely for additional training and support.

These seven steps are similar to those involved in any healthy growth process. There is still much to do. Let this be a source of excitement and challenge. And be patient with yourself. Remember that the ideal actor state is to feel genuine accomplishment over what you have just achieved and genuine motivation to achieve the next goal. This is a dynamic sense of being fully alive. You are a human work-in-progress. Once you achieve perfection, you might as well die.

Regard the development of your speech as never completed, always progressing towards greater ease and brilliance.

EVANGELINE MACHLIN, voice specialist

EXERCISE 8.4 MAKE A LIST, CHECK IT TWICE

1. Read each of the following sections, making a quick decision about how badly you need or want that activity.
2. On a scale of 1 to 10, rate the activity in relationship to you. How good an idea is this for you to pursue now? How much do you want it?
3. Once you've completed the chapter, go back and change any scores that are affected by the fact that you made some choices before reviewing everything.
4. Take your scores and use them to structure your efforts, dealing with the 10s first, then 9s, etc.

Owning

Blocks and strategies

Label the blocks you have recognized so far. Give them names other than those you have chosen for the voice itself. Think of them as your voice's disruptive, pesky neighbors. If you have trouble breaking through nasality, for example, you might call this problem "Nadine" or "Norm," shooting the name, of course, right through the nasal resonators. Make fun of it. "Well, Nadine is still here, still uninvited. Gotta send her on a trip." Or "Get off my back Norm. And out of my nose!!!!" Some habits stick harder than others. Give them extra time and attention. And extra humor!

College ain't so much where you been as how you talk when you get back.

OSSIE DAVIS, actor

Do you get feedback on your vocal life that you just don't yet hear yourself? Have you come to the conclusion that either everyone else is crazy or you simply don't get it? These blind (deaf) spots are ones where you need to listen more closely, spend more time with the recorder, probe and question other people for more detail. What you fail to sense yourself is the biggest barrier to your progress. There will be a day when you will hear. But you need to fight the temptation to throw up your hands and throw in the towel. Appreciate small victories.

I used to not be able to order pizzas on the phone. They'd say "We need to speak to your mom or dad." I would have to go down there and pick it up myself. Now that I've taken voice lessons, they'll deliver.

KATHY IRELAND, supermodel, designer

UNIT 8.1.2

Unfinished business

As you came to know and accept your voice, did you unearth some influences that you must go back and confront? Are there some conversations, even some confrontations, that must be had before you will ever be able to move forward? Schedule them. Exorcisms don't just happen. Someone makes them happen. Either talk to the person whose reaction had such a profound impact on you or devise a surrogate ritual. Have someone stand in, psychodrama style, for the real person, write a letter (send it or burn it), or some other process that lets you understand and let go. If you are not yet ready for this, put it on your calendar for some future date rather than back in the attic of your mind. Give yourself every chance to understand yourself.

The more you know yourself, the more you can offer as an actor.

REBEKAH DE MORNAY, actor

UNIT 8.1.3

Audiolization

Visualization is a widely proven technique in sports psychology and business. The act of picturing yourself in your victorious or successful state on a regular basis can accelerate progress. Hear the sound of the voice you would like someday to have. Don't pick one that is simply out of your range but get a clear profile of your real voice without its extra baggage and tedium, with increased clarity, support, texture, power or any other component you are seeking. At least once a day stop and listen

UNIT 8.2   **Healing**

UNIT 8.2.1   *The actual shrink*

(in your head) to this voice. Hear yourself speaking both onstage and off, in circumstances in which you would like to find yourself in the future.

Don't let more than five days go by without actually listening to your recorded self. You have probably almost made peace with your voice. Don't lose this connection. Don't let this relationship fade. Remember the machine can sit there while you're doing dishes, putting in your contacts or driving. Integrate your recording so that you don't have to stop your life to use it, but instead it becomes like your keys or your comb. Take it along, switch it on, and learn from it.

> **It's difficult to act other people if you don't really know who you are. It's confusing and disorienting.**
>
> **LYNN REDGRAVE, actor**

Are there personal issues that are relentlessly coming up and staying in your way? Do you know that just talking it out or devising a ritual is not going to take care of it? Does it go deeper, and is it more painful? Your theatre faculty members, no matter how informed and sympathetic, are unlikely to be trained therapists. This may be a counseling issue, and most campuses have counseling centers. Why not consult a professional now on ways of getting out of your own way. You should have nothing but respect for yourself for acknowledging and doing something about a problem too big to handle alone.

The Voice Shrink sections in Chapter 2 provided hang-up lists. Review these now. Which are not going to fix themselves? When you look at the areas where a quick fix is not possible, is there a pattern that emerges? Do you resist expressing yourself in ways that repeat themselves or under similar circumstances? Are you consistent in the kinds of instances where you are unwittingly unwilling to communicate fully?

> **The voice is an index of the mind and is capable of expressing all its varieties of feeling.**
>
> **QUINTILIAN, rhetorician**

Remedial work

Set up daily drills designed to address aspects of voice that aren't easy for you. Do you have a lazy tongue tip? Feature it in your exercises. Are there consonant combinations you always stumble over? Bring them to the front. Do you know that you need to work on placement for some sounds? Get this in your warm-up. Take the time to personalize all the standard work we have described to suit your own particular needs.

Incorporate work on written punctuation, making certain that each symbol on paper is actually incorporated through visualization into your speech.

A period is a stop sign. A semicolon is a rolling stop sign; a comma is an amber light.

ANDREW J. OFFUTT, writer

Focus on a problem a day. If breathiness is an issue, for an entire day, devote yourself to really getting a focused sound in your voice. Concentrate on an attitude counter to the one that has made you too breathy. Do the same for flatness, nasality, overuse of any single resonator, slurring, regional traps, voiced/voiceless inversions, anything on your personal list of habitual peeves.

Behavior modification

**I cannot sing the old songs
I sang long years ago,
For heart and voice would fail me,
And foolish tears would flow.**

CLARIBEL BARNARD, composer, *The Old Songs*

Have you postponed dealing with smoking or with regular secondary smoke contact? Do you have circumstances where you still allow yourself to become dehydrated or need to cough excessively? How often do you shout yourself hoarse or fail to warm up before extended use? How often do you push your voice without rest? How satisfied are you with your own vocal hygiene? How likely are you to push too far?

I gave a terrific scream at the end of the play and all the muscles in my back went into total spasm, because I was all wrapped up in the feeling and working only from instinct. You have to learn how to be fluid and facile, yet still express great emotion.

ANNETTE BENING, actor

Review this section in Chapter 2, with the idea of some permanent promises. It's time to start protecting your voice. Is there someone you know with a battered voice, whom you can use as a constant reminder of what you do not want to sound like in twenty years?

UNIT 8.3 Mastering

UNIT 8.3.1 *Transcription*

If you have not already done so, commit the IPA to memory and transcribe a passage at least once a month, like polishing shorthand skills. Free yourself from having to look up symbols. Find new transcription challenges. Sometimes work from manuscripts. Other times (especially when you hear an interesting new accent) try to transcribe what someone spoke. In particular, play with phonetically writing variations on perfect diction, noting the adjustments that people make when in a hurry or in less formal surroundings. Clarify for yourself the crucial differences between the written and the spoken word.

UNIT 8.3.2 *Memorization*

Free yourself from the need to carry this or any text around to remind you of sequences and lists for exercises. Take the time to get them in your head so that you can work any time, any place. Take your favorite drill sounds and sentences and write them on a note card that is portable and easy. Then gradually wean yourself so that you know them and no longer have an excuse for not running them.

Do the same with any of the A to Z sequences in the book. Put yourself in a position where whenever you have ten minutes, you can do a brief vocal work-out without extensive preparation. Of course, you won't always choose to use spare time in this way, but give yourself the option.

Categories

Deepen your recognition of vowels, consonants, and diphthongs so that you are clear how each is formed and where each is placed. Learn the technical as well as potential emotional differences in your parts of speech.

DON CAMPBELL, sound and healing expert

Have a good vowel movement every day.

Also clarify when sounds are voiced or voiceless, the specific kind and extent of pressure involved, and the circumstances in which each changes. Let your knowledge of words and sounds reach a new level of sophistication. Learn to appreciate each of the three major categories of sound in all its variations.

Expanding

Body to voice

Your voice deserves as much time as your body, and you have a lot of catching up to do. It is easy to feel too far behind and to give up. In Chapter 4, you were asked to devise a vocal work-out. Consider it just a first draft. Reserve a specific stretch of time three to five days a week when you can train. Commit to vocal health and fitness. Be very hard on yourself in this regard. Give yourself an affirmative action quota. In the same way that underrepresented people are being incorporated into crucial power positions, your voice — an underrepresented facet of the total you — must no longer be neglected. It deserves much attention to make up for much neglect.

Connect and overlap your physical and vocal work-outs. Combine them. Drill yourself on your toughest sounds as you run or walk. As you pump iron, pop consonants. Devise a vocal task to accompany each physical one. Work to come up with a perfect match. (Some of Robert's students devised something called "stairmaster scansion," scanning their verse pieces to the rhythm of the machine at the gym.) It will relieve the boredom and make both easier. You'll feel great about using time efficiently.

She works on a text through physicalizing the vowels and consonants in the body and through gymnastics where tone and text are explored together.

MIRKA YEMEN DZAKIS, director, described by Jacqueline Martin

UNIT 8.4.2   *Alignment on*

You have probably touched upon where you want your body to be. You have felt centered, relaxed, powerful, and ready. Give yourself some opportunity each day to enter that state. But also give yourself small reminders as you go along. What do you need an inner voice to tell you? "Drop your shoulders?" "Relax your neck?" "Unshlump?" "Unblock your air flow?" "Lose the chicken neck?" "Free the head to move up and out?" Do you need to remind yourself to let the torso lengthen? Let it widen? Uncurve your shoulders? Free your chest? Drop your chin? Hear these spoken gently, in a friendly, soothing tone, as aids in letting go, not barked as orders, or they will just make you all the more tense. Remember that your body wants to return to an aligned state it once had in childhood. Come up with a set of gentle suggestions. Remind yourself no matter where you are. You will probably instantly seem more relaxed and then more accessible to the person you're with, so the momentary time-cut will be barely noticed.

UNIT 8.4.3   *Floor on upward*

You can't spend your career on your back (unless you change careers), even though much good vocal work starts there. Every vocal challenge is easier from that position, but you can concentrate regularly on transferring floor awareness into standing, sitting, kneeling, and leaning effectiveness. Take the time to move directly from the floor into each of these positions, giving the body the immediate memory to take into adaptation.

When you move to stand up, try to recall the sensation you had on the floor and keep the sense of openness in your back.

CICELY BERRY, voice specialist

When you're at the wheel of a car, standing on an elevator, anywhere you can support your back for a moment, give yourself the sensation of floor alignment, then move away from the support and keep the muscle memory.

Breath power

Breathing is the all-important starting point, too often neglected because it just seems to happen. Devote some time each day to opening passages, activating the diaphragm, connecting breath to sound, to inhaling faster, deeper, more efficiently, more quietly, then to exhaling slower, more gradually, and without explosions of lost air.

Take each of the breathing exercises in this book and make them a natural, habitual part of your process. Use the healing breathing exercises in parts of your life where you wish to relax, to focus, to calm down. Integrate them into your day-to-day existence. Relearn what you once knew about breathing:

Children and animals breathe from the diaphragm. Others don't.

JERZY GROTOWSKI, acting visionary

Master breathing meditation exercises and experiment so that you come up with images that truly work for you. Start with simple pictures such as envisioning a colored light bulb deep in the torso whose light intensifies and dims with inhalation and exhalation. Or a simple pebble inside you bouncing as you breathe, being joined by other pebbles as energy increases. Experiment by changing the color of the bulb or making the pebbles into crystals. Come up with entirely new pictures that evoke a state of deep complete core breathing for you. Add stimuli from the other senses.

Develop a deep wisdom about the relationship between breath and emotion. Learn your personal patterns of breathing and feeling through observation without judgment. Make breath a subject you explore sufficiently so that you find many ways to tap this power. Research and then apply breathing exercises to decrease your appetite, to cool you down (like a personal air conditioner), to help you to focus, to energize, tranquilize, and bring on sleep. Experiment with altering your own physiological state and breathing for lasting power. Find what you need to breathe more effectively.

We can extract from the breath, the vital portion, the life force and that stays within the body. The energy is then within you and can be called forth whenever you need it.

KEN COHEN, chi kung teacher

UNIT 8.4.5   *Revolving variety*

Take each of the nine voice ingredients and revolve them over nine-day periods. Make it your task the first day to vary tempo. Place tempo high in your consciousness all day long in every kind of interaction. Listen to the tempos of others as well as your own. Catch the repetitive, tedious traps into which one can fall. Deliberately inject some alternatives. This will add variety and interest to your day, as well as help you to progress vocally. Then on the second day do rhythm, then articulation, pronunciation, pitch, volume, quality, word choice, vocal nonverbals and start over again.

Expand your own working vocabulary. Add a few new words (let the dictionary fall open or buy a word-for-the-day calendar) every day. Give yourself more choices so that you will be stronger in any circumstance.

A word has the potency to revive and make us free. It also has the power to blind, imprison and destroy.
RALPH ELLISON, author

Make a point of finding out which options you don't normally choose and then choose these more often. If you have an extensive academic vocabulary but are sluggish on slang, get to know some hip-hop types and learn the lingo. Or do the reverse. Widen your informal as well as formal choices. Get comfortable with all words.

UNIT 8.5   **Refining**

UNIT 8.5.1   *The sound of silence*

Speech is human, silence is divine, but dead. We must learn both arts.

THOMAS CARLYLE, essayist

Dump the garbage in your speech. Identify which words ("like," "you know," "fur shur," etc.) and sounds ("ummmm," "uhhh," "errr," etc.) are chosen by you so frequently that they dominate rather than support your communication. Separate what compels from what distracts.

Record yourself in standard everyday conversation often enough and long enough that you can sometimes forget the recorder is on. Are you afraid of silence? Do you sometimes make noise that in no way enhances? These are tiresome crutches and are reductive. Reliance on any single repetitive word, phrase or sound makes you seem less than you are. Do you sometimes prattle? Make a commitment to the pause, to intriguing breaks in your speech, to finding out when it is more effective not to speak. Be more discriminating about what comes out of your mouth. Develop the art of not speaking, for contrast and variety.

UNIT 8.5.2

Coloring

You can taste a word.

PEARL BAILEY, actor

Make your speech more onomatopoeic by coloring the sounds. When you want to make your listener feel as if they were there with you in the experience you are describing, attend to the sensual aspects of each word. When you want a specific emotional response (stunning an impertinent clerk, getting sympathy from a store manager, or calming someone who is angry), let words sound like the senses that surround them. When you are alone, alternate by going colorless for an immediate sense of the contrast, then letting the words out in their full flavors. When working on a speech or monologue, imagine that your listeners do not speak your language, but you still have the power to make them fully comprehend. In performance, let each speech find its movement forward.

Dramatic speech, unlike everyday conversation, has a specific pressure on it, an insistence that the words go somewhere, move towards a predetermined end, and advance the action.

J.L. STYAN, theorist/writer

UNIT 8.5.3

Three kinds of freedom

Practice your own regional/personal dialect periodically so that it is still in place. They always say that as soon as you drop, for example, the sound of your farming region in the Midwest, you get a call to audition to play a Midwestern farmer. Master the intricacies and varieties of the dialect that is most known to you. Move past just doing it to understanding how it works. Never let any speech pattern you have ever mastered get out of your grasp.

UNIT 8.5.4   *Temporary affectation*

Dare to be affected for a time. If you want to sound like a class act (and remember this is your choice), it will never happen until you risk moving through a self-conscious period where you labor over new sounds. Stop being terrified of sounding like a phony. Some people will think you're a pompous twit. Who cares? Warn those you care about that you are working on something new; explain exactly what the sounds are and why they give you so much trouble. They will probably be fascinated, infinitely supportive, and may even offer uninvited corrections when you slip. Almost anyone in your life worth having in your life will support you through a change you really want to make.

> **I was continuously struggling with the conscientious efforts of our players to underdo their parts lest they should be considered stagey. Much as if Titian had worked in black and grey lest he should be considered painty.**
>
> **GEORGE BERNARD SHAW, playwright**

Use encounters with strangers to help to empower the "aristocrat" in you. Remember that your most elevated speech is useful in many contexts, from getting a better table to not getting carded. It is particularly useful when you don't want people to mess with you. While much of the time you probably want to be warm and available, at other times you may wish to be intimidating.

UNIT 8.5.5   *Versing*

Take a new verse speech each week and scan it. Gradually work past marking it or physically scoring the manuscript. Try to do it in your head. It will take time, but there will be a day when — bang! — you look down at the page and the metre falls into place. The line is clear at a glance, and an intelligent scanning emerges out of your mouth. This is the point at which your work in the classics will become, if not effortless, far easier and more natural.

Work each day on generalizing your speech to network neutral and then elevating it to classical. As you run into different people, dare to go deep into your region, then into General American, Received Pronunciation, and Elevated Standard. Think of this as running arpeggios on a piano. Aspire to change accents as fast as Robin Williams can. If you can get a friend to play this game with you, all the better. You will surprise yourself how quickly you can change with practice.

Read a Shakespearean sonnet every day. Do it the first thing in the morning or the last thing at night. It's only fourteen lines, so it won't take long. Stay with one poem for as long as you like or move on every day and cycle through them. After a fairly brief time, you'll find the deeper layers of the language seeping into your consciousness. This is one pleasure that will ripen through repeated encounters.

Rhythm, metre, and timing are needed to create effects, which must then also appear to be absolutely spontaneous.

LAURENCE OLIVIER, actor

Once every month or two, memorize and develop a new classical verse monologue. No one ever seems to have enough of them for audition purposes, and these speeches have the energy of greatness in them. They have stood the test of time and let you rub up against greatness, some of which may rub off back on you! Consider using the "chestnuts" too familiar to be employed in auditions for your own private work-outs. Remember that these speeches became chestnuts precisely because they were so powerful and evocative that everyone was drawn to them. They are loaded.

Releasing
UNIT 8.6

Accenting
UNIT 8.6.1

When you own an accent, it releases new characters and new power in you. While in the beginning it usually takes weeks of steady daily work to master one accent, you cut this time down for the second, third, and subsequent ones you study because you get better at skipping steps and finding connections. Why not pick four or five you wish to add to your repertoire each term or as a great summer project? We have addressed the approaches. Now you have the basic tools. If you are interested in improvisational or satirical review work, you will wish to nail as many dialects as possible so that you can tap into them instantly in the middle of a session requiring immediate character detail and sharply defined attitude.

Move past your initial understanding of a general dialect into its varieties and subtleties. Get as many Southerners or Russians or Brits down as you can. Interview natives, rent DVDs, break the dialect itself down further into classes, sub-regions, and cultural differences. Test yourself by taking your dialect characters into the world, dressed appropriately, and ready to take on all distractions:

Too many accents are lost between the hotel room and the set. An actor will have it, and then all of a sudden, they're in five-inch heels, sideburns, or a corset and the accent's left behind.

JULIE ADAMS, dialect coach

Consider creating your own accent kits with the recorded and printed excerpts you find most useful from each of the systems. Set up files of material for yourself so that with twenty-four hours notice, you would know how to brush up an accent efficiently on request. Have an audition monologue memorized and ready to go in as many accents as you can.

UNIT 8.6.2

Character voicing

The more the merrier. If, in Chapter 6, you stumbled on certain voice categories or just avoided certain others, go back and get them. Improv work requires access to many voices at the drop of a tongue. But the more voices you have inside you, even when you are playing a straight role, the more likely you are to discover other vocal dimensions that will make that performance more interesting. You develop the capacity to expand any character's vocal expressiveness and to expand into any additional characters.

The student will finally have to speak with as many voices as the characters he has to create.

MARGARET BURY, designer

Devise a program. Aim to get a voice you hear (and record) from the tube or radio one day. The next day, get a real person from the drug store, the bank or Wendy's. Listen to all the voices out there. Push yourself past those that come easily toward those that challenge you and require care and detail.

Are there famous people you would love to imitate? Why not add one or two each term? Tell everyone you are working on your Marilyn or your Jack Nicholson and let them advise and critique you. It will be a fun running gag. You may be pathetic at first, but you will get better, and it will keep you listening and working on placement, tone, and timing. Try taping talk shows as raw material. The process is more than just diverting; it can be genuinely stretching for you as an artist.

UNIT 8.6.3

UNIT 8.6.4

Figure 8.2 Anna Deveare Smith. Photo by Mary Ellen Mark

I began transcribing talk-show interviews with famous people for my students to perform. It wasn't just about the success of doing a mimicry of Katharine Hepburn. The point is, if you talk and sit like her, you can feel like her.

ANNA DEAVERE SMITH, actor, playwright

Since professional voiceover artists often keep cards or computer documents on their various voices (see Chapter 6), naming each, writing a brief profile of the overall effect and what changes are made to achieve it, this can be useful to you as well. Consider starting a card file, or expanding yours if you have begun, so that you don't lose any but can bring back quickly anyone you have ever become.

Copy work

Pick a new piece of text each day and read it out loud. It may be the newspaper, a letter you receive or the liner notes on the CD you just bought. Let the text choose you by being there. Practice cold-reading techniques by getting your eyes off the page and into your partner's. Be less and less tied to the manuscript itself. Alternate by practicing mic techniques, recording and working on playing the mic like an instrument. These are skills that anyone can get better at, but only with regular, systematic attention.

Demos

Make a professionally recorded commercial voiceover demo. Surprisingly, many actors completely ignore this dimension of the profession. Develop this angle and it could be the area that brings you the most success. It's fine if that cat food commercial gives you the residuals to support you while you do Shakespeare for a theatre that hardly pays. Put together a home studio. Get an industrial and a cartoon demo together and really step into advanced work.

UNIT 8.6.5   *Songbird*

Take a singing class. Consider taking private voice, group voice, and if available, a voice for actors or musical theatre course, which focuses primarily on Broadway-style delivery. Study either German and Italian classical approaches, or both. The breathing exercises, the support, the control, all will carry over and help you to improve your speech.

I heard behind me a great voice as of a trumpet.

THE BIBLE, *Revelation*

Consider joining a vocal group, like a gospel choir or something fun, that gets you singing regularly and savoring musicality. Study music terminology, which can be a helpful way of understanding your own voice. Do you know these terms? *Piano* (soft), *pianissimo* (very soft), *mezzo piano* (medium soft), *mezzo forte* (medium loud), *fortissimo* (very loud), *sforzando* (suddenly loud), *crescendo* (gradually louder), *decrescendo* (gradually softer), and *piano subito* (suddenly soft)? Why learn them? They can increase your sensitivity to adjustments in volume. Because the element is so crucial in music, it can open up your speech possibilities. Do you actually make such distinctions when you talk? Be honest. Find the power of sforzando and the intrigue of decrescendo.

UNIT 8.7   Selecting

UNIT 8.7.1   *A better cave*

In Chapter 7, we reviewed Alexander and Feldenkrais, two physical programs likely to be taught with vocal training. Here are some of the vast range of others available: aikido; Aston patterning; bioenergetics; biofeedback; chi kung; chi yi; effector patterns; Gestalt; Hakomi; Hellerwork; karate; Laban; massage therapy; meditation; rebirthing; reflexology; Rolfing; shiatsu; t'ai chi ch'uan; Trager psychophysical integration; visualization; yoga; Zen sports. Yes, yet another A to Z sequence. Some of these areas of inquiry are concerned with how the body feels, some with how it relates, and others with how it perceives. All are sometimes employed by actors trying to align the cave in which the voice lives with the voice itself, to provide the voice with the most complete and comfortable home possible.

Try to get at least a passing acquaintance with each of the above, enough to be conversant. Determine which might be right for you. Questions to consider: what is it? How and where did it evolve? Is first-hand experience available in your community?

How and by whom is it primarily used outside the theatre? What is its potential within an actor training program? Is there a classic position/photo/drawing/tableau or movement by which you can remember the subject and not confuse it with others?

Remember that a relaxed yet ready physical state is what can ultimately free the voice. Respect your body as a prized instrument.

> **An actor is supposed to be a sensitive instrument. Isaac Stern takes good care of his violin. What if everybody jumped on his violin?**
>
> **MARILYN MONROE, actor**

Research the full spectrum of relaxation techniques. Since fear, stage fright, and anxiety play such a role in voice problems, it helps to know as many ways as possible to get centered and calm. When an approach strikes your fancy, continue to study it. Be on the alert for weekend workshops, lectures from experts, and new publications.

Expanded learning modes

UNIT 8.7.2

If you have found that you are largely visual, kinesthetic or auditory, consider expanding your learning process to include more of the other two. While it is good for you to know how you learn, you will not always be working with a director or partner whose pattern is the same as yours. Use this as a pathway to increasing rapport. Classes in neuro-linguistic programming may be available in your community. But even listening more carefully to the predicates that others use will help you to understand how they access information. See if (or "hear whether" or "get a feel for when") you can deliberately use predicates that you normally avoid in order to expand your range of expression.

Systemizing

UNIT 8.7.3

We have familiarized you with the various approaches to voice, but there is no reason you can't dig deeper independently. Get hold of the books. Seek out those who have studied the systems first-hand. Start with the one that seems most suited to your learning style. If that is Edith Skinner, aim to know more about the Skinner approach first-hand by the end of the term. Then move on to someone else. A working knowledge of each can only help you, because your director or coach may prefer an approach different to the one you end up studying in depth.

Prepare to interview and audition for advanced programs months ahead of the actual event. Write for all their printed materials so that you don't waste time asking questions that are answered on paper. Remember that it is fair game, in an audition, for the interviewer to ask to see anything on your resumé. Practice snatches of all roles in your repertoire, not just the ones you're planning to show. Practice interviewing friends and being interviewed in return. Ask others about the challenging questions that threw them off in interviews. Come up with challenging questions to ask back so that you appear lively, assertive, and vital.

Half of an audition is who you are as a person rather than as an actor. It becomes a question of whether or not they want to spend months working with you.

ROBERT SEAN LEONARD, actor

Video some of your simulated interviews and listen for an honest first impression based on the voice that is responding. Make every effort to get a sense of who you really sound like and appear to be in the interview. Consider how significant the voice is for leaving a lingering impression and how many actors put their voices in neutral under these circumstances for fear of making a wrong move and so end up lacking vocal presence. Aim to be remembered.

My first acting interview for a job, the man said to me, "Well, Jack, you're such an unusual person that I don't know exactly how we would use you, but when we need you, we'll need you very badly."

JACK NICHOLSON, actor

Consider aspiring to become a VASTA (Voice and Speech Trainers Association) member yourself someday. If you really like this work, examine the requirements and look into turning yourself into a trainer. Numerous voice coaches are professional actors, and it is not uncommon for one to work for a company as both performer and coach. This increases your potential marketability and keeps you very close to the performance process. Remember that many actors burn out or experience lean periods when they are "at liberty." The more you can do for a theatre, the more chance you have to spend time in a theatre. The idea of potentially guiding someone else may motivate you through some of the rough spots yourself. You may love the chance to share with others and to not have to focus all your voice knowledge inward.

CHAPTER 1

does this say about your ear at this point? How can your knowledge of your class' "mosts" and "leasts" help you to listen more carefully in the future?

Alternative assignment: If you are working alone, you could still benefit from filling out a ballot based on your perception of any group (co-workers, club members, etc.) of which you are a member, since it raises your powers of observation and perception.

UNIT 1.8   **The cave — your voice's home**

Your body is the mixing bowl or oven where the ingredients blend and bake. You should consider:

Body concept: how great or distressed you feel about how you look can influence strongly any sound you make. To what extent are you at peace with your body? Or are you always trying to adjust, hide or ignore some part of it?

Posture: how you stand, lean, tilt, and sit changes sound. Where you are centered, how aligned your spine is, and how collapsed, twisted or asymmetrical or closed-in your body is in repose can block or free the passage of air and stop or release the free flow of sound. The relationship of your head to your torso is particularly crucial to this connection.

Expression: any habitual way you place your face, such as jutting your jaw forward, flaring your nostrils, sucking in your cheeks or pursing your lips, will influence your speech, because you must always undo or alter this expression in order to completely shape certain sounds. Your facial muscles could be fighting you or helping you.

Breathing: the capacity to take in air swiftly and deeply and then let it out slowly and unobtrusively is important to acting, particularly in long, demanding monologues. If you now inhale and exhale almost exclusively in your upper chest or thorax, your breath is shallow. If you breathe down to your abdomen, it has greater depth. Some knowledge of your habitual patterns will help to shape your goals for expansion.

> **The first question I ask myself is: does this actor have any breathing difficulties? Not where or how he breathes, but *can* he breathe?**
>
> JERZY GROTOWSKI, theorist, director, actor trainer

- allergies;
- hearing problems;
- conditions that alter the nasal passage (deviated septum, sinusitis, swollen adenoids);
- throat conditions (post-nasal drip, swollen tonsils, pharyngitis);
- larynx and vocal fold conditions (laryngitis, nodules, polyps, papilloma, edema);
- respiratory conditions (asthma, bronchitis);
- nerve damage or sensory loss from injury or illness (stroke, thyroid surgery, or Parkinson's disease, among others);
- digestive disorders (gastro-esophageal reflux, bulimia);
- musculoskeletal tension syndromes (temporo-mandibular joint dysfunction (TMJ), muscular tension dysphonia, etc.).

If you experience a problem with your voice and can't ascribe it to any behavior, or if changes in your behavior don't seem to produce improvement, then the problem may be medical. Whom should you see? An otorhinolaryngologist (ear-nose-throat specialist) should cover all the bases. The best situation may be a group practice where several doctors each focus on a sub-specialty (allergy/asthma/immunology, otology, rhinology, laryngology). Sometimes they will have a voice and speech pathologist on staff as well. Ask local singing/speech teachers or theatre companies for a referral, since it is important to work with a doctor who understands the demands of the professional voice. Find one who has a record of success in treating professional singers and actors.

UNIT 2.4.1   *Vocal hygiene*

Sometimes you don't feel absolutely up to par but aren't sick enough to need a doctor. In situations like this, there are some things you can do for yourself to make your throat feel better and to help to improve the sound of your voice.

UNIT 2.7.5 *What to stress*

The term "operative words" is often given to the words that function as carriers of the message or significance in a line. How do you find these words? This issue is much more nuanced. It's easier to say what not to stress, because those categories of words interfere with understanding the primary meaning. But it isn't as easy to generalize about what you should stress. There are some things to look for, however.

Stress new idea words. Reduce importance for concepts that have already been stated.

To recap, here's a short list of words to avoid stressing:

- the word *not*
- pronouns (he, him, her, me, mine, I . . .)
- conjunctions (and, or, but . . .)
- prepositions (of, at, to, in, on . . .)
- articles (the, a, an).

You may have noticed, in all these "good" and "bad" versions, that you can act the bad versions rather well. It is quite possible to fill weak words with rich subtext. Stressing them can seem an inspiring way to personalize the text. It's just that you're the only one who will understand what you mean. The rest of us will be left wondering.

In reality, there is a hierarchy of stressing rather than an "on–off" switch of either hammered or whispered.

Don't stress any word that could be left out without changing the meaning. So get out your blue pencil and start crossing off words. Even complicated text can be reduced to simple sentences. That's not to say that anything an author wrote is unimportant, only that the audience needs to have important ideas put forward and discursive text placed in context.

Otherwise, it should be "uh." "An" is used before a vowel. When children are taught to read, their teacher often models "a" as "ay" and this transfers to a difference between natural speech and reading. You're more likely to hear actors use "ay" when reading than in their normal speech. This can inadvertently get memorized into the role, and it will make everything they say sound a little unnatural to the audience.

"A" is used before a consonant. Only in unusual stressing or when describing the letter A should it be pronounced like "ay."

2. Starting with whatever is a "normal" tonal quality for you, pick an easy mid-level pitch and say the sound "HEE" [hi] as in HEED three times on that pitch.
3. Maintain the same pitch, rhythm, volume, and vowel sound, and shift into the sharpest, most nasal quality you can. Say "HEE" [hi] three times.
4. Return to normal. Say "HEE" [hi] three times.
5. Shift to a hollow tonality (drop the back of your tongue, arch the back of the roof of your mouth by starting a yawn). Say "HEE" [hi] three times.
6. Return to normal. Say "HEE" [hi] three times.
7. Repeat steps 2–6 using a sustained "HEEEEEEEEEEE" [hiː] in each position once.
8. Using the "EEEEEE" [iː], go smoothly from normal to nasal to normal to hollow to normal without stopping the smooth flow of sound.
9. Repeat steps 2–8 using the same pattern on the vowel sounds [æ] as in *had*, [ɑ] as in *fa*ther, [u] as in *hoot*, and [ʌ] as in *hut*. Are some vowel sounds easier to place nasally or hollowly than others?
10. Pattern this into normal speech by counting while making these resonance shifts, then again while giving your name and address, then on a piece of text.
11. Note whether your voice feels more "centered," clearer, and freer.

UNIT 2.11.3 *Breathy or pressed voices*

The way the vocal folds come together and use the air stream to produce sound is a crucial element of vocal quality. When the folds don't meet completely, some air escapes through the center or back and isn't used to vibrate the folds. This results in a "breathy" sound. The opposite effect is achieved when the folds are pressed together too firmly (often the surrounding surfaces will also constrict). This gives a harsh, pinched sound. Though both can be used for character voices or effects, habitual use of either one is tiring for your voice. Both are correctable with some awareness and practice.

While it is important to honor the natural rhythmic structure of words, don't let that lead you into patterned or mindlessly predictable rhythms. Material requiring powerful defined rhythms can become boring if the actor doesn't find shading, nuance, and variety *within* the form.

EXERCISE 4.3.4 RHYTHM - FINDING FREEDOM WITHIN FORM

1. This selection has rhythmic formality. The 'rhythm is the essence of the material. Seek out ways to maintain that rhythm, but shade it with subtle differences in length to create and discover meaning, and communicate that message so it affects your listeners.

2. If working in a group, let one reader gc until another feels inspired to go back over the passage just read with greater balance of regularity and variety. Keep interrupting and trying another attack.

3. Look up the full versions of the poem and others like Longfellow's *The Song of Hiawatha* or Service's *The Cremation of Sam McGee* and try them. It can be challenging to find variety and interesting interpretations when you hit the 50th stanza of the same drum-beat rhythm.

4. While observing other actors work, ask yourself: what effect does the rhythm of the piece have on my metabolic rhythms (heartbeat, breathing)?

The Bells by Edgar Allen Poe

Hear the sledges with the bells —
Silver Bells!
What a world of merriment their melody foretells!
How they tinkle, tinkle, tinkle,
In the icy air of night!
While the stars that oversprinkle
All the heavens seem to twinkle
With a crystalline delight;
Keeping time, time, time,
In a sort of Runic rhyme

EXERCISE 4.9.2 JABBERWOCKING

This poem is wonderful for exploration because, much like an open scene, content and meaning is up to the interpreter. Unlike an open scene, it provides vast suggestion and stimuli.

1. Everyone should plan to perform the first stanza of the poem plus two others of their choice.
2. Each nonsense word must have a definte, recognizable meaning.
3. Jabberwocky may not be a dragon-like monster vaguely existing only in your imagination, open to free association by the audience. It must be a specific, recognizable, concrete thing or person.
4. Don't do a simple adventure story. Along with the nonsense words, real words may be given new meanings as long as you clearly communicate your intention for each.
5. Props are not allowed, but any kind of movement is permissible. Endow heavily.
6. Strive for the largest possible number of clear, original images, with maximum use of the voice as communicative tool.

Jabberwocky by Lewis Carroll[24]

(1)
'Twas brillig, and the slithy toves
Did gyre and gimble in the wabe;
All mimsy were the borogoves
And the mome raths outgrabe.

(2)
"Beware the Jabberwock, my son!
The jaws that bite, the claws that catch!
Beware the Jubjub bird, and shun
The frumious Bandersnatch!"

---

24 Concerning the pronunciation of these words, Carroll later said: "The 'i' in 'slithy' is long, as in 'writhe'; and 'toves' is pronounced so as to rhyme with 'groves.' Again, the first 'o' in 'borogoves' is pronounced like the 'o' in 'borrow.' I have heard people try to give it the sound of the 'o' in 'worry.' Such is Human Perversity."

pass, -es
passed
passable, -ness
passably
pass-book, -s
passer, -s
passer-by
passers-by
Passfield
passing
pass-key, -s
passman, -men
Passover, -s
passport, -s
password, -s
past
pastime, -s
pastor, -s
pastoral, -s
pastoralism
pastorate, -s
pasturage
pasture, -s
pastured
pasturing
(Cornish) pasty
path, -s
pathfinder, -s
Pathfinder
pathless
pathway, -s
perchance

planch, -es
planchette, -s
plant, -s
planted
planter, -s
planting
plaque
plaster, -s
plastered
plasterer, -s
plastering
prance, -s
Prance
pranced
prancer, -s
prancing

Q
quaff, -s
  [ɒ] RP, [ɑ] ES, GA
quaffed
quaffer, -s
quaffing

R
raft, -s
rafted
rafter, -s
raftered
rafting
ranch, -es, -er, -ed, -ing
rascal, -s

rascalities
rascality
rascally
rasp, -s
rasped
rasping
raspberries
raspberry
raspiness
raspy
rather
recast, -s
recasting
repass, -es
repassed
repassing
repast, -s
repasture
reprimand, -s
reprimanded
reprimanding

S
salve, -s
(ointment)
  [sɑɫv] RP
  [sav] ES
  [sæv] GA
salve, -s (rescue)
  [sæɫv] RP, ES, GA
salved
salving

sample, -s
sampled
sampler, -s
sampling
schoolmaster, -s
shaft, -s
Shaftsbury
shan't
slander, -s
slandered
slanderer
slandering
slanderous, ly
slanderousness
slant, -s
slanted
slanting, -ly
slantwise
soprano
staff, -s
staffed
staffing
stagecraft
stance, -s
stanch, -s
stanched
stanching
stanchion, -s
statecraft
steadfast, -ly
steadfastness
stedfast

Shakespeare will often insert a rhymed couplet in the middle of an otherwise unrhymed speech to call sudden attention to a key point or will give a character a couplet at the end of an unrhymed scene in order to forcefully bring the scene to a close. Even when characters speak nothing but couplets, they are consistently pleased with themselves for doing so. In this context, it simply becomes an everyday rather than a rare and major accomplishment. A character may move from blunt through poetic prose, to free verse, to metrically regular blank verse, to rhymed verse. At each stage, the level of achievement and satisfaction increases.

> **Then read from the treasured volume**
> **The Poem of thy choice,**
> **And lend to the rhyme of the poet**
> **The beauty of thy voice.**
>
> HENRY WADSWORTH LONGFELLOW, poet, *The Day is Done*

UNIT 5.7 Classical speech hints A to Z — antithesis to zone

We believe that the classics allow growth and fulfillment far beyond other material you might choose to practice. Because it is so challenging, it pushes you beyond your perceived limitations. If only you don't give up too early:

> **One must practice the classics long and hard. Americans seem to understand this about football, so why don't they see that it's true for classical acting? When I hear that Americans can't do the classics, I say that is absurd. They don't even try.**
>
> TINA PACKER, artistic director, Shakespeare and Company

The following hints and exercises will help you to get comfortable with both the act of elevating your speech beyond the ordinary and then placing that speech into verse format.

Antithesis: probably the most important rhetorical device used by classical writers, antithesis is putting one idea in opposition to another. Sometimes three or four words are placed in contrast to three or four others. The second or antithetical word (such as "angels" below contrasting "devils") tops or overcomes the first in emphasis. Try to overdo these in order to point them sufficiently. Example: Richard *III*, Act I, Scene II

1. A single change only. One factor for the thinnest possible accent (possibly just the resonance, for example).
2. Raise it to three.
3. Pick something that you consider a mid-range accent.
4. Organize what you think is thick but eminently clear.
5. Every change you've got.
6. Come up with ten practice sentences and move from 1 to 5 and back again, increasing the speed with which you move on to the next level.

EXERCISE 6.7.1.2 TEACHING THE ACCENT

You will have mastered the accent if you can pass on what you have learned to others. If you have been doing the UN exercise above, you have already taught: bits and pieces of the accent, but because of the smorgasbord nature of the exercise you have never stayed as a class with one or more than a few minutes.

1. Set up 30–45 minutes for each accent the class is studying, with one accent being taught in each class period for the next several weeks.
2. Teams should begin by preparing a handout. This is important, because it is what classmates will keep on file and use when they need this accent in the future. It should be an easy scan and include topics covered so far: images, values, influences, physical life, additions, subtractions, substitutions, quality, pitch, tempo, rhythm, volume, idiom/word choice, and nonverbals. Include sources for further study.
3. If possible, on your day of presentation, have the class leave the room while you "transform" the space with posters, banners, candles, music, whatever your imagination can produce to turn this room into another part of the world.
4. Pick a set of circumstances under which a group would be highly motivated to learn an accent: a big audition coming up, a spying expedition, an imminent takeover by foreign powers, a government-imposed mandate for a change in Standard Speech, or any simple survival tactic ("Big Daddy is about to return to the plantation and he just hates Yankees and Brits! Could y'all try real hard to git Southern? Ah'd hate to think what he might do if he found y'all out!"). It can be silly so long as we the learners know why we are here and what we want.

Howard Austin and Elizabeth Howard, *Born to Sing* (Vocal Power, 1985). A book and CD package with a thorough step-by-step approach and an effective section on various musical styles.

David Craig, *On Singing Onstage* (Applause Theatre Books, 1990). While arbitrary in tone, this text has much sound advice and particularly strong emphasis on phrasing.

Joe Deer and Rocco Dal Vera, *Acting in Musical Theatre: A Comprehensive Course* (Routledge, 2008). Probably the most complete guide to all aspects of musical performance, with multiple exercises and extensive practical advice. There are sections on musical theatre styles and pursuing careers not available in any other source.

Oscar Kosarin, *The Singing Actor* (Prentice Hall, 1983). Easy to read, with familiar show tunes as examples and an interesting exploration of the relationship between the speaking and the singing voice.

Tracey Moore, with Allison Bergman, *Acting the Song: Performance Skills for the Musical Theatre* (Allworth Press, 2008). A guide to planning and facilitating classes and workshops at every level, this book is particularly useful for those aspiring to teach in this field. A especially helpful section on auditioning.

Elaine Novak, *Performing in Musicals* (Schirmer Books, 1988). A comprehensive broad overview of musical theatre, with over a hundred pages of scenes and songs from famous musicals.

Fred Silver, *Auditioning for Musical Theatre* (Penguin Books, 1988). Full of original and challenging exercises, it could be titled *How to Act a Song.*

Singing should be a joyous release. Don't worry about whether you could compete professionally with other singers. You might be able to, but that's not the point. The world of vocal expression in singing is enormous, and expansive, and actors would do well to live in that large, bright place.

Singing also builds a larger, stronger, and more flexible vocal instrument. You can become a musical theatre performer without a voice to die for. You simply need to develop an outrageous, contagious way with a song. But even if your public never gets to hear you sing, they will enjoy the results when you act!

UNIT 6.14

Checking back

After completing the work in this chapter, go back and review some of your earlier work, recordings, and material you practiced, recalling your original attack. Recognize what you would now do differently. Not just what you would, but *could*

EXERCISE 7.9.1   DUELING THEORIES

1. Assign teams of actors to present one text each from those mentioned in this chapter. They can divide it into sections to study.

2. Each class throughout the first half of the term save 10 minutes for a presentation from one team on the basic nature of the text.

3. About halfway through the term the entire group should develop a list of "Most Common Voice and Speech Problems." This could be things like nasality, regional speech, upward inflection, weak projection, dropped final consonants.

4. Periodically set aside time to have the competition of the "Dueling Theories" for one certain problem. Each team chooses the solution posed by their author and presents it to the class, with an opportunity for a rebuttal.

5. The class (with particular input from individuals with the problem) selects which solutions they think will work best for them and reports on their progress at the next duel. (In some cases, what can be an excellent text may not be accessible to this approach because of the lack of a qualified teacher. In that event, present the theory as written, and make it a point to alert the class to any workshops available in the region in case some actors want to get a first-hand experience.)

UNIT 7.10

Advanced program checklist

After you graduate from your present program and decide to seek advanced training, how can you evaluate the strength of various voice and speech programs? Here are some signposts you can look for. When you read the literature from the school, check for answers. If you do not find it there, be sure to ask during your interview. You do not wish to commit two or three years of your life without a sense of what you are getting into.

- What is the breadth of the program; does it favor one voice system to the exclusion of others?
- How many full-time instructors do they have; what are their backgrounds, degrees, certifications?
- Whom do the teachers credit as their major influences?
- Do the faculty work as vocal coaches on productions; what is the degree to which the voice and acting programs are integrated?

4. The real shrink (hang-ups — promises).
5. Remedial work (daily drills — tendencies).
6. Behavior modification (habits — contact).
7. Transcription (text — speech).
8. Memorization (free from texts — short work-outs).
9. Categories (recognition — circumstances).
10. Body to voice (equal time — overlaps).
11. Alignment on (centering — reminders).
12. Floor upward (awareness — effectiveness).
13. Breath power (opening up — other avenues).
14. Variety (focus du jour — expanding vocabulary).
15. The sound of silence (clean-up — pause).
16. Coloring (onomatopoeia — forward movement).
17. Three kinds of freedom (personal — general — elevated).
18. Temporary affectation (risk — help from friends).
19. Versing (weekly scansion — adding monologues).
20. Accenting (expanding repertoire — subtleties).
21. Character voices (adding — devising a program).
22. Copy work (cold reading — mic technique).
23. Songbird (class — groups).
24. A better cave (body — home).
25. Expanded learning modes (rapport — predicates).
26. Systematizing (mastery — interview preparation).
27. Research (books on voice — CDs on voice).

Do these suggestions stagger you? Well, this is one subject in which you will never run out of new challenges and possible ways to train. You have been provided a banquet of choice. No one expects you to eat or drink it all. No one expects you to pursue everything offered in this chapter. You may reject most of the suggested activities as completely unsuitable for your game plan. Just have a game plan and always be attending to and activating your voice in some fashion. That is what matters.

"You have about forty different ways of sliding," people used to say to Ty Cobb. "How do you decide which way to slide?" "I don't think about it, I just slide," he answered. So it is with an actor's voice. You have worked so hard for so long that you don't have to be self-conscious and think about it. You just use it organically, as an instrument of your art.

JAMES EARL JONES, actor

The world is full of immobilized actors, who have frozen. They seem incapable of making choices and moving forward. And vocal choices are the easiest not to make. The world is equally full of those who choose but always safely. Yet safe is rarely a choice that leads to excitement. The fear of sounding dumb can block the potential to sound amazing.

Your motto should be "Dare to be stupid."

TIM ROBBINS, actor

The world is also full of people who do not recognize the profound influence and importance of the voice. You are no longer one of them. And this gives you tremendous power. No matter how much spectacle is in a play, a magical moment always comes when the actor simply stands still and speaks. The handling of that speech is often what is most remembered about the performance. No matter how much activity you may have in your social life, it is the moments when you just talk to each other that cement lifelong relationships. The times when you say what is in your heart are those that your friends remember. Because you now know about how the voice can shape these moments, you have the potential, onstage and off, to be unforgettable.

The world is full of couples and entire families who sit in desolate, bored silences together. There are many reasons why they end up this way, but we submit that those who have learned to love a well-turned phrase, an interesting inflection, and the sheer sensual pleasure of words are more likely to continue to attempt contact, relish repartee, and renew relationships. The voice is a primary tool for connection, and if you learn to love using it, you are more likely to connect.

Anytime you get bored or stuck, move over to some other venue. But keep your voice alive. It's worth it. It is worth it every time you are on the phone and your voice is all you have with which to communicate. When you are comforting a child, a sick friend lying in a dim room, or any suffering being whose eyes are momentarily closed in anguish, you will know what to do with your voice; and it will be worth it. When you speak with your lover in the dark, it will be worth it. At such moments, it is often not so much the words but the sounds that make the difference. At such moments, voice helps you to act your life.

It will be worth it when you get that great role with all those soliloquies. It will be worth it when you need to persuade someone to marry you, hire you or not to do something destructive. It will be worth it when you get that great laugh, gasp or sigh from the audience, not to mention that round of applause for a brilliant line reading. It will be worth it any time you know that what you said was fully supported by how you said it. They call what we do in the theatre plays, and it is easy to forget the original meaning of the word "play." It will be worth it as you hang out with friends, skillfully bouncing words, phrases, lines, puns, accents, routines, and voices back and forth and back and forth. It will be worth it because you will never, ever run out of ways to play.

Summary

In addition to the existing vocal systems you can study, it is possible for you to devise an independent, original lifelong program. Being imitated in depth and imitating someone else one last time is a valuable way to end class and begin solo work. It is important to savor every piece of information offered by your vocal mirror/partner. It is possible that never again will someone else focus so strongly on your voice. Each of the seven stages of growth (owning, healing, mastering, expanding, refining, releasing, and selecting) presented in the rest of this book offers more possible ways to continue to expand. Enough activities are offered here to keep you busy for a very long time. What you choose is much less important than that you choose and that you are always pursuing voice growth in some fashion. While your vocal work will probably never end, neither will your sense of enjoyment and discovery.

Note: forms for this chapter are available on the book's website.

Index

Note: postalveolar 151
posture 34, 217